Of Liberty and Necessity

In *Of Liberty and Necessity*, James A. Harris presents the first comprehensive account of the free will problem in eighteenth-century British philosophy. Harris proposes new interpretations of the positions of familiar figures such as Locke, Hume, Edwards, and Reid. He also gives careful attention to writers such as William King, Samuel Clarke, Anthony Collins, Lord Kames, James Beattie, David Hartley, Joseph Priestley, and Dugald Stewart, who, while well known in the eighteenth century, have since been largely ignored by historians of philosophy. Through detailed textual analysis, and by making precise use of a variety of different contexts, Harris elucidates the contribution that each of these writers makes to the eighteenth-century discussion of the will and its freedom.

In this period, the question of the nature of human freedom is posed principally in terms of the influence of motives upon the will. On one side of the debate are those who believe that we are free in our choices. A motive, these philosophers believe, constitutes a reason to act in a particular way, but it is up to us which motive we act upon. On the other side of the debate are those who believe that, on the contrary, there is no such thing as freedom of choice. According to these philosophers, one motive is always intrinsically stronger than the rest and so is the one that must determine choice. Several important issues are raised as this disagreement is explored and developed, including the nature of motives, the value of 'indifference' to the will's freedom, the distinction between 'moral' and 'physical' necessity, the relation between the will and the understanding, and the internal coherence of the concept of freedom of will.

One of Harris's primary objectives is to place this debate in the context of the eighteenth-century concern with replicating in the mental sphere what Newton had achieved in the philosophy of nature. Most of the philosophers discussed in *Of Liberty and Necessity* conceive of themselves as 'experimental' reasoners, and, when examining the will, focus primarily upon what experience reveals about the influence of motives upon choice. The nature and significance of introspection is therefore at the very centre of the free will problem in this period, as is the question of what can legitimately be inferred from observable regularities in human behaviour.

James A. Harris is Lecturer in Philosophy at the University of St Andrews.

OXFORD PHILOSOPHICAL MONOGRAPHS

OTHER TITLES IN THE SERIES

Of Liberty and Necessity

The Free Will Debate in Eighteenth-Century British Philosophy

James A. Harris

Lecturer in Philosophy, University of St Andrews

CLARENDON PRESS·OXFORD

OXFORD
UNIVERSITY PRESS

Great Clarendon Street, Oxford OX2 6DP

Oxford University Press is a department of the University of Oxford.
It furthers the University's objective of excellence in research, scholarship,
and education by publishing worldwide in

Oxford New York

Auckland Cape Town Dar es Salaam Hong Kong Karachi
Kuala Lumpur Madrid Melbourne Mexico City Nairobi
New Delhi Shanghai Taipei Toronto

With offices in

Argentina Austria Brazil Chile Czech Republic France Greece
Guatemala Hungary Italy Japan Poland Portugal Singapore
South Korea Switzerland Thailand Turkey Ukraine Vietnam

Oxford is a registered trade mark of Oxford University Press
in the UK and in certain other countries

Published in the United States
by Oxford University Press Inc., New York

British Library Cataloguing in Publication Data

Data available

Library of Congress Cataloging in Publication Data

Data available

Typeset by SPI Publisher Services, Pondicherry, India
Printed in Great Britain on acid-free paper by Biddles Ltd., King's Lynn, Norfolk

ISBN 978-0-19-926860-3 (Hbk.)   978-0-19-923475-2 (Pbk.)

1 3 5 7 9 10 8 6 4 2

For A. H. S.

PREFACE

Historical studies of philosophical ideas and arguments are sometimes motivated by an interest in what the philosophers of the past have to teach philosophers of the present day. Such an approach need not be predicated upon the assumption that the philosophers of the past in question were wiser and closer to the truth than philosophers of the present day. It could be that what is to be learned from are the mistakes of the past. Nevertheless, this approach to the history of philosophy justifies itself, when it is asked to do so, by adverting to the use of historical work for live and ongoing philosophical research projects. My concerns here are less ambitious. I mean to do no more than understand a particular period's treatment of the free will question in that period's own terms. I am interested, that is to say, in what is characteristic of eighteenth-century thought about the will, and in what differentiates it from the thought that went before and the thought that came after. While it is arguable that the central problems of philosophy are timeless, in the sense of being questions that all reflective people must find pressing, regardless of historical and geographical circumstance, it would be plainly false to claim that there is just one style of reasoning appropriate to all attempts to solve those problems. The eighteenth century in Britain echoes with declarations to the effect that a new, 'experimental', method is called for in the philosophy of mind. In what follows I hope to capture how this new philosophical method shapes discussion of the will and its freedom.

Just as an exercise of the present kind stands a chance of frustrating philosophers, so also it is all too likely not to satisfy historians. I say little about several contexts—religious, scientific, and political—consideration of which would be necessary to a full understanding of any eighteenth-century British philosophical dispute. My focus is upon the play of ideas, upon argument and counterargument, rather than upon what might be responsible for the fact that particular ideas and arguments appeal to particular people in particular times and places. This is, then, a fairly conventional work in the history of philosophical ideas. I do, however, believe that the kind of history of ideas that concentrates only upon canonical texts is bound to produce a more distorted view of its period than the kind that juxtaposes the canonical with the almost forgotten. Minor figures in the history of philosophy provide the background against which the achievements of the major figures can best be identified and understood. They often voice the received wisdom and generally held assumptions which one does well to keep in mind when assessing what a major figure is trying to do. To the extent, then, that I attend to writers who are no longer very widely read as well as to much more familiar figures, I do not ignore context altogether.

This book does not pretend to provide a comprehensive account of every aspect of the question concerning the nature and extent of human freedom as discussed in eighteenth-century British philosophy. The thread of argument that I follow is identified and characterized in the Introduction. In the texts that I focus upon, this thread is very often entangled with others, and it would require a much longer book to separate them all out, and to give equal attention to each. Several issues that are central to eighteenth-century discussions of freedom of will are therefore touched on only in passing. I say little about contemporary discussions of the relation of human freedom to divine foreknowledge and to predestination. Nor do I treat at any length the related issue of how to explain the presence of evil in a world supposedly under the governance of a supremely benevolent, intelligent, and powerful deity. I give much less space than might be expected by a reader familiar with the present-day free will debate to views about the conditions of moral responsibility, and about the moral basis and practical justification of punishment.

I do not marginalize these things because I consider them insignificant to the philosophers that feature in my narrative. The importance of religious issues, in particular, to almost all philosophers of the eighteenth century is difficult to exaggerate. While the official view, so to speak, in this period is that we come to know the mind of God through analogical study of the mind of man, it is surely very likely that theological presuppositions have a tendency to shape in advance a writer's conception of the powers of the human mind. It would be naive to imagine that religious belief never plays a role in the initial formation of a particular position with respect to the freedom of the will, and to take on trust statements to the effect that it is 'experience' and experience alone that has determined that position. However, detailed research on the interplay between theology and philosophy in the eighteenth century remains in its infancy. For far too long it was assumed that the philosophy in the texts of, for example, Locke or Reid could be understood and debated quite independently of the theology. The situation is improving, but a great deal more needs to be done before we will be in a position from which to see a Locke or a Reid in the round. The thread of argument that I follow here will, I hope, find a place in a history of eighteenth-century British philosophy, yet to be written, that does full justice to the complexity of the period's enquiries into the various powers of the human mind.

This book has its origins in an Oxford University D.Phil. thesis, and my thanks go first to my supervisor, Galen Strawson, who was throughout patient, encouraging, and helpful in every way. I hope he will forgive my continuing resistance to the notion that it is a task of the historian of philosophy to point out the relevance of old ideas to present-day debates. Ralph Walker supervised my work during my first year as a doctoral student, and continued to read through drafts when he had many other duties to attend to. Alexander Broadie, Dan Robinson, Paul Russell, Agnieszka Steczowicz, John Stephens, M. A. Stewart, and Wayne Waxman all provided very useful comments on parts of my thesis. David Wiggins was a great support while I was a graduate student at Oxford, and I should like to record my gratitude to him here. I am grateful also to the Humanities Research Board of the British Academy and the Royal Institute of Philosophy for financial support during my doctoral research. I finished my thesis at the University of Glasgow, and I thank the trustees of the Gifford Trust, and Alexander Broadie in particular, for the honour of election to a Gifford Research Fellowship.

As I have revised the thesis, I have sought to make the best possible use of the comments of my examiners, Michael Ayers and Knud Haakonssen. Since that first encounter in 2000, on the birthday of both Hume and Reid, Knud Haakonssen has been a constant source of wisdom and advice. M. A. Stewart has been another invaluable guide and teacher. It is, however, all too likely that this book will fail to meet the standards set by Haakonssen and Stewart for historians of eighteenth-century British philosophy. Those who have helped me minimize the number of mistakes and infelicities include John Hedley Brooke, Thomas Dixon, Allen Guelzo, Peter Millican, Victor Nuovo, Agnieszka Steczowicz, Matthew Stuart, Paul Wood, and an anonymous reader for Oxford University Press. I am especially grateful to Gideon Yaffe for having read the entire typescript with the care and acuity that characterizes his own work on the free will problem in eighteenth-century British philosophy. Needless to say, all remaining errors of fact and interpretation are wholly my own responsibility.

I turned my doctoral thesis into this book while a British Academy Postdoctoral Fellow. I hope that the Fellowship of the British Academy will be satisfied that I have made the most of the enormous privilege of three years of generous financial support. St Catherine's College, Oxford, was my academic home during my tenure of the British Academy Postdoctoral Fellowship, and I was made extremely welcome there by the Master and Fellows. I owe a special debt of gratitude to my 'mentor', Bill Brewer, for inviting me to come to St. Catherine's in the first place, and for ensuring that I had the time and space that I needed for my work. Almost all of the research for both thesis and book was done in the Upper Reading Room of the Bodleian Library, and I should like to express my gratitude to the staff of the Upper Reading Room for their unfailing amiability and helpfulness. Like every member of Oxford's Faculty of Philosophy, I have been aided in many ways by Karen Heald, the Faculty's Administrator. Encouragement and advice have been freely given me by my editor, Peter Momtchiloff, who has made the process of writing a first book much less intimidating than it might otherwise have been.

It would not have been possible for me to start on the road towards a career in academia without the support of my family. I am conscious that in particular I owe a great deal to my paternal grandparents, James Cole Harris and Melloney Harris, and it saddens me greatly that neither lived long enough to see tangible proof, as I hope, that I have not wasted the opportunities they helped provide me with.

ACKNOWLEDGEMENTS

I should like to thank the editors of the following journals for permission to use passages from previously published material: *Enlightenment and Dissent* ('Joseph Priestley and "the proper doctrine of philosophical necessity"', 20 (2001): 25–44); *Reid Studies* ('James Beattie, the doctrine of liberty, and the science of the mind', 5 (2002): 16–29); *The British Journal for the History of Philosophy* ('On Reid's "inconsistent triad": a reply to McDermid', 11 (2003): 121–7); 'Hume's reconciling project and "the common distinction betwixt *moral* and *physical* necessity"', 11 (2003): 451–71). I should also like to thank Thoemmes Press for permission to use passages from my 'Introduction' to Abraham Tucker, *The Light of Nature Pursued*, Bristol, 2003.

CONTENTS

Introduction
From Locke to Dugald Stewart

> It were better perhaps to treat of this abstruse subject after the manner
> of experimental philosophy, than to fill a thousand pages with meta-
> physical discussions concerning it.
>
> Colin Maclaurin, *An Account of Sir Isaac Newton's*
> *Philosophical Discoveries*, Book I

The eighteenth century covered in this book is a long one. It begins with the
appearance in 1690 of John Locke's *An Essay concerning Human Understanding*, and
closes in 1828 with the last of the works by Dugald Stewart published in his
own lifetime, *The Philosophy of the Active and Moral Powers of Man*. The idea that
Locke's *Essay* ushered in a new era in the history of British philosophy is
uncontroversial. It is true that no one could claim that there was immediate
and widespread agreement with the central doctrines put forward in the
Essay. Many of the early responses were very hostile, especially with respect to
Locke's attack on innate ideas, his account of personal identity, and his
apparent admission of the possibility of thinking matter. Locke was regarded
by some as indistinguishable from the deists and worse—John Toland,
Anthony Collins, Voltaire, and others—who were prominent among the
Essay's first admirers. It took forty years for the *Essay* to appear on the
curricula of the universities of England and Scotland, and even then its
position was not secure. But the opposition that Locke provoked is testimony
to the seriousness with which he was taken. In time, charges of secret
Socinianism or Spinozism became less frequent. Though there remained a
great deal of criticism of his positive views, Locke was increasingly recognized
as having had a significant and beneficial effect on the manner in which

philosophical questions were being discussed. Where before Locke there had been the barbarous terminology and innumerable distinctions within distinctions of medieval philosophy, afterwards, so it was claimed (with some unfairness to Hobbes), philosophy was written in plain English, with every effort made to define as clearly as possible the terms used and to minimize technicality.[1]

Fidelity to experience is the principal concern of the Lockean philosopher. In a reaction against the extravagant claims made on behalf of *a priori* reasoning in the age of Descartes, Spinoza, and Malebranche, eighteenth-century enquiry into both inanimate nature and the human mind is self-consciously limited to what can be given 'experimental' confirmation. In his *Cyclopædia* of 1728 Ephraim Chambers wrote that 'Experiments, within these fifty or sixty years, are come into such vogue, that nothing will pass in philosophy, but what is founded on experiment, or confirm'd by experiment, &c. so that the new philosophy is altogether experimental.'[2] In the eighteenth century, an 'experiment' is not necessarily an investigation specifically designed to test a certain theory, and carried out in a laboratory or in some other form of controlled conditions. Experimental philosophy is, simply, philosophy that aims to be true to the facts of experience, and the experience in question might well be that of everyday life. An important factor in Locke's success was the manner in which he succeeded in making it possible for his readers to think of themselves as practising philosophy when they compared the description of the mind given in the *Essay* with their own experience of themselves, their acquaintances, and the world in general.[3] In the Introduction to *A Treatise of Human Nature*, Hume puts Locke at the head of a list of 'some late philosophers in *England*, who have begun to put the science of man on a new footing, and have engaged the attention, and excited the curiosity of the public'.[4] Though these philosophers—in addition to Locke, he names Shaftesbury, Mandeville, Hutcheson, and Butler—'differ in many points among themselves', Hume later added, 'they seem all to agree in founding their accurate disquisitions of human nature entirely upon experience'.[5]

---

[1] For the reception of Locke in the eighteenth century, see, e.g., Maclean (1936), Yolton and Yolton (1985), pp. 1–37, Aarsleff (1994), Porter (2000), pp. 66–71.

[2] Chambers (1728), vol. i, p. 368.

[3] Stewart attributes Locke's success to the way in which he 'prepar[ed] the thinking part of his readers, to a degree till then unknown, for the unshackled use of their own reason' (Stewart (1854), p. 223).

[4] Hume (1739–40, 2000), p. 5.

[5] Ibid., p. 5; Hume (1740, 2000), p. 407.

The suggestion is that it is *because* the new wave of British philosophers rested their disquisitions upon experience that they excited public curiosity.

According to Bolingbroke, in reading the *Essay* one is 'led, as it were, thro a course of experimental philosophy. I am shewn my self; and in every instance there is an appeal to my perceptions, and to the reflection I make on my own intellectual operations.'[6] Locke's achievement, so those who came afterwards thought, was to show the way towards the replication in *moral* philosophy what had already been done in the philosophy of nature: towards, in other words, a 'Newtonianism of the mind'.[7] Sir James Mackintosh, for example, claimed that the *Essay* was 'the first considerable contribution in modern times towards the experimental philosophy of the human mind', and that 'before Locke, there was no example in intellectual philosophy of an ample enumeration of facts, collected and arranged for the express purpose of legitimate generalization'.[8] Mackintosh, like many other writers of the period, regarded Bacon as the source of modern experimentalism. Newton had shown what could be achieved in natural philosophy using Bacon's inductive method: Locke showed its fruitfulness in the philosophy of mind. The poet Edward Young had in his study busts of Newton and Locke, each with its motto: Newton's read 'Hic Natura Clavis est'; Locke's read 'Hic Hominis ostendit Tibi Te.'[9]

Entailed by the commitment to experimentalism that Locke shares with Newton is a clear sense of the distinction between questions that philosophy can answer and those that it cannot. Newton famously refuses to frame hypotheses about the cause of gravitational attraction; Locke says that he

---

[6] Quoted by MacLean (1936), pp. 11–12. Here Bolingbroke echoes Voltaire's pronouncement in his *Philosophical Letters*, written soon after his time in England in the second half of the 1720s, that where previous philosophers had only written 'the Romance of the Soul', Locke 'gave, with an Air of the greatest Modesty, the History of it' (Voltaire (1733), pp. 98–9). 'In the eyes of the eighteenth century,' Gerd Buchdahl writes, '[Locke] is the philosopher of "experience" *par excellence*' (Buchdahl (1961), p. 21).

[7] It would be an overstatement, and perhaps simply wrong, to say that Newton had a direct influence on the *Essay*: see Rogers (1978). My concern here is with the way in which Locke and Newton came to be associated with each other in eighteenth-century eyes: see Feingold (1988). The phrase 'Newton of the mind' appears to have been Kant's, in remarks on Rousseau: see Neiman (1994), pp. 36, 193–6.

[8] Mackintosh (1821), p. 240. A late-eighteenth-century German history of philosophy makes a similar point: 'discarding all systematic theories, [Locke] has, from actual experience and observation, delineated the features, and described the operations, of the human mind, with a degree of precision and minuteness, not found in Plato, Aristotle, or Des Cartes' (Enfield (1791), vol. ii, pp. 585–6).

[9] Feingold (1988), p. 299.

hopes 'to prevail with the busy Mind of Man, to be more cautious in meddling with things exceeding its Comprehension; to stop, when it is at the utmost of is Tether; and to sit down in a quiet ignorance of those Things, which, upon Examination, are found to be beyond the reach of our Capacities'.[10] One of the things of which we must remain ignorant, according to Locke, is 'whether any mere material Being thinks, or no': 'it being impossible for us, by the contemplation of our own *Ideas*, without revelation, to discover, whether Omnipotency has not given to some Systems of Matter fitly disposed, a power to perceive and think, or else joined and fixed to Matter so disposed, a thinking immaterial Substance'.[11] Locke begins the *Essay* by making it clear that his investigation into the capacities of the mind is to be carried out independently of the question of 'wherein its Essence consists'.[12] The mind–body question does not disappear completely from British philosophy of mind in the eighteenth century. On the contrary, and as already mentioned, Locke himself provoked a great deal of debate because he suggested that our ignorance of the essence of the mind leaves it open that, for all we know, thought might be a property of matter.[13] Nevertheless, it is for the most part true that self-consciously 'experimental' philosophers do not regard ontology as the foundation of inquiry into the mind's powers. Those who came after Locke believed that the question of what the mind is made of could be ignored while one sought to discover how it worked.[14]

The Free will Problem in the Eighteenth Century

My concern in this book is with eighteenth-century British discussion of the faculty of will. Locke defines the will as 'a *Power* to begin or forbear, to continue or end several actions of our minds, and motions of our Bodies,

---

[10] Locke (1690, 1975), pp. 44–5 (i.i.4).

[11] Ibid., pp. 540–1 (iv.iii.6).

[12] Ibid., p. 43 (i.i.2).

[13] This debate is chronicled in Yolton (1983).

[14] Gary Hatfield writes in a study of eighteenth-century psychology across Europe that 'Ontological questions were bracketed in order to concentrate on study of mental faculties through their empirical manifestations in mental phenomena and external behavior.... Psychological theorizing was only rarely pursued as part of an attempt to cast doubt on (or to secure) the existence of immaterial souls or their connection with things divine' (Hatfield (1995), p. 188). As Cassirer puts it, 'The metaphysics of the soul is to be replaced by a history of the soul, by that "historical, plain method" which Locke had maintained against Descartes' (Cassirer (1932, 1951), p. 99).

barely by a thought or preference of the mind ordering, or as it were commanding the doing or not doing such and such a particular action'.[15] This power, Locke adds in the second edition of the *Essay*, is not simply a matter of the reliable determination of one's actions by one's passions and desires. Exercise of the will is self-conscious selection of one particular course of action as the one to be pursued: to possess a will is to have the power to *choose* to act in one way rather than in another. 'The faculty of will', says Jonathan Edwards, 'is that faculty or power or principle of the mind by which it is capable of choosing: an act of the will is the same as an act of choosing or choice.'[16] Reid describes the will as, simply, 'our determination to act or not to act'. The will, Reid continues, cannot be defined, for 'the most simple acts of the mind do not admit of a logical definition': 'The way to form a clear notion of them is, to reflect attentively upon them as we feel them in ourselves.' Nevertheless, there are some means by which to distinguish volitions from other acts of the mind. When one wills something, one has a conception, more or less distinct, of what it is that one wills (this differentiates voluntary acts from things done from instinct or habit); what one wills is always an action of one's own (as is not true of desires and commands); what one wills (as opposed, again, to what one desires) is always something one believes oneself able to do; and, finally, 'in all determinations of the mind that are of any importance, there must be something in the preceeding state of the mind that disposes or inclines us to that determination'.[17] Not all, but by far the greater number of the philosophers of the period hold, with Reid, that, if the will is ever in a state of perfect indifference, the resultant actions are trivial to the point of insignificance. The business of the will is with the 'principles of action' that, according to Reid, God has given us to choose among. These principles are of various kinds. They include instincts and habits; appetites, desires, affections, and passions; and considerations of prudence and duty. All of these are very often described as 'motives'. One important element of eighteenth-century discussions of the will is the analysis and categorization of different kinds of motive. Here, however, I focus upon a different question, concerning the nature of the relation between motives, on the one hand, and acts of choice, on the other. At its starkest, the question is this: are we free in our volitions? or is

---

[15] Locke (1690, 1975), p. 236 (II.xxi.5).   [16] Edwards (1754, 1957), p. 137.

[17] Reid (1788, 1969), pp. 58–63 (II.i).

the influence of motives such that they do not merely 'dispose' or 'incline' choice, but in fact necessitate it?

This was of course by the time of the eighteenth century already an ancient question. Being an ancient question, it had many aspects, and there were various ways in which it could be framed. In different periods, people had found different things threatening to the freedom of the will. For around a century after the Reformation, doctrines of predestination and an inherited original sin were regarded by some as an obvious danger to man's sense of his moral responsibility for his actions—and as incompatible with the justice of divine punishment of human sin. During the seventeenth century, however, as the storm created by Luther and Calvin slowly died down, there gained ground the notion that it is not only in theology that problems are generated for belief in the freedom of our choices. Just in so far as acts of choice are part of the causal order of the universe, it began to be claimed, and irrespective of whether that causal order has a basis in the divine will, our volitions could be regarded as determined by factors over which we have no control. This line of thought, which had its proximate source in the more radical elements of Italian Renaissance humanism (in Pomponazzi, in particular), was articulated forcefully by Hobbes in a debate with the Bishop of Derry, John Bramhall.[18]

Bramhall's position, which he took himself to share with 'the much greater part of philosophers and Schoolmen', was that a human agent has absolute power over the choices he makes. No matter how strong the motive to act in a certain way, there is always the possibility of choosing to act in a different way. No normal, healthy human agent can ever truly claim that he *has* to choose as he does. In the case of any choice made in the past, it was possible for the agent to have chosen differently. But this is not to say that the will is indifferent to the deliverances of the understanding. Bramhall says that there is a middle way between motives having no influence on choice and their taking away the capacity of choosing differently. 'Motives determine not naturally but morally,' he says, 'which kind of determination may consist with true liberty'.[19] It will be seen in this study that the notion of a

---

[18] For the Renaissance debate, see Poppi (1988). Sleigh, Chappell, and Della Rocca (1998) is a general account of the seventeenth-century free will debate. The key texts in the Hobbes–Bramhall dispute are Hobbes (1654); Bramhall (1655); Hobbes (1656a), Bramhall (1658). A selection from these texts is provided in Chappell (ed.) (1999). The fullest accounts of the circumstances and content of the Hobbes–Bramhall dispute are given in Lessay (1993) and Foisneau (1999).

[19] Bramhall (1655), p. 167; Chappell (ed.) (1999), p. 56.

'moral necessity' supposedly distinct from 'natural' or, as some say, 'physical', or 'literal', necessity plays a central role in discussions of the will in the eighteenth century. It allows, or perhaps merely *appears* to allow, the believer in the freedom of the will to distinguish between, on the one hand, the way in which a cause determines its effect, and, on the other, the way in which a motive influences a choice. A motive, according to believer in the freedom of the will, is not, properly speaking, the cause of an act of will. A motive is better thought of as an *occasion* for the agent to exercise his will in a particular way. Most of those eighteenth-century philosophers who reject the idea that choice is necessitated by motives agree with the essential features of Bramhall's position. A small minority are suspicious even of the 'moral' necessitation of the will by motives, and affirm that freedom lies in the will's natural indifference.

I shall use the term 'libertarian' as shorthand for the view that the influence of motives, however characterized, is not such as to eliminate freedom of choice. It is perhaps worth drawing attention to the fact that *no* opponent of the doctrine of necessity believes that it is the mark of a free action that it lacks a cause. Nor is there any talk of the will as subject to some form of 'indeterministic' causation. The libertarian of the eighteenth century is a believer in what philosophers of today call 'agent causation'.[20] In other words, he holds that there is an alternative to regarding motives as the causes of choices and actions. Sometimes libertarians talk of the will as the cause of its own acts; at other times they talk of the agent as cause. That either way of talking is apt to sound strange to us now is a sign of significant differences between, so to speak, eighteenth and twenty-first-century philosophical environments. It is these differences (rather than the obvious similarities) that I hope this book will illuminate.

I shall follow late eighteenth-century usage and call those who believe that the influence of motives *is* such as to remove freedom of choice 'necessitarians'. 'Determinist' and 'determinism' are words coined in the nineteenth century.[21] It is very common for necessitarians to argue that, despite what libertarians might say, the libertarian position does involve a commitment to events without causes. Hobbes made this charge against

[20] For a representative sample of recent discussions of agent causation, see O'Connor (ed.) (1995). The most sustained recent elaboration of an agent causal theory of human action is O'Connor (2000).

[21] The *OED* cites one Sir William Hamilton's notes to his edition of Reid's collected works as the first use of the word 'determinism' (see Hamilton (1863), p. 87). In a letter to James Gregory,

Bramhall, and most eighteenth-century necessitarians follow suit. The libertarian picture of freedom, Hobbes claimed, 'implies a contradiction, and is non-sense'.[22] Bramhall would have it *both* that there is a cause—a motive, or set of motives—sufficient to explain a particular choice *and* that that choice might not have been made; and, Hobbes argues, this amounts to saying that the choice *both* has a cause *and* does not have a cause. For a cause of an event is by definition something sufficient to explain why the event took place when and where it did; and what is sufficient to explain an event is by definition something that necessitates that event; since if it were still possible for the event not to take place, it would be clear that the claim to sufficiency was not true.[23] A motive, then, cannot be *sufficient* to explain an action and yet not thereby *necessitate* that action. In so far as he rejects the doctrine of necessity, Bramhall must be affirming that choices are radically underdetermined by motives, and that free choice is arbitrary, random, and disconnected from the exercise of practical reason. Hobbes is, moreover, sharply critical of the notion of a merely 'moral' necessity. He says he can make no sense at all of a necessity which does not involve genuine necessitation. Necessity by definition takes away the freedom to choose and act otherwise than in line with one's motives. He also argues that there is no threat to freedom from the 'natural' necessitation of choice by motives, since liberty is simply a matter of not being prevented from acting in line with the most pressing motive. What we call the will is in fact simply the motive, or 'appetite', that immediately precedes action; and deliberation is 'nothing else but the *alternate* imagination of the *good* and *evil* sequels of action, or (which is the same thing) alternate *hope* and *fear*, or alternate *appetite* to do or quit the action of which [a man] *deliberateth*'.[24]

Reid says he believes that Alexander Crombie 'may claim the merit of adding the word *Libertarian* to the English language, as Priestley added that of Necessarian' (Reid (2002), pp. 234–5). William Belsham in fact uses the term 'libertarian' before Crombie. The *OED* lists the title of Dudgeon (1739) as the first use of 'necessitarian'.

[22] Hobbes (1654), p. 73; Chappell (ed.) (1999), p. 39.

[23] For discussion of Hobbes's definition of 'cause' see Brandt (1928); Leijenhorst (1996); Pécharman (1990); Zarka (2001). The connection made between causation and sufficiency is made before Hobbes by some in the Renaissance Aristotelian tradition. What is most obviously new in Hobbes is the notion that a cause is not by definition a substance: a Hobbesian cause may be a collection of accidents of two or more substances. Pécharman calls this 'la déréalisation de la cause' (p. 49). Leijenhorst notes how Hobbes blurs the traditional Thomistic distinction between 'internal conditions' and 'external circumstances', making both 'things requisite to produce the effect' (p. 432).

[24] Hobbes (1654), p. 68; Chappell (ed.) (1999), p. 37. For Hobbes's theory of mind, see Sorell (1986), ch. vii, and Gert (1996).

In all of this, especially in his claim that liberty is compatible with necessity, Hobbes was extremely influential. For present purposes, however, there is another element of his attack on the freedom of the will that is equally important. This is his use of the rhetoric of the new mechanistic science of motion.[25] The notion that 'a man originally can move himself', Hobbes claims, is one for which Bramhall 'will be able to find no Authority of any that have but tasted of the knowledge of motion'.[26] In the movements of the mind it is as it is in the movements of body: every change is caused by something external. Bramhall describes the influence of motives upon the will as a species of 'Metaphoricall motion', and compares it to the manner in which 'a man *drawes* a Child after him with the sight of a fair Apple, or a Shepheard *drawes* his sheep after him with the sight of a green bough'.[27] According to Hobbes, such talk is 'insignificant', or meaningless, and is a sign of his opponent's lack of 'philosophy'. 'Moral motion is a meer Word, without any Imagination of the mind correspondent to it.'[28] Hobbes repeatedly presents himself in the debate with Bramhall as one who has meditated closely upon 'this and other natural questions' while the Bishop relies solely on 'the authority of books'. Hobbes is a philosopher notoriously sceptical about the claims made by some of his contemporaries about the value of experience in the acquisition of knowledge, but he is, nevertheless, prepared to say that for his definitions of deliberation, of the will, and of freedom 'there can no other proof be offered but every mans own experience, by reflection on himself'. 'But to those that out of custom speak not what they conceive, but what they hear, and are not able, or will not take the pains to consider what they think when they hear such words', he continues, 'no Argument can be sufficient, because *experience* and *matter of fact* is not verified by other mens Arguments, but by every man's own *sence* and *memory*.'[29]

Throughout the eighteenth century, opponents of the freedom of the will, whether consciously or not, echo Hobbes's claim that experience provides sufficient proof of the necessitation of choice by motive. Necessitarians like to regard themselves as 'philosophical' reasoners: as, that is to say,

[25] For Hobbes's conception of natural philosophy, see Brandt (1928) and Jesseph (1996).

[26] Hobbes (1656a), p. 37.

[27] Bramhall (1655), p. 172; Chappell (ed.) (1999), pp. 57–8.

[28] Hobbes (1656a), p. 231.

[29] Hobbes (1654), pp. 74–5; Chappell (ed.) (1999), p. 39. In *De corpore* he remarks, similarly, that 'the causes of the motions of the mind are known, not only by ratiocination, but also by the experience of every man that takes the pains to observe these motions within himself' (Hobbes (1656b, 1839), p. 73).

followers of the methods of reasoning advocated by Bacon and Newton. They dwell, in particular, upon observed regularities in human behaviour, upon constant conjunctions of types of motives and types of actions, as proof that motives are the causes of actions in just the same sense as *natural* phenomena are causally related to each other. An important part of what keeps the free will debate going in this period, however, is the fact that those who believe in the will's freedom reject absolutely the charge that there is something, as we might say now, 'unscientific' about their conception of human action. From their point of view it is, rather, the proponents of necessity who cling to theories at the expense of facts, and who are guilty of inadequate attention to experience. What we experience when we reflect on ourselves, they believe, is the inability of motives, so to speak, to make our choices for us. Motives have an influence on choice that is comparable to advice. No matter how strong the inducements to act in one way, we are conscious of a capacity to choose to do something quite different. And even if this is not apparent at the time of action, it can become so later, with the onset of remorse. What is often called 'consciousness' is in this way an essential element of the libertarian claim that *experience* is of the will's freedom, rather than of its necessitation. The importance attached to the deliverances of introspection is one of the most striking features of eighteenth-century argument about the freedom of the will. Some of those who reject the doctrine of necessity believe that consciousness of the freedom of the will is so clear and undeniable that any argument that appears to speak for necessitarianism may be regarded as worthless even before its faults have been revealed. Others provide a detailed examination of the arguments the necessitarian uses to try to establish the determination of the will by motives. It is a common charge that the necessitarian exaggerates the uniformity of the connection between types of motive and types of action: that actions are more irregular and unpredictable than the necessitarian is prepared to admit. There is, in addition, a belief among libertarians that the doctrine of necessity is shown to be untenable by the practical consequences, in morals and in religion, of taking it as true. But the philosophers I discuss here do not rest their case solely on arguments from consequences. For all of them the free will question is in the first instance a question of empirical fact.

This concentration of attention upon the experience of choice and action is accompanied by the lack of concern with ontological issues characteristic of Lockean thought about the mind. In the seventeenth century, it is not uncommon for arguments to run directly from materialism to necessitarianism, and from the immateriality of the mind to libertarianism. Hobbes's necessitarianism is generally thought to be a consequence of his material-ism;[30] and so Cudworth is able to write that 'it is a sufficient confutation of [Hobbes] to show that there is another substance in the world besides body'.[31] In the eighteenth century, by contrast, this kind of argumentation is rare. Joseph Priestley, for example, claims that 'if man ... be wholly *material*, it will not be denied but that he must be a *mechanical being*';[32] but nevertheless makes an independent and wholly experimental case for the doctrine of necessity. He also argues that the immateriality of the soul would, even if true, fail to settle things in favour of the libertarian. If the mind is immaterial, he concedes, it follows that it is not subject to the laws of matter; 'but it does not, therefore, follow that it is subject to *no laws at all*, and consequently has a self-determining power, independent of all laws, or rule of its determin-ation'.[33] The libertarian position 'can derive no advantage from the com-monly received principles of the *immateriality of the human soul*.[34] Other eighteenth-century necessitarians, such as Kames, Edwards, Hartley, and Tucker, believe the mind to be immaterial; some libertarians, such as Reid and Stewart, see no reason why, if matter could take on mental properties, a wholly material being might not also have freedom of will. Reid writes:

If matter be what we conceived it to be, it is equally incapable of thinking and of acting freely. But if the properties from which we drew this conclusion, have no reality, as [Priestley] thinks he has proved; if it have the powers of attraction and repulsion, and require only a certain configuration to make it think rationally, it will be impossible to show any good reason why the same configuration may not make it act rationally and freely. If its reproach of solidity, inertness, and sluggish-ness be wiped off; and if it be raised in our esteem to a nearer approach to the nature of what we call spiritual and immaterial beings, why should it still be nothing but a mechanical being?[35]

Reid does not put this forward as a genuine possibility. There is plenty of evidence to suggest that he thought the arguments for the immateriality of

[30] See, e.g., Clarke (1738), vol. ii, p. 563.
[31] British Museum MS 4979, fol. 61; quoted in Mintz (1962), p. 127.
[32] Priestley (1782), vol. ii, p. xvii.
[33] Priestley (1779), p. 13.
[34] Priestley (1780b), p. 40.
[35] Reid (1788, 1969), pp. 356–7 (iv.xi). For an identical argument, see Stewart (1828), vol. ii, pp. 479–80. Priestley's opponent Lawrence Butterworth makes the same point: 'But were we to allow that man is *material*, and that his soul is no more than a property: yet it does not follow from thence, that he is incapable of acting of himself' (Butterworth (1792), p. 352).

the mind to be perfectly conclusive.[36] The remarkable thing is the fact that Reid, *qua* libertarian, does not believe it to be important whether the mind can be proven to be immaterial. Priestley and Reid differ about as deeply as is possible for two parties debating the free will question to differ, but they agree that theories about the essence of mind can be put to one side while the question is discussed. Because the philosophers to be discussed themselves regard it as irrelevant, the eighteenth-century debate about the possibility of thinking matter will not be brought to bear upon this study's account of the period's treatments of the relation between motives and volitions.

Summary of the Narrative

Eighteenth-century British philosophy may begin with Locke, but it was a source of frustration to many of the period's writers on the will that Locke himself failed to give a straight answer to the question of whether the will is left at liberty by the influence of motives. In the *Essay*'s chapter 'Of Power' Locke commits himself to neither the libertarian nor the necessitarian answer to this question. In Chapter 1 I suggest that Locke's project in 'Of Power' is to define freedom in such a way that it involves neither the indifference of the will nor the determination of choice by the understanding. Locke seems to have come to feel that in the first edition of the *Essay* he had recoiled too far from the liberty of indifference towards a doctrine of psychological determinism. His original position is that it is incoherent to attribute freedom to the will; he later introduces a 'power of suspension'; and in the fifth and final edition he allows that there is, after all, 'a case wherein a Man is at Liberty of *willing*'. What persuades Locke to change his view is in large part renewed attention to the experience of choice, and especially to the phenomenon of weakness of will. This devotion to accurate analysis of volition left Locke's contemporaries confused, and in the last part of Chapter 1 I give a representative sample of eighteenth-century criticism of the chapter 'Of Power'. Perhaps unsurprisingly, in light of this apparently widespread dissatisfaction, Locke's own contribution to the question of liberty and necessity does not play an important role in the eighteenth-century debate charted in this study. This should not be thought a reason to question the

---

[36] See Reid (1995), pp. 217–31; and also the first of the 'Three Lectures on the Nature and the Duration of the Soul' included in Reid (1785, 2002), pp. 617–18, 619.

importance of Locke to those who came after him. Locke's influence lay in his method, his style of philosophizing, rather than in his substantive philosophical doctrines.

Locke's method, however, did not take hold immediately. The principal protagonists of Chapter 2, Samuel Clarke and Anthony Collins, in effect resume the debate between Bramhall and Hobbes. But before I introduce Clarke and Collins, I describe the unusual definition of freedom presented by William King in *De Origine Mali*. King is a defender of the liberty of indifference: he believes that freedom is most purely realized in the exercise of a capacity to choose to act in a certain way regardless of the recommendations of the understanding. Clarke, like Locke, believes that to define freedom in this way is a serious mistake; and, following Bramhall, he seeks to negotiate a middle way between the indifference of the will, on the one hand, and the literal determination of the will by motives, on the other. The notion of 'moral necessity', as distinct from 'literal' or 'physical' necessity, is at the heart of Clarke's theory of freedom. It allows him to connect free choice with rationality (and goodness) without conceding that, at any one time, the influence of the understanding makes only one choice possible. Clarke also argues that a motive is not the kind of thing that can be a cause, and also that an action cannot, on pain of contradiction, be caused by something exterior to the agent. Clarke had a significant influence on all later libertarians. Collins's necessitarianism is identical to Hobbes's. Like Hobbes, he argues that libertarianism is defeated by a correct analysis of the concept of cause. But he also presents an extended analysis of what experience tells us about the operations of perception, judgment, choice, and action.

Clarke and Collins rely a good deal on *a priori* metaphysical argumentation of the kind that the characteristically eighteenth-century philosopher regards with suspicion. The first to approach the question of the nature of the influence of motives wholly in the spirit of Lockean experimentalism is Hume. Hume describes himself as a reconciler, and in Chapter 3 I give an interpretation of his 'reconciling project' that rests on the assumption that Hume is serious in wanting to show there to be underlying agreement between libertarians and necessitarians. Unlike Hobbes and Collins, Hume is not primarily concerned with showing it to be *impossible* that we might choose and act otherwise than we do. I suggest that the key to understanding Hume's strategy is the distinction between 'moral' and 'physical' necessity that libertarians such as Bramhall and Clarke attach so much importance to. What Hume does is show that all the doctrine of necessity amounts to, when properly understood, is something that the libertarian already concedes: that there is certain motives are regularly followed by certain actions, such that human action is largely uniform and so predictable. We cannot settle the metaphysical disputes that have traditionally divided libertarians and necessitarians, and so should give up on them, and focus upon experience; and when we do focus upon the experience of action, libertarians and necessitarians turn out to be in agreement.

There is, however, one important aspect of the experience of action that Hume has explained away in order to get the result that he wants. This is the first-person perspective, the agent's sense of not being determined by motives at the time of choice and action, and of having been able to have acted differently in retrospect. In Chapter 4 I describe the attempt made by another necessitarian, Lord Kames, to accommodate the agent's own perspective. There is a natural belief in necessity, he claims: Hume is correct about that. But there is in addition just as natural a belief that our choices and actions are not determined before they are made. Both practical, prudential reasoning and the operations of conscience depend on our believing the will to be free. Kames writes that 'man could not have been man, had he not been furnished with a feeling of contingency'. In order to resolve the paradox of directly contradictory natural beliefs, Kames hypothesizes that, though 'deceitful', the sense of freedom is an essential part of the fabric of the mind, given us by God in order that we be properly active and moral beings. God has to deceive us into thinking that we are free to ensure that we do not slip into sloth and fatalism. We should, therefore, be grateful that it is only in philosophical and reflective moments that we see through the deception. The idea that God might have to deceive us in order to realize his purposes was too much for Kames's contemporaries to take. Having given a brief account of the controversy generated by the hypothesis of a deceitful sense of freedom, I chart the alterations Kames makes to his view in later editions of his *Essays on the Principles of Morality and Natural Religion*.

In a pamphlet written in defence of Kames, Jonathan Edwards is invoked as proof of the fact that it is possible to be both a Christian and an opponent of the freedom of the will. Edwards's case for necessitarianism is the subject of Chapter 5. Edwards claimed not to have read Hobbes before he wrote his *Careful and Strict Inquiry into . . . Freedom of Will*, but he takes up the dilemma Hobbes had constructed for the libertarian, and gives it added sharpness. Either the believer in the liberty of the will in fact contradicts himself, by allowing the influence of motives on choice; or he is saying that free choices are undetermined and purely arbitrary. So Edwards argues. He attacks the libertarian picture of self-determination with great dialectical ingenuity. Hobbes and Locke had both dismissed the notion of the freedom of the will as involving an infinite regress of volitions; Edwards develops this line of argument, and shows that the notion, as he puts it, 'destroys itself'. Unlike Hobbes, however, Edwards finds use for the distinction between moral and physical necessity. The distinction is central to his claim that necessity as he understands it does not rule out human freedom and moral responsibility. Behind Edwards's necessitarianism is a view that he regards as a matter of everyday experience: that every event in nature, and every event in the minds of men, is directly the result of divine activity. I explore this aspect of Edwards's thought at the end of the chapter. The *Inquiry* was for the most part ignored by later opponents of the doctrine of necessity in Britain, and where it was not ignored, it was not taken very seriously. This is unfortunate, for it has a claim to being the eighteenth century's most powerful attack on the notion of the freedom of the will.

A reason why Edwards was for the most part ignored by British believers in the freedom of the will is perhaps to be found in Chapter 6. Here I introduce a line of thought according to which the introspective evidence of the freedom of the will, and of the falsity of necessitarianism, is so plain and strong that arguments which purport to identify contradictions and confusions in statements of the libertarian position can safely be disregarded. Johnson's dictum that 'All theory is against the freedom of the will; all experience for it' sums up this view very well. Others who adopt much the same approach to the question include Butler, Berkeley, and Richard Price. The liberty of the will, these men believe, is not only evident in experience, but is also the foundation of morality and religion. It is inconceivable, therefore, that there could be good reasons to doubt it. In Scotland this view manifests itself in the writings of two, at least, of the philosophers of common sense. I give a brief sketch of James Oswald's treatment of the will, but devote most of the chapter to the discussion of liberty and necessity found in James Beattie's *Essay on Truth*. According to Beattie, necessitarianism is a form of 'modern scepticism'. In other words, necessitarianism is meant to corrode and destroy the ordinary beliefs—particularly, again, the moral and religious beliefs—of ordinary people. It is, I suggest, Beattie's sense of the dangerousness of necessitarianism, and of the importance of belief in liberty, that explains the extraordinary violence of his attack on proponents of the doctrine of necessity—and on Hume in particular. Beattie is generally dismissed today as, in Hume's words, a 'bigotted silly Fellow', but in his own day he was enormously popular. What explains this is that many, if not most, of Beattie's contemporaries shared his sense of the importance of belief in liberty, and of the needlessness of engaging seriously with the arguments of necessitarians.

The success of the *Essay on Truth* prompted a broadside attack on the philosophy of common sense, not from a proponent of the scepticism Beattie denounces, but instead from Joseph Priestley, a philosopher peculiarly insensitive to the force of sceptical arguments of any kind. In his *Examination* of Reid, Beattie, and Oswald, Priestley charges the Scots with reinstating innate ideas with their talk of principles of common sense, and with generally abandoning the model of a science of the mind as laid out in Locke's *Essay*. What was essential to the Lockean project, according to Priestley, was the tracing of ideas to their source in sensation; and in David Hartley's *Observations on Man* showed how this was to be done. The association of ideas, in other words, was the central concept of any properly scientific account of the mind. In Chapter 7 I describe the necessitarian arguments of Hartley and Priestley, and try to determine what role associationalism plays in those arguments. I also examine the theory of the will developed by another Hartleyan philosopher, Abraham Tucker, in his enormous *The Light of Nature Pursued*. Tucker is principally concerned to show that freedom and providence are not in fact at odds with each other. It is in this connection that he differs most markedly from Hartley and Priestley, for both Hartley and Priestley believe that the doctrine of necessity entails that God is directly responsible for every human action. What, then, to do about the apparent prevalence of evil in the world? It is in providing an answer to this question that the association of ideas shows itself to be central to the solutions Hartley and Priestley give to the free will problem. Our current ideas about the nature of evil are the product of an inadequate understanding of the divine plan. In time, human beings will overcome their present ways of thinking, and associate all that happens with God's providential plan.

Like Priestley, if not more so, Thomas Reid is self-conscious in his presentation of himself as an 'experimental' reasoner. He believes that it is Hartleyan associationalism, and not the philosophy of common sense, that is at odds with the spirit of inductive inquiry into the operations of the mind. In Chapter 8 my intention is to supplement recent discussions of Reid's theory of action with an account of its place in Reid's reply to scepticism. Reid's account of freedom rests on a detailed analysis of the capacities that power over the will affords us: the capacities of mental attention, deliberation, and the making of resolutions. The centrality of belief in the freedom of the will to the practical life establishes it as a *natural* belief, a belief not the result of education or any other form of inculcation: as, in other words, a principle of common sense. The necessitarian can, of course, accept that the belief is natural, and argue that it is nevertheless false. Reid's response to the necessitarian is not, in the manner of Beattie, to point out the dangerous consequences of giving the belief up, and to attack the character of those who would have us do so. Nor is it to provide a direct argument for the belief's truth. It is, rather, to examine all the arguments which purport to demonstrate the truth of necessitarianism, and to show them to be wanting. Reid gives particular attention to arguments for necessity from the observable fact of the influence of motives on choice. He wants to show that there is nothing 'scientific', as we would say now, about belief in necessitarianism. According to Reid, the empirical evidence, properly understood, speaks rather for the liberty of the will.

The clash between Priestley and Reid over the freedom of the will is in a sense the climax of the free will debate in eighteenth-century British philosophy. For the next forty years, at least, necessitarians tended explicitly to align themselves with Priestley, and libertarians with Reid. In Chapter 9 I give a brief account of necessitarianism after Priestley, but focus upon the libertarian arguments of James Gregory and Dugald Stewart. Both Gregory and Stewart were personal friends of Reid's, and were significantly influenced in their approach to the free will problem by the *Essays on the Active Powers*. Nevertheless, they differed from Reid in interesting ways. Gregory thinks he can prove once and for all that the influence of motives upon human actions is not, as the necessitarian characteristically claims, the same as the influence of 'physical' causes upon their effects. His strategy is a *reductio ad absurdum* of the necessitarian view. Stewart, in contrast with both Gregory and Reid, appears not to think that the arguments of the necessitarian merit serious examination. He betrays something of Beattie's impatience with the idea that there is a substantive issue to be discussed in connection with the operations of the will. His principal discussion of liberty and necessity is to be found in an Appendix to *The Philosophy of the Active and Moral Powers of Man*. Stewart states that the *only* question which can be 'philosophically stated' on the subject of the will is whether or not 'the evidence of consciousness' is in favour of the scheme of free will or of the scheme of necessity. Stewart could not be regarded as a philosopher unaware of the explanatory scope of science, and of the science of the mind in particular. We see, therefore, that at the end of the 'long' eighteenth century described in this book, it is not by any means obvious to all that there is a problem combining belief in the freedom of the will with a serious concern with the development of a science of the human mind. In a brief Postscript I show that an 'experimental' debate between libertarians and necessitarians continues throughout the nineteenth century, and suggest that it is only in the early twentieth century that the terms of the free will debate change significantly.

The Lockean turn of eighteenth-century British philosophy thus failed to produce consensus as to the nature of the influence of motives upon the will. Libertarians and necessitarians were just as far apart at the end of the century as Bramhall and Hobbes had been 150 years earlier. One reason for this is that underlying general consensus as to the importance of experience to philosophy was profound disagreement about what exactly it meant, in Hume's phrase, 'to introduce the experimental method of reasoning into moral subjects'. On one side of this question were associationists like Hume, Hartley, Tucker, and Priestley; on the other were 'faculty psychologists' such as Kames, Beattie, Reid, and Stewart. It is not quite true to say that every associationist was a necessitarian, and every faculty psychologist was a libertarian. Nor is it true to say that every necessitarian was an associationist, and every libertarian a faculty psychologist. Nevertheless, it does seem to be true that, in the eighteenth century, and perhaps in the nineteenth century as well, one's stance with regard to the will and its freedom was to a significant extent shaped by one's understanding of what an empirical science of the mind should look like. Associationists tended to be necessitarians because the determination of choice by motives fits with the picture of the mind as a repetition-driven machine. Faculty psychologists tended to be libertarians because the autonomy of the will, its independence from the understanding, follows naturally from a view of the mind as a set of distinct and mutually irreducible functions or processes. It is a striking fact that both schools claim Locke's paternity for their version of the application of experimentalism to the mind. Locke invented the game, but left the rules so vague that it was never clear how the result was to be determined.

1

Locke's Chapter 'Of Power' and its Eighteenth-Century Reception

> Here even Locke, that cautious philosopher, was lost....
>
> Bolingbroke, *Fragments or Minutes of Essays*, Essay XLV

Locke's principal discussion of the nature of human freedom is in Chapter 21 of Book II of *An Essay concerning Human Understanding* (1690).[1] 'Of Power' is both the longest chapter of the *Essay* and the chapter that was most heavily revised, as Locke prepared his book for later editions. Soon after publication Locke changed his mind about several important matters, and presented a new account of freedom in the second (1694) edition of the *Essay*. Further significant changes were made for the fourth (1700) and fifth (1706) editions. The phenomena relevant to his enquiry in 'Of Power' appeared to Locke to be complex, and hence difficult to characterize accurately. In every edition, Locke is resistant to the idea that freedom consists in the *indifference* of the will to the deliverances of the understanding. It is manifest that our choices are strongly influenced by what the intellect tells us is the best course of action to follow; and it is hard to see why we should value the capacity to ignore the intellect and choose irrationally. In the first version of the *Essay*, this line of thought issues in the claim that the will is determined in its choices by what the understanding presents as being 'the greater good'. Correspondence with William Molyneux then persuaded Locke that in coupling volition and understanding in this way, one runs the risk of allowing freedom to disappear altogether. Moral responsibility is threatened as a result; but so is

---

[1] All quotations from the *Essay* will be from Locke (1690, 1975). References given in the main body of the text will be to section numbers of II.xxi rather than page numbers. Where a passage does not appear in all five editions, a number in bold will indicate which editions it is found in.

fidelity to the experience of choice. Locke is concerned particularly with the kind of mental conflict manifest in what philosophers now term 'weakness of will'. He wants to make sense of our capacity to choose to act badly while knowing what the best thing to do is, for, given familiar facts about human weakness and perverseness, it will not do for a philosopher to exaggerate our propensity to rational behaviour. In the first three sections of this chapter I shall give a summary account of Locke's attempts to find the right way of describing the relation between the will and the understanding. This is familiar ground, perhaps, but what I mean to add to existing accounts of 'Of Power' is a reminder of the prominence there of the discourse of experimental inquiry into the powers of the mind. Locke is interested in more than the mere *concept* of freedom. He intends to be true to the experience of freedom, to the experience of what deliberation and choice-making are actually like.

Locke is sometimes interpreted as presenting in 'Of Power' what would now be called a 'compatibilist' theory of freedom and moral responsibility. That is, he is read as being interested in showing that freedom, properly defined, is compatible with 'determinism'. On this reading Locke is principally concerned with 'articulating, filling in, and deepening Hobbes's analysis of freedom'.[2] Yet there is no explicit argument for anything like Hobbesian necessitarianism anywhere in the *Essay*, nor any explicit argument to the effect that freedom as Locke understands it is compatible with such necessitarianism.[3] Nor, it must immediately be said, is there an argument *against*

---

[2] Rickless (2001), p. 254. For claims that Locke seeks to show that moral responsibility (or freedom) is compatible with 'determinism', see, e.g., Jolley (1999), ch. 7, *passim*; Chappell (2000), pp. 236–7; Rickless (2000), p. 59; Yaffe (2000), pp. 4 and 142–3 n. 5. This consensus has been challenged by Schouls (1992), who argues that 'Locke's intention . . . was to present a consistent libertarian doctrine' (p. 119). Colman (1983), ch. 8, questions whether Locke is properly seen as a determinist, and so does Lowe (1995), p. 136. Yaffe (2000) presents a rich account of Lockean freedom, and argues that (while remaining compatibilist) Locke's decided view is that Hobbes's theory of freedom is inadequate: 'Locke's view is distinctive precisely by virtue of what he *adds* to Hobbes's view' (p. 74). Rickless (2001) argues that Locke remains more of a Hobbesian than Yaffe allows.

[3] Passages sometimes cited from the *Essay* in support of the claim that Locke is a determinist are at iv.x.3–4: 'bare *nothing can no more produce any real Being, than it can be equal to two right Angles*'; and 'what had its Being and Beginning from another, must also have all that which is in, and belongs to its Being from another too' (see Chappell (2000), p. 248 n. 2). But neither of these passages amounts to an argument for determinism. To claim that nothing comes from nothing and that what is brought into existence by something else must owe all its powers to its creator is compatible with the notion of a created being able to cause its own actions. Another passage that

Hobbesian necessity, nor a case made for its *incompatibility* with freedom and responsibility. Locke appears not to want to address the metaphysical—and theological—problems surrounding human freedom at all.[4] I believe that Locke intended his account of liberty to be entirely neutral with respect to the grand questions surrounding human volition and action, and shall not attempt to settle the question of whether or not Locke believed freedom to be compatible with necessitarianism as argued for by Hobbes.[5] Locke is a philosopher peculiarly alive to complexity and difficulty. He is, as Boling-broke has it, pre-eminently a *cautious* philosopher, one who shies away from clear and decisive pronouncements, and who is always ready to revise and restate in order to improve in accuracy of formulation. Elegance and clarity are not his *forte*. Elegance and clarity mattered to the philosophers of the eighteenth century, however, and, even though almost all who come after Locke protest their respect for him, wherever 'Of Power' is discussed, it is with dissatisfaction. Later philosophers wanted a clear answer to the questions posed by Hobbes, and they were only frustrated by what they found in Locke. Libertarians regarded Locke as having conceded too much to the necessitarian cause; necessitarians saw him as muddying a question that Hobbes had been the first to state perspicuously. In the final section of the chapter I shall give a representative sample of the complaints voiced by eighteenth-century philosophers about Locke's hesitancies and ambiguities.

has been claimed to show Locke's determinism is at ı.iii.14 (see Yaffe (2000), p. 143 n. 5), where Locke says that part of the evidence that there are no innate moral principles is that some deny the existence of all moral rules on the grounds that 'Men are no other than bare Machins.' This is an obscure passage, but it seems to me that all that Locke says there is that morality and mechanism 'are not very easy to be reconciled, or made consistent'; and that leaves it wide open whether or not Locke thought they can, in fact, be reconciled and made consistent.

[4] Nicholas Jolley has claimed that, unlike elsewhere in the *Essay*, 'in Locke's discussion of free will agnosticism plays no part; where freedom of the will is at issue, he conveys no sense that there are metaphysical facts which are hidden from out mental view' (Jolley (1999), p. 140). This is hard to square with Locke's repeated declarations to the effect that, while he is sure that we are free, he cannot see how to reconcile our freedom with divine omnipotence and omniscience: see, eg, ıv.xvii.10; Locke (1954), p. 276; and Locke (1979), pp. 625–6.

[5] I do not mean to deny that it could be that Locke did in fact believe in the doctrine of necessity, nor that it could be that he also believed freedom to be compatible with necessitation. At various places in 'Of Power' Locke says things that are most easily explained if he did hold these two beliefs. My point is that he does not argue explicitly and directly either for necessitarianism or for compatibilism.

First Thoughts about Freedom and Choice

Current in the Remonstrant culture in which Locke was immersed while in exile in Holland in the 1680s was a distinctive understanding of human freedom.[6] The Remonstrants rejected altogether the Calvinist doctrines of an inherited 'original sin' and predestination, along with the doctrine of an 'efficacious grace' that, once given, prevented the recipient from ever relapsing into sinfulness. They argued that Calvinism tended towards fatalism, and believed fervently in the natural freedom of the will. Essential to the will's freedom, they believed, was what they termed its *indifference*. Locke's friend Philip van Limborch had claimed that it is in the nature of the freedom of the will that we are able either to obey or disobey what the understanding dictates that we should do:

The true Liberty therefore of the Will consists in an active Indifference, whereby, having all things requisite for Action, it may act or not act, and may do this rather than that. And this Liberty is so far essential to the Will, that Man had it not only in a State of Innocence; but has it in every State or Condition whatsoever, the State of Sin not excepted. For Sin as 'tis an Act of a free Power, cannot destroy the Power of the Will; because, by its inordinacy, 'tis not contrary to the Liberty of the Will, but to Virtue.[7]

It was Locke's view that such a freedom as this is not worth the name. Freedom is surely something valuable, and there is nothing valuable about being able to set aside the deliverances of reason. In 'Of Power', as throughout Book II of the *Essay*, Locke's project is the clarification of ideas. He begins with the idea of power in general, separates out the idea of passive power, power to be changed, from the idea of active power, power to effect change; and he finds that our only idea of active power is taken from 'reflection on what passes in our selves, were we find by Experience, that barely by willing it, barely by a thought of the Mind, we can move the parts of our Bodies, which were before at rest' (§ 4). Our idea of active power, in other words, is an idea of volition; and '[f]rom the consideration of the extent of power of the mind over the actions of Man, which every one finds in himself, arise the *Ideas* of *Liberty* and *Necessity*' (§ 7). Locke appears more interested in the idea of freedom than he is in the idea of necessity. The question that concerns him

---

[6] For helpful introductions to Remonstrant, or (as it was often called) 'Arminian', thought, see Harrison (1937) and Colie (1957). For the rise of Arminianism in England in the first half of the seventeenth century, see Tyacke (1987).

[7] Limborch (1713), vol. I, p. 141.

most is not whether liberty is compatible with necessity, but rather how liberty is to be defined. One way to understand what Locke is doing in the various versions of 'Of Power' is to see him as struggling to produce a better definition of liberty than that offered by the Remonstrants.[8]

The first step to this end was to make it plain that freedom is not, and cannot be, a property of the will. Locke's introductory definition of liberty and its contrary runs as follows:

the *Idea* of *Liberty*, is the *Idea* of a Power in any Agent to do or forbear any particular Action, according to the determination or thought of the mind, whereby either of them is preferr'd to the other; where either of them is not in the Power of the Agent to be produced by him according to his *Volition*, there he is not at *Liberty*, that Agent is under *Necessity*.

(§ 9)

Unlike Hobbes in his more polemical moments, Locke insists that in order for something properly to be called either free or unfree, it must be a thinking being in possession of a capacity of making choices. A river can therefore neither be free nor unfree in its motions. Nor is freedom simply a matter of being able to do what one has an inclination to do. It matters to Locke, as it sometimes seems not to matter to Hobbes, that if (contrary to fact) one were to have an inclination to do something else, or to do nothing at all, one should be free to do that as well. But Locke agrees with Hobbes that it does not make sense to talk of freedom of the *will*. The idea of freedom is not an idea of something belonging to the will, Locke says, but rather of something belonging to the agent: that is, it is an idea of the agent's being able to do, or, 'having a power' to do, what he has a mind to do. For we say that an agent is not free when, and only when, he does not have that ability or power—when he is restrained in some way from doing what he wants to do, or under compulsion, either to do something else, or to do what he wants to do whether or not he wants to. To possess a will is to have one kind of power, the power, as Locke puts it, to prefer one thought or action to another; to have liberty is to have another kind of power, the power to do or

---

[8] Locke was not alone in seeking a theory of freedom that made no reference to indifference. Cudworth is engaged in the same project in his extensive manuscript writings on the topic: see Passmore (1951), pp. 59–65. See also Cudworth's *Treatise of Freewill*, which remained unpublished until 1838, especially ch. IX: Cudworth (1838, 1996), pp. 176–8, where Cudworth criticizes those modern philosophers and theologians 'who zealously maintain the phenomenon of *liberum arbitrium*, or freewill, [and] think there is no other way to do it but only to make an indifferent and blind will fortuitously determining itself'.

forbear from doing as one prefers. To talk of the freedom of the will is thus to attribute one power to another power, and that, Locke says, is to talk absurdly: 'For who is it that sees not, that *Powers* belong only to *Agents*, and are *Attributes only of Substances, and not of Powers* themselves?' (§ 16). What has made it seem as though freedom might be attributed to (or denied) the will is a regrettable tendency to regard the powers of the mind, such as the understanding and the will, as 'some real Beings in the Soul' that themselves perform individual acts of understanding and choice (§ 6). Like many philosophers of his time, including Remonstrants like van Limborch, Locke rejects absolutely the supposedly divided mind of scholastic psychology.[9] The will is simply one capacity among several that a human being has, and is no more an agent than, say, the sense of sight. That said, Locke recognizes the difficulty, if not impossibility, of ceasing to talk in terms of the will preferring this, ordering that, or being determined by a third thing. What concerns him is that some are not sufficiently attuned to the artificial and metaphorical nature of such talk.[10]

The only kind of freedom that it is possible to make sense of, then, is freedom of action. Locke knows that this is not going to satisfy some people. It is sometimes thought, he acknowledges, 'that a Man is not free at all, if he be not as free to will, as he is to act, what he wills' (§ 22). Having pointed out that one cannot choose not to choose when issued a 'proposal of present Action', and that choice is therefore always *in some sense* necessary (§§ 23–4), Locke turns to the question of whether we can be said to be free to choose our preferences, and concludes swiftly that here, once again, there is patent absurdity:

For to ask, whether a Man be at liberty to will either Motion, or Rest; Speaking, or Silence; which he pleases, is to ask, whether a Man can *will*, what he *wills*; or be pleased with what he is pleased with. A Question, which, I think, needs no

---

[9] The seventeenth-century concern with the unity of the mind is a central theme of James (1997). For Cudworth against faculty psychology, see Passmore (1951), pp. 54–7. Limborch is careful to be seen not to be separating the understanding and will from the soul itself: see Limborch (1713), vol. I, pp. 137–8. So is another Remonstrant writer, Simon Episcopius: see Episcopius (1678), vol. II, pp. 199–200. (Episcopius even writes that 'ex hac distinctione ortas esse omnes circa doctrinam de libero arbitrio difficultas' ('all the difficulties about the doctrine of free will arise from this distinction': i.e., the distinction between the faculty of will, on the one hand, and the mind, on the other).)

[10] Locke charges the Remonstrants with such negligence in a letter to van Limborch: Locke (1976–89), vol. vii, pp. 503–4.

answer: and they, who can make a Question of it, must suppose one Will to determine the Acts of another, and another to determinate that; and so on *in infinitum.*

(§ 25)

Now it is not clear exactly what Locke is saying in this passage. It might be that he is saying that it is so obviously *false* that a man can will what he wills (after all, we cannot help liking what we like) that there is no point in making a question about it. On the other hand, it might be that he is saying that it is so obviously *true* that we can will what we will (after all, if one *is* doing something it is plain that one *can* do it) that there is no sense in making a question about it.[11] Context suggests to me that Locke means the first thing, and that he makes himself hard to understand because in this particular passage he talks simply in terms of willing and being pleased, when what he is seeking to determine is '*Whether a Man be at liberty to will which of two he pleases, Motion or Rest*' (§ 25, emphasis added). In other words, the question is not really whether we can like what we like, but whether, given a choice between two courses of action, it is up to us which of the two we prefer. And, so Locke claims, it is just a fact that one of the two courses of action will please us more than the other; and in preferring that course of action, one is *already* willing to do it.[12] 'Is then a Man indifferent to be pleased, or not pleased, more with one thing than another?', Locke asks is in the first edition version of 'Of Power'; 'Is it in his choice, whether he will, or will not be better pleased with one thing than another? And to this, I think, every one's Experience is ready to make answer, No' (1 § 28). It follows that 'the Will, or Preference, is determined by something without it self' (1 § 29); and what determines preference is conception of which course of action is apt to produce most pleasure, or least pain. What determines preference, in other words, is our sense of wherein consists the greater good, we being creatures who can imagine no greater good than maximum pleasure, or minimum pain. And in so far as we are incapable of being insensible to considerations of pleasure and pain, it is obvious that indifference is no constituent of human freedom.

---

[11] Cp. Rickless (2000), pp. 62–5; disagreeing with Chappell (1994), p. 108.

[12] As will be seen below, in the second and later editions Locke disengages the will from conceptions of the greater good. This has the effect of making interpretation of § 25 even less straightforward than it is in the first edition.

Second Thoughts

Soon after the publication of the first edition of the *Essay*, it came to seem to Locke that he had somewhat overstated his case against a liberty of indifference. Locke was helped to appreciate this by William Molyneux, who in a letter he sent to Locke in 1692 complained that the thread of Locke's 'Discourse about Mans Liberty and Necessity' 'seems so wonderfully fine spun..., that at last the Great Question of Liberty and Necessity seems to vanish'.[13] The 'great question', Molyneux makes plain, is that of whether or not men are genuinely morally accountable for their actions. By depicting the will as determined by conceptions of the greatest good, he says, 'you seem to make all Sins to proceed from our Understandings, or to be against Conscience; and not at all from the Depravity of our Wills'; and 'it seems harsh to say, that a Man shall be Damn'd, because he understands no better than he does'.[14] Locke has recoiled all the way from the indifference of the will to a position where choice, and with it the freedom that confers responsibility and liability, threatens to be subsumed by the operations of the understanding. We do not choose to believe what the understanding represents to us as true; so, if the understanding is what determines our actions, it looks as though, by the same token, we cannot really be said to choose to act as we do. And just as people are not punished for not knowing more than they do, nor for not being better reasoners than they are, why should they be punished for acting badly, if every voluntary action is determined by the understanding? Locke accepted that a new account of the determination of choice was needed. However, the way in which he presents that new account suggests that what he seeks to capture is not, in the first instance, the necessary and sufficient conditions of moral responsibility, but rather (a not unrelated matter) the experience of being able to acknowledge wherein lies the greater good, and yet choose to act to further some other, more short-term, interest. There are times, this is to say, when it is manifest that the greater good fails to move us to act. Locke had not ignored the problem of weakness of will in the first edition account, but he

[13] Locke (1976–89), vol. iv, pp. 600–1. It is not perfectly clear what point Molyneux is making when he calls Locke's account 'wonderfully fine spun'. Like Yaffe ((2000), p. 42), I think he is saying that Locke's theory of freedom needs further refinement. Matthew Stuart, in an unpublished work on Locke's metaphysics, points out that to call something 'fine spun' normally carries implications of excessive subtlety and refinement, and suggests that Molyneux's point is that Locke has already made things needlessly complicated.

[14] Locke (1976–89), vol. iv, p. 601.

now thinks his solution of the problem to be inadequate.[15] The experience of freedom is sometimes—too often—that of finding it hard to summon the resolve to do what one knows one really ought to do, and this experience needs to be better accommodated.

Before Locke presents his new account of the determination of choice, however, he makes two important preliminary moves. Both would seem to be designed to capture aspects of the 'phenomenology' of freedom that are at risk of disappearing in the first edition version of 'Of Power'. The first edition has it that will must be 'determined by something without it self', and that that 'something' is 'the greater good' (1 § 29). In the second edition, by contrast, Locke writes as follows:

To the Question, what is it determines the Will? The true and proper Answer is, The Mind. For that which determines the general power of directing, to this or that particular direction, is nothing but the Agent it self Exercising the power it had, that particular way.

(2–5 § 29)

Locke does not make much of this, and moves on quickly to the question of what moves the mind to choose one course of action as opposed to another. But it is worth drawing attention to the passage's significance, for here Locke appears to be saying that, properly speaking, it is 'the Agent it self', and not any particular conception the agent has of his best interests, that is causally responsible for an act of choice. The point would appear to be that whatever it is that, as we say, determines our choices, does not literally *determine* them. Rather the agent chooses on the basis—to continue to talk in the terms of the first edition of 'Of Power'—of what is presented to his understanding as the best course of action. Regardless of how much freedom there is in that choice, still, it is the agent who makes it. This in fact was already implicit in Locke's criticism of those who turn powers of the mind into distinct agents. The following passage is found in all editions:

I grant, that this or that actual Thought may be the occasion of Volition, or exercising the power a Man has to chuse; or the actual choice of the Mind, the cause of actual thinking on this or that thing: As the actual singing of such a Tune, may be the occasion of dancing such a Dance, and the actual dancing of such a

---

[15] In fact, much of the first edition account of weakness of will is retained in later editions. Locke decided, not that it was in need of wholesale replacement, but that it needed supplementation with a better explanation of how short-term interests can defeat long-term ones. For Locke on weakness of will, and Leibniz's criticisms of Locke's account, see Vailati (1990).

Dance, the occasion of singing such a Tune. But in all these, it is not one *power* that operates on another: But it is the Mind that operates, and exerts these Powers; it is the Man that does the Action, it is the Agent that has power, or is able to do.

(§ 19)

It seems to me likely that the use of the vocabulary of occasionalism is self-conscious here. A thought may provide the *occasion* for a choice, but does not literally cause or make that choice. It is the man, and not the thought, that 'does the Action'. Presumably Locke now wants to foreground this point so as to ward off the worry that on his account of freedom, choices are things that are made *for* the agent, rather than *by* him.[16]

The task that Locke has before him in the second and later editions of the essay is to find a role for genuine acts of choice in the aetiology of action without sliding back into the grip of the indifference theory. To portray the will as determined by conceptions of the greater good was to portray choices as things that happen and not as things that are made, and to undermine the status of the will considered as a distinct power of the mind. This surely explains why Locke's next move in his revision of 'Of Power' is to make it clear that he regards there to be a distinction between, on the one hand, the kind of preference that is a *willing* of, say, motion over rest, and, on the other, the kind of preference that amounts only to *desiring* motion more than rest. Terms such as 'chusing' and 'preferring' can signify desire as well as volition, but, so Locke claims, reflection on what passes in the mind makes it plain there are important differences between volition and desire. Hobbes, like Locke, had argued against the notion of the voluntariness of volitions, but, as he did so, *identified* the will with the passions, such as desire, fear, and hope, that determine choice and action.[17] But the distinctness of volition from desire is shown by the fact that one cannot will, but can desire, the actions of another person; and that, with respect to one's own actions, one can voluntarily do what one does not desire to do, and desire to do what one does not will to do. Volition, unlike desire, is, Locke says, 'conversant about

---

[16] Schouls (1992), p. 128, makes these points well. Gideon Yaffe has pointed out to me that establishing that choices are made by the agent, and not for him by his motives, is something that a philosopher has to show that he has accomplished, not something we can trust him to have accomplished merely because he says it matters. This is true. But it is the simple fact that Locke says that it matters that is significant for present purposes.

[17] One imagines that Hobbes is one of those whom Locke has in mind when he says that he finds 'the Will often confounded with several of the Affections, especially *Desire*; and one put for the other, and that by Men, who would not willingly be thought, not to have had very distinct notions of things, and not to have writ very clearly about them' (2–5 § 30).

nothing, but our own Actions; terminates there, and reaches no farther', being 'nothing but that particular determination of the mind, whereby, barely by a thought, the mind endeavours to give rise, continuation, or stop to any Action, which it takes to be in its power' (2–5 § 30). Under pressure, I may do something which, as Locke puts it, 'tends one way', while my desire 'tends another, and that the direct contrary': Locke's example is being compelled to try to persuade someone to do something that one does not want to be done (2–5 § 30). A man suffering from gout wants to be rid of the pain in his feet, but may not choose to do anything about it, for fear of spreading the disease to another, 'more vital', part of his body. These examples are meant to show desiring and willing to be two distinct acts of the mind. The distinction will be essential to Locke's means of making sense of the psychological conflicts that he sees as central to the experience of freedom.

Having made these two preliminary clarifications, Locke moves on to the main question at hand: if the greater good does not determine, or occasion, the agent's choices, then what does? The answer to this question is, as Locke puts it in one of several formulations, 'the *uneasiness* of *desire*, fixed on some absent good, either negative, as indolency to one in pain; or positive, as enjoyment of pleasure' (2–5 § 33).[18] The main problem for the first edition account, Locke says, is the fact that '*good*, the *greater good*, though apprehended and acknowledged to be so, does not determine the *will*, until our desire, raised proportionably to it, makes us *uneasy* in the want of it' (2–5 § 35). This is a plain fact of experience. But there are reasons to explain why it is so. One such reason is that, in any deliberative situation, our first priority is always to relieve ourselves of any pain or uneasiness we might be subject to. Pursuit of the greater good is therefore permanently liable to being deflected by any fleeting pain or uneasiness, and therefore, in order to maintain its grip on our deliberations, the pain or uneasiness produced by a sense of the lack of the

---

[18] Yaffe (2000), p. 147 n. 26 is one of those unsure whether or not Locke means to *identify* uneasiness with desire. At 2–5 § 31, for instance, Locke says that 'Thus *Uneasiness* we may call, as it is, *Desire*.' But at 2–5 § 39 Locke emphasizes that 'most of the other Passions', such as aversion, fear, anger, envy, and shame, *also* give rise to uneasiness—which suggests that desire and uneasiness cannot simply be identified. A desire makes one uneasy, Locke seems to be saying, but this does not mean that desire is uneasiness: one can surely have a desire (for example, to be a millionaire) which does not occasion uneasiness. Locke appears to have taken the notion of 'uneasiness' from Malebranche: see Vienne (1991), who suggests that Locke's revisions of 'Of Power' for the second edition of the *Essay* 'are the fruit of an interpretative reading by Locke of Malebranche's theses' (p. 99). 'Uneasiness' appears to be a word intended to capture at least some of the connotations of Malebranche's notion of *inquiétude*: see Vienne (1991), p. 101.

greater good has to be greater than any other pain. A second reason is that pain or uneasiness, no matter how trivial its cause, is by its nature present, and the greater good, no matter how great, by its nature absent. This again means that, in order to motivate us to action, the pain or uneasiness felt in the absence of the greater good has to be more acute than other pains. What determines the will, then, is always the greatest uneasiness, or, at least, the uneasiness 'which is the most pressing of those, that are judged capable of being then removed' (2–5 § 40). Part of what attracts Locke to this new account of the determination of choice is that it is to a certain extent up to the agent which uneasiness he feels to be the most pressing. We have seen that in the first edition, Locke asks rhetorically whether it is 'in our choice' which of two things we are better pleased with. The answer, obviously, is No. In the second edition, however, Locke draws attention to the fact that, just as we can learn to enjoy foods and drinks we dislike at first, and just as we can wean ourselves from enjoying what we know is bad for us, so also we can cultivate a taste for virtue, and a concomitant distaste at vice (see (2–5 § 69)). Our preferences are to a large extent artificial, and created for us by such things as fashion, common opinion, education, and custom; as such, they can be altered, if not immediately, then at least over time. In this way we can learn to make ourselves feel more uneasy at the absence of our greatest good than at any other perceived lack. A man blames himself, Locke points out, 'when Happiness is lost, and misery overtakes him' (2–5 § 69): why would he do so if he did not believe it was in his power to have lived differently?

Space is created in the deliberative economy for the possibility of altering the relative strengths of uneasinesses by the introduction in the second edition of a power to resist the pressure exerted by their influence:

For the mind having in most cases, as is evident in Experience, a power to *suspend* the execution and satisfaction of any of its desires, and so all, one after another, is at liberty to consider the objects of them; examine them on all sides, and weigh them with others. In this lies the liberty Man has; and from the not using of it right comes all that variety of mistakes, errors, and faults which we run into, in the conduct of our lives, and our endeavours after happiness; whilst we precipitate the determinations of our *wills*, and engage too soon before due *Examination*.

(2–5 § 47)

Two things are significant in this passage. The first is the claim that liberty lies in the capacity to arrest the operations of the will, so as to make sure that what seems most preferable really is so. There is in fact more to freedom, it would seem, than mere freedom of action, freedom from external restraint and compulsion. Hence even if (what, as we shall see, is not altogether obvious now) there is no sense to talk of freedom of the *will*, still, freedom is manifest in something as it were internal, something psychological. (Presumably, though, Locke still believes that *in addition to* this internal something, it is important that there be absence of external restraint and compulsion.) The second thing worth noting is the claim that the existence of a power of suspension is 'evident in Experience'. What is driving the revision of the first edition account of freedom is first and foremost a sense on Locke's part that that initial attempt failed as an account of the *experience* of freedom.[19] In 'Of Power' Locke is not merely analysing the *concept* of freedom, as if the question might remain open whether or not that concept is ever applicable to the human case. At every turn, on the contrary, he evinces the psychologist's concern with capturing how the mind actually works. And, as others had pointed out before him, an ability to step back from the scene of action, to suspend proceedings in order better to understand the nature of our real interests, is indeed a prominent feature of human agency.[20]

Third Thoughts?

In 1701 and 1702, van Limborch and Locke exchanged several letters about the chapter 'Of Power'. A principal subject of discussion was the extent to

[19] In the *Essay's* 'Epistle to Reader' Locke writes that he changed his mind about the determinants of choice '[u]pon a closer inspection into the working of Men's Minds, and a stricter examination of those motives and views, they are turn'd by' (p. 11); writing to van Limborch, Locke says that 'in writing about these things [i.e., the will and its supposed indifference] I have neither followed other men's opinions nor so much as consulted any writings at all, but have set forth in the most suitable words in my power what the things themselves have taught me, so far as they could be compassed [assequi] by investigation [indigatione] and meditation [meditatione]' (Locke (1976–89), vol. vii, p. 328).

[20] For what Locke's doctrine of suspension may owe to Malebranche, see Vienne (1991), esp. p. 102. Schneewind (1998, p. 146, n14) notes that '[t]he idea of will as suspension of desire was...common', and cites William Ames: 'The *Will* can at pleasure *suspend* its acts about that which is *apprehended* and *judged* to be good, without any *foregoing act of judgement*, that it doe so' (Ames (1639), p. 23). It seems, though, that Ames regards this power of suspension as a kind of disability: it distracts us from the guidance of conscience and the understanding, and enables us to do what we know is sinful. Darwall (1995), ch. 6, emphasizes the similarities between Locke's revised account of freedom and the position developed by Cudworth in his manuscript writings on the topic; the power of suspension, however, is not one of the sixteen points of comparison between Locke and Cudworth listed on pp. 173–5.

which a power of suspension invested the will with the indifference that Locke regarded as irrelevant to human freedom, but that the Remonstrants insisted upon as essential. In his first letter to Locke, van Limborch expresses his satisfaction that he and Locke appear not to differ over anything of importance.[21] By 'indifference', he explains, the Remonstrants mean only 'that before that [final] decree of the will a man has the liberty to determine himself to this or that side, and is not determined to one only of opposites'; and 'when that decree of the will, or act of willing, is added, that indifference is taken away, and the power is determined to acting or not acting'.[22] In this, van Limborch claims, 'we agree'. His next letter makes explicit reference to § 47 of the revised version of the chapter as the place where Locke introduces indifference back into his account of freedom.[23] Van Limborch takes the power of suspension to give the agent the freedom of will (as opposed to freedom of action) that Locke has claimed it is impossible to make sense of. Liberty, he says, 'consists solely in a power by which a man can determine, or not determine, an action of willing'.[24] And with a power of suspension comes, precisely, a power by which a man can, as van Limborch puts it, 'determine himself'.

According to van Limborch, the 'internal' aspect of freedom is the will's independence from the determinations of the understanding—or, rather, the freedom of the *agent* in his choices to ignore what the understanding recommends to be done. The only alternative to the view Locke puts forward in the first edition version of 'Of Power', this is to say, is the directly contrary view that the understanding, properly speaking, has *no influence at all* on our volitions. When the understanding has done its work, the will remains indifferent, or, as van Limborch puts it in his third letter to Locke on this matter, 'the power [potentia] is determined to neither, and . . . therefore of two opposites [a man] can choose whichever he pleases'.[25] This is not to say that the free agent is 'set as it were in equilibrium and does not incline to one side more than to the other': we are always urged to one side of a question by

---

[21] In his review of the fifth edition of the *Essay* in the *Bibliothèque Choisie*, Jean le Clerc, another Remonstrant, and also another friend of Locke's, claims that the sentiment of those who ground liberty in indifference 'est parfaitment conforme à la définition, que [Locke] a lui même donnée de la Liberté' (le Clerc (1707), p. 102). Locke was antagonistic toward the liberty of indifference, le Clerc believes, only because he did not properly understand it.

[22] Locke (1976–89), vol. vii, p. 276.

[23] Ibid., p. 370.

[24] Ibid., p. 368.

[25] Ibid., p. 453.

our passions, and by custom and habit. Even so, 'although [a man] may be inclined to one more than to the other, yet he has not lost dominion over his action, but can even determine himself to the other'.[26] And he is able to do so in virtue of the power of suspension. The question for Locke, then, is whether the introduction of such a power really does go along with the indifference that he consistently shows himself—in the later editions just as much as in the first—to be opposed to (see, e.g., **2–5** § 71). Does a power of suspension set Locke's account of freedom against itself?[27]

Locke's replies to van Limborch suggest that he himself was quite sure that his account of freedom does not entail the indifference of the will. He continues in fact to find incoherent the notion of such an indifference:

to argue as to whether a man, before the last judgement of the understanding, has liberty to determine himself to one or other of opposites seems to me to be arguing about nothing at all or about an impossibility. For who would ask, or what does it avail to ask, whether a man can determine himself to one or other of opposites when he is in a state in which he is altogether unable to determine himself? For before the judgement of the understanding he is altogether unable to determine himself, and so it is idle to inquire whether in that state he has liberty to determine himself to one or other alternative when he is altogether unable to determine himself to either.[28]

One can only be said to be able to determine himself, or make a choice to do one thing rather than another, when the last judgment of the understanding has been made. But once that judgment has been made, the choice is made also. '[L]iberty cannot consist in a power of determining an action of willing contrary to the judgement of the understanding', Locke writes, 'because a man does not possess such a power.'[29] This is not, however, to say that a man always acts in line with 'mature and right judgement'.[30] Often we do not deliberate carefully, or fail to deliberate at all, and so fail to do what is in our best interests. Suspension of judgment gives us the opportunity to make sure that we deliberate properly, and, in the process, to ensure that we have a clear enough understanding of what is in our best interests to be made more

---

[26] Ibid., p. 455.

[27] The case for the view that Locke does introduce incoherence into his account with the power of suspension is powerfully made by Chappell (1994); see also Chappell (2000). For a reply to Chappell on Locke's behalf, see Yaffe (2001). For additional worries about the coherence of Locke's account, see Magri (2000).

[28] Locke (1976–89), vol. vii, p. 329.

[29] Ibid., p. 410.   [30] Ibid., p. 411.

uneasy about our lack of it than about our lack of anything else. Suspension therefore does not give us the ability to ignore the last judgment of the understanding altogether, and, by the same token, does not give us freedom of will. Nothing in the correspondence with van Limborch gives reason to believe that Locke ever changed his mind about this.[31]

Nevertheless, in the final, posthumous, edition of the *Essay*, a paragraph is added which has seemed to some to indicate that, in the end, Locke came to accept that a power of suspension does, at least sometimes, confer freedom of will upon an agent.[32] In that paragraph, Locke writes that

> there is a case wherein a Man is at Liberty in respect of *willing*, and that is the chusing of a remote Good as an end to be pursued. Here a Man may suspend the act of his choice from being determined for or against the thing proposed, till he has examined, whether it be really of a nature in it self and consequences to make him happy, or no.
>
> (5 § 56)

It is this 'Liberty in respect of *willing*', Locke goes on to claim, that explains 'how it comes to pass, that a Man may justly incur punishment, though it be certain that in all the particular actions that he *wills*, he does, and necessarily does will that, which he then judges to be good' (5 § 56). The freedom of will being discussed here, however, is clearly not a freedom of indifference. In fact, Locke seems to me to be saying nothing in this passage that is at odds with what he writes to van Limborch.[33] We have freedom enough to enable us to make sure that what we do is what is best for us in the long term: our choices are not determined by whatever happens to be the most pressing

---

[31] Locke does, it is true, write to van Limborch that 'there are some cases in which a man is unable not to will, and in all those cases of willing a man is not free because he is unable not to act. In the rest, where he was able to will or not to will, he is free' (Locke (1976–89), vol. vii, p. 680). I take it, however, that Locke's point here is that in the cases where a man is free in this sense of 'free', he is able for a time to suspend choice while he deliberates about what to do; there is no suggestion that the agent is freed from the necessity of making *some* decision eventually, nor that the understanding does not determine that decision when it is made.

[32] See Chappell (1994), p. 118. Chappell suggests that Locke added this passage because he had finally been persuaded by van Limborch of the freedom (in some circumstances) of the will.

[33] The point being made here is surely the same as that made in the passage from the correspondence with van Limborch discussed in note 32 above. Thus I agree with the conclusion reached in Rickless (2000): the power of suspension gives us freedom to ensure that what we do in the future is for the best. It does not enable us to defer making choices about what to do at the present moment.

uneasiness. But we do not have a freedom that would leave us indifferent to what the understanding tells us is in our best interests.

'Of Power' in the Eighteenth Century

Eighteenth-century treatments of the question of liberty and necessity very often begin with an ostentatious display of definitions. Anthony Collins, for example, explains 'the sense of the Question' as follows:

Man is a *necessary Agent*, if all his actions are so determin'd by the causes preceding each action, that not one past action could possibly not have come to pass, or have been otherwise than it hath been; nor one future action can possibly not come to pass, or be otherwise than it shall be. He is a *free Agent*, if he is able, at any time under the circumstances and causes he then is, to do different things: or, in other words, if he is not unavoidably determin'd in every point of time by the circumstances he is in, and causes he is under, to do that one thing he does, and not possibly do any other.[34]

It is a striking, and frustrating, feature of 'Of Power' that it fails to make clear whether men are free or necessary agents in these senses of 'free' and 'necessary'.[35] It appears that in the first edition he does not attach importance to the ability to choose otherwise. He is careful to say that, in order that an action be free, it must be possible for the agent to have done another thing, or refrained from acting altogether, had he chosen to. The libertarian, however, insists also on the freedom of the act of choice, and Locke finds no place for that kind of freedom in his first thoughts on the subject. When he alters 'Of Power' for the second edition of the *Essay*, however, Locke makes himself harder to understand in this connection. The power of suspension is meant to give the agent a certain amount of control over his choices, and it is coupled with an insistence on the distinction between will and desire, and on the agent himself as the determinant of the will. But the power of suspension does not give the will independence from the recommendations of the understanding. Moreover, the question must arise as to whether or not the agent is free in his acts of suspension. That is: is it up to the agent

[34] Collins (1717), p. 11.

[35] This has been noted by at least one modern commentator: '[Locke's] whole account is not the smallest use in enabling us to answer the question: is it ever true to say of a man who does action A in a given situation, that he *could have done* action B without any change at all in the antecedent circumstances, mental and physical?' (O'Connor (1967), pp. 116–17).

whether or not he suspends action and deliberates properly as to what is in his long-term interests? If so, then what makes it so seems likely to have to be a prior act of suspension in order to decide whether or not to suspend choice; and thus the first step has been taken towards a regress *in infinitum* of acts of suspension.[36] On the other hand, if it is not up to the agent whether or not he suspends choice and action, then if he does not exercise the power of suspension and acts wrongly, how is he to be held accountable for acting that way? If what makes him accountable is, simply, the voluntariness of the action, then the power of suspension would seem to turn out to be irrelevant to accountability after all—contrary to what Locke claims in the additions to § 56 made for the fifth edition version of 'Of Power'.

For his part, Collins cites the treatment of liberty in 'Of Power' as support for a Hobbesian necessitarianism. The essence of Lockean freedom according to Collins is a '*liberty or freedom from outward impediments of action*, and not a *Freedom or Liberty from Necessity*'.[37] And Locke expresses well the absurdity of asking whether we are free in our choices.[38] However, when treating the other aspect of the supposed freedom of the will, the notion of a freedom 'to will, or not to will', Locke risks muddying the water with his talk of a power of suspension. Suspending, Collins argues, 'is itself an *act of willing*': 'it is willing to defer willing about the matter propos'd', and therefore a power of suspension does not endow the agent with the power not to will at all with respect to some proposed course of action.[39] 'In fine, tho' great stress is laid on the case of *suspending the will*, to prove *liberty*, yet there is no difference between that and the most common cases of willing and chusing upon the manifest excellency of one object before another.'[40] Collins does not discuss the passages from the later versions of 'Of Power' in which Locke allows for a freedom over the will and gives the power of suspension as the source of that freedom, but it is reasonably plain that Collins preferred Locke's first thoughts on liberty to his second. Jonathan Edwards plainly felt the same

---

[36] On Yaffe's reading of Locke, this is not a serious concern. Yaffe argues that for full-fledged Lockean freedom, all that is needed is the power to suspend for long enough to ensure that one has deliberated correctly. There is no need for the power to suspend the uneasiness that prompts suspension. See Yaffe (2000), pp. 58–9.

[37] Collins (1717), p. 13; citing II.xxi.8.

[38] See Collins (1717), pp. 40–2; citing II.xxi.25.

[39] Collins (1717), pp. 38–9.

[40] Ibid., p. 39. William King's translator and commentator, William Law, on the other hand, argues that Locke's notion of suspension is radically at odds with the essentially necessitarian tenor of the chapter 'Of Power': see King (1731), pp. 246–60 fn and 263–65 fn.

way. In the very first section of his *Inquiry into . . . the Freedom of the Will*, Edwards criticizes the distinction between volitions, on the one hand, and desires, on the other. He doubts, for instance, that it is ever really true that our desires and volitions 'can ever properly be said to run counter': in the terms of Locke's putative example of the contradiction of will and desire, the man forced to try to persuade someone to do what he does not want to be done wants to do one thing (to speak certain words) and does not want the other thing.[41]

According to Edwards, it involves 'little, if anything, short of a direct and plain contradiction' to deny that the will is determined by the greatest apparent good.[42] In a set of notes now known as 'The Mind' Edwards attacks Locke directly, arguing that uneasiness is not relevant when forbearance, rather than action, is at issue. If I decide to remain sitting and not to get up, I remain sitting voluntarily, but my choice need not have been determined by any uneasiness at my present circumstances.[43] Another significant addition to the revised version of 'Of Power', the power of suspension, is also severely criticized by Edwards—although without mentioning Locke by name. The Lockean claim is that what liberty of will we have consists in a determination to suspend action; Edwards wants to know 'wherein consists the will's freedom with respect to this act of suspension?'[44] The only answer he can imagine is that this freedom consists in an ability to defer—that is, suspend—the decision whether or not to suspend. And this is absurd in two ways: first, in so far as it involves doing the same thing twice, since 'during the space of suspension, to consider whether to suspend, the act is *ipso facto* suspended'; secondly, in so far as it threatens to generate an infinite regression of acts of suspension.[45] There is another problem with suspension as freedom as well: it puts freedom in the wrong place, not in choice itself, but in a determination to defer choice. For Edwards, then, as for Collins, the changes Locke made to 'Of Power' serve only to confuse matters, and to render impossible a straightforward formulation of the necessitarian position. Both Collins and Edwards appeal to Locke's authority wherever they can, yet find his considered theory of freedom unaccountably at odds with itself.

Joseph Priestley is more forthright. 'It is universally acknowledged', he says, 'that [Locke's] chapter on *power* is . . . remarkably confused; all his *general maxims* being perfectly consistent with, and implying, the doctrine of

---

[41] Edwards (1754, 1957), pp. 138–40. [42] Ibid., p. 143.

[43] Edwards (1980), p. 385 (§ 70 of 'The Mind'). [44] Edwards (1754, 1957), p. 210.

[45] Ibid., pp. 210–11.

necessity, and being manifestly inconsistent with the liberty which, after writing a long time like a Necessarian, he attributes to man.'[46] The general maxims in question are Locke's claims that there is no sense to talking of freedom of the will, and that the opposite of freedom is constraint and compulsion. These, to Priestley's mind, go naturally with a necessitarian answer to the question posed by Hobbes. It is the doctrine of suspension that creates confusion. Like Collins and Edwards, Priestley takes Locke to be a necessitarian who misguidedly sought to accommodate in his theory of freedom some of the elements of libertarianism, and as a result made a mess of his answer to Hobbes's question.[47] Priestley's follower Thomas Belsham notes that some libertarians restrict their supposed power of self-determination to 'some mental operations only: such, for example, as the act of suspending the choice, of deliberating, of choosing out of contending motives, and the like'; and points out that, however the self-determining power is limited, 'the question still recurs, Can you suspend, deliberate, &c. without a reason for it, without inclination to it, and where you have the strongest motives to the contrary?'[48] In a footnote he writes that Locke was the first to introduce 'this curious limitation of free will to the act of deliberation only', and asks:

Could this sagacious writer really fall into such an unaccountable confusion of ideas? Or was Mr. Locke apprehensive that if he avowed necessarianism, he should be exposed to the invidious charge of Hobbism, and atheism? Perhaps, indeed, Mr. Locke himself might not see the reconcileableness of the necessity of human actions to moral agency and accountableness; and, through a virtuous though unnecessary fear of moral consequences, might be driven to this miserable refuge.[49]

Belsham refers the reader to an essay by his brother William on Locke's chapter 'Of Power', in which there is expressed astonishment 'at the obscurity and perplexity in which this interesting topic, under [Locke's] management of it, seems involved'.[50] For much of 'Of Power', according to William

---

[46] Priestley (1782), vol. ii, p. xxvi. 'I am rather surprised', he continues, 'that Mr. Locke, who seems to have been so much indebted to Mr. Hobbes for the clear view that he has given us of several principles in human nature, should have availed himself so little of what he might have learned from him on this subject'.

[47] See Priestley (1782), vol. ii, p. 7 ('In fact, all the liberty that Mr. Locke contends for, is perfectly consistent with the doctrine of philosophical necessity, though he does not seem to have been aware of it.')

[48] Thomas Belsham (1801), p. 231.

[49] Ibid., p. 232 fn.

[50] William Belsham (1789–91), vol. i, p. 18.

Belsham, Locke writes like a necessitarian, only to introduce gross inconsistency into his account with the notion that a power of suspension gives us freedom of will. On the contrary, William Belsham claims, suspension is always 'the result of motives'. 'Surely the hypothesis of Philosophical Liberty', he exclaims, 'never had a more imbecile advocate!'[51]

Just as necessitarians like to believe that Locke was really a confused member of their party, so libertarians hold that Locke was, despite some unfortunate phraseology, one of them. Priestley's critic Joseph Berington claims that the system he proposes 'is no other than the original doctrine of Mr. Locke'—albeit 'exhibited, perhaps, in a more striking and less complex point of view'.[52] John Palmer acknowledges that 'Mr. Locke... has indeed expressed himself in such a manner, as, in the opinion of some of his most judicious readers, is less easy to be understood'; but argues that Locke 'does not maintain the invariable determination of the will, which [Priestley] imputes to him'.[53] The power of suspension, Palmer continues,

implies in it, as far as it extends, the very power of self-determination on which the whole controversy turns. For if the mind has such a power, so that it can examine the objects of its present desires and compare them with others, it may then, in consequence of such examination, suppress the present desire, and excite a contrary one; which is totally repugnant to the doctrine of Philosophical Necessity.[54]

James Gregory regards Locke as a libertarian much like himself, particularly in so far as he shows an awareness of the inappropriateness of talking of motives as genuine causes:

Yet in the course of his inquiries, and even in that very chapter (*Of Power*) in which it was of the utmost consequence for him to guard against such ambiguities, he got into a puzzle by means of them, as he very candidly acknowledges, (sect. 71.), and endeavours to get out as well as he can. But in this he hath not succeeded. The whole train of reasoning in that chapter, and particularly in that 71st section of it, is

---

[51] Ibid., vol. i, p. 30. Another necessitarian unhappy at Locke's treatment of the question is William Corry: 'Mr Locke, surprized to find that the result of his philosophical inquiries led him to conclusions contradictory to certain early received prejudices, or opinions, from which he was determined not to depart, vainly endeavours to distinguish away those conclusions by fine-spun metaphysical refinements, in a manner, surely, most unworthy of a writer of his great penetration and candour' ([Corry] (1761), p. 6). The 'early received prejudices' in question appear to centre on the view that human beings are free in their choices and actions.

[52] Berington (1776), p. 212.

[53] Palmer (1779), pp. 12, 14.

[54] Ibid., pp. 14–15.

perverted, and rendered unsatisfactory, and in many places almost unintelligible, in consequence of that very ambiguous and metaphorical use of such common expressions as those under consideration.[55]

Dugald Stewart, too, expresses frustration at Locke's way of proceeding in 'Of Power'. He notes that Locke's initial definitions of liberty and power 'approach, indeed, very nearly to the definitions of liberty and necessity given by Hobbes, Collins, and Edwards'; but goes on to claim that 'Locke, in order to do justice to his own decided opinion on the subject, ought to have included also in his idea of liberty, a *power* over the determinations of the will.'[56] 'That Locke conceived himself to be an advocate for *free-will*,' Stewart says, 'appears indisputably from many expressions in his chapter on power';

and yet, in that very chapter, he has made various concessions to his adversaries, in which he seems to yield all that was contended for by Hobbes and Collins: And, accordingly, he is ranked with some appearance of truth, by Priestley, with those who, while they opposed verbally the scheme of necessity, have adopted it substantially, without being aware of their mistake.[57]

Stewart would appear to speak for the majority of Locke's eighteenth-century readers when he remarks that 'On the subject of Free Will, Locke is more indistinct, undecided, and inconsistent, than might have been expected from his powerful mind, when directed to so important a question.'[58]

[55] Gregory (1792), p. ccxxvii. [56] Stewart (1828), vol. ii, p. 475.
[57] Stewart (1854), p. 296 fn. [58] Ibid., p. 296 fn.

2

King, Clarke, Collins

Here therefore, seems at last really to lie the fundamental Errour both of those who argue against the *Liberty of the Will*, and of those who but too confusedly defend it: They do not make a clear distinction between *moral Motives*, and *Causes Physically Efficient*; Which Two things have no similitude at all.

Samuel Clarke, *A Demonstration of the Being and Attributes of God*, Section x

In the *Essay*'s chapter 'Of Power' Locke appears self-consciously to turn his back on metaphysical issues, and to focus instead upon giving an accurate account of the *experience* of freedom. At first he seems to agree with Hobbes, and portrays freedom as a property of actions only; later a certain amount of freedom of choice is added to the picture. Many subsequent contributors to the free will debate found Locke's account insufficiently clear and decisive as regards the questions concerning freedom of choice as debated by Bramhall and Hobbes. The philosophers to be discussed in this chapter return to those questions, and, in particular, to the issue of how motives bear upon the will, the faculty of choice. William King takes an extreme libertarian position: he argues that all influence upon the will is incompatible with freedom, and seeks attempts to rehabilitate the liberty of indifference that is Locke's principal target in the *Essay*'s chapter 'Of Power'. King made his career in the Anglican church in Ireland, and was rewarded for loyalty to the Protestant cause with the bishopric of Dublin in 1691. Samuel Clarke was also a man of the Anglican church, who, despite a reputation for heterodoxy, remained rector of St James's, Piccadilly, from 1709 until his death. Like Locke, Samuel Clarke views the cause of liberty as endangered principally by poor definitions of freedom (such as King's), and, like Bramhall, sees the distinction between 'moral' and 'physical' necessity as the basis of the libertarian reply to Hobbes. The anti-clerical deist Anthony Collins responds to Clarke exactly as Hobbes responded to Bramhall. The debate between Clarke and Collins sets the terms for discussions of liberty and necessity for the rest of the century. For all subsequent writers on the topic, the principal issue is the influence of motives upon choices, and whether that influence is such as to rule out a freedom to choose more than one course of action in any one particular set of circumstances.

William King and the Liberty of Indifference

In October 1692 William Molyneux enclosed in a letter to Locke comments made on the *Essay concerning Human Understanding* by William King.[1] Like many readers of Locke, King finds the chapter 'Of Power' particularly unsatisfactory. At this time, of course, King knew only the first edition of the *Essay*, and so his complaint is not that later alterations and additions introduce ambiguity and incoherence into Locke's account of freedom. It is, rather, that Locke has failed to show that there is absurdity to the notion of freedom of the *will*, as opposed to freedom of *action*. Why may I ask 'whether my will be not free, that is whether I might not have been born for choosing what I did chuse'? '[I]t is tru that the will is the power of doing or for bearing an action. I hope we may ask whether this power determines it self to one of these or is determined by something without. if it be, all its actions are as necessary as the falling of a stone, and it is a *passive* and consequently a necessary agent. that is, it doth not act but as it is acted upon.'[2] There is more to freedom than having the power to do what one wills: one is 'a great deal freer ... if that will be not crambed down his throat, but proceed meerly from the active power of the soul. without any thing from without determining it to will or not to will'.[3] The will, King writes, is an active power that determines itself in its choices. King's understanding of self-determination appears to amount to precisely the liberty of indifference criticized by Locke. It is 'a power to chuse or not to chuse to prefer or not to prefer'. If the will were determined, as Locke says it is in the first edition version of 'Of Power', by the greater good, then there would be no freedom, for the idea of the greater good is 'impressed on the mind by outward objects and outward objects are ordered by God in an absolutely necessary chain and so God necessitates a man as

---

[1] For an account of King's intellectual context, see Berman (1982).
[2] Locke (1976–89), vol. iv, pp. 539–40.   [3] Ibid., p. 540.

much to kill his father as the sun to move.'[4] Like several later libertarians (especially those discussed in Chapter 6 below), King believes that there is no need to take seriously arguments which purport to show freedom of the will to be impossible. No 'sophistry' will ever destroy this 'native idea of liberty', he says, 'and all arguments against are but like Zeno's argument against motion and proceed merely from our ignorance of spirits'.[5]

King presents his theory of freedom in fully worked-out form in *De Origine Mali* (1702). As its title indicates, this is a theodicy, an attempt to explain the existence of evil in a universe created and governed by a God who is omnipotent, supremely wise, and supremely benevolent. King does not refer to other philosophers by name, but his principal target is almost certainly Pierre Bayle, who in various articles of his *Dictionaire historique et critique* (1695–6) had appeared to insinuate that the only satisfactory explanation of evil is the Manichaean hypothesis of an original and distinct malevolent principle, with which divine goodness is permanently at odds.[6] The task King sets himself in *De Origine Mali* is to show that Bayle is wrong, and that a place can be found for evil in the order of providence. A large part of the book is concerned with evils of imperfection (the absence of perfections or advantages present in other parts of creation) and with natural evil; and King's accommodation of these need not concern us here. It is only in the treatment of moral evil that the will and its freedom are introduced. Moral evil is defined as 'vicious Elections, that is, such as are hurtful to ourselves, or others'. The principal claim King makes with regard to this kind of evil is already implicit in his remarks on Locke: that it is only possible to acquit God of responsibility for evil if the wills of those who perpetrate it are free. King does not, however, limit himself to an explanation of how it is possible that there is evil in the universe. He intends also to prove that a universe in which there is evil is, by virtue of the freedom of will which makes it possible, a superior universe to any other we can conceive of. The purely theological aspects of King's chapter 'De Malo morali' I propose also to put to one side. The only part of the chapter directly relevant to the concerns of this study is the first section, 'De Natura Electionum'.[7]

---

[4] Ibid., p. 541.

[5] Ibid., p. 540.

[6] King was not the only contemporary British philosopher exercised by Bayle's apparent defence of Manichaeanism: see also, e.g., John Clarke (1720).

[7] All quotations from *De Origine Mali* will be from Edmund Law's 1731 translation into English (i.e., from King (1731)). In this chapter references to this work will be given in the main body of the text.

King's first move in his analysis of choice is to identify the shortcomings of other theories of freedom. He begins with those (he probably has in mind Hobbes and Spinoza) who argue that the will is determined by appetite, and who seek to retain freedom of action by means of a distinction between the voluntary and the compelled. As might be expected from his remarks on Locke, King does not believe this to be a theory of *freedom* at all. His argument against it is from its consequences. The first of these is the removal of all contingency from human affairs, something we are clearly meant to regard as so absurd as not to warrant comment; the other consequences in various ways alter the significance of moral distinctions, and change the basis of moral and judicial practices. King acknowledges the weakness of arguments from bad consequences, but, he says, 'when these are acknowledg'd by the Authors themselves; and, if believ'd, would prove detrimental to Morality, they bring no small prejudice against an Opinion which is attended with them, and recommend us to some other as more probable, tho' it be not supported by any stronger Reasons' (*Origin of Evil*, p. 159). King then turns to a different account of freedom, which gives the will freedom from the appetites, but portrays it as determined by the understanding's conception of the greatest good. A role for a power of suspension, such as makes the agent able to ensure that it is the *greatest* good that determines choice, might mean that King has in mind here strands of Locke's revised theory of freedom. The chief element of this second theory, however, is its rationalism, and so a theory such as Bramhall's would also fit the description King gives. Again, King cannot make sense of this theory as a theory of *freedom*. There is a promise of a power of self-determination in the mediation of the understanding between appetite and choice, but, when more closely examined, the promise turns out to be deceptive. For a choice determined by the understanding is a choice determined by something over which we have no control; and, in any case, the understanding is weak, and often fails us when it comes to determining the greatest good. It could be said that freedom lies in being able (should one so choose) to ignore the recommendations of the understanding; but such a freedom would seem more likely to be a danger than a benefit. The conclusion King draws is that in order to give a coherent account of the freedom, such as also makes clear the advantages of being free, the will needs to be decoupled from the understanding, and regarded as a wholly inde-pendent and self-determining power.

According to King, it is in the very nature of active, as opposed to passive, power 'to *make* an Object agreeable to itself, *i. e.* good, by its own proper act'

(*Origin of Evil*, p. 181). On the two views so far considered, the will is determined by something else's—either appetite's, or the understanding's—conception of the good. For a person to be genuinely free, though, he has able to choose for himself wherein lies the good. Then he will not be at the mercy of the circumstances he happens to find himself in. King is not conceiving here of a power to find the good in whatever one chooses to find it in. He accepts that no one can find pleasure in pain, or satisfaction in hunger or thirst. Nor does he have in mind a power of choice that is so independent of the understanding as to enable choices of what one knows to be impossible. Rather, he is concerned with choosing itself as a good: with the act of choice, not the thing chosen. There is a happiness felt in the complete and proper exercise of all the powers one has, and therefore there is a happiness in making completely free choices, choices not determined by anything other than, as we might say, willfulness itself. The understanding bears on such choices in so far as it distinguishes between the possible and the impossible; but it has no further influence. Full exercise of the power of choice enables one to choose independently of the understanding. More importantly, however, it enables one to choose against the bias of one's appetites. One cannot find pleasure in an unsatisfied appetite; but one can find pleasure, King believes, in *choosing* to ignore the demands of appetite; and sometimes this pleasure is greater than the pain of an unsatisfied appetite. King imagines that such a power of free choice might be given 'that the Agent might have wherein to please itself, when those things which are agreeable to the natural Appetites cannot be had, as it very often happens' (*Origin of Evil*, pp. 178–9). He is at pains to make it clear that in his conception of freedom there is 'no room for Chance, if by Chance be understood that which happens beside the Intention of the Agent' (*Origin of Evil*, p. 181). Nor is choice inherently unreasonable, since it is realized not so much in choosing a lesser good over a greater as in *making* a greater good what either before had no good in it all, or less good than something else. Moreover, in exercising the power of choice actively, an agent is 'the true *Cause* of his Actions, and...whatever he does may justly be imputed to him' (*Origin of Evil*, p. 182). King believes he has explained why such a freedom might be bestowed by an intelligent and benevolent God, and how it is that misuse of it would be the agent's own, and not God's, responsibility.

King holds both that it is one of the perfections of God to possess freedom in this complete sense, and that this divine attribute is, in principle, communicable to human beings. He also takes there to be reasons to believe that we actually possess freedom as he has described it (see *Origin of Evil*, pp. 197–212). These reasons are all empirical. The first is provided by 'consciousness', or introspective reflection. 'We experience in ourselves a Principle of this kind, *i.e.* a free one, to such a degree of certainty', King claims, 'that if our Minds be consulted we can hardly doubt of it' (*Origin of Evil*, p. 198). Philosophers might sometimes say they doubt of it, but only when wrapped up in puzzles of their own creation: the vulgar *never* doubt of it, and this is one of the respects in which they are wiser than the philosophers. The second piece of evidence is the fact that 'we experience in ourselves the Signs and Properties which belong to this power' (*Origin of Evil*, p. 200): we attribute our actions to ourselves; we are able to oppose the appetites and even reason, and can find pleasure in doing so; and we are able to habituate ourselves into believing obvious untruths and into taking evil things for good. Thirdly, King argues, some of the choices we make are so absurd as to be inexplicable save on the hypothesis of complete freedom of choice. Thus freedom is not intrinsically good. When joined with warring appetites and a limited understanding, it can be used badly, and bring harm to its possessor. The bulk of the rest of the chapter on moral evil is given over to an explanation of 'How Evil Elections are consistent with the Power and Goodness of God' (*Origin of Evil*, pp. 222–97).

Samuel Clarke and 'Moral' Necessity

Two years after the publication of King's *De Origine Mali*, Samuel Clarke, then chaplain to the Bishop of Norwich, gave the first of two series of Boyle Lectures at St. Paul's Cathedral. The lectures were later published with the title *A Demonstration of the Being and Attributes of God: More Particularly in Answer to Mr. Hobbs, Spinoza, And their Followers. Wherein the Notion of Liberty is Stated, and the Possibility and Certainty of it Proved, in Opposition to Necessity and Fate.*[8] The liberty with which Clarke concerns himself in this work is in the first instance the liberty of God. Clarke takes denial of the existence of God to be indistinguishable from a denial of the principal attributes of God. An atheist, in other

[8] The edition of the *Demonstration* used here is that in Volume II of the 1738 edition of Clarke's *Works* (i.e., Clarke (1738)). References to the *Demonstration* will be made in the main body of the text. There is extensive explication and analysis of Clarke's arguments in the *Demonstration* in Ferguson (1974). For a general account of Clarke's life and ideas, see Ferguson (1976). Clarke's treatment of the free will question is discussed in Rowe (1991), ch. 2.

words, is one who denies that God is a necessarily existing being, necessarily infinite and omnipresent, necessarily one, possessed of intelligence and liberty and choice, infinitely wise, and morally perfect. Each of these attributes is as important as the rest, and to deny God one is to deny him all of them. The liberty of the divine creator of the universe occupies a special place in Clarke's theology. For at the heart of his treatment of natural religion is an attempt to find a middle way between voluntarism, on the one hand, and Spinozistic necessitarianism, on the other. Voluntarism is characteristic of much Calvinist theology, and amounts to the view that God's creative act was unconstrained by pre-existing notions of goodness and justice. The voluntarist believes that notions of goodness and justice are themselves the work of God. On this view, God's freedom is similar in character to the liberty of indifference explored by King. Every one of God's choices is completely arbitrary, and expressive primarily of his unlimited power. On the Spinozistic picture, by contrast, it is impossible that the universe be any different from how it is. Spinoza's 'main purpose', Clarke says, 'was to make us believe that there is no such thing as *Power* or *Liberty* in the Universe, but that every particular thing in the World is by an Absolute Necessity just what it is, and could not possibly have been in any respect otherwise' (*Demonstration*, p. 542). Clarke takes Spinozism to be self-evidently absurd. It is obvious, he repeatedly claims, that the world and everything in it could have been different from how it actually is. The laws of motion, the number and movements of the planets, the number and nature of the species of animals and plants, the number of legs and eyes on a horse or an ox: there is no absolute necessity detectable in any of these things. And yet it will not do to say that God's creative choices were arbitrary. It is in God's nature to be wise and good, and it is in order to maximize the beauty, order, and well-being of the whole of creation that God acts as he does. There is a sense, then, in which God has to act as he does, but the necessity is 'a Necessity, not of Nature and Fate, but of Fitness and Wisdom', such as is 'consistent with the greatest Freedom and most perfect Choice' (*Demonstration*, p. 551).

Clarke holds that it can be proven *a priori* that there has to be a being in the universe that has the power of beginning motion. (To have a power of beginning motion is according to Clarke what it is to be free: this is why, as we will see below, he believes it to be a contradiction in terms to speak of an *agent* as necessitated in its actions.) Everything that exists must have a cause of its being, either in itself, or in another thing. It cannot be that everything that exists has the cause of its being in another thing, for that would be to postulate an infinity of dependent beings, and such an infinity Clarke believes to be 'plainly impossible, and *contradictory* to it self' (see *Demonstration*, pp. 525–7). So there must be at least one being that has its cause of existence in itself, and which has in itself a principle of acting, a power of beginning motion. Such a being exists necessarily, and, Clarke argues, must be able to do everything that is not logically impossible. There is no logical impossibility to the idea of an infinite power creating other beings also endowed with the power of beginning motion, and with a liberty of will or choice. And so it is possible for an infinite power to create other beings, which do not exist necessarily, but which do possess a freedom analogous to the freedom of God. For evidence that God has in fact created such beings, Clarke asks the reader to consult his own experience of himself:

For the Arguments drawn from continual Experience and Observation, to prove that we *have* such a Power, are so strong; that nothing less than a strict Demonstration that the thing is absolutely impossible, and that it implies an express contradiction, can make us in the least doubt that we have it not. We have all the same Experience, the same Marks and Evidence exactly, of our really having really a Power of *Self-Motion*; as the most rigid Fatalist could possibly contrive to require, if he was to make the *Supposition* of Man's being indued with that Power. There is no one thing, that such a Man can imagine *ought* to follow from the Supposition of *Self-Motion*, which every Man does not now as much feel and *actually* experience in Himself, as it can possibly be imagined any man would do, supposing the Thing were true.

(*Demonstration*, p. 558)

With this, Clarke turns immediately to refutation of the arguments of those who believe they can show a power of self-motion, and freedom of will, to be in some sense contradictory or impossible. The manner in which he thus attempts to shift the burden of proof onto the necessitarian anticipates much libertarian argument in the eighteenth century. The libertarian of this period tends to believe that the strongest evidence for the reality of free will is to be found in intuitive self-awareness. Introspection so powerfully speaks for the libertarian position that there are no arguments, as such, needed to justify belief in libertarian freedom. It should be noted, however, that there is one important respect in which later libertarians differ from Clarke: less confident than he of the powers of *a priori* argumentation, they tend to believe our idea of divine freedom is taken from the human case, and not the other way around.

Clarke's case for the freedom of the human will, then, is principally to be found in his replies to the arguments of his necessitarian opponents: Spinoza,

Hobbes, 'and their followers'. He considers several such arguments. One necessitarian argument rests upon the necessity of an external cause for every determination of the will, just as for every motion in the body. Clarke replies that such an argument must apply to the will of God just as much as to the human will, points to his own proof of the absolute necessity for there being a being possessed of a power of self-motion, and reiterates his case for the possibility and actuality of the transfer of such a power to human beings. Another argument for necessitarianism hinges on the assumption of the materiality of the mind. '[S]ince 'tis manifest that Matter has not in it self a Power of Beginning Motion', Clarke paraphrases, 'or giving it self any manner of Determination whatsoever; therefore 'tis evident likewise, that 'tis impossible there should be any such thing as Freedom of Will' (*Demonstration*, p. 559). Even though he follows Locke in maintaining the inscrutability of the substances or essences of all things (see, e.g., *Demonstration*, p. 537), Clarke believes materialism to be demonstrably false. His case against it is complex and protracted, and need not concern us here.[9] It is significant, though, that Clarke asserts that even if thought really were only an affection of matter, that would not prove freedom of will to be impossible:

For since it has already been demonstrated, that Thinking and Willing cannot possibly be Effects or Compositions of Figure and Motion; Whosoever will make Thinking and Willing to be Qualities or Affections of *Matter*, must suppose *Matter* capable of certain Properties entirely different from Figure and Motion. And if it be capable of Properties entirely different from Figure and Motion; then it can never be proved from the Effects of Figure and Motion being all Necessary, that the Effects of other and totally distinct Properties must likewise be Necessary.

(*Demonstration*, p. 563)

As we saw in the Introduction, Reid was to argue in exactly the same way more than eighty years later.[10] A third argument for necessity considered by Clarke is from divine prescience. Clarke makes the standard libertarian reply that foreknowledge, in the divine case as in the human, cannot by itself render an event necessary. Foreknowledge is comparable to any other kind of knowledge: knowing that something is the case does not make that thing the case, and nor does knowing that something *will* be the case make that thing come to pass (see *Demonstration*, pp. 566–8).

[9] See *Demonstration*, pp. 561–3. See Gay (1963) for an account of some connections between Clarke's rejection of materialism and his theory of freedom.

[10] See Reid (1788, 1969), pp. 356–7 (IV.xi).

For the purposes of this study, what is most significant in Clarke's criticisms of necessitarian argumentation is his response to the claim that the impossibility of freedom follows from the necessity of the will's being determined by the last judgment of the understanding. Here Clarke appears to have something like Locke's view in the first edition of the *Essay*.[11] He ignores the fact that the proponent of such a view does not take himself to be arguing against human freedom as such, but rather to be *redefining* freedom. Freedom for Clarke, if it is anything at all, is libertarian freedom, freedom of will or choice; such a freedom as is, he says, 'not at all *prevented* by *Chains* or *Prisons*' (*Demonstration*, p. 566). And, like Bramhall, he rejects the idea that the judgments of the understanding might *literally* necessitate the choices we make. His first reply to the necessitarian is to argue that 'the Necessity of the Will's being determined by the last Judgment of the Understanding is ... only a Necessity upon Supposition; that is to say, a Necessity that a man should *Will* a thing, when 'tis *supposed* that he *does Will it*' (*Demonstration*, p. 564). What Clarke means here is made clearer when he explains that there is a necessary connection between a final judgment and volition just in so far as a final judgment is what a volition *is*. The necessity in this case is of a trivial kind: necessarily, a thing that exists cannot, while it exists, not exist. This of course does not answer the necessitarian's question, which concerns the connection between the understanding and the will considered as two different things. Here is Clarke's reply to that question:

if the *Act of Volition* be distinguished from the *last Judgment of the Understanding*; then the *Act of Volition*, or rather the *Beginning of Action*, consequent upon the last *Judgment of the Understanding*, is not *determined* or *caused* by that last Judgment, as by the *physical Efficient*, but only as the *Moral Motive*. For the true, proper, immediate, *physical Efficient Cause* of Action, is the *Power of Self-Motion* in Men, which exerts itself *freely* in consequence of the *last Judgment of the Understanding*. But the *last Judgment of the Understanding*, is not itself a *physical Efficient*, but merely a *Moral Motive*, upon which the *physical Efficient* or *motive Power* begins to Act. The *Necessity*, therefore, by which the *Power of Acting* follows the *Judgment of the Understanding*, is only a *Moral Necessity*; that is, *no Necessity at all*, in the Sense wherein the Opposers of Liberty understand *Necessity*. For *Moral Necessity*, is evidently consistent with the most perfect *Natural Liberty*.

(*Demonstration*, p. 565)

[11] He might have Hobbes in his sights as well. However, Hobbes's characteristic way of stating his position is that the will is determined by *appetite* rather than by the understanding. In fact, Hobbes *identifies* the will with the appetite that wins out in the 'alternate succession of contrary appetites' that is deliberation as he understands it.

It is with men as it is with God. Insight into the good and true determines our choices, but it does not do so literally, or 'physically'. We retain the capacity to ignore what the understanding tells us, and to choose the worse thing, while knowing the better. There is a sense in which a healthy and sane man *cannot* commit suicide. He simply sees no reason to, for example, jump off a cliff once he has climbed to its top. But this does not mean it is properly speaking impossible for him to do so, even while he remains healthy and sane.

What Clarke is seeking is, again, a middle way between the two extremes of necessitarianism and voluntarism. He does not accept the view that the determinants of choice render choice absolutely necessary. On the other hand, without mentioning the author of *De Origine Mali* by name, he rejects King's view that we are most free when we choose for the sheer pleasure of choosing, indifferent to the deliverances of the understanding. The two views share an assumption to the effect that, in so far as motives determine the will, they take away its freedom. It is in failing to see that motives determine the will in a completely different way from the way in which physical causes determine their effects that there lies 'the fundamental Errour, both of those who argue against the *Liberty of the Will*, and of those who but too confusedly defend it' (*Demonstration*, p. 565).

In correspondence with John Bulkeley, a 'Gentleman from the University of Cambridge', Clarke adds a further element to his argument for the liberty of the will. Bulkeley declares himself unable to see how the middle way Clarke seeks to navigate does not end up in Hobbesianism. Just as a judgment of the understanding is necessitated by the true and good, Bulkeley urges, so also, surely, the will is necessitated by the understanding. The necessity in question might, in order to be rendered consistent with freedom, be thought of as 'not an *external Necessity* or *blind Impulse*, but a Necessity Internal, which results from the very Being and Constitution of rational Nature';[12] but it is all the same a necessity that makes it literally impossible for anything other than one decision to be made. It would be no imperfection in God if he were unable to do anything other than what is just and good; by the same token, it would be no imperfection in man. Bulkeley, like the Locke of the first edition of the *Essay*, is content to attribute sin to an imperfection of the human understanding. Clarke's reply to Bulkeley is to explain in more detail why it is that it is impossible for the judgment literally, or

---

[12] Clarke (1738), vol. iv, p. 715. The debate with Bulkeley was originally published with the Leibniz–Clarke correspondence.

physically, to determine the will. The reason is that the judgment is wholly *passive*, while the will is intrinsically *active*. Something that is passive cannot, Clarke argues, determine the state of something that is active. Bulkeley has failed to take into account the pure activity of the faculty of will.[13] No matter how little reason there is to pursue a certain course of action, Clarke is saying, the active nature of the will ensures that there is a sense in which it is possible to decide to do what is completely irrational and purposeless. God 'always *acts* or *does* what is Just and Good, *freely*; that is, having at the same Time a full *natural* or *physical Power* of acting differently'.[14] If he did not have this power, he could not properly be said to be just and good, since, so Clarke claims, it is intrinsic to a just or good action that the agent might have chosen not to do it.

The middle way that Clarke is looking for is less easy to characterize than he admits. The power a free agent has to ignore the last judgment of the understanding must, presumably, be more than a 'physical power of acting differently'. It must be a power to choose to act differently, not simply a power to act differently *if the agent were to choose to act differently*. And the nature of such a power is not clear. This is a point pressed by Leibniz in his own correspondence with Clarke. In his 'Fourth Paper', Clarke alleges, Leibniz deploys the principle of sufficient reason in such a way as to lead to 'universal necessity and fate'. Leibniz does so

by supposing that motives have the same relation to the will of an intelligent agent, as weights have to a balance; so that of two things absolutely indifferent, an intelligent agent can no more choose either, than a balance can move itself when the weights on both sides are equal. But the difference lies here. A balance is no agent, but is merely passive and acted upon by the weights; so that, when the weights are equal, there is nothing to move it. But intelligent beings are agents; not passive, in being moved by motives, as a balance is by weights; but they have active powers and do move themselves, sometimes upon the view of strong motives, sometimes upon weak ones, and sometimes when things are absolutely indifferent. In which latter case, there may be very good reason to act, though two or more ways of acting may be absolutely indifferent.[15]

Leibniz, in reply, declares that he accepts that there is no literal or physical causal relation between motives and choices. '[P]roperly speaking', he says, 'motives do not act upon the mind, as weights do upon the balance;

---

[13] See Clarke (1738), vol. iv, pp. 714, 716. [14] Ibid., p. 717.
[15] Leibniz and Clarke (1717, 1956), p. 45.

but 'tis rather the mind that acts by virtue of the motives, which are its dispositions to act'.[16] This is not sufficient, however, to establish freedom as Clarke understands it. For Clarke's picture of decision-making, as Leibniz puts it, 'divide[s] the mind from the motives': it seems to require that there be additional motives, upon which the mind chooses to act upon the motives it is provided with by the understanding. These second-order motives are unnecessary, Leibniz argues: first-order motives provided by the understanding provide all the reasons necessary for rational decision-making. Leibniz also says he can make no sense of there being a reason to act where there is no motive: a will without motive would be 'blind' and 'owing to mere chance'.[17] Moreover, an agent faced with two motives perfectly equal in strength could not find reason to choose one at the expense of the other.

Clarke's response to Leibniz in his 'Fifth Paper' is essentially the same as his response to Bulkeley. He does not really address the problem Leibniz has identified. As will be seen in Chapter 5 below, that problem is expanded upon and made more pressing still by Jonathan Edwards—but is in fact never seriously addressed by any libertarian of the eighteenth century. Before we move on from Clarke to Collins, it is perhaps worth underlining the fact that nowhere in his writings on liberty does Clarke allow that a free action is an uncaused action. It does not, so he claims, follow from the fact that motives are not the cause of choices that choices have no cause. Clarke's position, as we have seen, is that 'the true, proper, immediate, physical cause of action is the power of self-motion in men, which exerts itself freely in consequence of the last judgment of the understanding'.[18]

Anthony Collins's Return to Hobbes

One of Anthony Collins's first works, published in 1710, was a reply to a sermon given by King on predestination and divine foreknowledge in their relation to human freedom. King had argued, probably with Bayle in his sights, that it is possible to reconcile predestination and foreknowledge with the freedom of human agents, but only when it is remembered that there is

---

[16] Ibid., p. 59.

[17] Ibid., p. 79.

[18] For more detailed discussion of the parts of the Leibniz–Clarke debate which touch upon free will, see Vailati (1997), ch. 3.

only a distant, 'analogical', relation between the divine attributes and their instantiation in the human case. Thus what it means for a human being to have foreknowledge of an event is different from what it means for God to know that it will happen before it does, and we know so little of God's nature that we have no reason to think it impossible that God should foresee without in any way obstructing or limiting our freedom of choice. The answer to those who claim that foreknowledge is inherently incompatible with contingency and freedom is that 'though such *Fore-knowledge* and *Decrees*, as are in our Understandings and Wills, cannot consist with *Contingency*, if we suppose them certain, yet what we call so in God may, being quite of a different Nature, and only called by those Names, by Reason of some *Analogy* and *Proportion*, which are between them'.[19] To Collins this appears to amount to an unwarranted surrender to the atheistical sceptic of the main point he seeks to establish, which is that reason is useless in theological matters. What King concedes, in effect, is that the sceptic is *right* when he claims that foreknowledge is incompatible with human freedom, and when he claims, more generally, that there is no reasoned reply to make to Manichaeanism. King's position is, in the end, indistinguishable from that of the atheist. 'I do not see how his Grace will be able to prove the Existence of one Eternal Immutable Being', Collins says, 'if the Atheist should think it worth his while to dispute that Point with his Grace.'[20] The right way of approaching the question of foreknowledge and freedom Collins had already indicated three years earlier, in his *Essay concerning the Use of Reason*. There he claims that, in fact, the matter is so clear 'that I cannot forbear thinking, that nothing but the Interest of some, or Prejudice of others, in behalf of receiv'd Systems, could make it a question of difficulty'.[21] It is plain that if liberty is understood as involving contingency and a power of self-determination, then liberty is indeed inconsistent with divine prescience; for if an action is foreknown, it is certain that it will be done. It is, however, just as plain that liberty understood in such a way is, as Collins puts it, 'inconsistent with Truth'.[22] For 'the greatest Freedom or Liberty we can conceive to belong to any Being' is, simply, an agent's 'Power to do or forbear several Actions, according to the Determination of his Mind', which is to say, a 'Liberty or Freedom from Compulsion'.[23] And such freedom is perfectly compatible with foreknow-

---

[19] King (1709, 1727), p. 46.   [20] Collins (1710), p. 15.   [21] Collins (1707), p. 45.
[22] Ibid., p. 47.   [23] Ibid., p. 47.

ledge, since it gives no role to contingency, and allows that free actions are wholly determined by the determinations of the agent's mind.[24]

Collins returns to the question of freedom and necessity in his *Philosophical Inquiry concerning Human Liberty* of 1717.[25] Collins's concern with clarity and aversion to the obscure and mysterious is a prominent feature of the *Inquiry*. Once clear and accurate definitions are given of the principal terms of the dispute, and of freedom in particular, Collins believes, it will be seen that there is no difficulty in reconciling the opposing parties. For the only coherent definition of freedom is compatible with the necessitation of human action. This fact allows Collins to make a claim characteristic of eighteenth-century necessitarianism: that libertarians, did they but know it, are already in agreement with their opponents. Collins believes, or pretends to believe, that there is nothing to the doctrine of necessity that the libertarian need object to. Thus he is keen to make it clear from the first that, though he denies liberty 'in a certain meaning of that word' (*Inquiry*, p. ii), he does not deny it altogether. The essence of the position advocated in the *Inquiry* is the Hobbesian doctrine that to hold the doctrine of necessity is *not* the same thing as to deny the freedom of all human actions. Indeed, Collins goes further than Hobbes in his attempt to put an end to the disagreement between libertarians and necessitarians. We saw in the Introduction that Hobbes is contemptuous in his dismissal of the notion of 'moral necessity' employed by Bramhall in order to explain the influence of the understanding on the will. Collins, by contrast, knowing that 'moral necessity' is at the heart of Clarke's style of libertarianism, adopts the term to his own purposes. '[W]hen I affirm *necessity*', he says; 'I contend only for what is call'd *moral necessity*, meaning thereby, *that a man, who is an intelligent and sensible being, is determin'd by his reason and his senses*; and I deny man to be subject to such necessity, as is in clocks, watches, and such other beings, which for want of *sensation* and *intelligence* are subject to an *absolute, physical, or mechanical necessity*' (*Inquiry*, p. iii). Of course, this is not in fact all that Clarke or Bramhall mean to signal by the distinction between moral and physical necessity; but it is a sign of Clarke's influence on subsequent treatments of the free will question

---

[24] There is disagreement in the literature on Collins as to whether he is sincere in his vindication of the reasonableness of religious belief. O'Higgins (1970) believes that he is, and portrays Collins as anti-clerical and anti-Christian, but as a believer in God and a future life; Berman (1988), ch. 3, believes that he is not, and sees Collins as an atheist in disguise. For discussion of King's sermon on predestination, see Berman (1976).

[25] In the present chapter references to this work will be made in the main body of the text.

that Collins makes such a claim. In other respects, Collins follows Hobbes's lead. He argues that necessity, and not a liberty of self-determination, is the foundation of morality, and that a liberty of self-determination would in fact be an 'imperfection', dangerous to those who possessed it, and subversive of the authority of morals and positive law. These claims will not be discussed here. I shall focus instead on Collins's discussion of the libertarian claim that experience testifies to the falsity of necessitarianism, and his reiteration of Hobbes' argument for necessity from the definition of the term 'cause'.[26]

'[E]xperience', Collins says, 'is urg'd with great triumph, by the patrons of Liberty' (Inquiry, p.12). It seems to be King, in particular, that Collins has in mind: King is described as '[a] famous Author, who appeals to common experience, for a proof of liberty', and Collins cites criticisms of King's appeal to experience by Leibniz and 'the Journalists of Paris' (Inquiry, pp. 21, 28, 29–30). The only other writer referred to by name as resting the case for liberty on experience is 'the late Bishop of Sarum', Gilbert Burnet.[27] As we have seen, it is indeed experience, or 'consciousness', that King invokes to justify the claim that God not only can, but also actually has, endowed human beings with a power to free choice. Collins adopts a two-part strategy. First, he seeks to show that it is much less plain than a philosopher such as King thinks that experience testifies to our possessing a freedom that is incompatible with the determination of choice by reason and the senses. Those who make this claim sometimes seem to be talking about freedom as Collins himself understands it; sometimes they will say that the question of liberty and necessity is a very difficult one, which sits ill with the claim that liberty is a plain fact of experience; some libertarians do not rest their case on experience, and prefer to cite the supposed consequences of the doctrine of necessity as proof of liberty; and some philosophers (Collins instances Bayle and Leibniz) are prepared to argue that, even if it seems that there is experience of free choice, in reality choice is determined by factors beneath the level of consciousness (see Inquiry, pp. 12–31). Collins concludes that 'liberty is not a plain matter of experience' (Inquiry, p. 31).

The second part of his response to the libertarian argument from experience is an attempt to clear matters up by means of a careful examination of, as he puts it, 'the various actions of Men which can be conceiv'd to concern

---

[26] For additional discussion of Collins's criticisms of libertarianism, see Rowe (1991), ch. 3.

[27] Collins quotes from Burnet's Exposition of the Thirty-Nine Articles of the Church of England (1699).

this subject', by which he means the perception of ideas, the judging of propositions, volition, and doing as one wills. Collins means to show that in each of these kinds of actions, the mind is subject to necessity. It is obvious, and is conceded by libertarians (for instance, by Clarke in his correspondence with Bulkeley), that perception and judgment do not involve freedom of any kind. The libertarian, moreover, does not rest his case on an experience of freedom to do or not to do as one wills. It is the will itself, and whether or not we have control over its determinations, that is the crux of the matter between the libertarian and his opponent.[28] Collins's position, of course, is that we do not have such control. His main reason for asserting this is taken from Locke: 'Willing or preferring', Collins says, 'is the same with respect to good and evil, that judging is with respect to truth or falshood' (*Inquiry*, p. 41). It is as impossible to choose misery instead of happiness in exactly the way in which it is impossible to *prefer* misery to happiness. Preferences are not up to us; volitions are preferences; so volitions are not up to us. What about cases where there is no perceptible difference between two or more courses of action—where, in other words, there is no preference either way? Collins answers that such cases are not those that should matter most to the libertarian; that cases of pure indifference are very rare indeed; and that where there is *no* perceptible difference, choice is impossible. There is, therefore, no experience of freedom as the libertarian understands freedom. Indeed, 'it is a matter of experience, that man is ever determin'd in his willing or acts of volition and choice' (*Inquiry*, p. 52).

Collins, like Hobbes, thinks that he can show that man is a necessary agent merely by means of analysis of the concept of 'cause'. Every action has a beginning; whatever has a beginning has a cause; and every cause is a necessary, or (as we might say) *necessitating* cause. So every action is necessary. As I hope to have made clear, the libertarian does not deny the second premise. What he does deny is that every cause is a necessary cause. Here is Collins's argument for that claim:

if a cause be not a necessary cause, it is no cause at all. For if causes are not necessary causes; then causes are not suited to, or are indifferent to effects; and the *Epicurean System* of chance is rendered possible.... If [causes] be suited to some particular effect and not to others, they can be no causes at all to those others. And therefore a cause

[28] There is also the question of, in Collins's words, '[w]hether we are at liberty to will, or not to will'—in particular, whether we have, as he thinks Locke thinks we have, the power to suspend willing and not make a decision at all. Collins's position is that '*suspending to will*, is itself an *act of willing*', and so is not a special case. See *Inquiry*, pp. 37–40.

not suited to the effect; and no cause; are the same thing. And if a cause not suited to the effect, is no cause; then a cause suited to the effect is a necessary cause: for if it does not produce the effect, it is not suited to it, or is no cause at all.

(*Inquiry*, pp. 58–9)

The conclusion that Collins draws is that '[l]iberty, or a power to act or not to act, to do this or another thing under the same causes, is an *impossibility*'; it is also, he says provocatively, '*atheistical*' (*Inquiry*, p. 59). In this way Collins, surely self-consciously, uses Clarke's argument for the necessary existence of a first cause of the universe against Clarke's own conception of freedom. What Collins means by a cause being 'suited to' its effect would seem to be that a cause is, by definition, sufficient for its effect to take place.[29] And, as with Hobbes, the idea here is that what is *sufficient* for an event is, by definition, such as to make it necessary that that event takes place. Collins is not afraid of collapsing causal necessity into logical necessity: 'I do allow', he says in reply to an imagined objection to his account of liberty, '*that if all events are necessary, it was as impossible for* Julius Caesar *not to have died in the Senate, as it is impossible for two and two to make six*' (*Inquiry*, p. 107). It is, he adds, in fact impossible to so much as *conceive* of Caesar as having died anywhere else than in the Senate.[30]

The Clarkean Reply to Collins

In the same year that Collins published the *Inquiry*, Clarke issued a brief reply. The reply gives prominence to the claim that 'a *Necessary Agent* or *Necessary Action* is a *Contradiction in Terms*': 'For whatever *acts Necessarily*, does not *act at all*, but is only *acted upon*; is not at all an *Agent*, but a mere *Patient*; does not *move*, but

---

[29] Gideon Yaffe has suggested to me a different way of understanding Collins's talk of causes being 'suited to' their effects. Collins might grant his opponent the claim that sometimes causes do not necessitate their effects. He then tries to imagine how the opponent might answer the question, 'So why did *x* happen rather than not-*x*?' He imagines the opponent saying: 'Because *x* is suited to the cause, and not-*x* is not suited.' That is, the opponent claims that there is a fitness relation between certain causes and their non-necessitated effects which explains why they occurred instead of alternatives to them. Collins's response is to say that that amounts to another way of saying that such causes necessitate their effects. I do not think this is incompatible with my reading.

[30] It is precisely in order to avoid this conclusion that Leibniz distinguishes between 'absolute' necessity (where denial of the proposition produces a contradiction) and 'hypothetical' necessity (where no contradiction is yielded by a denial). Leibniz's claim to be able to reconcile necessity and freedom rests on the fact that the necessitation of human action is not absolute. When he

is moved only.'[31] To be an agent is to have a power to begin motion, and, Clarke argues, motion cannot begin necessarily. Motion can be transmitted from one body to another in such a way that the resulting movement is necessary, but the source of the motion must—simply in order to be a *source*—be able to initiate motion freely. A source of motion might be either God or a rational being endowed by God with a power of self-determination. Clarke writes that '*All Power of Acting*, essentially implies at the same time a *Power of not Acting*: Otherwise it is not *Acting*, but barely a *being acted upon* by That Power (whatever it be) which Causes the Action.'[32] Clarke also explains in a little more detail than in his other writings on liberty and necessity why it is that a motive cannot be a cause. One reason, as we have seen, is that they are passive; another is now said to be that they are 'mere abstract notions'. 'May not an *abstract Notion*', Clarke asks rhetorically, 'as well *strike a Ball*, as be the *efficient Cause of Motion in a Man's Body*.'[33] It is not clear what Clarke means by calling motives 'mere abstract notions'. It appears that what he intends to draw attention to is the fact that motives are not *substances*.[34] Substances can be agents, and motives, not being substances, cannot. But Clarke does not tell the reader whether there are further implications of passivity in the fact that motives are *notions*, and *abstract* notions at that.

Clarke charges Collins with misunderstanding the indifference that is essential to freedom as the libertarian understands it. Throughout the *Inquiry*, Collins confounds '*Indifference* as to *Power*, (that is, an *equal Physical Power* either of *acting* or of *forbearing to act*)' with '*Indifference* as to *Inclination*, (that is, an *equal Approbation* or *Liking of one thing* or *the contrary*)'.[35] The libertarian is interested only in the former kind of indifference. Collins ignores the fact that possession of a power of self-determination does not entail that motives have no influence at all on choice. Collins, in other words, is blind to the real significance of the

claims, as he frequently does, the motives incline the will without necessitating it, what he means is that they do not *absolutely* necessitate it. But the connection is necessary in just the same sense as is any law of material nature. This is of course why Clarke rejects freedom as Leibniz defines it. For Leibniz's distinction between absolute and hypothetical necessity, see, e.g., his discussion of Hobbes at the end of the *Theodicy*: Leibniz (1710, 1985), p. 395.

[31] Clarke (1738), vol. iv, p. 722.

[32] Ibid., p. 722.

[33] Ibid., p. 723.

[34] Thus he says that Collins is guilty of 'supposing *Reasons* or *Motives* ... to make the same *necessary Impulse* upon *intelligent* Subjects, as *Matter in Motion* does upon *unintelligent Subjects*; which is supposing *abstract Notions* to be *Substances*' (Clarke (1738), vol. iv, p. 725).

[35] Ibid., p. 724.

distinction between moral and physical necessity. He thinks that to allow for the libertarian to allow any influence to motives is to concede the game to the necessitarian. But the Clarkean libertarian, as we have seen, believes that there is a middle way between 'indifference as to inclination' and literal determination by motives of choice and action. Clarke emphasizes that '*Moral Necessity*, in true and Philosophical Strictness, is not indeed any *Necessity* at all, but 'tis merely a *figurative Manner of Speaking*, which, like all other *figurative* Expressions, has nothing of *Physical Reality* in it.'[36] There is no truth in Collins's claim that he asserts nothing the libertarian is concerned to deny.

Twelve years later, in 1729, there appeared a *Dissertation on Liberty and Necessity ... With some Remarks upon the Reverend Dr. Clarke's Reasoning on this Point*, 'By A. C. Esq.' It is tempting to assume that 'A. C.' is Anthony Collins, but Collins's biographer disputes the attribution.[37] The most interesting point made in the *Dissertation* is a claim to the effect that Clarke begs the question by assuming that human beings are agents in Clarke's metaphysically loaded sense of the term: 'He supposes a *Self-Moving Faculty*, which is the point in dispute, and then argues that 'tis not *Passive*.'[38] This is not absolutely fair, of course, for Clarke argues in the *Demonstration* that 'continual experience and observation' provide compelling evidence that God has endowed us with a power of self-motion. A further claim made in the *Dissertation* is that, since we do not know what the substance of the soul is, and are conscious only of its operations, in explaining those operations 'we are reduced to the necessity of drawing parallels from matter'.[39] And drawing such parallels, so it is argued, intimates that the soul is always acted upon by the last judgment of the understanding.

The *Dissertation* in turn provoked responses from Clarkean libertarians. (Clarke himself died in 1729.) John Jackson, in *A Vindication of Humane Liberty*, seeks to exploit the fact that the author of the *Dissertation* denies that his argument for necessity extends to the divine as well as to the human case.[40]

---

[36] Thus he says that Collins is guilty of 'supposing *Reasons* or *Motives* ... to make the same *necessary Impulse* upon *intelligent* Subjects, as *Matter in Motion* does upon *unintelligent Subjects*; which is supposing *abstract Notions* to be *Substances*' (Clarke (1738), vol. iv, p. 725).

[37] See O'Higgins (1970), p. 109.

[38] A. C. (1729), p. 11.

[39] Ibid., p. 13.

[40] 'A. C.' writes: 'Our Knowledge is too imperfect to account for the Manner in which the *Deity* acts; but surely it is no just Consequence, that because our Actions are determined by the Last Judgment of the Understanding, and therefore necessary, that his are too; That were to prove things we are in the dark about, by other things still farther removed from our Comprehension' (p. 12). This sits ill with the spirit of Collins's attempt to vindicate the use of reason in theological matters, and is perhaps another piece of evidence that the *Dissertation* was written by someone else.

Jackson replies that 'as necessity of judgement does not make God a merely *passive* being, so neither can it make man a merely passive being, or take away his agency'.[41] 'It cannot be rightly argued', Jackson says, 'that where the action does instantaneously follow the judgement, there the action is not free. For this is the case with respect to the agency of God, which nevertheless A.C. acknowledges to be free; and it may be so, for aught he knows, in the exertion of the humane soul.'[42] In both the divine and the human case, there is only a relation of 'concomitancy' between judgment and action. The same style of argument is adopted by Phillips Gretton, who seeks to show that the case made in the *Inquiry* and the *Dissertation* for the necessitation of human action proves also that God is not a free agent. And if the divine mind is free in its choices, then so may be the human mind.[43]

Libertarianism after Clarke

The 1730s saw something of a revival of King's theory of human freedom. In 1731 *De origine mali* was translated into English by Edmund Law, and published with extensive explanatory notes. 'Our author's notion of *indifference*', Law writes in the notes to his translation, 'has been grossly misunderstood by all his adversaries, who have accordingly rais'd terrible outcries against it, as destroying the essential, and immutable distinction between good and evil; subverting appetites, making reason and judgment useless, and confounding everything'.[44] Law seeks to clarify King's conception of liberty, partly by

---

[41] Jackson (1730), p. 8.

[42] Ibid., pp. 41–2.

[43] See Gretton (1730).

[44] King (1731), p. 174n. Among King's critics had been Bayle, Leibniz, and Collins. In the *Réponse aux questions d'un provincial*, Bayle argues 'Que la liberté d'indifférence à l'égard du bien en général seroit une imperfection': 'Tous les conseils, et tous les raisonnemens du monde pourront être très-inutiles; vous lui éclairerez, vous lui convaincrez l'esprit, et néanmoins sa volonté fera la fiere, et demeurera immobile comme un rocher' (Bayle (1727), vol. iii, p. 679). Leibniz is unable to see how it can be the case that liberty as King understands it might add to human happiness: 'on the contrary, there is nothing more imperfect; it would render knowledge and goodness futile, and would reduce everything to chance, with no rules, and no measures that could be taken' (Leibniz (1710, 1985), p. 425). The criticisms made of King by Bayle and Leibniz are repeated (sometimes without acknowledgement) by Collins in the *Inquiry*. Collins argues that, with the exercise of a power of choice as defined by King, 'man would ... be the most irrational and inconsistent being, and by consequence, the most *imperfect* understanding being, which can be conceiv'd' (*Inquiry*, p. 65).

restricting its scope. He notes that ' 'Tis not an absolute indifference ... of the *man* or mind in general, nor of the *senses*, perception or judgment, which [King] contends for; but it relates wholly to that *particular power* of the mind which we call *willing* ... '.[45] Law also replies to the Leibnizian argument, repeated by Collins, that it does not follow from the fact that we are not conscious of motives determining choice that there are not in play motives of which we are not aware. In the case of mental realm, Law argues, not to be perceived and not to exist amount to the same thing: 'To feel no pain, to be conscious of no idea, is to have none: and in like manner to perceive no motive or reason of action, is the same as not to act upon any, or to perceive that we act without one.'[46] Isaac Watts also took his conception of freedom from King.[47] Watts refuses to allow that there might be a distinction to be drawn between literal necessitation of the will by motives and a non-literal, figurative, merely 'moral' necessitation. Liberty, he says, 'is utterly inconsistent with all necessity'.[48] And experience shows that, in many cases, 'the will is determined neither by present uneasiness, nor by the greatest apparent good, nor by the last dictate of the understanding, nor by anything else, but merely by itself as a sovereign and self-determining power of the soul'.[49]

Nevertheless, the cases of Law and Watts notwithstanding, it is Clarke's middle way between indifference theories and necessitarianism that later libertarians attempt to follow. The will, according to Samuel Fancourt, 'is not in its nature indifferent to all objects, after evidence has been examined'; 'such is the make of the will, it does in its own nature follow (supposing it to come *now* to a determination) what appears at this time, and upon summing up the evidence, to be of the greatest weight, or best for itself.'[50] 'It is the property and perfection of a *rational agent* to act upon precedent rational

---

[45] King (1731), p. 174 fn.

[46] Ibid., p. 199 fn. It is perhaps also worth noting the following remark of Law's: 'Dr *Clarke's* argument for absolute freedom, because all motives or sensations are mere abstract notions, and have no physical power, seems not conclusive, or at least not clear' (King (1731), p. 167 fn).

[47] In *On the Freedom of the Will in God and Creatures*, Watts denies that liberty is compatible with the influence of motives upon the will, and admits that he is 'indebted to Bishop *King* in his treatise of the *Origin of Evil*, many years ago, for my first thoughts of this kind': Watts (1732), p. 27.

[48] Ibid., p. 9.

[49] Ibid., pp. 25–6. In his notes to his translation of *De origine mali*, Law defends King's conception of liberty; but is also careful to restrict its scope: ''Tis not an absolute indifference ... of the *man* or mind in general, nor of the *senses*, perception or judgment, which [King] contends for; but it relates wholly to that *particular power* of the mind which we call *willing* ...' (King (1731), p. 174 fn).

[50] Fancourt (1729), pp. 18, 19.

motives and considerations', writes John Jackson; 'Reason is given us to direct our *choice* aright. But it is no consequence, that, because we make *reason* the ground of our actions, our actions are not *free*.'[51] Jackson argues, indeed, 'that the more *rationally* men act, the more *freely* they act'.[52] Continuing Clarke's debate with Bulkeley, Samuel Strutt reiterates the claim that the will closely follows judgment—though he is careful to insist that these two things 'have *no connection or relation* to each other': 'All that can be said, consistent with the truth, concerning human nature, is, that we generally, and almost always do act, in consequence of the last judgment of the understanding.'[53] We will see in the next chapter that this insistence on the influence of understanding upon the will is crucial to Hume's attempt to do better than Collins in persuading libertarians that their position is, despite appearances, compatible with necessitarianism.[54]

[51] Jackson (1730), p. 47.

[52] Ibid., p. 47.

[53] Strutt (1730), pp. 16–17.

[54] Collins's deist and anti-clerical reputation ensured that he had little direct influence on the subsequent debate. Priestley is unusual among British necessitarians in acknowledging Collins's influence. Priestley says that it was Collins who first convinced him of the truth of necessitarianism (Priestley (1782), vol. ii, p. xxvi), and published an edition of the *Inquiry* in 1790. It would seem that, on the whole, Collins was taken more seriously in France than in England: see O'Higgins (1970), pp. 217–20.

3

Hume's Reconciling Project

> We change no circumstance in the received orthodox system with
> regard to the will, but only in that with regard to material objects
> and causes.
>
> Hume, *An Enquiry concerning Human Understanding*, Section VIII

On the title page of *A Treatise of Human Nature*, Hume describes his first book as 'an attempt to introduce the experimental method of reasoning into moral subjects'. The experimental method had been identified by Bacon, described by Hume in *The History of England* as having 'pointed out at a distance the road to true philosophy';[1] and had been perfected by Newton, 'the greatest and rarest genius that ever arose for the ornament and instruction of the species'. Newton was, Hume writes in the *History*, '[c]autious in admitting no principles but such as were founded on experiment; but resolute to adopt every such principle, however new or unusual'. His achievement was 'to draw off the veil from some of the mysteries of nature', but, so Hume claims, Newton also drew attention to limits of explanation, particularly mechanical explanation, 'and thereby restored [nature's] ultimate secrets to that obscurity, in which they ever did and ever will remain'.[2] The Introduction to the *Treatise* leaves the reader in little doubt that Hume took his task to be the development of a Newtonianism of the mind: what he himself terms a 'science of man'. '[T]he only solid foundation we can give to this science itself must be laid on experience and observation', Hume writes.[3] '[W]e must endeavour to render all our principles as universal as possible', he adds, 'by tracing up our experiments to the utmost, and explaining all effects from the simplest and

---

[1] Hume (1778, 1983), vol. v, p. 153.

[2] Ibid., vol. vi, p. 542.

[3] Hume (1739–40, 2000), p. 4. All subsequent references to the *Treatise* in this chapter will be in the main body of the text.

fewest causes' (*Treatise*, p. 5). The Newtonian character of Hume's ambition is made plain when, in Book I of the *Treatise*, Hume characterizes the way ideas are associated with each other in the mind as 'a kind of ATTRACTION, which in the mental world will be found to have as extraordinary effects as in the natural, and to show itself in as many and as various forms' (*Treatise*, p. 14 (I.i.4)).[4] In addition to Newton's explanatory ambitiousness, Hume takes on Newton's sense of the limits of explanation, declaring that 'any hypothesis, that pretends to discover the ultimate original qualities of human nature, ought at first to be rejected as presumptuous and chimerical' (*Treatise*, p. 5). Just as Newton refuses to frame hypotheses about what is responsible for the fundamental laws of nature being as they are, so also Hume will abjure metaphysical questions in his science of the mind—in particular, the 'absolutely unintelligible' question of what the mind is made of.[5] There is, though, one important difference between natural and moral philosophy. In setting out to examine principles governing the operations of the mind, one can all too easily disturb the mind's natural workings. It is hard, if not impossible, for a philosopher to catch himself in the act of reasoning and feeling as normal people do. 'We must therefore glean up our experiments in this science from a cautious observation of human life', Hume says, 'and take them as they appear in the common course of the world, by men's behaviour in company, in affairs, and in their pleasures' (*Treatise*, p. 6). Eschewal of metaphysics and attention to common life are prominent features of Hume's treatment of the question of liberty and necessity.[6]

---

[4] In the *Abstract* of the *Treatise* he describes association as the 'cement' of the mental universe. '[I]f any thing can entitle the author [of the *Treatise*] to so glorious name as that of *inventor*', he says, ''tis the use he makes of the principle of the association of ideas, which enters into most of his philosophy' ((1740, 2000), pp. 417, 416). Hume is, indeed, an innovator here. Locke had described the association of ideas as a 'sort of Madness'. He added a chapter on the topic to the fourth edition of *Essay* as a means of explaining better the ways in which reason is overcome and perverted by miseducation and prejudice (Locke (1690, 1975), pp. 394–401 (II.xxxiii)). The same suspicion of the effects of association is evident in the early works of Francis Hutcheson (see Broadie (2002)). There is a large literature devoted to Hume's philosophical method and its debt to the culture of Newtonian science: see, e.g., Kuypers (1930), chs. 1–3; Noxon (1973); Forbes (1975), ch. 1; Jones (1982), ch. 1; Wright (1983), ch. 5; Barfoot (1990); Force (1990); and McIntyre (1994) (which makes a useful comparison between Hume and Collins).

[5] For Hume's discussion of the ontology of mind, see *Treatise* I.iv.6.

[6] This chapter is an expansion and (at certain points) reformulation of the argument of Harris (2003c).

'Of Liberty and Necessity' in the *Treatise* and in the First *Enquiry*

In the *Treatise*, Hume's discussion of the question of liberty and necessity is found in Book II, 'Of the Passions'. The will, Hume admits, is not properly speaking a passion, but demands to be discussed in this context of a treatment of the passions because 'the full understanding of its nature and properties, is necessary to the explanation of them' (*Treatise*, p. 257 (II.iii.1)). Yet it is made immediately apparent that Hume believes that there is little, if anything, to be said about the will.[7] He says that he regards it as 'nothing but *the internal impression we feel and are conscious of, when we knowingly give rise to any new motion of our body, or new perception of our mind*' (*Treatise*, p. 257 (II.iii.1)). He adds that this impression is 'impossible to define, and needless to describe any farther'. The point of this is presumably to make it clear that the Humean will is not a distinct faculty or power of the human mind. Hume turns straightaway to 'that long disputed question concerning *liberty and necessity*; which occurs so naturally in treating of the will', but his characterization of the will as a sort of epiphenomenal accompaniment of intentional action directs investigation away from the usual question of the freedom, or lack thereof, of human choices. In Hume's hands, the question concerning liberty and necessity concerns the liberty and necessity of *actions*, rather than of *volitions*. What is at issue is how motives are connected with bodily movements. We see in this, I think, the importance of 'the common course of the world' to Hume's science of the mind; and also the difference between Hume's understanding of the experimental method and Locke's. Where Locke dedicated himself to a minute examination of what introspection told him about the making of choices, and sought to give an accurate picture of choice from the standpoint, as it were, of the chooser, Hume formulates his answer to the question of liberty and necessity from the standpoint of the observer of the human scene. He explicitly rejects the idea that introspection is reliable as a guide to understanding human freedom, and, as we will see, constructs an elaborate means of explaining away whatever 'consciousness' there may be of freedom of the libertarian sort.

The *Treatise* discussion of liberty and necessity sees Hume appear to regard necessity and liberty as incompatible. He argues for necessity and against liberty. He writes that 'According to my definitions, necessity makes an

---

[7] Hume's definition of the will is discussed by Stalley (1986).

essential part of causation; and consequently, liberty, by removing necessity, removes also causes, and is the very same thing with chance' (*Treatise*, p. 261 (II.iii.2))—though this is tempered by an invocation of the distinction 'betwixt the liberty of *spontaneity*, as it is call'd in the schools, and the liberty of *indifference*, betwixt that which is oppos'd to violence, and that which means a negation of necessity and causes' (*Treatise*, p. 262 (II.iii.2)). In the section 'Of Liberty and Necessity' included in *An Enquiry concerning Human Understanding*, however, Hume's approach is different. His concern in the later treatment of the question is not to argue against liberty by arguing for necessity, but rather 'to make it appear, that all men have ever agreed in the doctrines both of necessity and of liberty, according to any reasonable sense, which can be put on these terms; and that the whole controversy has hitherto turned merely upon words'.[8] He declares that his is a 'reconciling project' (*Enquiry*, p. 72). The *Treatise*'s lack of success seems to have prompted Hume to wish to clarify his approach to metaphysical questions. He appears to have worried that his first book was seen to be dogmatically destructive when it was meant to be only agnostic, in the way that all 'experimental' reasoning is agnostic, about metaphysical matters. In a letter he explains that he came to regret 'the positive Air, which prevails in [the *Treatise*], and which may be imputed to the Ardor of Youth'.[9] In accord with the wish expressed by Hume in the 'Advertisement' prefixed to the first *Enquiry*, I shall base my interpretation of Hume's treatment of liberty and necessity upon his second thoughts, rather than upon his first.[10]

Hume's clarification of the implications of his approach to the free will question begins in the *Abstract* of Books I and II of the *Treatise* published in 1740. There Hume highlights 'what our author says concerning *free-will*', and claims that his manner of examining the relation between motives and actions 'puts the whole controversy in a new light'.[11] He claims to have shown that it is possible to affirm the doctrine of necessity without saying

---

[8] Hume (1748, 2000), p. 63. All subsequent references to the first *Enquiry* in this chapter will be made in the main body of the text. For discussion of the significance of the claim that the dispute 'has hitherto turned merely upon words', see Russell (1983); Flew (1984); Russell (1985).

[9] Hume (1932), vol. i, p. 187.

[10] The 'Advertisement' prefixed to the first *Enquiry* by Hume asks that 'the following Pieces ... alone be regarded as containing [the Author's] philosophical sentiments and principles' (*Enquiry*, p. 1). For discussion of the question of whether, despite the Advertisement, Hume interpretation should focus upon the *Treatise* or the *Enquiry*, and for reasons to favour the *Enquiry*, see Buckle (2001), ch. 1 and Millican (2002a).

[11] Hume (1740, 2000), pp. 415, 416.

anything likely to raise objections in even 'the most zealous advocates for free-will'. His reason for making this claim is that he has brought to the question 'a new definition of necessity'. It would seem, then, that in order to come to an understanding of Hume's reconciling project, one must first ensure that one is clear about what is new in his definition of necessity. That is, one must distinguish Hume's definition from that of his predecessors in the necessitarian tradition. I shall begin with an interpretation of Humean necessity considered quite generally, and then turn to his application of his new definition of necessity to human actions. After that I shall address his understanding of liberty, and his claim that necessity as he has defined it is compatible with liberty as understood by its most zealous advocates.[12]

Necessity in the Operations of Matter

It is often said that Hume's approach to the question of liberty and necessity differs only in inessentials from Hobbes's.[13] If this were really so, Hume's talk of bringing to the question a new definition of necessity and thereby putting the whole controversy in a new light would have to be read as, at best, somewhat disingenuous. There are in fact good reasons to think that there must be important differences between Hobbes's understanding of necessity and Hume's. For one thing, as we have seen, Hobbes believes that the doctrine of necessity follows straightforwardly the principle that every event has a cause; while Hume, in the *Treatise*, argues that there is no good reason to believe in that principle—explicitly attacking Hobbes as he does so (see *Treatise*, pp. 56–8 (1.iii.3)). Moreover, Hobbes identifies causal necessity with logical necessity; while Hume argues that there is no contradiction involved in any conceivable alteration of the normal course of nature (see *Enquiry*, p. 31). Hume does, it is true, introduce the doctrine of necessity in a

---

[12] Hume's treatment of liberty and necessity has received less coverage in the secondary literature than other aspects of his philosophy because it has been generally assumed that he diverges only in inessentials from a tradition of compatibilism that, supposedly, stretches from Hobbes and Locke to Ayer and Schlick. For reasons to be suspicious of this assumption, see Russell (1995a), pp. 3–7, and *passim*; and also Botterill (2002).

[13] Thus, e.g., Flew (1961, p. 142): 'In his attempt at reconciliation he had in Hobbes a[n] ... immediate predecessor'; Penelhum (2000, p. 158): 'What he says is anticipated in Chapter xxi of Hobbes's *Leviathan*'; Stroud (1977, p. 153): 'The general strategy of his "reconciling project" is ... found in all essential respects in Hobbes.'

way that suggests that he has put his worries about the fixity of the laws of nature to the back of his mind:

It is universally allowed, that matter, in all its operations, is actuated by a necessary force, and that every natural effect is so precisely determined by the energy of its cause, that no other effect, in such particular circumstances, could possibly have resulted from it. The degree and direction of every motion is, by the laws of nature, prescribed with such exactness, that a living creature may as soon arise from the shock of two bodies, as motion, in any other degree or direction than what is actually produced by it.

(*Enquiry*, p. 63)

But he nowhere endorses what is 'universally allowed'.[14] Rather, he asks where this belief in the actuation of the operations of matter by a necessary force might come from. Taking it as obvious that the belief cannot be derived from *a priori* reasoning, Hume looks to experience, which turns out to be able to explain the belief, but not to justify it. This is of course not surprising. In Section IV of the *Enquiry* he argued that no amount of experience is able to justify the belief that how things have been is a reliable guide to how they will be in the future.[15]

Whence does the idea of necessity arise, when we apply it to the operation of bodies? This is a question to which Hume gave a novel, not to say revolutionary, answer in Section VII of the *Enquiry*. The answer has two principal aspects, one negative, the other positive. Construed negatively, the answer is that the idea of necessity has its source in neither sensation nor reflection on individual instances of causal interaction. Like Locke, Hume holds that our experience of the external world of material bodies is of an inscrutable succession of distinct events. 'When we look about us towards external objects, and consider the operation of causes', he claims, 'we are

---

[14] Here I disagree with, e.g., Garrett (1997), p. 128 and Buckle (2001), p. 216. Most readers of Hume appear to believe that in this passage Hume is stating his own view. I suggest that Hume is better seen as doing no more than presenting an extended *ad hominem* argument to the effect that, if you believe that matter is necessitated in its operations, by parity of reasoning you should also believe that human actions are necessitated.

[15] Hume's treatment of induction is, it seems to me, sufficient to show that he does not subscribe to determinism of any kind, whether Hobbesian or merely nomological. Recent work on Hume on induction (e.g., Garrett (1997), ch. 7, and Owen (2000)) suggests that what Hume means to show is that a 'uniformity principle' (a principle to the effect that the laws of nature are unchanging) plays no role at all in our reasoning from causes to effects—an interpretation which fits nicely with Hume's general agnosticism, as I read him, about things as they are in themselves.

never able, in a single instance, to discover any power or necessary connexion; any quality, which binds the effect to the cause, and renders the one an infallible consequence of the other. We only find, that the one does actually, in fact, follow the other' (*Enquiry*, p. 51). Our experience of the world is not such as to indicate that what happens around us is a matter of chance. There is order in the form of the regular conjunctions of types of event: billiard balls interact with other in a limited and predictable number of ways, heat is a constant attendant of flame. Nevertheless, experience gives us no insight whatsoever into why things happen in these regular and predictable ways. All we perceive is one event following another. Hume takes this view further than Locke, though, in so far as he rejects the notion that the idea of power or necessary connection (Hume takes these to be synonyms) might be derived from introspective awareness of the operations of the mind. 'It may be said', he acknowledges, 'that we are every moment conscious of internal power; while we feel that, by a direct command of our will, we can move the organs of our body, or direct the faculties of our mind' (*Enquiry*, p. 52). In fact, however, all we are conscious of is the fact that motions of the body follow upon the commands of the will; and we have no idea at all as to how it is that volition produces bodily movement. Our experience of ourselves is therefore no different from our experience of the world outside of ourselves: in both cases, experience presents us only with successive events. Even if there is order and regularity to a domain experience, there is lacking insight into what, if anything, is responsible for that order and regularity. Hume knows that some of his contemporaries will say a lack of experience of power and necessity in the operations of material bodies and in the mind provides reason to believe that in every case it is God that makes effect follow cause. Occasionalism is incredible on its own terms, Hume replies; and, anyway, it does not solve the problem, for no explanation is given by the occasionalists of where we obtain our idea of the 'manner or force' by which the supreme mind operates.[16]

It is a cardinal principle with Hume that we cannot have an idea of something without first having had a sensory or inward impression of it. It would appear, then, that, we have no idea of a necessary connection between material bodies, and that therefore talk of the actuation of matter in all its operations by a necessary force is, to use Hume's own words, 'absolutely

---

[16] Hume's relationship with occasionalism is more interesting than Hume himself admits: see, e.g., Wright (1991) and McCracken (1983), ch. 7.

without any meaning' (*Enquiry*, p. 58). This is a conclusion Hume seeks to avoid. We start talking in terms of causal connections, he observes, as soon as we have a certain amount of experience of one particular species of event being constantly conjoined with another. We naturally call the event that comes first a cause, and the event that follows an effect. And what goes along with this way of talking is the supposition of 'some connexion between them; some power in the one, by which it infallibly produces the other, and operates with the greatest certainty and strongest necessity' (*Enquiry*, p. 59). Perhaps, then, the idea of a necessary connection is in some way itself an effect of repeated experience of conjunctions of particular species of events. If so, the idea is obviously not derived from the experiences themselves, since they do not change simply by being repeated, and we have already established that no one of them evidences necessary connection between cause and effect. What repeated experience of conjunctions of particular species of events produces is not, in the first instance at least, an idea, but rather a certain *habit*. When presented with one of a pair of usually conjoined events, our thoughts naturally proceed to the other; and, Hume suggests, this habit, or 'customary transition of the imagination', is the best place to look for the source of the idea of necessary connection between bodies. Certainly, there is nowhere else to look. The positive aspect of Hume's account of the origins of the idea of necessary connection develops out of this suggestion. The thought is that the habitual transition of the mind is accompanied by a particular feeling of compulsion, or, as we may say, of certainty. I *feel* sure that the usual effect will follow a certain event, and this feeling is then somehow—Hume does not properly explain how—projected onto the world. Thus, while the idea of necessity is really an idea of something going on in the mind, we mistake it for an idea of something out in the world, for something that connects events and that *makes* things happen as they do.[17]

Hume expresses no view as to the truth or falsity of what is 'universally allowed' about the operations of matter. His first concern is with the

---

[17] There is a great deal that is mysterious in all of this. In the *Treatise* Hume talks of the mind's 'great propensity to spread itself on external objects, and to conjoin with them any internal impressions, which they occasion, and which always make their appearance at the same time that these objects discover themselves to the senses' (p. 112 (I.iii.14))—but how, exactly, the mind does this is not explained. In particular, Hume says nothing about how a (presumably) contentless feeling of determination is transmuted into a belief about the metaphysical structure of reality. For a discussion of projection in Hume, see Kail (2001).

explanation of the general belief in the existence of 'necessary forces', and with showing that the belief does not have its foundation in insight into the secret workings of material substances. Its origins lie instead in peculiar features of how the mind responds to observed regularities; and this means that what is universally allowed dramatically outstrips its experiential base. The moral Hume draws is that necessity as we can conceive of it is not what it has been thought to be. It amounts only to observed regularity and a concomitant disposition to predict effects given the occurrence of causes. This is the sole kind of necessity of which we have a clear idea. When we talk about necessity in this sense, we know what we are talking about, while when we talk about some other kind, grounded in God's will, or in the hidden essences of substances, or in accidental properties superadded to substances, or in the active powers of Newtonian ether, we are really just juggling with words.[18] This is not to say that one or other of those ways of talking might not be true—just that we have no means of giving determinate meaning to our words and of settling the question. We would do well, then, to give up on the question of the efficacy of causes, and to focus instead upon what accurate observation tells us is followed by what, and to try to sort merely accidental conjunctions from event pairings that can be brought under scientific laws. When we do that the old metaphysical question of liberty and necessity simply disappears, leaving behind a set of purely empirical questions about human behaviour and its predictability.

All Men have ever Agreed in the Doctrine of Necessity

In the exchange between Clarke and Collins there is what looks like a situation of stalemate in the debate about the causation of human actions. Each side is able to accuse the other of begging the question in the way in which it defines the terms central to the dispute. Collins begs the question with his definition of cause: his claim that a 'suitable' cause is by definition a 'necessary', or necessitating, cause is precisely what the libertarian denies. The libertarian (as Collins well knew) holds both that free actions are caused (by the agent, or by his will) and that the agent has what Clarke terms 'a full natural or physical power of acting differently'. For his part, Clarke insists

---

[18] These are all theories mentioned by Hume in the *Letter from a Gentleman to his Friend in Edinburgh* (Hume (1745), pp. 27–9).

that freedom from necessity follows directly from a proper definition of what it is to be an agent. A necessitated agent is a contradiction in terms. 'A. C.' (perhaps Collins, perhaps not) complains, not without justification, that Clarke assumes without argument that his definition of action is the one applicable to the human case. This was the state of the question of liberty and necessity when Hume was developing his philosophical ideas in the 1730s. Hume believed that he had a means, in the form of a 'new definition of necessity', of moving the debate on, or, perhaps better, of ending the debate altogether. In order to see how Hume's new theory of necessity might have the effect that Hume believes it will, it is important to bear in mind what work it needs to do. On the one hand, Hume has to convince the libertarian that his theory of necessity, whatever it ultimately amounts to, does not rule out Clarke's 'full natural or physical power of acting differently' as incoherent or impossible. The necessity, in other words, needs to be somewhat weaker than that defended by Collins, and before him by Hobbes. On the other hand, the necessity must not be so weak as to allow for the re-introduction of the liberty of indifference that the necessitarian regards as antithetical to freedom worth the name. Motives must remain the determinants of action. The kind of necessity able to fulfil these two requirements is, precisely, the *moral* necessity appealed to by both Bramhall and Clarke in their attempts to define a middle way between necessitarianism and the liberty of indifference.

What is not in dispute between necessitarians and libertarians (King and his followers excepted) is the influence of motives upon our choices and actions. The necessitarian, of course, insists upon such influence, and claims that it rules out freedom as the libertarian understands it: that it rules out, in other words, a power of acting differently. But a libertarian such as Bramhall or Clarke also admits the influence of motives. This is perhaps a point that is worth emphasizing, in light of the fact that necessitarians often chose to ignore it in the hope of making the libertarian position appear maximally unattractive. As we saw in Chapter 2, the libertarian literature of the first half of the eighteenth century is replete with advertisements of the difference between the liberty of indifference and liberty as properly understood, and with calls for recognition of the influence of motives. This admission— indeed, insistence—on the part of libertarians of the influence of motives upon free choice and action went along with an admission of what clearly follows from it, that free action is *predictable* action. Contrary to what the opponents of libertarianism claim, there is no necessary connection between libertarian freedom, properly defined, and the randomness and unpredictability of purely arbitrary choice. God, though free, is predictable, because his choices are guided by comprehensible standards of rationality and goodness; and, by the same token, human agents are predictable in so far as their actions are guided by the faculty of judgment. Clarke says that we can be sure that God *must* 'act with altogether as much Certainty and *unalterable Steddiness*; as even the Necessity of Fate can be supposed to do'.[19] But God is of course free in his choices nevertheless. When it is said of someone that he cannot tell a lie, what is meant is not that he could not tell a lie even if he wanted and decided to. Rather, we mean that we can rely on him not wanting and deciding to.[20] The power to act differently is thus not a power that need ever be exercised in order for an agent to count as free. This aspect of the libertarian position is crucial to Hume's reconciling project. It allows him, as we will shortly see, to claim that with respect to *empirical* matters, matters pertaining to how human beings are observed to behave, there is no disagreement between necessitarians and libertarians. Hume's tactic, in fact, is to take things the libertarian himself regards as characteristic of his position—the conjunction of motives and actions, and the consequent predictability of actions—and to make them the sole premises of his argument for necessity.

Like Collins before him, Hume believes that the libertarian already grants the central necessitarian tenet: that motives are the causes of human actions. But what Collins meant when he called motives the causes of the human actions ensured that in reality Clarke did not and could not allow the necessity for which Collins contended. Collins's Hobbesian conception of causation explicitly rules out as impossible Clarke's 'full natural or physical power of acting differently'. Hume's tactic is simply to refrain from talking in terms of metaphysical impossibilities, and to remain, as it were, on the empirical surface of things. Examination of human behaviour and of our predictive propensities with respect to our fellow human beings shows, according to Hume, that 'all mankind have ever agreed in the doctrine of necessity, and that they have hitherto disputed, merely for not understand-

---

[19] Clarke (1738), vol. ii, p. 573.

[20] Here the notion of 'moral necessity' connects with that of 'moral certainty', defined in the *OED* as 'a degree of probability so great as to admit of no reasonable doubt', such as 'rests on a knowledge of the general tendencies of human nature, or of the character of particular individuals or classes of men; often in looser use, applied to all evidence which is merely probable and not demonstrative' ('Moral', *a*, § 11).

ing each other'. They have hitherto disputed, in other words, because libertarians have misunderstood the doctrine of necessity, and because necessitarians have misunderstood the nature of liberty. Hume's clarification of the meaning of necessitarianism has two stages. He seeks to establish, first, the constant conjunction of motives and voluntary actions; and secondly, that this conjunction is the basis of the inferences—the predictions and explanations—we make concerning human actions. Both stages of the argument are purely 'experimental' in character. The experiments that Hume rests his case upon are drawn from observation of the behaviour of men in society. When Collins gave an empirical argument for necessity, he focused upon internal acts of the mind, and, in particular, on the relation between the judgment and the will. Locke looks inside himself, and at choice and the suspension of choice, for data to base his account of freedom upon. And for Hobbes, too, the case for necessitarianism rests on proof of the universal determination of *choice* by *judgment*. But Hume looks *outside* of himself, and grounds his necessitarianism on what is acknowledged to be true of the actions of men 'in all nations and ages'. This is particularly obvious in the *Enquiry* version of the argument, where Hume places special emphasis upon *history* as a valuable source of support for the necessitarian position. History's 'chief use', Hume goes so far as to say, 'is only to discover the constant and universal principles of human nature, by showing men in all varieties of circumstances and situations, and furnishing us with materials, from which we may form our observations, and become acquainted with the regular springs of human action and behaviour' (*Enquiry*, p. 64).

In the *Treatise* Hume sets out to 'prove from experience, that our actions have a constant union with our motives, tempers, and circumstances' (*Treatise*, p. 258 (ii.iii.1)). In the *Enquiry* he describes the first stage of his argument slightly differently. Just before he moves on to the second stage, he claims to have shown 'not only that the conjunction between motives and voluntary actions is as regular and uniform, as that between the cause and effect as any part of nature; but also that this regular conjunction has been universally acknowledged among mankind, and has never been the subject of dispute, either in philosophy or common life' (*Enquiry*, p. 67). In the later account Hume is more careful to make it clear that he is arguing only that there is no distinction to be drawn between the regularity of events in nature and the regularity of events in the social and political spheres. This in turn makes it clear that he is absolved from having to establish that there are, as a matter of fact, exceptionless laws governing human behaviour. He points out that such things as character, prejudice, and opinion prevent it from being true that all men will act in exactly the same way when placed in the same circumstances. But this is not an obstacle in the way of proving a constant union of action and motive, since exact uniformity in every respect is not to be found in the natural realm either. In the philosophy of nature, there are 'irregular' events in abundance; but the scientist does not, when faced with such events, conclude that in such cases causation has ceased to operate, that the laws of nature have been suspended. On the contrary, he assumes that here there are previously unsuspected causes at work, and then begins work on trying to discover what they may be. The physician who finds that a medicine does not have its usual effect on the symptoms of an illness knows, as Hume puts it, 'that a human body is a mighty complicated machine: That many secret powers lurk in it, which are altogether beyond our comprehension: That to us it must often appear very uncertain in its operations: And that therefore the irregular events, which outwardly discover themselves, can be no proof, that the laws of nature are not observed with the greatest regularity in its internal operations and government' (*Enquiry*, p. 67). And the same goes for human actions. The properly philosophical response to an unexpected or uncharacteristic action is to refine one's understanding of human nature, not to assume that no laws at all govern such cases. The libertarian therefore has the same reason to think that human actions are necessitated as he does to believe in the necessitation of events in nature.

The constant conjunction of motives and actions is not, though, something that is maintained only by philosophers (or social scientists) who are able to respond appropriately to 'irregular events'. Hume also describes it as a matter of 'common life'. What he means is that it is something we assume in our everyday dealings with other people. This, again, is a claim more prominent in the *Enquiry* than in the *Treatise*. Hume chooses it to emphasize it, presumably, in order to stress that the necessity he is arguing for is something that no one should be afraid of. Necessitarianism as he is presenting it is not a revisionary doctrine at odds with common sense. It is, rather, already a feature, and a central feature at that, of the world of conversation and business. We declare our belief in the uniformity of human nature when, for example, we find incredible a traveller's tales of a people 'entirely divested of avarice, ambition, or revenge; who knew no pleasure but friendship, generosity, and public spirit' (*Enquiry*, p. 64); and, more generally, when we use our experience of the world as a means of establishing what the real meaning of a someone's actions or words is. We all assume that the older and more experienced a person is, the wiser, less gullible, and more prudent he is likely to be; and that assumption would be completely baseless were there no uniformity in human actions, and were every episode in common life 'irregular and anomalous'. As we have seen, Hume does not try to push this claim of belief in uniformity and regularity too far. As a matter of course we acknowledge that a multiplicity of factors comes into play in the determination of behaviour in any one particular case. Manners and conduct are known to be shaped in great part by 'the great force of custom and education', by the differences between the sexes, and by the age of the individual concerned.[21] But these things, it is nevertheless generally believed, determine behaviour in an orderly way. '[F]rom observing the variety of conduct in different men', Hume says, 'we are enabled to form a greater variety of maxims, which still suppose a degree of uniformity and regularity' (*Enquiry*, p. 65). That is, we form maxims about ways in which education, sex, and age affect people's character and actions. 'Even the characters, which are peculiar to each individual', he says, 'have a uniformity in their influence; otherwise our acquaintance with the persons, and our observation of their conduct, could never teach us their dispositions, or serve to direct our behaviour with regard to them' (*Enquiry*, p. 66).

The second stage of Hume's necessitarian argument is the proof that 'that this experienced uniformity in human actions is a source, whereby we draw *inferences* concerning them' (*Enquiry*, p. 68). He seeks to show that it is essential to *both* ordinary everyday life *and* most of 'the speculative parts of learning' that past experience of people's behaviour is a reasonable basis for predictions as to what they will do in the future. This is so obvious, Hume thinks, and follows so closely from what has just been established, that a case hardly needs to be made. The 'poorest artificer', the manufacturer, the historian, the politician, the moral scientist, the critic: each uses his experience of the uniformity of human nature as a means of directing his labours. Once more, Hume is principally concerned to draw attention to the fact that there is no difference between assumptions we make concerning the uniformity of the

---

[21] A striking omission here is the influence of climate. Montesquieu had famously argued for the importance of climatic differences to the explanation of differences in the laws governing human societies; Hume rejects this mode of explanation in his essay 'Of National Characters', arguing that 'If we run over the globe, or revolve the annals of history, we shall discover every where signs of a sympathy or contagion of manners, none of the influence of air or climate' (Hume (1987), p. 204).

material realm, on the one hand, and the social realm, on the other. '[W]hen we consider how aptly *natural* and *moral* evidence link together, and form only one chain of argument', he writes, 'we shall make no scruple to allow, that they are of the same nature, and derived from the same principles' (*Enquiry*, p. 69). The prisoner without money and influence can be just as sure that his gaolers will not release him before the date of his execution as that the bars and locks on his cell will continue to keep him confined. Here, again, it does not matter whether or not there are in fact psychological, social, or economic laws which justify the prisoner in this belief. The point is that, as Hume puts it, 'the mind feels no difference' between cases where it runs along trains of ideas concerning the guards and cases where it runs along trains of ideas concerning his physical situation: 'The same experienced union has the same effect on the mind, whether the united objects be motives, volitions, and actions; or figure and motion' (*Enquiry*, p. 69). To continue with the case of the prisoner: it is *possible* that the guards might relent and free him out of pure capriciousness; but it is *possible* also 'that a sudden earthquake might arise' and shake and tumble the prison around his ears. In general, we are no less confident that people will continue to behave as they have always done in the past as we are that the laws of nature will remain the same in the future.

This concludes Hume's argument for necessity—or, rather, Hume's argument for the proposition 'that all mankind have ever agreed in the doctrine of necessity'. In this argument Hume makes no claim that the mainstream libertarian of his day was concerned to deny. The libertarian who continues to balk at the doctrine of necessity really is just quibbling about a word. Far from taking up necessity as Hobbes understood it, Hume has eviscerated necessitarianism of its metaphysics, and has redefined it as something the libertarian has no reason to recoil from. Hume's own way of summarizing his argument is worth quoting in full:

Necessity may be defined in two ways, conformably to the two definitions of *cause*, of which it makes an essential part. It consists either in the *constant conjunction of like objects*, or in the *inference of the understanding from one object to another*. Now necessity, in both of these senses, (which, indeed, are at bottom, the same) has universally, though tacitly, in the schools, in the pulpit, and in common life, been allowed to belong to the will of man; and no one has ever pretended to deny, that we can draw inferences concerning human actions, and that those inferences are founded on the experienced union of like actions, with like motives, inclinations, and circumstances. The only particular, in which any one can differ, is, that either, perhaps, he will refuse to give the name of *necessity* to this property of human actions: But as long as the meaning is understood, I hope the name can do no harm: Or that he will maintain it possible to discover something farther in the operations of matter. But this, it must be acknowledged, can be of no consequence to morality or religion, whatever it may be to natural philosophy or metaphysics. We may here be mistaken in asserting, that there is no idea of any other necessity in the actions of body: But surely we ascribe nothing to the actions of the mind, but what every one does, and must readily allow of. We change no circumstance in the received orthodox system with regard to the will, but only in that with regard to material objects and causes. Nothing therefore can be more innocent, at least, than this doctrine.

(*Enquiry*, pp. 73–4; cp. *Treatise*, p. 263 (ii.iii.2))

I think Hume can be taken at his word here. Where Hobbes and Collins rest their case for the compatibility of liberty and necessity upon a revised definition of freedom—freedom of action, as opposed to freedom of will— Hume's reconciling project begins with a radical redefinition of necessity.[22]

All Men have ever Agreed in the Doctrine of Liberty

Let us turn with Hume to the second part of his reconciling project: to the claim that, in addition to being of one mind about necessity, 'all mankind have ever agreed in the doctrine of liberty'. Hume asks, 'what is meant by *liberty*, when applied to voluntary actions?':

We surely cannot mean, that actions have so little connexion with motives, inclinations, and circumstances, that one does not follow with a certain degree of uniformity from the other, and that one affords no inferences by which we can conclude the existence of the other. For these are plain and acknowledged matters of fact. By *liberty*, then, we can only mean *a power of acting or not acting, according to the determinations of the will*; that is, if we choose to remain at rest we may; if we chose to move, we may also. Now this hypothetical liberty is universally allowed to belong to every one, who is not a prisoner and in chains. Here then is no subject of dispute.

(*Enquiry*, p. 72)

Hume is right, of course, that no one denies the connection of actions with motives, inclinations, and circumstances; and that one part of freedom is freedom of action. But, as he knew, the libertarian believes there to be more

---

[22] Thus I think that Hume moves further away from Collins than is allowed in Russell (1995b). When it comes to questions of metaphysics—the existence of God, the ontology of mind, liberty and necessity—Collins is a dogmatist where Hume is a sceptic.

to freedom than this. The libertarian regards freedom of will as an essential component of freedom. It matters to him that, with everything held constant, an agent be able to *choose* either to move or remain at rest. This is what Clarke means by a 'full natural or physical power of acting differently'. Clarke writes in the *Demonstration* that the 'Power of *Agency* or *Free Choice* . . . is not at all *prevented* by *Chains* or *Prison*'.[23] This suggests that freedom of choice in fact matters *more* than freedom of action: that an agent can remain free in the ways that matter even if he has no freedom of movement. How, then, can Hume claim that there is here no subject of dispute?

Hume's first answer to such a question follows from the demand that a definition of liberty be 'consistent with plain matter of fact'. There is no *experience* of an ability to act contrary to the influence of motives, inclinations, and circumstances. Hume believes that this is conceded by the libertarian who allows that particular kinds of actions reliably follow particular kinds of motives (given particular kinds of inclinations, and particular kinds of circumstances). He therefore moves directly onto a second reason to deny that there is real dispute about the definition of freedom: freedom, however defined, must be 'consistent with itself'. '[I]t is pretended', Hume writes, 'that some causes are necessary, some not necessary' (*Enquiry*, p. 72). However, 'Let any one *define* a cause, without comprehending, as part of the definition, a *necessary connexion* with its effect; and let him show distinctly the origin of the idea, expressed by the definition; and I shall readily give up the whole controversy.' There is no way for the libertarian to portray free actions as *caused* without at the same time conceding the truth of the doctrine of necessity. The notion of an action caused but not necessitated is incoherent. The only notion of cause we have has as part of its definition a necessary connection of cause with effect. So where there is no necessary connection, there is no causation; and where there is no causation, there is chance—'which is universally allowed to have no existence' (*Enquiry*, p. 73). Although this is presented as a conceptual point, it is rooted in Hume's account of the origins of the idea of cause. A Humean definition proceeds by means of a tracing back of an idea to its source in an impression. It is unintelligible *for us*—for 'all mankind'—that there might be a cause that is not 'necessary', or necessitating, because our possession of the idea of cause depends on experience of the regular conjunction of types of events, and the consequent impression of felt determination in the mind, from which the idea of

---

[23] Clarke (1738), vol. ii, p. 566.

necessary connection derives. Hume has no means of showing a non-necessitating cause to be impossible in and of itself. It remains possible, for example, that other beings, who do not need impressions to have ideas, or who have some form of intuitive insight into how causes produce their effects, might have such a notion. Hume is asking the libertarian to focus upon where we get our idea of cause from, and to tell him where to find a means of giving sense to the notion of a non-necessitating cause. If it transpires that there is no empirical source for such a notion, this should not worry the libertarian unduly, because the necessity involved in necessitating causes is, so far as we know, only a projection.[24]

According to the libertarian, however, there is more to the experience of freedom than observation of the constant conjunction of motives and actions. In addition there is what introspective awareness tells us about our powers. There is the sense we have, in other words, of being in control of our choices, and of being able to act and choose otherwise than we do. In the previous chapter we saw that 'consciousness' of this kind of power is an important part of the libertarian arguments of King and Clarke; and that Collins treats the argument from introspective awareness as a crucial element of the position he opposes.[25] Collins claims that it is only the 'vulgar', 'bred up to believe *Liberty* or *Freedom*', who 'think themselves secure of success, constantly appealing to *Experience* for a proof of their freedom, and being persuaded that they feel themselves free on a thousand occasions', while, in fact, '[t]hey either attend not to, or see not, the causes of their actions, especially in matters of little moment, and thence conclude, they are free, or not moved by causes, to do what they do'.[26] In this Collins follows Hobbes. 'A woodden Top that is lashed by the Boyes', Hobbes says in his debate with Bramhall,

[24] I should acknowledge that in this paragraph I make a contentious assumption about Hume's empiricism. On another reading of Hume, the fact that we have no idea of (for example) a non-necessitating cause justifies the claim that such an idea is intrinsically incoherent, and also justifies the further claim that such a cause is impossible. I do not think that this reading is plausible, but cannot argue the point here.

[25] Another example: George Cheyne writes that 'Some men indeed deny that we have any free-will at all; but these need only examin their own consciences to be convinc'd of their mistake' (Cheyne (1715), p. 138). 'Conscience' and 'consciousness' sometimes mean the same thing in this period. The *OED* lists as one obsolete meaning of 'conscience' 'Inward knowledge or consciousness; internal conviction', and quotes Swift: 'The word Conscience properly signifies, that knowledge which a man hath within himself of his own thoughts and actions' (i.1.a).

[26] Collins (1717), pp. 12–13.

and runs about sometimes to one Wall, sometimes to another, sometimes spinning, sometimes hitting men on the shins, if it were sensible of its own motion, would think it proceeded from its own Will, unless it felt what lasht it. And is a man any wiser, when he runs to one place for a Benefice, to another for a Bargain, and troubles the world with writing errors and requiring answers, because he thinks he doth it without other causes than his own Will, and seeth not what are the lashings that cause his Will?[27]

For Collins, as for Hobbes, the case for necessitarianism rests securely on *a priori* argumentation, and so there is no danger that experience might threaten it. Nor is there any risk that questions may appear to be being begged when 'consciousness' is given less importance than other relevant modes of experience. Hume's position as a necessitarian is novel because his proof of necessity is purely empirical. He does risk begging the question when he privileges the standpoint of the observer over the first-person standpoint of the agent himself. Two strategies, therefore, are open to him. He can deny that consciousness does speak for liberty; or he can admit that there is a sense of liberty to the first-person 'agentic' perspective, and then attempt to explain it away. He takes up the latter option.[28]

In the *Treatise* the supposed experience of freedom of choice is given prominence as one of three 'reasons for the prevalence of the doctrine of liberty, however absurd it may be in one sense, and unintelligible in another' (*Treatise*, p. 262 (ii.iii.2)). In the *Enquiry*, by contrast, Hume's treatment of it is

---

[27] Hobbes (1656), p. 41. Spinoza adopts the same strategy. As his first example of how 'error consists in privation', he adduces the way in which men are deceived in thinking themselves free: 'a belief that consists only in this, that they are conscious of their actions and ignorant of the causes by which they are determined' (*Ethics*, Part ii, Scholium to Proposition 35: Spinoza (1982), p. 86). In a letter, Spinoza asks the physician G. H. Schuller to conceive a moving stone which 'thinks, and knows that it is endeavouring, as far as in it lies, to continue in motion.' Such a stone, Spinoza continues, 'since it is conscious only of its endeavour and is not at all indifferent, will think it is completely free, and that it continues in motion for no other reason than it so wishes. This, then, is that human freedom which all men boast of possessing, and which consists solely in this, that men are conscious of their desire and unaware of the causes by which they are determined (Letter 58: Spinoza (1982), p. 250). Spinoza may be criticizing Descartes here: 'That there is freedom in our will, and that we have power in many cases to give or withhold our assent at will', Descartes says, 'is so evident that it must be counted among the first and most common notions that are innate in us' (*The Principles of Philosophy*, Part i, Paragraph 39: Descartes (1984–5), vol. i, pp. 205–6).

[28] Dugald Stewart claims that Hartley was the first necessitarian to deny that there is consciousness of freedom: see Dugald Stewart (1828), vol. ii, p. 510.

relegated to a concluding footnote to his case for the doctrine of necessity (at *Enquiry*, pp. 71–2). It is not obvious why Hume made this particular change to his way of treating the question of liberty and necessity. The *Enquiry's* arrangement does, however, allow Hume to collect all considerations relevant to the clarification of the *ideas* of liberty and necessity in Part i, and to devote Part ii solely to the interests of morality and religion. His way of explaining away the 'false sensation or seeming experience which we have, or may have, of liberty or indifference' is essentially the same in the two discussions. The 'sensation or seeming experience' is 'false' in the sense that it is deceptive: it fools us into thinking that we are not determined in our actions by our motives. Just as '[t]he necessity of any action, whether of matter or of the mind, is not properly a quality in the agent, but in any thinking or intelligent being, who may consider the action', so also the appearance of an *absence* of necessity is a matter of a certain feeling or sensation in the mind. The feeling in question is 'a certain looseness' felt when we pass from an idea of a cause to an idea of its effect in circumstances where we are not absolutely sure what the effect will be. When we act, Hume says, we are 'sensible of something like' this 'looseness or indifference', even though, as the libertarian concedes, we rarely feel it when we observe human actions as a spectator. And the resemblance between the two feelings prompts us to believe that choice and action is in fact determined by nothing, just as the 'certain looseness' felt when we are unsure what effect will follow a cause prompts the naive person to believe that the effect, when it comes, is a matter of contingency.

We form the belief that we could have acted in a way different from how we actually chose to act, Hume suggests, when we are told by the necessitarian that this is not in fact possible: then we feel that the will 'moves easily every way, and produces an image of itself . . . even on that side, on which it did not settle'. Moreover, we think we can prove that we were not subject to necessity in what we did, when we show that in similar circumstances we can do something different to what we did before. But, Hume says, in so doing we only show that the desire of showing our liberty can act as a motive; we do not show that our actions have no motives at all. '[H]owever we may imagine we feel a liberty within ourselves', Hume says; 'a spectator can commonly infer our actions from our motives and character; and even where he cannot, he concludes in general, that he might, were he perfectly acquainted with every circumstance of our situation and temper, and the most secret springs of our complexion and disposition.' And this is 'the very essence of necessity', according to Hume's definition of the term.[29] In Part II of *Enquiry* version 'Of Liberty and Necessity', he goes on to consider standard objections to the doctrine of necessity from morality and religion. He argues that the moral assessment of actions is not only compatible with, but also depends upon, the doctrine of necessity; and that while there are problems reconciling necessity with theism, these problems are testimony to the weakness of human reason, rather than signs of the falsity of necessitarianism.[30]

Interpretations of Hume's Reconciling Project

On one reading of Hume, he is able to promise a reconciliation of the doctrines of liberty and necessity because he has argued that there is nothing more to necessary connection than the constant conjunction of types of events. Because there is nothing to a cause that enables it to make its effect come about, because all there is to a causal relation is one kind of thing following another kind of thing, the libertarian's worries about regarding motives as causes of volitions and actions are shown to be groundless. Hume is taken to have shown, or to have tried to show, something about the world as it is in itself—that there are just regularities 'all the way down'. And this is supposed to be a discovery that should obviate the libertarian's reservations about the claim that a free action can be 'literally' or 'physically' caused by its motive. There are at least three problems with this as an interpretation of Hume's reconciling project. The first is that it would seem to be important to

---

[29] In the *Treatise*, but not in the first *Enquiry*, Hume considers first what might be termed the *retrospective* aspect of the argument from consciousness:

> After we have perform'd any action; tho' we confess we were influenc'd by particular views and motives; 'tis difficult for us to perswade ourselves we were govern'd by necessity, and that 'twas utterly impossible for us to have acted otherwise; the idea of necessity seeming to imply something of force, and violence, and constraint, of which we are not sensible.
>
> (p. 262 (II.iii.2))

The problem here is the obscurity of the ordinary idea of necessitation. Hume's solution is to suggest that, once it is recognized that necessity is grounded only in regularity of connection of motive and action, along with consequent predictability, there will be no reason to suppose an absence of necessity where there is an absence of an appearance of violence and constraint.

[30] The best account of Hume on moral responsibility is Russell (1995a). See also Botterill (2002). I make some suggestions about the context of Hume's consideration of the theological dimension of the free will problem in Harris (2005). For an early text of Hume's on the problem of evil, Stewart (1990). The (pretended?) fideism of Hume's theodicy is very reminiscent of Bayle, and also of Mandeville's *Free Thoughts on Religion*.

freedom as we ordinarily conceive of it that it be more than a mere coincidence that certain actions follow certain motives. It would seem to be significant, morally speaking (but not just morally speaking), that we act in a certain way *because* of a certain sentiment or belief, and it is not clear how this way of reading Hume captures that kind of 'because'.[31] The second problem is that it is not obvious how a claim about the source of our ideas can function as a justification for a claim about the world as it is in itself. Why should it follow from the fact that we cannot conceive of real and productive connections between causes and effects that no such connections exist? The general tenor of Hume's philosophy is sceptical, in the sense of manifesting an acute awareness of the limits of our understanding of both ourselves and the world around us; and it sits ill with such a philosophical posture to claim that there is nothing at all connecting any and every cause with any and every effect. This is a metaphysical claim, a claim about causes as such, and so not a claim that could be given a basis in experimental philosophizing.[32] The third problem facing this reading is that in Hume's texts there are many passages where Hume refers to secret connections, hidden powers, concealed forces, and the like, passages which are hard to square with a Hume intent on voiding the universe of causal relations as traditionally conceived.[33]

It seems to other readers of Hume to be so much common sense that there has to be more to the universe than brute regularity—that there cannot be regularity 'all the way down'. These people take advantage of the language of secret connections and so forth, and claim that Hume shares their understanding of common sense. Far from emptying the universe of causal powers, they argue, Hume positively believes in the existence of powers, powers which we cannot conceive of, but which we may suppose to exist nonetheless.[34] I do not think that this is plausible. Hume's scepticism is thorough-going enough, I would argue, to issue in a complete suspension

---

[31] See Russell (1995a), pp. 53–5.

[32] This is a point made by all proponents of the 'sceptical realist' interpretation of Hume: see, e.g., Wright (1983), ch. 4; Craig (1987), ch. 2, and Strawson (1989); and also the papers by these authors collected in Read and Richman (2000).

[33] This is another point frequently made by members of the 'sceptical realist' school of Hume interpretation. For a discussion of the significance of these passages, see, e.g., Millican (2002b), pp. 142–5.

[34] See, e.g., Wright (2000), p. 96 ('Hume clearly continued to endorse the speculation that there are active, motion-producing powers in nature itself'); and Strawson (2000), p. 42 ('He takes it for granted that there must be something about the world in virtue of which it is regular'). For a case for the importance of the supposition/conception distinction, see, e.g., Wright (2000), pp. 89–90.

of judgment as regards whether there is more to the universe, causally speaking, than we can conceive of. Despite talk of secret connections, Hume's considered position with respect to the internal operations of matter is one of studied agnosticism. There is therefore no justification for recoiling all the way from the view that Hume believes there is no such thing as a necessary connection anywhere in nature to an interpretation according to which Hume definitely believes that there is more to the material world than we can know. Hume leaves it a completely open question whether there are secret *connections* between things that appear to be merely *conjoined*.[35] It is important that this be recognized because what Hume wants to establish with regard to the question of liberty and necessity is that the operations of mind are necessary in just the same sense as are the operations of matter. If, then, he presents the material world as plainly governed by unalterable necessity, if he commits himself to a 'deterministic' conception of nature, then this is going to have implications for his theory of freedom. It would mean, for one thing, that there was nothing new in his definition of necessity after all. Hume would become a necessitarian of the same kind as Hobbes and Collins, and, despite what he says in the *Abstract* to the *Treatise*, would have little to add to their case for the compatibility of liberty and necessity.[36]

The care with which Hume tries to avoid committing himself to meta-physical (and theological) positions that the libertarian rejected was as little appreciated in his own day as it has been since. The very notion of a defence of necessity was indelibly associated in most eighteenth-century minds with Hobbism, Spinozism, fatalism, immorality, and atheism. Hume's first readers were unable, or unwilling, to recognize what was new in his version of the necessitarian scheme. In one of the very earliest published responses to the *Treatise*, an anonymous contributor to *Commonsense: or, The Englishman's Journal* seeks to prevent Hume's necessitarian argument 'from having any *mischievous* effect upon the opinions or morals of mankind'.[37] Having quoted the passage from *Treatise* II.iii.1 in which Hume presents his new definition of necessity, the author of the letter declares that he 'shall take no notice of this *novel* sort of diction, because most *metaphysicians*, to the great prejudice of science, affect

---

[35] Thus I agree with Winkler (1991) and Blackburn (1990)—and also with Bennett (2001), vol. ii, pp. 279–81.

[36] Millican (2002a), p. 59, draws attention to the lack of interest shown by proponents of the 'sceptical realist' reading of Hume in the consequences of their view for Hume's treatment of liberty and necessity.

[37] *Commonsense*, 5 July, 1740: 1–2, p. 1.

to think, and to express their thoughts, in a method *peculiar* to themselves'.[38] The Irish bishop Robert Clayton writes that if Hume is right in believing that liberty amounts only to an absence of constraint, 'then indeed, according to the doctrine of some of our modern French philosophers, man is a machine',[39] and Joseph Highmore claims that Hume 'maintains absolute uncontroulable necessity, in the moral and the natural world'.[40] John Leland, in the second edition of his *View of the Principal Deistic Writers*, accuses Hume of using his doctrine of cause and effect 'for overthrowing the liberty of human actions': the doctrine is employed 'to confound all difference between physical and moral causes', so as to make out that 'the latter have the same kind of causality as the former'.[41] The difference between Hume's necessitarianism, on the one hand, and that of Hobbes, Spinoza, and Collins was thus almost universally ignored. There was no recognition of the pains taken by Hume, in all of his philosophy, to draw a distinction between, on the one hand, what we have clear ideas of, and, on the other, the nature of things as they are in themselves. Hume was seen for the rest of the eighteenth century as being devoted to the overthrow of common sense—and of morality and religion as well.[42]

[38] Ibid., p. 1.

[39] Clayton (1753), p. 6.

[40] Highmore (1766), vol. ii, p. 40.

[41] Leland (1754–60), vol. ii, pp. 21, 8.

[42] I should like to emphasize that it is not my view that Hume *succeeded* in showing that there is nothing to necessitarianism, properly understood, that is threatening to the commitments of the libertarian. Contemporary libertarians were not unreasonable in their suspicions of Hume's treatment of their position. If it is *possible* that there is more to the causal relation than we know about, then it is possible that there is no freedom such as the libertarian understands it; and so Humean agnosticism is bound to be unsatisfying from the libertarian point of view. Moreover, in his undermining of the experiential basis of the libertarian conception of freedom, Hume is doing more damage to the libertarian cause than he is willing to admit, particularly in a philosophical climate which valued experiential evidence above all else. My concern here has been with how Hume presents his treatment of the question of liberty and necessity, and with why he might have thought—or, perhaps, why he merely pretended he thought—that his new definition of necessity 'puts the whole controversy in a new light'.

4

Kames's Hypothesis

Few productions of late years have occasioned more speculations and
controversy than these Essays.

Objections against the Essays on Morality and Natural Religion Examined

In 1751 the Scottish jurist Henry Home published *Essays concerning the Principles
of Morality and Natural Religion.*[1] A year later, Home became a judge of the Court
of Session, Scotland's highest civil court, and took up the title Lord Kames.
His ambitions may explain why the *Essays* were published anonymously.
Kames, as Home is always called, writes in his book's Advertisement that
the essays 'are not thrown together without connection'. Part I comprises
three essays. The first is 'designed to illustrate the nature of man, as a social
being'; the second and longest essay 'considers [man] as a subject of morality.
And as morality supposes freedom of action, this introduces the third essay,
which is a disquisition on liberty and necessity.' The second part of the book
is in essence a reply to the sceptical account of human nature proposed by
Kames's friend and sometime *protegé* David Hume. Here, the Advertisement
continues, '[a] plan is prosecuted, in support of the authority of our senses,
internal and external; where it is occasionally shown, that our reasonings in
some of the most important subjects, rest ultimately upon sense and
feeling'.[2] A reviewer of the *Essays* in the July 1751 edition of *The Monthly Review*

---

[1] For Kames's life, see Lehmann (1971) and Ross (1972). For general accounts of the *Essays*, see
McGuinness (1970), ch. 2; Lehmann (1971), ch. XI; Ross (1972), ch. 6. On topics related to the
concerns of this book, see also Helo (2001).

[2] Hume said of Kames's *Essays* that '[t]hey are well wrote; and are an unusual instance of an
obliging method of answering a Book' (letter to Michael Ramsay, 22 June 1751: Hume (1932),
vol. i, p. 160). 'Philosophers must judge of the question', Hume continues; 'but the Clergy have
already decided, & say he is as bad as me. Nay some affirm him to be worse, as much as a
treacherous friend is worse than an open enemy.'

has praise for the fact that their author employs 'the only true method', that of building his moral enquiries 'upon a strict examination of the structure and fabric of the human mind, and the frame and connexion of its various powers and affections', and of 'trying the conclusions he draws from the principles of our frame by their true touch-stone, that of facts and experiments'.[3] As was the custom in the eighteenth century, the reviewer does little more than provide an extended paraphrase, with many quotations, of the book's principal arguments. He notes, however, that the essay 'Of Liberty and Necessity' sets the question 'in a very uncommon point of view': 'In handling this point, our author goes into an unbeaten tract, and lays down an hypothesis, which, for aught we know, is entirely new, but such a one, as we apprehend, will give little satisfaction to any considerate reader.'[4] Kames is a necessitarian; but, unlike Hobbes, Collins, and Hume, he believes that neither agency nor moral responsibility are compatible with the doctrine of necessity. In order to live active and fully virtuous lives, Kames argues, we need to believe something false: we need to believe that there is contingency in the universe, that our actions and choices are not determined by our motives, and that it is always possible for us to act otherwise than we in fact do. And, fortunately for us, we believe these things as a matter of instinct. Each of us is fashioned by God so as naturally to believe that the doctrine of necessity does not apply to him. God, that is to say, is a deceiver. He has to be a deceiver if there is to be cultivated in us a concern for the moral values upon which the possibility of human society depends.

'Perhaps no opinion on the subject of necessity was ever offered to the public which excited more general opposition than this hypothesis of a deceitful sense': so wrote Dugald Stewart.[5] The *Essays* were criticized by different people in different ways. George Anderson, the driving force behind the attempt to expel Kames from the Church, sees Kames as having been seduced by the anti-rationalism characteristic of the writings of Shaftesbury and Hutcheson. Anderson argues that what he calls 'the sensitive philosophy' 'takes morality off the old and solid foundation, to place it upon an internal sensation, to be understood according to everyone's fancy'.[6] Freedom lies in the correct use of reason, according to Anderson; and Clarke, in his explication of the distinction between moral and physical necessity, showed clearly how to combine the influence of motives with the reality of liberty. As will be seen in the next chapter, Jonathan Edwards too charges

---

[3] [Anon] (1751), p. 129.   [4] Ibid., pp. 129, 142.   [5] Stewart (1828), vol. ii, p. 506.
[6] Anderson (1753), p. 12.

Kames with having paid too little attention to the difference between moral and physical necessity. Others complain that, on the contrary, Kames places too much trust in reason, and too little in the evidence of internal sensation. According to an author signing himself 'Phileleutherus', Kames attempts to reach too far into 'superior things' in his argument that the only way of reconciling providence with human accountability is by means of a deceitful sense of liberty.[7] He would have done better to trust in what consciousness and conscience tell us about human freedom, and to have been properly sceptical of any hypothesis that falsifies beliefs that we cannot renounce. Here 'Phileleutherus' and Anderson are in agreement. Both maintain that if we can be deceived in our consciousness of the operations of our own minds, we stand to be deceived in everything. Kames's hypothesis puts the status of consciousness at the centre of eighteenth-century argumentation about the freedom of the human will. Having given an account of the argument of Kames's essay 'Of liberty and necessity', I shall describe in more detail the reaction it met with, and the changes made by Kames in subsequent editions of the *Essays*. The chapter will conclude with a brief consideration of Kames's relation to the philosophy of common sense.

Liberty and Necessity in the First Edition of the *Essays*

Kames's argument for necessity is, like Hume's, an argument from the influence of motives on human choices and actions. His starting point is the fact that '[i]t is admitted by all men, that we act from motives'.[8] Sometimes, he says, it is also admitted that the influence of motives is *plainly* such as to make a certain course of action necessary: 'in the judgment and feeling of all mankind, a motive may, in certain circumstances, carry in it the power of rendering an action necessary' (*Essays*, p. 166). Kames illustrates this as follows:

A criminal walks to the scaffold in the midst of his guards. No man will deny that he is under an absolute necessity in this case. Why? because he knows, that if he refuses to go, they will drag him. I ask, Is this a physical necessity or a moral one? The answer, at first view, is not obvious; for the distinction between these two seems lost. And yet, strictly speaking, it is only a moral necessity: for it is the force of the motive which determines the criminal to walk to the scaffold: to wit, that resistance is vain,

---

[7] [Phileleutherus] (1751), p. 64.

[8] Kames (1751), p. 159. All subsequent references to this edition of the *Essays* will be made in the main body of the text.

because the guards are neither to be forced nor corrupted. The idea of necessity, however, in the minds of the spectators, when they view the criminal in this situation, is not less strong, than if they saw him bound and carried on a sledge.

(*Essays*, pp. 165–6)

There are other times, however, when it is not so obvious that action is necessitated by motives, when our feelings speak in favour of liberty rather than necessity. '[I]n the greater part of human actions', Kames writes, 'there is a real feeling of liberty. When the mind hesitates between two things, examines and compares, and at last comes to a resolution, is there any compulsion or necessity here?' (*Essays*, pp. 166–7). Kames responds to this with the charge that the only alternative to the necessitation of action by motives is action upon which motives have no influence at all. Motiveless action is, he says, both alien to ordinary experience and intrinsically absurd; but allow that motives have some influence, and you must allow that actions are necessary. For resolutions are made, not by a freely choosing agent, but rather, in a real sense, by the motives themselves. Motives are of different kinds, and have different strengths; and 'it is involved in the very idea of the strongest motive, that it must have the strongest effect in determining the mind. This can no more be doubted of, than that, in a balance, the greatest weight must turn the scale' (*Essays*, p. 167). There is a 'real feeling of liberty' only because, as with a pair of scales, there tends to be a certain amount of oscillation before it is determined which is the heavier motive, and because we are not always able to tell, from introspection, what the result of the weighing process will be.

The fact that the mind is constrained in its exertions of power makes it plain that, as was suggested by his description of the situation of the prisoner, Kames does not take there to be a significant difference between 'moral' and 'physical' necessity. What does a libertarian like Clarke gain, he asks, 'by showing, that we have a power of beginning motion, if that power never is, never can be, exerted, unless in consequence of some volition or choice, which is necessarily caused?' (*Essays*, p. 172). As Hobbes and Collins had argued, moral necessity rules out a freedom to do otherwise just as surely as does physical necessity: 'to say that moral necessity, is no necessity at all, because it is not physical necessity,...is no better, than to argue, that physical necessity is no necessity at all, because it is not moral necessity' (*Essays*, p. 173). Nevertheless, and despite this argument to the conclusion that actions are necessitated by motives, Kames does not take the strongest motive to be the *cause*—at least, not the *efficient* cause—of the action it necessitates. In this connection he sides with Clarke against Collins: 'the immediate efficient cause of motion is not the motive, but the will to act'. 'No person ever held', Kames writes, 'that the pleasure of a summer-evening, when a man goes abroad into the fields, is the immediate cause of the motion of his feet' (*Essays*, pp. 171–2). The strongest motive determines the will, which is to say that the will is not in our power; but, still, an exercise of the will is needed if motives are to produce action. In a footnote to his essay 'Of our Idea of Power', Kames adopts the characteristically libertarian view that motives are best conceived of as 'occasions', rather than causes, of action. 'It is the mind which exerts the action', he writes; 'only 'tis so framed, that it cannot exert its powers, otherways than upon the presenting of certain perceptions to it' (*Essays*, p. 288 fn).

Kames's position is thus a curious one. Most necessitarians from Hobbes onwards take motives to be causes. Kames accepts a key element of eighteenth-century libertarianism, Clarke's claim that motives cannot be causes, but still denies that we have freedom as the libertarian understands it. It is clear, however, that despite the fact that he does not take motives to be causes, Kames's necessitarianism is more traditional and straightforward than Hume's. For Hume's claim that there is no difference between moral and physical necessity can be seen as amounting to a reduction of the latter of the former, and does not rule out, as Kames does, the ability to do otherwise that is essential to freedom as the libertarian understands it. Like Hume, Kames takes it to be a matter of ordinary, natural belief that actions are necessitated by motives. There is, he says, a 'natural feeling' 'that motives are so connected with their proper motives, as necessarily to arise from the temper, character, and other circumstances of the agent' (*Essays*, p. 160). But repeated experience of the constant conjunction of certain motives with certain actions is not the source of this feeling. Kames is explicit about this in the essay 'Of our Idea of Power', where he writes that

Such is the human constitution, that we act necessarily, upon the existence of certain perceptions or motives. The prospect of victuals makes a hungry man accelerate his pace. Respect to an antient family moves him to take a wife. An object of distress prompts him to lay out his money, or venture his person. Yet no man dreams a motive to be the *cause* of action; tho', if the doctrine of necessity hold true, here is not only a constant, but a necessary connection.

(*Essays*, p. 288; emphasis added)

That we can observe constant conjunctions without forming the belief in a causal connection shows that constant conjunction is not sufficient to generate the idea of power. What prompts us to believe in necessary connection is not Humean custom or habit, but rather what Kames terms 'an impression of sight'.

This does not mean that we *literally* perceive exercises of causal power, for Kames accepts that all that is ever perceived is mere constant conjunction. He speaks of a 'peculiar manner of perception' by which 'we discover a relation betwixt certain objects, which makes one to be termed the cause, the other the effect' (*Essays*, p. 278). In a move characteristic of common sense philosophy, he then denies that this 'manner of perception' can be explained. 'All that can be done in this case', he says,

> is to request of the reader, to attend to what passes in his mind, when he sees one billiard ball struck against another, or a tree, which the wind is blowing down, or a stone thrown into the air out of one's hand. We are obviously so constituted, as not only to perceive one body acting, and exerting its power; but also to perceive, that the change in the other body is produced by *means* of that action or exertion of power. This change we perceive to be an *effect*; and we perceive a necessary connection betwixt the action and the effect, so as that the one must unavoidably follow the other.
>
> (*Essays*, p. 279)

We perceive the existence of a causal relation immediately. 'The first time a child lifts a bit of bread', Kames writes, 'the perception it has of this action, not only includes a conjunction of the hand with the bread, and that the motion of the latter follows the motion of the former; but it likeways includes that peculiar modification, which is exprest by a power in the hand to lift the bread' (*Essays*, p. 280). The crucial difference between Kames and Hume here is that, according to the former, one does not have to look to the imagination and its associative proclivities in order to explain, for example, why we believe objects to be causally related.

In the first edition of the *Essays on the Principles of Morality and Natural Religion*, Kames joins the libertarians in regarding the doctrine of necessity as subversive of commitment to the cause of virtue. There are two elements to Kames's incompatibilism. He claims first that without what he calls 'a feeling of contingency', 'some feeling of things possible and contingent, things dependent upon himself to cause', an agent would have no reason to exercise his capacity for practical deliberation. 'Then, indeed', Kames says, 'the *ignava ratio*, the inactive doctrine of the Stoicks, would have followed' (*Essays*, pp. 188–9). Believing that he has no capacity to make a difference to the order of things, the agent would adopt the position of the fatalist who, because he thinks that whatever will be, will be, fails to reflect on what alternative courses of action might be available to him, and lets himself be pushed around by his instincts and appetites. But this is not how it is with us. We are more than animals reliant on instincts to persuade us, for example, to plant seeds at one time of year, and then harvest them at another. We reflect on what is to be done, and how best to do it, and therefore act as if the doctrine of necessity were false. Kames does not entertain the idea that the feeling of contingency can be explained away, as Hume explains it away, as a sense of uncertainty as to what will happen next. He understands it as a positive sense of things being up to the agent to bring to actuality, rather than as a merely negative sense of future events being underdetermined by the present. We have been framed with this feeling of contingency in order that we make proper use of the faculty of reason: 'reason and thought could not have been exercised in the way they are, that is, man could not have been man, had he not been furnished with a feeling of contingency' (*Essays*, p. 190).

The feeling of contingency applies to events. The second element of Kames's incompatibilist argument is a 'feeling of liberty' applied to agents. As *spectators* of the actions of others, our sense of the influence of motives tends to convince us that actions are subject to necessity. 'Here we have a very weak feeling if any at all,' he says, 'of liberty as distinguished from necessity.' As *agents*, our feelings are different. Normally, 'a man has a feeling of liberty, or of a power of acting otherways than he is doing'. When we reflect on past actions, in particular, the feeling of liberty is unmistakable and undeniable. Kames writes that 'it is principally in reflecting and passing judgment upon a past action, that the feeling of liberty is sensible and strong' (*Essays*, pp. 193–4). Kames's principal datum in this connection is what he calls 'the pain, the *cruciatus* of remorse'. When we reflect on something we know we should not have done, we are very often all too painfully aware that it was perfectly possible for us to have done something else instead, no matter how strong was the pressure of motives upon us. For there is, Kames says, more to remorse than a simple dislike for what was done. The action will strike us as not only hateful and regrettable, but as *wrong*, which is to say, as a violation of rules which we have it in our power either to obey or to disobey. It is impossible, according to Kames, to square the idea that an action is morally wrong—or right—with the idea that that action was necessitated.

'The operations of moral conscience plainly proceed upon the supposition', Kames writes, 'that there is such a power in man of directing his actions, as rendered it possible for the person accused, to have acted a better part' (*Essays*, pp. 194–5). The libertarian claim that necessity destroys accountability has, Kames thinks, never been answered. It is, when one reflects upon it, a striking fact that Hume gives no consideration at all to the experience of remorse in his account of what he terms the 'false sensation or seeming experience which we have, or may have, of liberty or indifference, in many of our actions'.[9] The only evidence of repentance that he considers is that which is testified to by being 'attended with a reformation of life and manners'.[10] This omission helps to make sense of the charge made by all the philosophers of common sense that Hume is insufficiently attentive to the deliverances of 'consciousness'. At the very least, it makes it apparent that different 'experimental' accounts of human action place emphasis upon different aspects of the phenomenology of agency.

Kames argues in this way that it is a matter of 'natural feeling' *both* that the will is free *and* that actions are necessitated by motives. Here there are 'feelings, which on both sides are natural, and yet clash with each other', and so, in this case at least, 'the feelings ... can be no test of truth; because in contradictory propositions, truth cannot ly on both sides' (*Essays*, p. 161). To solve the problem, Kames devises a 'hypothesis' able to 'solve all the phenomena': he suggests that the feeling of liberty is a deceitful sense given us by nature to provide 'the foundation of all the labour, care and industry of mankind'. 'Let us fairly own', he writes, 'that the truth of things is on the side of necessity; but that it was necessary for man to be formed, with such feelings and notions of contingency, as would fit him for the part he has to act' (*Essays*, pp. 184–7). These feelings, or 'natural principles', are 'too deeply rooted, to give way to philosophy'. The deception practised upon us here is, however, wholly benevolent. The fact that we cannot rid ourselves of our false belief in contingency and liberty displays 'the greatest wisdom, and the greatest goodness'. If we acted upon the system of necessity, we would, it is true, still love virtue as 'the best constitution of nature, and the only sure foundation of happiness'. But that would be all. The higher parts of morality—self-approbation, remorse, generous indignation at the wrongdoing, the sense of the justice of the punishment of crimes and of reward of worthy and generous actions—would disappear. There would be love and hatred, sorrow

[9] Hume (1748, 2000), p. 71 fn.   [10] Ibid., p. 75.

and pity; but 'the sense of *duty*, of being *obliged* to certain things we *ought* to perform must be quite extinguished; for we can have no sense of moral *obligation*, without supposing a power in the agent over his actions' (*Essays*, pp. 203–6).[11]

Kames ends the essay 'Of Liberty and Necessity' with replies to three obvious objections to the hypothesis of a deceitful sense of liberty. It might be asked whether deceit is a secure or honourable foundation for virtue. Kames answers that the deceit, since it pertains to the obligatoriness of right actions, 'affects only a certain modification of our ideas of virtue and vice': the foundation of virtue, its conduciveness to human happiness, remains untouched (*Essays*, p. 209). He also claims that the honour of virtue is augmented by the fact that 'a sort of extraordinary machinery is introduced for its sake'. Doesn't Kames's scheme represent God as acting deceitfully by his creatures, 'as if he were unable, to carry on the government of this world, did his creatures conceive things, according to the real truth' (*Essays*, pp. 211–12)? Kames answers that not all our senses are given us for discovering the truth: some of them we have in order, rather, to be happy and virtuous.[12] Furthermore, it is wrong to judge God by our own standards: we should be willing to accept that deceit might be part of a scheme whose perfection we cannot fully comprehend. Deceit, as such, is no more difficult to reconcile with God's goodness than the appearance of moral evil and disorder within the order of creation. And, finally, God's deceitfulness is explained and justified by the facts, first, that 'it is a more perfect state of things, and more worthy of the Deity, to have all events going on with unbroken order, in a fixed train of causes and effects; than to have everything desultory and contingent' (*Essays*, p. 213), and, secondly, that it is for the best that man should act as if he were a free agent. If it was necessary for man to be given this delusive sense of freedom, why was he given the ability to discover the deception? Kames answers that the discovery has no bad consequences and one good consequence, which is to say, an addition to the argument for God's existence and his wisdom and providence; for '[n]othing carries with it

---

[11] In his discussion of justice in *The Theory of Moral Sentiments*, Smith expresses a debt to 'that remarkable distinction between justice and all the other social virtues, which has of late been insisted upon by an author of very great and original genius'—that is, by Kames: see Smith (1759, 1984), p. 81 (ii.ii.i). The anonymous *Some late Opinions concerning the Foundation of Morality* of 1753 also commends Kames for 'stating so clearly the sentiment of duty or moral obligation, and distinguishing it from the sentiment of simple moral approbation': [Anon] (1753), p. 8.

[12] Kames draws an analogy here with our perceptions of secondary qualities such as colour, which are misleading, but useful nevertheless.

more express characters of design' than this 'wonderful' reconciliation of liberty with necessity, than this 'marvelous adjustment' (*Essays*, pp. 216–17). It is in order that we perceive the intricacy of the stratagem, according to Kames, that God lets us see so far into his counsels.

The Reception of the First Edition

There is, I think, every reason to take Kames to be sincere in his claim that he has found new evidence of divine wisdom and benevolence. Insistence on the visibility of providence is everywhere in the *Essays*; it is impossible to imagine that it might all be nothing more than irony. The book concludes with a ringing celebration of the wonders worked by the 'Eternal Mind' and 'Sovereign Architect of All' (*Essays*, pp. 389–94), traditionally supposed to have been contributed by Hugh Blair, at the time second minister of the Canongate in Edinburgh.[13] Nevertheless, Kames's essay on liberty and necessity immediately attracted harsh criticism from those unable to tolerate the idea that duty and obligation might depend upon an illusion. 'Were I to plead the cause of atheism', George Anderson writes in his *Estimate of the Profit and Loss of Religion* (1753), 'I could not think of a stronger argument against the being of God, than "if he is at all, he must be a deceiver".'[14] In the seventeenth century, Anderson notes, 'it was universally agreed, that, without the persuasion *that God cannot deceive us*, we can be sure of nothing'.[15] He continues:

if I can be deceived in any thing that I am conscious of, then I may be deceived in every thing: I do not doubt that I reason, that I affirm, that I deny, and that I doubt, but by being conscious that I do. And they, that pretended to doubt of every thing, never doubted that they did doubt. We feel, and are conscious, that we are free agents; and therefore we actually are in truth and reality such: or consciousness is no foundation of any truth, or certainty; no, not of our own being.[16]

As his hostility to 'sensitive philosophy' shows, Anderson is no common sense philosopher; but here he makes a point that we will return to below when discussing the libertarian arguments of Beattie, Reid, and Stewart. Like the common sense philosophers, Anderson finds uncontainable scepticism in the idea that we might be deceived by consciousness. According to Anderson, human freedom is reconciled with divine prescience and decrees when it is

---

[13] For an account of Kames's natural theology, see Ross (2000).

[14] Anderson (1753), p. 114.   [15] Ibid., p. 122.   [16] Ibid., pp. 122–3.

recognized that God stands outside space and time. Human actions are not literally foreseen or determined before they happen, because from God's point of view there is no before or after: 'to him, nothing is future, nothing past; but all things are always naked and open to his omniscience'.[17]

Anderson closes the *Estimate* with an argument in favour of enforcement of correct religious belief and practice by the magistrate. Shaftesbury was wrong when he said that we have wit enough to save our own souls.[18] In order to hinder atheists from doing harm to others, these 'demented men' should be excommunicated.[19] We are left in no doubt that Anderson has Kames (whom throughout he refers to as 'Sopho') and Hume in mind here. In 1755, Anderson and his faction in the Church of Scotland moved to put theory into practice.[20] Their opening salvo was *An Analysis of the Moral and Religious Sentiments Contained in the Writings of Sopho and David Hume, Esq*, addressed to 'The Members of the ensuing General Assembly of the Church of *Scotland*'. This pamphlet, now thought to be the work of John Bonar of Cockpen, is an attempt to show Kames and Hume to be condemned by their own words. Both, we are asked to believe, have been engaged in a 'public attack . . . on the great principles and duties of natural and revealed religion'.[21] Quotations are assembled to show that Kames holds, among other things, that 'Man is a mere machine, under irresistible necessity in all his actions', that 'Though man be thus necessarily determined in all his actions, yet does he believe himself free, God having implanted into his nature this deceitful feeling of liberty', that 'This deceitful feeling of liberty is the only foundation of virtue', and 'That since man is thus necessarily determined in all his actions, and can have nothing more than a deceitful feeling of liberty, it follows as a necessary consequence, that there can be no sin or moral evil in the world.'[22] Bonar insinuates that these propositions are themselves necessary consequences of Kames's belief, expressed in an essay 'Of the Laws of Motion', that matter is

[17] Anderson (1753), p. 117.

[18] See Shaftesbury's *Letter concerning Enthusiasm*: Shaftesbury (1711, 1999), esp. p. 12, where Shaftesbury says that if a government can at least 'keep us sober and honest', 'it is likely we shall have as much ability in our spiritual as in our temporal affairs, and, if we can but be trusted, we shall have wit enough to save ourselves when no prejudice lies in the way'.

[19] Anderson (1753), pp. 389–90, and pp. 377–92.

[20] For an account of this episode, see Ross (1972), ch. 8. Ramsey of Ochtertyre comments that 'this rash and futile attempt to check the progress of freethinking, convinced the philosophers of Edinburgh that they had no longer anything to dread from the Church courts' (Ramsey (1888), vol. i, p. 317).

[21] [Bonar] (1755), p. 2.

[22] Ibid., pp. 14, 16, 20, 21.

not passive, as was generally believed at this time, but rather active, or, as Bonar puts it on Kames's behalf, 'possessed of a power of self-motion'.[23] This view is supposed by Bonar to amount to the Epicurean principle that the universe needed no creator and has therefore existed for all eternity, and to allow for the possibility that matter is able to take on the capacity for thought. Bonar fails to acknowledge that Kames makes no reference to the arguments of the essay on motion in his discussion of the question of liberty and necessity.[24]

A reply to the *Analysis* was not long in coming. Kames's defenders first published some 'observations' on Bonar's pamphlet, prefaced with the additional observation that the Church of Scotland was itself established 'by means of free inquiry'. 'The proper objects of censure and reproof', Kames's champion writes, 'are not freedom of thought, but licentiousness of action; not erroneous speculation, but crimes pernicious to society.'[25] There follows a description of how Kames's views are misrepresented in the *Analysis*. Kames, we are told, 'meant to inculcate no physical necessity': 'it is not a blind fatal necessity that is argued for, but a necessity derived from the will of the Deity'.[26] Furthermore, 'It will scarcely be denied that the doctrine of this church is the same, and that *Calvin, Beza, Turretin*, have all maintained it in their several systems.'[27] The claim that Kame's necessitarianism is indistinguishable from Calvinist predestination is developed in more detail in *Objections against the Essays on Morality and Natural Religion Examined* (1756).[28] This work argues, with the support of extensive quotation, that the view that liberty of spontaneity is sufficient for moral responsibility is to be

[23] Ibid., p. 6. Kames's essay on motion was published in 1754 along with a variety of other papers read to the Edinburgh Philosophical Society. 'Matter, so far as we can discover, is certainly not endued with thought or voluntary motion', Kames writes; 'and yet, that it is endued with a power of motion in certain circumstances, appears to me an extreme clear point' (Kames (1754), p. 7). John Stewart, professor of natural philosophy at Edinburgh University, replied to Kames's essay, reaffirming the orthodox Newtonian view that 'body itself is absolutely inactive'. Kames had debated this point early on in his career with Andrew Baxter (see Ross (1972), pp. 63–7), and was to return to it again in his correspondence with Reid (see Ross (1972), pp. 360–2).

[24] Kames explicitly rejects the materialist hypothesis in his *Sketches of the History of Man*: see Kames (1778), vol. i, p. 342.

[25] [Anon] (1755), p. 2.

[26] Ibid., p. 18.

[27] Ibid., p. 18.

[28] The 'substance' of this pamphlet is reprinted in the second and third editions of the *Essays*: see [Kames] (1758), pp. 164–78; Kames (1779), pp. 207–21. Ross thinks that Kames himself may have written it, possibly with the help of Hugh Blair and Robert Wallace: Ross (1972), p. 156.

found in Calvin, Turretine, Pictet, and Jonathan Edwards. Kames is thus in agreement with 'all the most noted systems of theology, composed by Calvinist divines, and taught in our universities'.[29] The author also defends Kames against the charge of having claimed that 'men cannot really sin against God'. Kames does not acquit the sinner of his sin; nor does he deny the reality of moral evil. And, again, the idea that God might permit evil in order that a greater good might come of it has precedents in the Calvinist tradition: Calvin himself, John Knox, Samuel Rutherford, and Jonathan Edwards are cited as evidence.

There is, it has to be admitted, nothing very convincing in these claims that Kames is still working within the Calvinist theological framework. James McCosh remarks that the doctrine of necessity as upheld by Kames 'looks as if it were the residuum of the doctrine of predestination, when the flowing waters of the stream had been dried up by an arid period'.[30] It might be argued that, on the contrary, the religion of which Kames's form of necessitarianism is a part marks a radical break with Calvin's Augustinian brand of Christianity. Kames, like Shaftesbury and Hutcheson, and like most of the Scottish *literati* of his day, is a devotee of what Richard Sher has called 'Christian Stoicism'.[31] At the heart of this school of religious thought is the optimistic providentialism ('whatever is, is right') mocked, not only by Hume at the end of the *Enquiry*'s section 'Of Liberty and Necessity', but also by 'orthodox' polemicists such as Anderson and John Witherspoon.[32] Kames's

---

[29] [Anon] (1756), p. 14.

[30] McCosh (1875), p. 176. McCosh finds it striking that the doctrine of necessity 'was upheld by three men, who arose about the same period and in much the same district of the country,— David [sic] Dudgeon, David Hume, and Henry Home' (p. 176). William Dudgeon's understanding of the doctrine is much the same as Kames's: one of his books is entitled *A view of the Necessitarian or Best Scheme* (Dudgeon (1739, 1765)). The difference between Kames's and Dudgeon's necessitarianism, on the one hand, and Hume's on the other, makes it appear to me unlikely that Dudgeon had any influence upon the development of Hume's views on this topic (cp. Russell (1999)).

[31] See Sher (1985). The central tenet of this religion, Sher writes, 'is that to attain true happiness people should concentrate on being benevolent in thought and deed, leaving results, outcomes, and consequences in the capable hands of the deity' (p. 179).

[32] See esp. the 'Athenian Creed' proposed by Witherspoon in his *Ecclesiastical Characteristics*. This has the aspiring 'moderate man' declare that he believes

that there is no ill in the universe, nor any such thing as virtue absolutely considered; that those things vulgarly called *sins*, are only errors in the judgment, and foils to set off the beauty of Nature, or patches to adorn her face; that the whole race of intelligent beings, even the devils themselves, (if there are any), shall finally be happy; so that Judas Iscariot is by this time a glorified saint, and it is good for him that he hath been born.

(Witherspoon (1763), p. 41)

conception of the human relationship with God is quite different from Calvin's. In his natural state, according to Kames, man is the recipient of divine benevolence, rather than, in Edwards's famous phrase, a sinner in the hands of an angry God. Everything that God made good remains good in Kames's scheme of things. It is as if the Fall had not happened. It is only 'enthusiasts', Kames says in his *Sketches of the History of Man*, who 'contradict our Saviour, by making his yoke severe, and his burden heavy'.[33]

The heated atmosphere generated by the attempt to prosecute Kames and Hume was not, perhaps, conducive to close reading and careful philosophical argument. A more subtle criticism of Kames's *Essays* than either Anderson's or Bonar's had appeared very soon after the book appeared, entitled *A Letter to a Friend*, and signed 'Phileleutherus'. Much of this is devoted to the essay 'Of Liberty and Necessity'. The author first attacks Kames's premises, and then his conclusions. Kames's necessitarian argument, he says, rests on three propositions: 'That the mind cannot act without motives; That the mind, when it acts upon motives, acts necessarily, and cannot resist them; and also, That the motives are not only necessary in their influence, but even in their existence, and violently obtrude upon the mind.'[34] Each of these propositions is, according to Phileleutherus, contradicted by consciousness. '[A] very little reflection' tells us that 'where two means, or two ends are supposed equal, there the mind chuses the one preferably to the other arbitrarily, and without any prepollent motive':[35] so much for the first of Kames's premises. As for the second, 'since the soul can act without motives, it must have a force within itself independent of motives; and without determining the extent of this force, it may at least be supposed equal to the influence of considerable motives; and therefore sufficient to prevent their effect, that is, to resist them'.[36] Even when motives act upon the mind, and influence our choices, 'we are intimately conscious of a power of hesitating, deliberating, and examining things with great attention and care, before we proceed to the action excited to'.[37] The necessitarian position is that all motives are generated by causes outside the mind, and that they act upon the mind like

---

[33] Kames (1778), vol. iii, p. 390. In a letter to Miss Catherine Gordon dated 13 November 1764, Kames writes that 'Gaiety . . . is the noblest expression of [a] religious turn . . .' (cited by Lehmann (1971), p. 281).

[34] [Phileleutherus] (1751), p. 27.

[35] Ibid., p. 28.

[36] Ibid., pp. 30–1.

[37] Ibid., p. 32.

weights act upon a balance. Turning to the third of Kames's premises, Phileleutherus replies that under the influence of such 'external' motives, the mind 'must often be in a fluctuating state, unavoidably tossed backwards and forwards, by broken and precarious operations': 'The motives, in this case, like weights thrown at random into the scales, acting by an uncertain direction, must exclude all regular conduct, and produce the strangest disorder imaginable'.[38] Phileleutherus brings to our attention 'the case, where the motive of action springs from the mind itself'. He does not explain exactly what he means, but perhaps the motives in question are the product of reflection, or of conscience. These do not 'start out of nothing, and begin to exist without any cause': 'We are intimately conscious that the mind is the cause of internal motives, and must also have direction of external ones'—if the disorder just described is to be avoided.[39] When the mind deliberates, motives and reasons 'are its servants, quite obedient to its commands, and by no means its masters; for we must be sensible, that the mind calls up ideas, and brings them under view at pleasure, and attends to, and compares them in the same manner'.[40]

Having rejected the premises of Kames's necessitarian argument, Phileleutherus turns to its conclusions, to try them also 'by their true touchstone, that of facts and experiments'.[41] ('For...had this method been strictly followed, the world would not have been perplexed with many inconsistent systems, which unhappily have rendered morality a difficult and intricate science.') He focuses in particular upon the way in which Kames attempts to avoid the difficulties attaching to the idea that God might be the cause of evil, by claiming that, in fact, there is no such thing as sin. This, Phileleutherus remarks, 'cuts the Gordian knot instead of loosing it'.[42] As Kames himself admits, this conclusion is violently at odds with our natural feelings of self-approbation, remorse, indignation, and so on. Kames sets reason at odds with our consciousness of liberty, and with the moral awareness that comes with that consciousness. And this should have given him pause for thought. For he is contradicted by 'obstinate facts, of which we have certain experience': most importantly, the existence of 'an established course of things, a moral order and connexion, which the notion of necessity cannot affect'.[43] According to Phileleutherus, Kames is led to try to deny these facts because he is too confident of his own powers of insight. He is more certain than he has right

---

[38] [Phileleutherus] (1751), p. 32.   [39] Ibid., pp. 33–4.   [40] Ibid., p. 36.
[41] Ibid., p. 40.   [42] Ibid., p. 44.   [43] Ibid., p. 55.

to be that it is impossible to reconcile divine prescience and decrees with human freedom and responsibility. It is true wisdom

not to suffer our minds to take an unbounded flight into the superior regions, whereby we might lose sight of nature entirely; but to advert to our present circumstances and situation, to the present imperfection of our faculties and condition, and thence learn that true modesty, which (if we trust Plato's sentiments) is at once a decent ornament to the soul, and its strongest guard and security against error.[44]

It is wisdom, in particular, to trust our senses, as answering the good ends for which God has given them, and as serving the common purposes of life. Of course, the senses can deceive and mislead us, and then we look to reason for advice. But it is inconceivable that deception should extend to our consciousness of the operations of our own minds, to 'our intimate feelings and perceptions of things'. Then we would be 'thrown into unavoidable error': 'For these very perceptions are the principles and foundation of all our reasonings, and if they are false, our reasonings must be so too, and that without any possible remedy.'[45]

Liberty and Necessity in the Second and Third Editions

Helped, no doubt, by the controversy generated by Anderson's attempt to have him expelled from the Church of Scotland, Kames came to accept, both that the notion of a deceitful sense was a mistake, and that he was wrong to claim that moral necessity is incompatible with moral accountability. He issued a second (but still anonymous) edition of the *Essays* in 1758, having made significant changes to the essay 'Of Liberty and Necessity'.[46] It now appears to him 'a harsh doctrine, that virtue in any part should be founded on a delusion'.[47] He argues instead that the doctrine of necessity is *consistent* with our moral sentiments. The first stage of the argument involves an increased amount of attention to the distinction between moral and physical necessity: Kames says that, while man is passive under physical necessity, he is

---

[44] Ibid., p. 65.

[45] Ibid., p. 58.

[46] Kames also lessens the emphasis he originally placed on belief being a matter of feeling, often replacing the word 'feeling' with 'perception'.

[47] [Kames] (1758), pp. 157–8 fn.

active under moral necessity;[48] that an action done as a matter of moral necessity is always voluntary, for 'a moral cause operates not by force or coaction, but by solicitation and persuasion';[49] that while physical necessity is disagreeable, acting under moral necessity is 'always agreeable';[50] and that moral necessities do not *feel* like necessities, and that 'we have no intuitive perception, nor direct consciousness, of the necessary connection that links will to desire'.[51] This last point is important, because it explains why most people have a natural prejudice against the idea of their actions being governed by a necessity of any kind. The truth of the doctrine of necessity is, Kames writes, 'not otherwise discoverable, but by deep thinking, and by a long chain of abstract reasoning', and is therefore 'known to philosophers only'.[52] The second stage of Kames's new compatibilist argument is the claim that the object of praise or blame is not the possessor of a supposedly free will but rather the state of character that prompted the action in question. With respect to virtue, Kames writes that 'if virtue ought to be rewarded, that man hath the best claim, who is virtuous of his nature, and upon whom a vitious motive never hath the smallest influence'.[53] This is the case in first-person self-reproach as well as in the blame of others: Kames now believes a coward blames himself for his cowardly nature, even though he accepts that he cannot help being the coward that he is. The content of the 'could have done otherwise' element of self-blame is now described in terms of a sense of not having been compelled to act by force or physical power. In fact, belief in a liberty of indifference 'would in some measure cramp the moral sense, and blunt the sentiments arising from it', since, as we have already seen, one who wavers and has to choose is less praise-worthy than one for whom there is no question of doing anything but the right thing.[54] Kames is prepared to admit that there remains a delusive notion of liberty of indifference in the first-person, present-moment perspective upon action, and explains this in the same terms as he did in the first edition, as an illusion that protects us from the lazy argument. But this illusion is now separated from the basis of our moral judgements, both first and third-person. We do not have to believe something false in order to believe someone genuinely to warrant praise or blame.

---

[48] [Kames] (1758), p. 132.   [49] Ibid., p. 133.   [50] Ibid., p. 133.   [51] Ibid., p. 134.
[52] Ibid., p. 134.   [53] Ibid., pp. 142–3.   [54] Ibid., p. 145.

Later, Kames changed his mind again about the phenomenology of agency. In *Sketches of the History of Man*, Kames asserts that we do, after all, have a distinct sense of being able to act against motives:

During a fit of bitter remorse for having slain my favourite servant in a violent passion, without just provocation, I accuse myself for having given way to passion; and acknowledge that could and ought to have restrained it. Here we find remorse founded on a system ... that acknowledges no necessary connection between an action and its motive; but, on the contrary, supposes that it is a man's power to resist his passion, and that he ought to resist it.[55]

Now, though, this perception is explained away, not in terms of a necessary illusion, as in the first edition of the *Essays*, but as the result of 'the irregular influence of passion on our opinions and sentiments'.[56] Passions naturally seek their own gratification, and the horror that we feel at some of the things we do finds no relief in the idea that all actions are necessitated by motives. 'A man who has done an action that he repents of and that affects him with anguish', Kames explains, 'abhors himself, and is odious in his own eyes: he wishes to find himself guilty; and the thought that his guilt is beyond the possibility of excuse, gratifies his passion.'[57] When the same man does something that he does not regret, by contrast, he is afterwards afflicted by no such feelings, and is perfectly reconciled to the doctrine of necessity. There is no real deceit in feelings of remorse, however, since the notion of being able to act against our motives is dispelled as soon as the passion cools. This new interpretation of the feeling of remorse is incorporated into the third and final edition of the *Essays*, published in 1779, this time with Kames's name on the title page. There he adds that the theory 'is equally applicable' to what a bystander feels witness to a terrible crime: 'The indignation of the bystander, is equally gratified, by thinking as the guilty person does.'[58] The crucial point difference between the revised theory and the position of the first edition is that, as Kames puts it, 'any notion we have of a power to act against motives is a delusion of passion, *not of nature*'.[59] The error is fleeting, and

[55] Ibid., vol. iv, p. 114.

[56] The theory is developed first in Kames's *Elements of Criticism*: see Kames (1762), vol. i, pp. 183–200.

[57] Kames (1778), vol. iv, p. 116. Laurie puts the point nicely: 'the illusion of freedom occurs only when the mind is ... warped by emotion' (Laurie (1902), p. 107).

[58] Kames (1779), pp. 178–9.

[59] Ibid., p. 179; emphasis added.

is not a permanent, God-given, feature of our mental constitution. 'And now', Kames writes in the Preface to the third edition of the *Essays*, 'rejoice with me, my good reader, in being at last relieved from so many distressing errors.'[60]

Kames and the Philosophy of Common Sense

It is characteristic of the philosophy of common sense to lend particular importance to introspection in the prosecution of scientific enquiry into the operations and powers of the human mind. This will be seen in subsequent chapters when we examine the approach to the problem of liberty and necessity taken by Beattie, Reid, and Stewart. What Reid calls 'the way of reflection' is, according to these philosophers, the only sure means of capturing what is distinctive about the human mind, of preventing the contamination of psychology with false analogies taken from natural philosophy. This prioritization of consciousness is especially significant in investigation into the operations of the faculty of will. For it might plausibly be thought that to ignore introspective testimony, and to focus, like Hume, on data provided by third-person observation, is to make it very hard to gain a clear picture of the aetiology of human action. There are other features of Kames's philosophy which suggest that, though he does not describe himself as a philosopher of common sense, he is naturally grouped with Beattie, Oswald, Reid, and Stewart. In Part Two of the *Essays*, Kames develops a reply to Hume that founds fundamental principles of belief—in the enduring identity of the self, in the authority of the senses, in the connection of causes and effects, in the uniformity of nature, even in the existence of God—upon *feelings*. These principles cannot be given a basis in reason: this Kames, like Beattie and Reid, concedes to Hume. But this concession does not generate scepticism, since the feelings which testify to the truth of the principles are too firmly rooted in human nature for us to be able to doubt that, for example, the past is a reliable guide to how the future will be.

Natural beliefs, or feelings, are conceived of, by Kames as by Reid and Beattie, as natural in the sense of being elements of the human constitution. They are given us by our maker; and they are evidence of our maker's benevolence and wisdom. Furthermore, it is because our basic principles of

---

[60] Kames (1779), p. vii.

belief are natural, in the sense of being the work of God, and a benevolent and wise God at that, that they can be relied upon. The point here is not that our natural feelings can be trusted because God has been proved, *a priori*, not to be a deceiver. Rather, they can be trusted because they form part of an immense design which could only have a wise and benevolent author.[61] Kames, as we have seen above, thinks that the deceitful sense of liberty is part of the evidence of divine providence. 'That artificial light, in which the feeling of liberty presents the moral world to our view', he says, 'answers all the good purposes of making the actions of man entirely dependent upon himself' (*Essays*, p. 206). It is here that the case for Kames's having a place among the philosophers of common sense breaks down. For it is essential to the common sense position that there be no distinction between the veridical and the deceitful among *natural* principles of belief. Beattie writes that if the real existence of a sense of 'moral liberty' be acknowledged, 'it cannot be proved to be fallacious without any arguments, which may not also prove every power of nature fallacious, and consequently, to show that man ought not to believe anything at all'.[62] Reid says that the notion of a fallacious sense 'is dishonourable to our maker, and lays a foundation for universal scepticism'.[63] To both Beattie and Reid, it matters that there be shown to be no conflict among the various 'principles of common sense'. For no one of these principles has greater authority than any other: they stand or fall together. Kames, then, turns out to be a sceptic despite himself. According to Beattie and Reid, though, the way to avoid the scepticism implicit in the first edition of the *Essays* does not lie in the reinterpretation of the phenomena of the moral life found in later editions of the book. It lies where 'Phileleutherus' had suggested it does, in a closer examination of what consciousness tells us about the relation between motives and choices.

---

[61] This, I take it, is what David Fate Norton means when he describes Hume's Scottish critics as advocates of 'providential naturalism': see, e.g., Norton (1982), pp. 202–5; and Norton (1976), pp. 318–20.

[62] Beattie (1771), p. 74.

[63] Reid (1788, 1969), p. 304 (iv.vi).

5

Jonathan Edwards against Arminianism

This work...is one of the most closely reasoned, elaborate, acute, serious, and sensible among modern productions. No metaphysician can read it without feeling a wish to have been the author of it.

Hazlitt, 'On Liberty and Necessity'

Histories of American philosophy usually begin with Jonathan Edwards.[1] He was born in Connecticut, he made his name as a revivalist preacher and controversialist at Northampton, Massachusetts, and when in 1754 he published the book with which we will be concerned in this chapter, *A careful and strict Enquiry into The modern prevailing Notions of that Freedom of Will, Which is supposed to be essential to Moral Agency, Virtue and Vice, Reward and Punishment, Praise and Blame*, he was the minister at Stockbridge, out at the western edge of New England. He died four years later at Princeton without having once crossed the Atlantic to Britain.[2] In the *Enquiry*, Edwards's target is what he calls 'Arminianism'. Where most Christian contributors to the free will debate of this period believe that the interests of morality and religion depend on a vindication of the libertarian position, Edwards maintains the traditional Calvinist view that it is, on the contrary, belief in the freedom of the will that undermines what is essential to Christianity. 'Arminianism' is not for Edwards simply a matter of declared adherence to the doctrines put forward by the Dutch anti-Calvinist theologian Jacobus Arminius at the end of the sixteenth century, and condemned at the Synod of Dordrecht in 1618–19.[3] In order

---

[1] For a recent example, see Kuklick (2001).
[2] A good modern biography is Marsden (2003).
[3] For an account of Arminius and Arminianism, see Harrison (1937).

to count as an Arminian in Edwards's eyes it was sufficient to allow the human will a degree of freedom, such that men and women might play *some* part, no matter how slight, in their own regeneration from sin. My principal concern in this chapter is to present a clear account of Edwards's argument against freedom of the will. This will lead us on to an examination of Edwards's understanding of the causal relation. Despite apparent similarities between Edwards and Hobbes, it will turn out that Edwards shares with occasionalists such as Berkeley a deep-seated antipathy to mechanistic philosophies of nature. But first, perhaps, it is necessary to justify the inclusion of the first American philosopher in a study of eighteenth-century philosophy in Britain.

Edwards as Lockean Philosopher

In 1949, Perry Miller published a revolutionary book about Edwards that had at its centre the claim that 'The simplest, and most precise, definition of Edwards's thought is that it was Puritanism recast in the idiom of empirical psychology.'[4] Miller writes that Edwards read the *Essay concerning Human Understanding* 'with ecstasy, the burden of an insupportable weight lifted with every page'.[5] The relief afforded Edwards by Locke lay, according to Miller, in the offer of an intelligible account of how the will of God interacts with the mind of man. The passivity of perception as described by the empiricist, criticized by many at the time and since, was precisely what attracted Edwards to Lockeanism. As in sense perception, so in the accession of grace: the mind contributes nothing of itself. Locke, in Miller's account, taught Edwards how to be rigorously 'naturalistic', how to incorporate religious experience into the new world described in Newton's *Principia*. As Miller puts it: 'His supernaturalism was naturalized, or if you will, he supernaturalized nature, and introduced the divine element into the world, not as a substance or a quantity, not as a compound of already existing things or an addition to them, but as "what some metaphysicians call a new simple idea".'[6] Locke is the most significant influence also upon Edwards's account of the will, Miller argues. Naturalism and anti-Arminianism both demanded the dissolution of the traditional framework of distinct and autonomous mental 'faculties'; for at the very heart of Arminianism is

---

[4] Miller (1973), p. 62.   [5] Ibid., p. 55.   [6] Ibid., p. 187.

the notion that the will has a power of self-determination, and a self-determining will is impossible to find a place for (according to Miller) in a world governed by exceptionless laws of nature. Edwards found the possibility of replacing the traditional picture of the mind in the Lockean claim that what had been called faculties are really only different capacities or powers possessed by the agent. The question regarding the will then becomes, not whether the *will* itself is free, but rather whether the will gives freedom to the *person* who possesses it. And an affirmative answer to this new question does not in any way threaten to subvert the order of nature. Freedom is no longer an ability to turn against and transform one's character: instead, it is simply a matter of not being prevented from acting one's desires and instincts, and, as such, is no different in men from what it is in animals. Indeed, Miller says, Edwards goes even further than Locke in the 'assertion of the unitary and functional nature of the organism'.[7] His 'naturalism' pushes him to the conclusion that Hobbes had reached a hundred years earlier: that there is, properly speaking, no such thing as the will at all, if 'volition' is conceived of as a mental act distinct from desire.[8] It is Locke's own project that Edwards completes when he devotes the first section of Part I of the *Enquiry* to arguing, against Locke, that 'A man never, in any instance, wills anything contrary to his desires, or desires anything contrary to his will.'[9]

In an anthology of writings by Edwards and Benjamin Franklin, Carl Van Doren had described Edwards as having been 'tragically born out of his true century'.[10] Miller's intention was to show that, on the contrary, Edwards was very much a man of his time, attuned perfectly to the challenge supposedly

---

[7] Miller (1973), p. 254.

[8] This is emphasized also in Murphy (1959). The upshot of Edwards's argument, according to Murphy, is that, properly speaking, there is no causation of acts of will by motives: the will simply *is* the strongest motive.

[9] Edwards (1754, 1857), p. 139. All subsequent references to the *Enquiry* in this chapter will be made in the main body of the text.

[10] Quoted by Weber (1981), p. ix. Franklin published a short 'dissertation' on liberty and necessity in 1725. He argues that if God is omnipotent, then 'there can be nothing either existing or acting in the Universe *against* or *without* his consent'; and that it follows from this that no creature can have 'such a Thing as Liberty, Free-will or Power to do, or refrain from Action' (Franklin (1725), pp. 5, 10). Franklin goes on to argue 'that all Things exist now in a Manner agreeable to [God's] Will, and in consequence of that are all equally Good, and therefore equally esteem'd by Him' (p. 14). There is thus an affinity between the views of Franklin and those of Hartley and Priestley, to be discussed below in Chapter 7. Edwards emphatically denies that either the impossibility of human freedom or the unreality of evil follows from divine omnipotence.

posed to Christianity by the seventeenth century's scientific revolution.[11] However, his picture of Edwards as a naturalizer of religious experience, while it revitalized Edwards's scholarship, did not win many adherents: it was implausible from the first, perhaps, that the great proponent of the reasonableness of Christianity might have found a disciple in one for whom faith is, if not a surrender of reason to emotion, then just as much a conative as a cognitive act.[12] It has recently been argued—by Michael McClymond—that Edwards's account of spiritual perception is designed as, precisely, a rebuttal of Locke's tendency to collapse religious experience into 'inspiration' and 'enthusiasm'.[13] More than one writer on Edwards has suggested that Cambridge Platonism was a more significant influence upon his thought than Lockean 'empiricism'.[14] Are there reasons to be doubtful also of Miller's claim that Locke is central to Edwards's book on the will?

I suggested in the Introduction that what is most characteristic of Locke, and hence of Lockeanism, is the *method* employed in the *Essay*, the insistence that theory be determined only by the most careful attention to experience; and it is to be admitted that 'experimentalism' is almost completely absent from Edwards's *Enquiry*. While Edwards does conform to eighteenth-century practice in so far as he refrains from mixing up his analysis of the will with speculations concerning the relation between matter and mind, there is none of Locke's attachment to the 'Historical, plain method' in his argument against 'Arminianism'. Edwards does not, like a good Baconian, begin with effects given in experience, and then proceed to postulation of causes. Edwards is concerned to show that Arminianism is 'plainly absurd' and 'manifestly inconsistent', not merely that it has no basis in human experience. He approaches the free will question confident that it can be settled before experience of any kind needs to be taken into account. Thus he resolutely refuses to acknowledge the existence of the sense of contingency and freedom that so greatly concerns Kames in the first edition of his *Essays*;

---

[11] Indeed, it often seems that Miller wants to establish Edwards as a man of our time as well. Miller, writing in the aftermath of the Second World War, appears to have found in Edwards's bleak Calvinism a more adequate response to the horrors of the age than 'liberalism' was able to provide.

[12] See Cherry (1966), pp. 18–19, and p. 221, n. 30; and Erdt (1980), *passim*, esp. ch. 2 (on 'the sense of the heart' as 'the essence of religious experience').

[13] See McClymond (1998), pp. 14–16.

[14] See especially Elwood (1960), Wallace Anderson (1980), Fiering (1981). See also Helm (1969) ('Edwards used Lockean empiricism as a *model* for religious experience and nothing more' (p. 54)). For a reassertion of the importance of Locke to Edwards, see Lee (2000), pp. 117–25.

and fails to address the Humean question of whether or not human behaviour is as regular in its permutations as the phenomena of nature. Edwards uses purely *a priori* reasoning to demolish the libertarian position, and to that extent has more in common with Hobbes and Collins than with the experimentalists of his own century. Edwards not only rejects Locke's method; he also attacks key features of Locke's considered account of human liberty: the distinction between desires and volitions, and also the claim that the will is determined by uneasiness rather than by perception of the greater good,[15] and the notion that the locus of autonomy is a 'power of suspension' in the will (see *Freedom of the Will*, pp. 209–12). The differences between Edwards's theory of freedom and Locke's are, it might well be said, more obvious than the similarities.

There is, nevertheless, a sense in which the *Enquiry* is a Lockean text: it is Lockean just in so far as it takes 'Of Power' as its point of departure. Edwards finds a place among more obviously 'experimental' philosophers of mind such as Tucker, Priestley, Reid, and Stewart because, like them, he is motivated by the desire to clear up a question that Locke had left unsatisfactorily confused and ambiguous. A wish to be true to the spirit of Locke's initial intuitions—to defend them, as it were, against Locke's own second thoughts—is at the heart of the *Enquiry*. A sceptic as to Edwards's right to have a chapter devoted to him in a book about eighteenth-century British philosophy might say that this is beside the point, and that the fact is that Edwards's contribution to the project of formulating a coherent version of Lockeanism about the will was ignored on the European side of the Atlantic. Neither Price nor Beattie nor Reid nor Stewart engages with his arguments. Edwards, the sceptic might continue, belongs to another narrative altogether, which is to say, to the story of Calvinist theology in America.[16] And this is doubtless true. It is also true, though, that the British libertarians of the eighteenth century *should* have answered Edwards. The *Enquiry* deserves to be included in this study simply because the case it mounts against libertarian freedom is such a powerful one.[17]

---

[15] See especially § 70 of 'The Mind': Edwards (1980), p. 385; and also *Freedom of the Will*, pp. 143–6.

[16] See Guelzo (1989) for the first hundred years of that story, and Edwards's central place in it. Guelzo says that 'Almost every theological party, faction, or movement in New England from 1758...until 1858...defined itself in some way or other according to "Edwards on the will"' (p. 208).

[17] It is perhaps worth adding that, despite the fact that it was published in Boston, 42 of the 298 subscribers to the first edition of the *Enquiry* were Scottish (including Hugh Blair, Kames's defender, and John Witherspoon, scourge of the moderates). Several subsequent editions were

The Refutation of Libertarianism (1):
the Regress Argument

The word 'liberty' 'as used by Arminians, Pelagians and others, who oppose the Calvinists' has, Edwards writes, three things belonging to its meaning:

1. That it consists in a self-determining power in the will, or a certain sovereignty the will has over itself, and its own acts, whereby it determines its own volitions; so as not to be dependent in its determinations, on any cause without itself, nor determined by anything prior to its acts. 2. Indifference belongs to liberty in their notion of it, or that the mind, previous to the act of volition be, *in equilibrio*. 3. Contingence is another thing that belongs and is essential to it; not in common acceptation of the word, . . . , but as opposed to all necessity, or any fixed and certain connection with some previous ground or reason of its existence.

(Freedom of the Will, pp. 164–5)

Part II of the *Enquiry* is given over to a consideration of 'Whether There is or Can Be Any Such Sort of Freedom of Will, as that Wherein Arminians Place the Essence of the Liberty of All Moral Agents; and Whether Any Such Thing Ever Was or Can Be Conceived of' (*Freedom of the Will*, p. 169). This is more than a merely philosophical question for Edwards. A passage in his book on original sin has it that if the anti-Calvinists can vindicate their conception of liberty, 'then they have an impregnable castle, to which they may repair, and remain invincible, in all the controversies they have with the reformed divines, concerning *original sin*, the *sovereignty* of grace, *election, redemption, conversion*, the *efficacious operation* of the Holy Spirit, the nature of saving *faith*, *perseverance* of the saints, and other principles of like kind'.[18]

For Edwards, as for Calvin before him, the freedom of the human will is incompatible with the absolute dominion of God; and from absolute dominion of God directly follow all the principal teachings of Christianity. Moreover, along with Arminianism about the human capacity for self-transformation tended to go confidence in the Church's ability to cultivate those capacities in all who called themselves Christians; and with that confidence in the efficacy of Christian ritual tended to go an acceptance of

published in London. Edwards cared about how he was interpreted in Britain: when Kames's supporters numbered him among the Calvinists whose doctrine of necessity is identical to that presented in the *Essays on the Principles of Morality and Natural Religion*, Edwards made sure that his response was published in Edinburgh by his friend John Erskine.

[18] Edwards (1758b, 1970), p. 376.

the authority of bishops to determine what ritual should consist in. Arminianism thus represented everything that the 'Puritans' had sought to escape in leaving old England for New.[19] Yet Edwards's argument against Arminianism has no theological premises; nor does Edwards follow Calvin in making constant appeal to the authority of Scripture. Though Edwards does point out (in Sections 11 and 12 of Part II) that Arminian freedom is inconsistent with God's certain foreknowledge of future actions, this is not where the weight of his argument lies. The doctrines of revealed religion do not need to be brought into the controversy, because, according to Edwards, the Arminian position is internally unstable. There is, in fact, no position there for the Calvinist to attack. Either the Arminian is saying something self-contradictory; or he is, without acknowledging it, in agreement with the Calvinist.

Edwards begins his consideration of Arminian freedom with a show of generosity. He says that the Arminians cannot really mean that the will determines itself: that would be an obvious absurdity, in the light of what Locke has shown concerning the impossibility of coherently attributing powers to powers. As Locke says, 'we may as properly say, that 'tis the singing *Faculty* sings, and the dancing *Faculty* dances; as that the *Will* chuses, or that the Understanding conceives'.[20] 'So when it is said, the will decides or determines', Edwards writes, 'the meaning must be, that the person in the exercise of a power of willing and choosing, or the soul acting voluntarily, determines' (*Freedom of the Will*, p. 172). The Arminian position is that the person in exercising his power of will (that is, in making choices) is not determined by anything either 'without' himself or 'prior' to the act of choice itself. Edwards homes in on the problem of how, exactly, a person is to determine his own will. It is agreed on both sides that the mark of a free act of any kind is that it is voluntary, or chosen. So, presumably, if an act of the will is to be free, it too must be voluntary. That is, in Edwards's words, 'the soul determines all the free acts of the will in the exercise of a power of willing; or, which is the same thing, it determines them of choice; it determines its own acts by choosing its own acts' (*Freedom of the Will*, p. 172). Thus the person freely chooses by choosing his choices. But if the choice of a choice is to be free, it too must be chosen; and the choice of a choice of a choice must also be chosen; and so on, until there is reached the first act of choice in the series, the act by which the person initiates the series of choices

[19] Cp. Alexander Allen (1889), pp. 282–3 ('Everything vital was at stake in the doctrine of the human will'); see also Ramsey (1957), pp. 31–2.
[20] Locke (1690, 1975), p. 242 (II.xxi.17).

of choices by which a free act of choice is made. And here the Arminian is faced with a dilemma fatal to his conception of freedom. For what causes that first act of choice? If the Arminian answers that the first act of choice is chosen, then he contradicts himself: for then the 'first' act of choice has an act of choice that precedes it, and is therefore not the first act of choice. But if the Arminian answers that the first act of choice is not chosen by a prior act of choice, then that first act of choice, by the Arminian's own lights, is not a free act of choice. And, argues Edwards, 'if that first act of the will, which determines and fixes subsequent acts, be not free, none of the following acts, which are determined by it, can be free' (*Freedom of the Will*, p. 173). It does not matter how many choices of choices occur between the first act of will and the supposedly free act of choice that is the product of the intervening choices: the fact that the first one is not free, because not chosen, means that none of the rest of them can be. 'Thus, this Arminian notion of liberty of the will, consisting in the will's self-determination, is repugnant to itself, and shuts itself wholly out of the world' (*Freedom of the Will*, p. 174).[21]

Edwards did not invent this argument. Locke says that 'they, who can make a Question' of 'whether a Man can *will*, what he *wills*' 'must suppose one will to determine the Acts of another, and another to determine that; and so on *in infinitum*'.[22] But this is a remark made in passing. It shows that Locke takes it to be obvious that the will is, as he puts it, 'determined by something without it'.[23] Establishing this, however, is not Locke's primary concern. He is much more interested in the question of what it is that determines the will, a question that cannot be answered without empirical enquiry. And reflection on experience of what prompts human beings to make the choices they make turns out to leave it unclear whether or not the determination of the will by things without it is always such as to rob the agent of the freedom that the Arminian is concerned to vindicate. It transpires that Locke allows a measure of control over choice, in the form of the power in the mind 'to *suspend* the execution and satisfaction of any of its desires, and so all, one after another'.[24] This power, Locke then says, is 'the source of all liberty'. In reply to the hypothesis of a power of suspension, but

---

[21] For a helpful account of Edwards's argument, see Chai (1998), pp. 95–113.

[22] Locke (1690, 1975), p. 247 (II.xxi.25).

[23] Hobbes writes: 'I acknowledge this *Liberty*, that I *can* do, if I *will*, but to say, I can *will* if I *will*, I take to be an absurd speech' (Hobbes (1654), p. 3; Chappell (ed.), p. 16); but, like Locke, does not make much of it.

[24] Locke (1690, 1975), p. 263 (II.xxi.47).

without mentioning Locke, Edwards applies the same reasoning that Locke uses to dismiss the idea of a man willing what he wills. If liberty consists solely in a power of suspension, 'then wherein consists the will's freedom with respect to this act of suspension' (*Freedom of the Will*, p. 210)? The answer must be, if liberty really does consist *solely* in a power of suspension, that liberty with respect to this act of suspension consists in a power of suspension. And this is absurd in two ways: it makes no sense to talk of suspending or deferring something that is already suspended or deferred; and, as a condition upon free choice, it results in an infinite regress of acts of suspension.

It is clear, then, that if the libertarian, or 'Arminian', is to find a means of answering the argument sketched by Locke and fully worked out by Edwards, his strategy is going to have to be to formulate an account of control over choices that does not have room within it for an regression of exercises of control over exercises of control. Edwards himself suggests two ways in which the Arminian might try to evade the force of his argument. One attempts to avoid the problem of a regression of acts of will by claiming 'that the faculty or power of the will, or the soul in the use of that power, determines its own volitions; and that it does so without any act going before the act determined' (*Freedom of the Will*, p. 175). The agent determines his volitions, that is, directly or immediately: he does not have to do something *in order to* make a choice. Edwards gives several replies to this purported answer (see *Freedom of the Will*, pp. 175–6), but the essence of his response is that there is no means of making sense of the activity of an agent with respect to the will except in terms of volition itself. If the soul determines its volitions it must be active in doing so; and for the soul to be active is, Arminians themselves insist, for it to exercise the power of choice.

The other strategy of evasion has it that, while the agent is active in determining his volitions, and while the determination is therefore an act, 'yet there is no need of supposing this act to be prior to the volition determined; but the will or soul determines the act of the will *in willing*; it determines its own volition, *in* the very act of volition; it directs and limits the act of the will, causing it to be so and not otherwise, *in* exerting the act, without any preceding act to excite that' (*Freedom of the Will*, p. 176). This, Edwards comments, might mean three different things. It could mean that the determining act (the exercise of the will) goes before the act determined (the making of the choice) only 'in the order of nature', and not 'in the order of time': just as when one body causes another to move, contact can be said to happen at the same time as the beginning of the motion of the second body, without this suggesting that there is no distinction between cause and effect. But that there is does not help at all, for the regress opens up just as plainly in the order of nature as it does in the order of time. On a second possible interpretation, the suggestion could be that the determining act and the act determined are identical, the very same act of mind. This, though, is to make the exertion both cause and effect, as if one were to say that the action of breaking a window is the same event as the breaking of the window.[25] To say that the choice is caused, and yet not caused by anything antecedent or distinct from it, would appear to be, again, a contradiction. A third interpretation involves acceptance of the inference just drawn: that is, of the claim 'that the soul's exertion of such a particular act of will, is a thing that comes to pass *of itself*, without any cause; and that there is absolutely no ground or reason of the soul's being determined to exert such a volition, and make such a choice, rather than another' (*Freedom of the Will*, pp. 178–9). But this is either a failure to answer the original question of what determines the will; or a positive assertion that the answer to the question is that *nothing* does, that free acts of the will 'arise from nothing; no cause, no power, no influence, being at all concerned in the matter' (*Freedom of the Will*, p. 179).

The Refutation of Libertarianism (II): Volitions and their Causes

At this point Edwards has obtained the result that every necessitarian in the eighteenth century desires: he has shown, to his own satisfaction at least, that the libertarian position amounts to the claim that a free act does not have a cause. Edwards proceeds to rub salt in the wound by drawing attention to the fact that it is a 'dictate of common sense' that every event has a cause, and by pointing out that 'If this grand principle of common sense be taken away, all arguing from effects to causes ceaseth, and so all knowledge of any existence, besides what we have by the most direct and immediate intuition'; and that '[p]articularly all our proof of the being of God ceases' (*Freedom of the Will*, p. 181). If the libertarians were to say that there is something special about free acts of will, such that they, unlike all

---

[25] I owe this way of posing the problem to Maria Alvarez.

other things, can come into existence without any cause, then, Edwards says, the libertarians would be contradicting themselves yet again: 'for they would be giving an account of some ground of the existence of a thing, when at the same time they would maintain there is no ground of its existence' (*Freedom of the Will*, p. 185). The only kind of thing that needs no cause is a thing that has always existed, that is 'self-existent, or necessary in the nature of things', and no libertarian thinks a free act of will to be that kind of thing.

Edwards addresses an attempt by Isaac Watts to distinguish between two different applications of the principle that every event must have a cause. In the material world, Watts says, it is true 'that nothing is, or comes to pass, without a sufficient reason why it is, and why it is in this manner rather than another'; but 'spirits' are active by nature, and are able to bring about choices freely, simply by means of an exercise of the will.[26] A free choice has its cause in the pure activity of the mind, and is therefore not an effect without a cause. Edwards replies that this is to fail to understand what a cause is. Activity of the mind is, on the proposed account, the cause of all free choices; but what is needed in each case is an explanation of why the mind exerts itself in one way rather than another. Activity of the mind is always the same; determinations of the will differ; so activity of the mind cannot be the cause of the determinations of the will; and this, as Edwards says, 'is contrary to the supposition' (*Freedom of the Will*, p. 188). With the coherence of self-determination by acts of choice undermined, and with un-caused self-determination a non-starter, all that is left the Arminian is self-determination by means of some other faculty of the mind. But if the will were determined by the understanding, for example, or by any other faculty, 'then *the will* don't determine *itself*; and so the self-determining power of the will is given up': 'So that let Arminians turn which way they please with their notion of liberty, consisting in the will's determining its own acts, their notion destroys itself' (*Freedom of the Will*, p. 191).

In addition to a self-determining power in the will, 'Arminian' freedom as Edwards defined it contained the notions of the indifference of the will and of contingency of choices. We have seen that both Hume and Kames allow that a feeling of indifference is a component of the decision-making process, though neither regards the feeling as an obstacle for his necessitarian argument. Edwards, on the other hand, argues that the very idea of a choice

---

[26] Watts (1732), pp. 68–9; cited *Freedom of the Will*, p. 186.

made in circumstances of indifference is simply incoherent. Focusing upon liberty of indifference as described by Watts, he claims that to say that the will chooses between various options while regarding those options as equally preferable 'is the very same thing as to say, the mind has a preference, at the same time that it has no preference' (*Freedom of the Will*, p. 196). Again: 'To suppose the will to act at all in a state of perfect indifference, either to determine itself, or to do anything else, is to assert that the mind chooses without choosing' (*Freedom of the Will*, p. 198). Edwards acknowledges that not every opponent of necessity rests his case on the radical form of indifference espoused by Watts (and by King before him). But, he says, there is no logical room for degrees of indifference. To talk of motives inclining without 'literally' necessitating choice is 'grossly absurd', for it amounts to talk of preferences which are not 'literally' preferred: 'if there be the least degree of antecedent preponderation of the will, it must be perfectly abolished, before the will can be at liberty to determine itself the contrary way' (*Freedom of the Will*, p. 205).

Like other necessitarians of his age, Edwards draws an analogy between the determinations of the will and the operations of a balance: 'Choice and preference can no more be in a state of indifference', he says, 'than motion can be in a state of rest, or than the preponderation of the scale of a balance can be in a state of equilibrium' (*Freedom of the Will*, p. 207). One cannot choose between two very similar things—two eggs, for example—without finding one more attractive than the other, for, as Edwards understands choice, to choose something simply is to find it more attractive than its alternatives. And choice is made possible by the (presumably contingent) fact that, no matter how similar the things to be chosen between may be, it will always be the case that, as Edwards puts it, 'one will prevail in the eye, or in idea beyond others' (*Freedom of the Will*, p. 199). The ideas of the mind are continually varying, Edwards says, and these changes are quite involuntary; without there needing to be a prior act of the will, very similar objects will be differentiated in some small way, by the play of light upon them, perhaps, or by a change in their relations with other things. It is also relevant, first, that choice is, properly speaking, of actions and not of things, so that two things may appear identical, and the mind still be able to differentiate between 'taking or touching' one rather than the other; and, secondly, that an agent may be indifferent 'with respect to what is to be done in a more distant and general view of it', and yet not indifferent 'with respect to the next immediate act, viewed with its particular and present circumstances' (see *Freedom of the Will*, pp. 200–1).[27] Those eighteenth-century libertarians who do not emphasize the importance of the will's indifference make much, as we saw in Chapter 2, of the distinction between, on the one hand, how motives determine choice and, on the other, how physical objects determine the actions of other physical objects. Edwards, like Hobbes and Collins, replies that there is only one kind of causal relation. Either the effect is wholly determined by its cause, or it is not; and if it is not, then the 'effect' is in fact an event without a cause. The notion of an 'effect' with only a contingent relation to its cause is a contradiction in terms (see *Freedom of the Will*, pp. 213–16).

This concludes Edwards's attack on the three components of Arminian liberty. However, he goes on to argue that to say, as do Clarke and his followers, that the determinations of the will always follow the dictates of the understanding is to concede everything that the necessitarian hopes to establish. Edwards maintains this partly because, as will be explained below, he takes perfect predictability to be what the doctrine of necessity amounts to in the human case. But he also gives an argument to show that there is no means of conceding the influence of the understanding on the will without also conceding that it is impossible to act against the understanding's deliverances. The libertarian who holds that it is up to us whether we act in accord with the last dictate of the understanding must say that we choose whether so to act; and then the question must arise as to what motivates the choice to act in line with what the understanding recommends. For such a choice to be possible, there must be what Edwards terms 'some antecedent light in the understanding concerning the greatest apparent good or evil' (*Freedom of the Will*, p. 221), and then the choice is not free after all. The libertarian can of course postulate another act of choice, a determination to act in line with the understanding's sense of the greatest apparent good or evil; but that choice, again, could only be made in the light of a sense of the greatest or most eligible good; and so a possibly infinite regress of acts of

---

[27] In one of his few discussions on the experience of choice, Edwards analyses the acts of mind involved in choosing at random to touch one square of a chessboard rather than the other sixty-three squares. In such a case, he says, there are three 'steps of the mind's proceeding (though all may be done as it were in a moment)': first a 'general determination' to touch one of the squares; secondly, another general determination on the mind's part to 'give itself up to accident, in some certain way; as to touch that which shall be most in the eye or mind at that time, or to some other suchlike accident'; and, thirdly, a 'particular' determination to touch the square that turns out to be 'most in the eye or mind at that time' (see *Freedom of the Will*, pp. 198–9).

choice opens up once more. Thus Edwards is in a position to claim that volition is in every case 'necessarily connected with the influence of motives': for choice in indifference, without motives, is incoherent; and once the influence of motives is conceded, it appears that motives can only influence by wholly determining choice; 'And if volitions are properly the effects of their motives, then they are necessarily connected with their motives' (*Freedom of the Will*, p. 225). From his case *against* the Arminian scheme Edwards has produced an argument *for* the Calvinist position. No examination of actual relations between different kinds of motives and different kinds of actions, nor even of common beliefs about such relations, has proved necessary. Edwards's conception of agency—of actions as determined by motives over which we have no control—is vindicated simply because it is the only conception not vitiated by self-contradiction.

Edwards and Hobbes Compared

We saw in the previous chapter that Edwards was appealed to as an example of a theologically sound defender of the doctrine of necessity. Edwards, however, bridled at the idea that his views were similar to Kames's. In a pair of open letters to his friend John Erskine in Edinburgh—letters appended to the third and all subsequent editions of the *Enquiry*—Edwards seeks to make it clear that, on his view, as not on Kames's, the fact that all human choices and actions are determined by motives does *not* entail that no human choice or action is free. Surprisingly, in view of the criticisms of Clarke adumbrated above, the distinction between moral and 'physical' or 'natural' necessity turns out to be integral to Edwards's explanation of how the necessary connection of volitions with motives is compatible with our liberty and accountability. It is clear that Edwards will reject the libertarian claim that going along with the distinction between moral necessity and natural necessity is a difference between two quite different kinds of cause, such that agents may be said to cause their actions while preserving the ability to act otherwise than they actually do. All events are necessitated by their causes, Edwards believes: there is no such thing as an 'effect' contingently related to its cause. Edwards must therefore understand the difference between moral and natural necessity simply in terms of the difference in the relevant *relata*. There is moral necessity where the causal relation obtains between 'moral' things, natural where the relation is between 'natural' things. The relation itself is the same in the two cases. 'I suppose', Edwards says, 'that necessity which is called natural, in distinction from moral necessity, is so called, because "mere nature", as the word is vulgarly used, is concerned, without anything of choice' (*Freedom of the Will*, p. 158). Where a thing is done because it was chosen, there is neither compulsion nor constraint; and where there is neither compulsion nor constraint, then, according to Edwards, there is freedom of action. No delusion is involved in belief in freedom, nor in the belief in moral responsibility that goes with it.

Dugald Stewart notes that 'it is remarkable how completely Collins has anticipated Dr Jonathan Edwards, the most celebrated, and indisputably the ablest champion, in later times, of the scheme of necessity'.[28] In its central arguments, Collins's case for necessity and against libertarianism is the same as Hobbes's. Can it be said, then, his necessitarianism is Hobbesian in character? Hobbes destroys the traditional distinction between natural and intelligent causes by claiming that a cause, no matter what kind of thing it is, is a cause only in so far as it is sufficient to produce a given effect.[29] It follows directly from this definition of 'cause' that all causes necessitate their effects, since if one thing is genuinely sufficient for the bringing into being of another, then that first thing cannot but bring the second into being. If it were possible for the first thing to exist without the second following, then the first thing would show itself not, in fact, to be the second's cause. Edwards, too, holds that every cause must provide a complete explanation of its effects: it is part of his case against Arminianism that a bare act of will is not sufficient to explain why one course of action is chosen rather than another (see *Freedom of the Will*, pp. 177–8, 187–8). He also, like Hobbes, refuses to admit there to be a difference in the kinds of necessity produced by moral and natural causes: the distinction between moral and natural necessity is a matter only of the difference in the *relata*. And, again like Hobbes, he seeks to preserve moral responsibility with a distinction between voluntary action, on the one hand, and cases of compulsion and restraint on the other.

Something that Edwards says in his reply to Kames suggests, however, that things are not so straightforward here as they might seem. He claims that in the *Enquiry* he has 'largely declared, that the connection between antecedent

---

[28] Stewart (1828), vol. II, p. 500. Stewart also says that 'it must be owned that the objections urged by Collins and Edwards to the doctrine of Freewill are of an incomparably more imposing and popular nature, than the very subtle and shadowy arguments by which they have tried to reconcile their scheme with man's moral agency' (Stewart (1828), vol. II, p. 499).

[29] See above, p. 8.

things and consequent ones, which takes place with regard to the acts of men's wills, which is called moral necessity, is called by the name "necessity" improperly ...: and that such a necessity as attends the acts of men's wills, is more properly called "certainty", than necessity ...'.[30] There are many things, Edwards says in the *Enquiry*, which count as causes even though they do not have what he terms 'a positive efficiency or influence to produce a thing, or bring it to pass'. What is essential to a cause is simply that it 'have the nature of a ground or reason why some things are, rather than others; or why they are otherwise' (*Freedom of the Will*, p. 180). Edwards appears to be being careful here to prevent the possibility of someone understanding his 'moral' causes to act in a mechanistic fashion. Motives, he seems to be saying, are things that make particular actions *certain*, rather than things that, as it were, force actions to be performed. And this would appear to differentiate his understanding of necessity from that of Hobbes and Collins.

Edwards says, in fact, that, quite generally, 'Metaphysical or philosophical necessity is nothing different from certainty' (*Freedom of the Will*, p. 151). He is quick to add that he is talking about not 'the certainty of knowledge, but the certainty that is in things themselves, which is the foundation of the certainty of knowledge of them; or that wherein lies the ground of the infallibility of the proposition which affirms them' (*Freedom of the Will*, pp. 151–2). But he does seem to be suggesting that it is not only in the case of moral causes that there is no sense to talk of a cause giving rise to an effect by means of an exercise of force or power. To explain what is meant by causal necessity, he says, it is not enough to say that it is 'that by which a thing cannot but be, or whereby it cannot be otherwise', since then we are still owed an account of what 'cannot' means in this context. According to Edwards, 'Philosophical necessity is really nothing else than the full and final connection between the things signified by the subject and the predicate of a proposition, which affirms something to be true' (*Freedom of the Will*, p. 152). It is not perfectly clear what this means. In some cases, the 'full and final connection' will be guaranteed by the fact that to deny the proposition results in a contradiction, or 'gross absurdity' (see *Freedom of the Will*, pp. 152–3). But what of other cases, where what is being described is a matter of fact? Edwards seems to be saying that then the 'full and final connection' is established by the fact that there is a regularity and uniformity in the order of nature such that it has always been the case that subject and predicate have gone together. Such a

---

[30] Edwards (1758a, 1957), p. 456.

regularity and uniformity is, of course, a thing of the past; but it amounts to a 'full and *final* connection', and pertains to the future too, because it allows us to be absolutely *certain* of what will be connected with what in the future. This certainty, as we have just seen Edwards insist, is more than a mere confidence in how things will be in the future: it is justified belief that how things have been in the past demonstrates how things have to be in the future. Edwards does not engage with matters of fact in the *Enquiry*, but he does in *Original Sin*, and there it is clear that he takes the transition from claims about past experience to claims about necessities to be quite unproblematic. Having examined 'what appears in fact of the sinfulness of mankind', Edwards concludes that there is in human nature a propensity to sin 'of the highest kind, a propensity that is *invincible*, or a tendency which really amounts to a fixed constant unfailing *necessity*'.[31] The fact that human beings are uniformly and universally sinful when deprived of God's grace justifies the claim that without grace it is (morally) impossible for us *not* to sin.

In the light of Hume's scepticism about the rational basis of induction, it is worth asking how Edwards might have thought experience of past regularities justifies claims about future possibilities and impossibilities. If Edwards's necessitarianism is not Hobbesian in character, if there is in causes no 'positive efficiency' or 'influence', one is left wondering what it is, exactly, that underwrites the relation between cause and effect, and guarantees that given one event, another *has* to follow. Edwards, I think, points towards an explanation of causal necessity in *Original Sin* when he considers a potential objection to the position he has been expounding. It is important to Edwards that sin happen only because God permits it to happen. The Manichean notion of the independence of sin from God's will is anathema to Edwards just as it is for Augustine and Calvin. So Edwards must refute the idea that sin, after the Fall, 'comes in a course of nature', and, as such, is nothing to do with God.[32] The worry for Edwards here is that the 'course of nature' might be thought of as 'a proper active cause, which will work and go on by itself, without God, if he lets or permits it'.[33] Of course God created the order of nature; but, it might be said, all he did was set up its initial conditions and its laws of operation. After that, he withdrew his agency, and let things take their own course. In doing so, God in a very general sense permitted

[31] Edwards (1758b, 1970), p. 123.

[32] Ibid., p. 384.

[33] Ibid., p. 384. Here Edwards is citing John Taylor's *Scripture Doctrine of Original Sin*, the book that *Original Sin* is meant to refute: see Taylor (1740), p. 410.

everything to happen that followed from the initial conditions and the laws of nature; but he also renounced direct control of nature, and cannot therefore be held directly responsible for what transpires there.

Edwards's response is 'that the course of nature is nothing without God'.[34] This is meant quite literally. Like Descartes in the Third Meditation, Edwards believes that it is the agency of God, and only the agency of God, that keeps the universe in existence from moment to moment. At any one moment in time, there is nothing in nature sufficient to bring about what follows at the next moment in time. The laws of nature do not have the capacity, by themselves, to ensure that things will carry on in accord with them. In one of his hundreds of notes on theological questions, now known collectively as 'The Miscellanies', Edwards writes that 'there is no other law than only the infinite wisdom of all things, who in one simple, unchangeable, perpetual action comprehends all existence in its utmost compass and extent and infinite series'.[35] Another note says: 'In natural things, means of effects, in metaphysical strictness, are not the proper causes of the effects but only occasions. God produces all effects; but yet he ties natural events to the operation of such means, or causes them to be consequent on such means according to fixed, determinate, and unchangeable rules which are called the laws of nature.'[36] This, presumably, is the answer Edwards would have given had he been asked why he is confident that past regularity is evidence of how things have to be, and so of how they will be in the future. Past regularity is the direct result of the will of God, and therefore there is no more reason to think that the laws of nature will change than there is to think that there will be alterations in the divine will.

Edwards was, of course, not the first philosopher to recoil from the idea that created substances might have powers of their own all the way to an all-out denial of the existence in nature of 'second causes'. But the rigorousness of his occasionalism is striking nevertheless. In his early and unpublished work 'The Mind', Edwards argues that it is not just the motion of bodies that is the result of the direct action of God. Solidity itself is, he says, 'as much action or the immediate result of action as gravity':

Gravity by all will be confessed to be immediately from some active influence. Being a continual tendency in bodies to move, and being that which will set them in

---

[34] Edwards (1758b, 1970), p. 384.

[35] Miscellany § 1263; cited in Elwood (1960), p. 55.

[36] Miscellany § 629: Edwards (2000), p. 157.

motion though before at perfect rest, it must be the effect of something acting on that body. And it is as clear that action is as requisite to stop a body that is already in motion, as in order to set bodies a-moving that are at perfect rest. Now we see continually that there is a stopping of all motion at the limits of such and such parts of space, only this stoppage is modified and diversified according to certain laws. For we get the idea and apprehension of solidity only and entirely from the observation we make of that ceasing of motion, at the limits of some parts of space, that already is, and that beginning of motion that till now was not, according to a certain constant manner.

And why is not every whit as reasonable that we should attribute this action or effect to the influence of some agent, as that other action or effect we call gravity, which is likewise derived from our observation of the beginning and ceasing of motion according to a certain method?[37]

Edwards is suspicious of the idea that there is anything more to bodies than what we observe to be their properties. When it is said that there must be something which, as Edwards puts it, 'upholds the properties of bodies', something which gives a natural body its unity and impenetrability, Edwards will reply that no sense can be made of such a thing, unless what is meant is 'he by whom all things subsist'.[38] In *Original Sin* Edwards argues that 'it appears, if we consider matters strictly, there is no such thing as identity or oneness in created objects, existing at different times, but what depends on *God's sovereign constitution*'.[39] This is to say, in effect, that substances, conceived of in the normal way as entities which do not depend for their continued existence on any other entity, do not exist; or that the only substance is God.[40] In Edwards's thought, though, this notion has no pantheistic implications. God is not thereby naturalized; nor is nature deified. In 'The Mind', Edwards explains (if that is the right word) as follows:

And indeed, the secret lies here: that which truly is the substance of all bodies is the infinitely exact and precise and perfectly stable idea in God's mind, together with his stable will that the same shall gradually be communicated to us, and to other minds, according to certain fixed and established methods and laws: or in somewhat different language, the infinitely exact and precise divine idea, together with an

---

[37] 'The Mind', § 61: Edwards (1980), pp. 377–8.

[38] Ibid., p. 380.

[39] Edwards (1758b, 1970), p. 404.

[40] Edwards's attack upon the traditional notion of substance is the principal concern of Lee (2000).

answerable, perfectly exact, precise and stable will with respect to correspondent communications to created minds, and effects on their minds.[41]

There is, it seems, nothing at all of Hobbes in Edwards's understanding of the basis of necessitarianism. On the contrary, Edwards would appear to have deduced from the metaphysic of occasionalism something rather similar to Berkeley's immaterialism.[42]

American Supernaturalism and British Naturalism

The occasionalist metaphysic of God's continuous and direct action upon his creation was not, for Edwards, an abstract matter, derived, as it was for some in the seventeenth century, from metaphysical difficulties in making sense of causal interaction between finite substances while one remained within the Cartesian system. It seems that Edwards believed there to be constant and irrefutable *experience* of the dependence of everything upon the divine will. This is reasonably plain even if we remain neutral with respect to the question, raised by Miller, of the degree to which Edwards 'naturalizes' religious experience. Dependence upon God is, in the first instance, evidenced in one's experience of oneself; and according to Edwards it is, or should be, just as vivid in the 'natural man', the man who is turned away from God, as it is in the man possessed of grace. Edwards's most famous work, the sermon 'Sinners in the Hands of an Angry God' (given at Enfield in 1741), is suffused with a sense of the utter helplessness of man in his natural condition. 'The unseen, unthought of ways and means of persons going suddenly out of the world are innumerable and inconceivable', Edwards writes; 'Unconverted men walk over the pit of hell on a rotten covering, and there are innumerable places in this covering so weak that they won't bear

---

[41] Edwards (1980), p. 344. See also pp. 380, 398.

[42] It seems now to be a matter of consensus that Edwards developed his version of idealism without having read Berkeley. See Anderson (1980), pp. 76–7, and the works cited there; see also McClymond (1998), p. 128, n. 46. For a comparison between the idealisms of Edwards and Berkeley, see Anderson (1980), pp. 102–3. There is no trace of Edwards's peculiar metaphysics in the *Enquiry*. As Georges Lyon points out, 'Presque partout, l'auteur y parle la langue du réalisme courant, comme s'il y avait effectivement un monde extérieur et comme si les objets de la perception possédaient hors de l'esprit une réalité' (Lyon (1888), p. 434). Certainly, the argument against Arminianism does not depend upon Edwards's extreme form of idealism.

their weight, and these places are not seen.'[43] 'Universal experience', he continues, bears testimony to the fact that 'Natural men's prudence and care to preserve their own lives, or the care of others to preserve them, don't secure 'em a moment.'[44] The natural man's sense of his own sinfulness must convince him that it is only God's interposition that keeps him out of the fires of hell.

This aspect of Edwards's thought is, however, easily exaggerated in its importance.[45] Edwards is far more interested in the experience of dependence upon God contained within the overwhelming surprise that is the accession of grace. This is everywhere in Edwards. He argues, time and time again, that men and women play no part at all in their redemption. There is not even cooperation between man and God. As he put it in the Public Lecture he gave in Boston in July 1731: 'The nature and contrivance of our redemption is such, that the redeemed are in every thing directly, immediately, and directly dependent on God: they are dependent on him for all, and are dependent on him every way.'[46] God, for Edwards, is principally experienced as an active force that can wholly remake one's self and the way one sees the world. Again, in this Edwards is radically at odds with Hobbesianism, with its *deus absconditus*, hidden behind the world he has created, and about whom we can know nothing more than the bare fact that he exists.

It is in his sense of God as a violently transformative force, as a cause of transfiguration of the self, that Edwards is most at odds with the Scottish clergymen who invoked his name in their defence of Kames against Anderson and the 'Orthodox' faction of the Church of Scotland. As we saw in the last chapter, Kames takes divine benevolence to be visible in the natural condition of man. The peroration to the *Essays on the Principles of Morality and Natural Religion* asks:

[D]o not all these wonders, O *Eternal Mind!* Sovereign Architect of all! form a hymn to thy praise? If in the dead inanimate works of nature, thou art seen; if in the verdure of the fields and the azure of the skies, the ignorant rustic admires thy creative

---

[43] Edwards (1741, 1999), p. 53.

[44] Ibid., p. 53.

[45] Elwood says that 'Today most students of American thought recognize that the famous Enfield sermon is not nearly so representative of Edwards as it is of his time' (Elwood (1960), p. 2). As Cherry notes, even in 'Sinners in the Hands of an Angry God' there is 'a stream of hope and mercy running through the exposition of the wrath of God' (Cherry (1966), p. 69).

[46] Edwards (1731, 1999), p. 202. The sermon was first preached in Northampton in the autumn of 1730.

power; how blind must that man be, who, looking into his own nature, contemplating this living structure, this moral frame, discerns not thy forming hand? What various and complicated machinery is here! and regulated with what exquisite art!

(*Freedom of the Will*, pp. 389–90)

Hutcheson, too, had claimed that divine providence manifests itself just as clearly in the moral as in the material sphere, and especially in the fact that each of us has built into his constitution principles of action necessary and sufficient for a life of virtue and happiness. In his augural lecture at Glasgow, for example, he argues that 'the benevolence of the Deity . . . is obvious from man's very constitution; since the most beneficent Father of all has . . . provided and equipped us for all that is excellent and virtuous, and indeed joyful and agreeable'.[47] Edwards, by contrast, holds that the natural condition of man is explicable only in terms of the doctrine of original sin. He devotes a dissertation to drawing a distinction between 'true virtue', on the one hand, and 'natural virtue' on the other.[48] True virtue 'consists in love to Being in general', which is to say, in love to God: 'it may be asserted in general that nothing is of the nature of true virtue, in which God is not the *first* and the *last*'.[49] Natural virtue, no matter how purely a matter of selfless generosity or 'pity', whether or not regulated and directed by conscience, is inevitably limited in scope, and focused upon one part of the system of 'Being' at the expense of other parts.[50] Edwards does not dwell upon human selfishness. His point is that a morality that extends no further than a natural concern for other human beings is not a complete morality, and certainly not one in which God makes himself manifest. Edwards shares with critics of Calvinism a desire to make moral sense of God's providence. He is not content to leave it a brute inexplicable fact that unregenerate men and women are punished for sins it is necessary that they permit. However, in continuing to conceive of true virtue as something supernatural, Edwards sets himself against, not only the Scottish Moderates, but also eighteenth-century British moral

---

[47] Hutcheson (1730, 1993), p. 147.

[48] Norman Fiering has argued that Hutcheson is Edwards's principal target in the dissertation on true virtue (see Fiering (1981), pp. 337–40). This is disputed by Paul Ramsey in his edition of Edwards's ethical writings: see Ramsey (1989), pp. 692–3, fn. 1. On the specifically American context of the dissertation, see Chamberlain (1990), pp. 242–9.

[49] Edwards (1765, 1989), pp. 541, 560.

[50] Chamberlain summarizes Edwards's view as being that 'Such affections as justice, desert, gratitude, anger and pity, although contributing to the well-being of society, fall short of truly public benevolence' (Chamberlain (1990), pp. 276–7).

philosophy considered more generally. Like John Wesley, who admired him,[51] Edwards must have seemed to many of his British contemporaries exactly what Miller claims he was not, an alien figure speaking the 'enthusiastic' language of another age.

[51] Wesley produced an edition of Edwards's *Religious Affections* in 1773. It should be said that Wesley's admiration for Edwards was not unqualified. In the brief letter to the reader that prefaces his edition of *Religious Affections*, he describes the original work as a 'dangerous heap, wherein much wholesome food is mixt with much deadly poison' (Edwards (1806), p. 3). Wesley attacks Edwards's necessitarianism in his pamphlet *Thoughts upon Necessity* (Wesley (1774)), and elsewhere openly proclaimed himself an Arminian: see Rivers (1991–2000), vol. i, pp. 213–14. However, he, like Edwards, laid great emphasis on the doctrine of original sin, and rejected altogether the Hutchesonian religion of benevolence to one's fellow men. Rivers quotes a passage from Wesley's *Journal* in which he says that Hutcheson 'is a beautiful writer, but his scheme cannot stand unless the Bible falls' (Rivers (1991–2000), vol. i, p. 230).

6

The Bare Authority of Feeling: James Beattie in Context

But, Sir, as for the doctrine of Necessity, no man believes it. If a man should give me arguments that I cannot see, though I could not answer them, should I believe that I do not see?

Johnson in conversation with Boswell, 23 June 1784

At Boston in 1770 appeared an anonymous work entitled *An Examination of the late Reverend President Edwards's Enquiry on Freedom of Will*. The author of this, the first in a long line of American replies to Edwards on the will, was James Dana, then minister of an independent church at Wallingford, Connecticut.[1] In the opening part of his *Examination*, Dana attacks the 'foundation principle' of Edwards's argument, the claim that the will is necessarily determined by the strongest motive, arguing that it begs the question as to what causes an object to appear most agreeable to the will. Edwards does not answer this question, and this means that, contrary to what he supposes, he has not shown what determines volition. The second part of the *Examination* comprises a review of the consequences of Edwards's necessitarianism: Dana is particularly keen to make it clear that Edwards must accept that God is the author of sin, and to point out the 'remarkable coincidence' between Edwards's system and those of Hume, Hobbes, Spinoza, 'or any of the old heathen Philosophers'.[2] Dana's own view is, as he puts it in the title of the book's third part, 'that *internal moral* Liberty, as distinguished from *external* or natural, belongs to moral Agency', but he proposes no positive argument for

[1] For an account of the context of Dana's attack on Edwards, see Guelzo (1989), ch. 5.
[2] Dana (1770), p. 84. In his book's Appendix Dana provides quotations '[e]xhibiting a specimen of coincidence between the principles of Mr Edwards's book, and those of antient and modern Fatalists'.

the libertarian position. He regards it as sufficient to establish that a power of self-determination is integral to our ordinary, everyday idea of moral agency. This, Dana claims, is 'self-evident'.[3] And the fact that we treat each other as possessing libertarian freedom when we praise, blame, command, exhort, promise, warn, threaten, and so on, shows, according to Dana, that even if Edwards's scheme is 'true in *theory*, it is not applicable to practice'. For so long as we are 'immediately conscious of liberty', no merely theoretical problems attaching to the doctrine of liberty provide good reasons to give the doctrine up. What Dana calls 'metaphysical reasoning' is all too likely to obscure practical subjects. 'Let a man look into his own heart, and he cannot but perceive internal freedom—*Inward freedom*—For if freedom be not in the *mind* it is no where. And liberty in the mind implies *self-determination*.'[4]

In this chapter I shall show that it is not unusual for eighteenth-century British defenders of libertarianism to regard immediate inward consciousness of a power of self-determination as sufficient proof of the falsity of the necessitarian position. This inward consciousness is sometimes characterized in moral terms: in the first instance, it is direct awareness of it having been possible for one not to have chosen to do the wrong thing. Consciousness of liberty manifests itself also in our normal and untutored reactions to the actions of others: when we respond to others as moral agents, so the claim goes, we are aware of reacting to them as if they have a power of self-determination. What we will be concerned with here is the idea that the vivacity of this sense of freedom overcomes all speculative or 'metaphysical' difficulties with the concept of self-determination, and establishes the reality of liberty even while one might not be able to answer every problem the necessitarian puts in the libertarian's way. The doctrine of necessity is shown to be false, so it is often said, simply in so far as it is not possible to act upon it, simply in so far as one cannot be a *practical* necessitarian. Dr Johnson's most famous contribution to philosophy is his purported refutation of Berkeley's immaterialism. Equally notable is his dismissal of the problem of liberty and necessity: 'Sir', Boswell reports him saying, 'we *know* our will is free, and *there's* an end on't.'[5] And again: 'All theory is against the freedom of the will; all experience for it.'[6] Johnson, of course, fails utterly in his answer to Berkeley; but several of his more philosophically sophisticated contemporaries— Butler, Berkeley himself, and Richard Price—adopt a similar approach to

---

[3] Dana (1770), p. 89.   [4] Ibid., p. v.   [5] Boswell (1791, 1934–50), vol. ii, p. 82.
[6] Ibid., vol. iii, p. 291.

the free will problem. A willingness to take the evidence of consciousness at face value, and to accept the reality of a capacity for self-determination as a basic principle which neither needs nor can have reasoned support, is characteristic also of the Scottish philosophers of common sense. Reid, the most sophisticated exponent of the common sense philosophy, is the subject of Chapter 8; Dugald Stewart, Reid's disciple, will be discussed in Chapter 9. Here I shall briefly discuss James Oswald and James Balfour, and then turn to James Beattie, a philosopher who, though now known principally for having been called by Hume a 'bigotted silly Fellow', was extremely popular in his day.[7]

Butler, Berkeley, Price, Oswald, Balfour

Joseph Butler discusses the question of liberty and necessity in Chapter 6 of the *Analogy of Religion* (1736). The discussion is rather oblique. The *Analogy* as a whole is designed to show that the arguments that a deist accepts as proof of the tenets of natural religion are sufficient also to establish the religion revealed to Christians in the Bible; and Butler's principal purpose in Chapter 6 is to prove that, even if the doctrine of necessity is supposed true, it is reconcilable with revealed religion. Even if we are subject to necessity, he argues, still it is a manifest fact that we are rewarded and punished by our fellow men, and it is therefore possible that we will be rewarded or punished by God in the life to come. But this is also to say, according to Butler, that even if in fact we are necessitated in our actions, 'the analogy of nature shows us that the opinion of Necessity, considered as practical, is false'.[8] Butler assumes that a necessitarian is one who believes that, 'since he cannot possibly behave otherwise than he does, he is not a subject of blame or commendation, nor can he deserve to be rewarded or punished'. A child brought up to believe this of himself would soon find that others held him accountable for his actions, and reproach and punishment would, in the end, convince him that there must be something wrong with the system he had been educated into. The practical falsity of necessitarianism would reveal itself in other ways too, as the child learned that it is absurd to infer from the

---

[7] Hume's dismissal of Beattie is in a letter to his printer, William Strahan: see Hume (1732), vol. i, p. 301.

[8] Butler (1736, 1897), vol. i, p. 159.

fact that one is 'fated' to die at a particular time that no care needs to be taken in preserving one's life. It is plain, therefore, that

> though it were admitted that this opinion of Necessity were speculatively true, yet, with regard to practice, it is as if it were false, so far as our experience reaches; that is, to the whole of our present life. For the constitution of the present world, and the condition in which we are actually placed, is as if we are free. And it may perhaps justly be concluded that since the whole process of action, through every step of it, suspense, deliberating, inclining one way, determining, and at last doing as we determine, is as if we were free, therefore we are so.[9]

Butler does not take this last suggestion any further. He admits later in the chapter that 'the doctrine of Liberty, though we experience its truth, may be perplexed with difficulties which run up into the most abstruse of all speculations';[10] and he nowhere addresses the free will question directly. Butler appears uninterested in purely speculative questions. As J. B. Schneewind has noted, it is no coincidence that Butler's principal contribution to moral philosophy is made in a series of sermons.[11] His concerns are first and foremost practical ones. 'Knowledge is not our proper happiness', Butler claims in the fifteenth of the sermons preached at the Rolls Chapel; 'Our province is virtue and religion, life and manners; the science of improving the temper, and making the heart better.'[12]

A similar insouciance about the difficulties attaching to speculative vindication of the doctrine of liberty is to be found in Berkeley's *Alciphron* (1732). Late in the dialogue, Berkeley has Alciphron, the 'minute philosopher' whose principal objection to Christianity is that its doctrines are contrary to reason, argue that the Christian religion supposes accountability, that accountability supposes human liberty, and that human liberty is 'a thing impossible'.[13] Introspection proves that judgments of the understanding necessarily determine the will, Alciphron claims; also, the prescience of God entails that we lack freedom, since 'what is certain is necessary'.[14] Euphranor replies, first, that there is nothing in mere certainty as such that implies constraint or is any way inconsistent with our responsibility for our actions. Then he makes the characteristically Berkeleyan move of claiming that the vocabulary in which Alciphron has made out his case for necessity—the vocabulary of 'actions of the mind', such as mind, judgment,

---

[9] Butler (1736, 1897), vol. i, p. 145.   [10] Ibid., p. 149.   [11] Schneewind (1998), p. 342.
[12] Butler (1726, 1897), vol. ii, pp. 270, 272–3.   [13] Berkeley (1732, 1950), vol. iii, p. 309.
[14] Ibid., pp. 311, 312.

and will, and of 'power, faculty, act, determination, indifference, freedom, necessity, and the like'—is a vocabulary of general terms which purport to denote distinct abstract ideas. Like his creator, Euphranor believes that there are no such things as abstract general ideas, and that mistakes in metaphysics begin as soon as general terms are introduced in place of the language of the particular and concrete. Applying this to the question of the possibility of human freedom, Euphranor replies to Alciphron much as Butler—or, indeed, Johnson—might have done. He compares those who deny human freedom to those who have thought they could show that there is no such thing as motion: 'Walking before them was thought the proper way to confute those ingenious men. It is no less evident that man is a free agent: and though, by abstracted reasonings, you should puzzle me, and seem to prove the contrary, yet, so long as I am conscious of my own actions, this inward evidence of plain fact will bear me up against all your reasonings, however subtle and refined.'[15] As for the problem of what human freedom actually amounts to, Euphranor declines to solve it. It is an 'idle' question to ask whether a man can will what he wills: 'The notions of guilt and merit, justice and reward, are in the minds of men antecedent to all metaphysical disquisitions; and, according to those received natural notions, it is not doubted that man is accountable, that he acts, and is self-determined.'[16]

We see in both Butler's *Analogy* and *Alciphron* a tendency to equate the affirmation of necessity with a denial of human accountability. In both works, the necessitarian is depicted as accepting, what most actual necessitarians were at pains to deny, that his scheme is impossible to reconcile with punishment and reward. The doctrine of necessity can therefore be refuted by, simply, the sense that all men have of being morally responsible for their actions. Later libertarians were doubtless reassured that they were justified in this characterization of the position of their opponents by the first edition of Kames's *Essays on the Principles of Morality and Religion*. Here, at last, was a patron of necessity willing to face up to the consequences of his position. And yet here also was a necessitarian who accepted that our feelings tell us that we are free and morally responsible, and who, moreover, claimed that divine providence is responsible for the deceit. Richard Price, for one, can make no sense of this paradox, complaining in a footnote to the *Review of the Principle Questions and Difficulties in Morals* (1758) that 'if, as this author [i.e., Kames] asserts, morality implies liberty, and liberty there neither is, nor can be; it follows,

---

[15] Ibid., p. 314.   [16] Ibid., p. 316.

surely, that there neither is, nor can be morality, nor consequently religion; and that the subjects of his Essays are, *the principles of what has no existence, of an impossibility*.[17] Treating 'the nature, requisites, and essentials of *practical virtue*', Price writes as if it is impossible to deny that a morally accountable being possesses libertarian freedom of will: 'Virtue supposes determination, and determination supposes a determiner; and a determiner that determines not himself, is a palpable contradiction.'[18] He asks, 'who must not *feel* the absurdity of saying, *my* volitions are produced by a *foreign* cause, that is, are not *mine*; I determine *voluntarily*, and yet *necessarily*?'[19] He declines 'to enter much further into a question, which has been so strangely darkened by fallacious reasonings, and where men are so apt to fall into a confusion of ideas'; the crucial thing, admitted even by a necessitarian such as Kames, is that 'The whole language of mankind, all their practical sentiments and schemes, and the whole frame and order of human affairs, are founded upon the notion of liberty, and are utterly inconsistent with the supposition, that nothing is made to depend on ourselves, or that our purposes and determinations are not subject to our own command, but all the result of an invincible, natural necessity.'[20] In another footnote, and possibly with Hume in mind, Price remarks that there is 'very little mysterious' in the fact of a constant conjunction of particular motives and actions, since motives bear upon actions as 'the *accounts* or *occasions* of our *putting ourselves* into motion'.[21] The distinction between 'accounts or occasions' and efficient causes is, we are given to understand, so clear as not to need either defence or explication.

At the time when Price was writing his *Review*, the groundwork was being laid at Aberdeen by Thomas Reid and George Campbell for what became known as the philosophy of common sense.[22] The first to apply the characteristic *modus operandi* of common sense philosophy to the question of liberty and necessity was James Oswald, minister at Methven, Perthshire. Oswald's *Appeal to Common Sense in Behalf of Religion*, published in two volumes, the first in 1766, the second in 1772, reads at times like an attack on philosophy itself.[23] Oswald distinguishes between 'reason' and 'reasoning', and valorizes the

---

[17] Price (1758), p. 318 fn. [18] Ibid., p. 316. [19] Ibid., p. 316.

[20] Ibid., pp. 317–18. [21] Ibid., p. 319 fn.

[22] The discussions of the Aberdeen Philosophical Society, popularly known as the 'Wise Club', were very important to the development of the philosophy of common sense: see Wood (1998a); Ulman (1990), and (for the papers Reid presented to the Society between 1758 and 1763), Reid (1764, 1997), pp. 266–315.

[23] It is hard to disagree with McCosh's opinion that making one's way through the platitudes with which the *Appeal* is replete is a 'dreary task' (McCosh (1875), p. 230). Laurie says that 'it has

former while questioning the value of the latter. He criticizes Kames for depicting belief in fundamental principles as a matter of feeling, rather than reason; but claims also that 'a too great fondness of cultivating and employing our reasoning powers', and consequent neglect of the role of perception and judgment, is 'one of the chief sources of the ignorance, the mistakes, and the follies of mankind'.[24] '[T]he modern hypothesis', according to Oswald, is that 'primary' truths are to be proved 'by trains of subtle reasoning', either through being traced back to the testimony of the senses, or through being derived from 'the axioms of the schools'.[25] One of the deleterious consequences of this hypothesis is seen in the fact that Hume and Kames, 'with several others of distinguished ability, have offered a chain of strict reasoning, in proof that man hath, in no case, a power of self-determination; but is, in all his actions, determined by what they call a moral necessity, which they affirm to be as real a necessity as any other'.[26] Oswald goes on to point out that 'The advocates of necessity have, in spite of their hypothesis, the same consciousness of good and evil desert, and do condemn or excuse themselves in much the same manner, as they would have done if they had believed themselves free agents.'[27] Here he echoes Butler, Berkeley, and Price; but Oswald does not feel obliged, as they do, to admit that there are difficulties in making sense of the possibility of libertarian freedom. Such supposed difficulties are the result of attaching too much importance to 'reasoning', which he calls in one place 'the epidemical distemper of the human mind'.[28] Writing on 'moral government', Oswald dismisses as 'nothing other than reasoning' the idea—probably he has Hartley's *Observations on Man* in mind—that God's goodness implies that he desires the happiness of each one of his creatures.[29] To suggest that a God primarily concerned with justice and punishment might be a vindictive God is to judge God by human standards of goodness, and to ignore the fact that we are frequently painfully conscious of *deserving* punishment. '[I]n proportion to the degree of common sense a man retains', Oswald writes, 'he will believe, that the supreme ruler conducts

been justly objected that Oswald's mode of treatment does not simplify, but destroys, philosophy' (Laurie (1902), p. 169).

[24] Oswald (1766), p. 26. Regarding Kames, Oswald says that he 'hath confuted Mr. Hume upon principles too near akin to his [i.e., Hume's] own' (Oswald (1766), p. 112).

[25] See Oswald (1768), p. 57.

[26] Oswald (1766), pp. 94–5.

[27] Ibid., pp. 97–8.

[28] Ibid., pp. 58–9.

[29] Oswald (1772), p. 157.

himself with propriety; and of consequence will look for his favour or displeasure, as he does good or evil; and this is all that was ever meant by moral government, or just administration.'[30] Oswald declines to define common sense: he says that his task is simply that of 'setting before the reader the primary truths of religion and morality'.[31] He is quite untroubled by the problem of distinguishing between common sense, on the one hand, and mere prejudice on the other; and it is in this that he shows himself a different kind of philosopher from Campbell and Reid, and also, as will be seen below, from Beattie too. Oswald has none of the typical Enlightenment philosopher's anxieties about the ease with which natural sentiment can be turned by miseducation or factionalism into 'enthusiasm'.[32]

Before we turn to Beattie's defence of liberty in the *Essay on Truth*, another contributor to the debate about human freedom merits acknowledgement. This is James Balfour, who was appointed Professor of Moral Philosophy at Edinburgh in 1754, and transferred to the chair of the law of nature and nations ten years later. Having written a reply to Hume's moral philosophy in 1753, he published in 1768 a collection of three 'philosophical essays', of which the third is 'Of Liberty and Necessity'. Balfour is not a self-professed philosopher of common sense, but this essay displays the Scottish philosophy's characteristic emphasis upon what 'consciousness' tells us about the powers of the mind. The belief that man is a free agent, and has 'in himself a proper principle of action', Balfour writes, 'seems naturally to arise from the consciousness of our own minds when we engage in any kind of action; and as this consciousness is immediate, and always attends us, this opinion therefore seems to have been the most common and prevailing one'.[33] Much of the essay is given over to detailed criticism of the argument that the doctrine of necessity is proven by the fact that our actions are always determined by motives. Balfour denies that motives are properly regarded as causes: a motive, he says, 'is nothing but a quality, or mode of [an active being]; and it is the being itself that acts'.[34] It is in any case not true that the

---

[30] Oswald (1772), pp. 171–2.

[31] Ibid., p. v.

[32] Gavin Ardley depicts Oswald as part of what might be called the Scottish Counter-Enlightenment: his endeavour is 'a critique of the modern world, a world then taking form under his eyes; especially in so far as that world received a pretended rationale from the then popular philosophers' (Ardley (1980), p. x). Ardley compares Oswald with Burke: Oswald, he says, 'was shocked into philosophy by the national events of his time' (p. 1). Ardley also makes the truly bizarre claim that Oswald is more 'discerning' than either Beattie or Reid (p. ix).

[33] Balfour (1768), p. 134.   [34] Ibid., pp. 145–6.

mind always acts from motives: 'immediate consciousness' tells us that when we are faced with two or more 'equipollent' motives, we are able to choose even though in a state of indifference. And our experience in such cases informs us that, even when the mind acts from a motive, it does not do so as a matter of necessity, but always retains the power to resist the motive's influence. Balfour says that 'we feel, whilst we deliberate, a secret power in the mind over the motives which may be presented to it, in virtue of which it suspends their influence; and when it yields to any of them, it is still with this consciousness, that it could have resisted them; and that therefore the mind itself is properly the agent and by no means the motive'.[35] This consciousness of not being a mere machine, Balfour continues, 'affords a stronger evidence than a thousand arguments'.[36] Balfour admits that both divine prescience and the divine decrees (i.e., predestination) create serious difficulties for belief in the reality of human liberty, but makes the standard reply that these matters exceed our understanding. 'Instead, therefore, of pursuing a subject so very difficult and abstruse', he concludes, 'it may be of much greater use and benefit to us, to consider the natural tendency and consequences of the different opinions of liberty and necessity.'[37] While we believe we are free, we will do what we can to ensure our own happiness; belief in the doctrine of necessity, on the other hand, will 'reduce us to state of total indifference and stupidity; than which nothing can be more pernicious to society as well as to the individual'.[38]

Beattie's Way with the Sceptic

James Beattie was Professor of Moral Philosophy at Marischal College, Aberdeen, from 1760 until 1796.[39] The work that made his name as a philosopher was *An Essay on the Nature and Immutability of Truth, in opposition to Sophistry and Scepticism*, published in 1770, and in its sixth edition six years later.

---

[35] Ibid., pp. 166–7.   [36] Ibid., p. 166.   [37] Ibid., p. 184.

[38] Ibid., pp. 185–6. Balfour considered the question of liberty and necessity again in his *Philosophical Dissertations*, focusing this time principally upon the arguments of Kames's *Sketches of the History of Man*: see Balfour (1782), pp. 45–70.

[39] For a good, brief account of Beattie's life and work, see Morère (1999). A much fuller account is given in Morère (1980): this is by far the most comprehensive study of Beattie and his place in eighteenth-century British thought. The best biography is Margaret Forbes (1904); for many of Beattie's letters, see Sir William Forbes (1806). Beattie (2004) is a complete collection of his letters.

Beattie's first interest had been in poetry and criticism, and in a Postscript added to the second edition of the *Essay on Truth* he admits that he has 'neither head nor heart' for the work involved in undoing the confusions and sophistries of the sceptic. 'But', he continues, 'when doctrines are published subversive of morality and religion;—doctrines, of which I perceive and have it in my power to expose the absurdity, my duty to the public forbids me to be silent; especially when I see, that, by the influence of fashion, folly, or more criminal causes, those doctrines spread wider every day, diffusing ignorance, misery, and licentiousness, where-ever they prevail.'[40] The *Essay on Truth* was born of a sense on the part of both Beattie and others in Aberdeen that the danger posed by scepticism to morality and religion was more pressing than had so far been acknowledged.[41] A book like Reid's *Inquiry into the Human Mind* was not what the situation called for: Hume had to be thoroughly and finally discredited, his reputation completely destroyed, in order to protect general confidence in what Beattie terms 'old truths'.[42]

The *Essay on Truth* began as a paper given to the Aberdeen Philosophical Society on 28 January 1766 concerning 'The difference between Common Sense, and Reason'.[43] Unlike Oswald, Beattie was not concerned to impugn

[40] Beattie (1771), p. 535. All subsequent references in this chapter to the *Essay* will be made in the main body of the text.

[41] Campbell, Alexander Gerard, and the professor of medicine (first at Aberdeen, and from 1766 at Edinburgh) John Gregory were instrumental in persuading Beattie to write and publish the *Essay*: see esp. letters from Gregory to Beattie in Sir William Forbes (1806), vol. i. See also Phillipson (1978), which argues that the *Essay on Truth* has its origins in Aberdonian worries about the corruption of Scottish morals by a newly worldly and fashionable (and Humean) Edinburgh; and, for an account of the genesis of the *Essay*, Robinson (1996a).

[42] So seriously does Beattie take the danger posed by scepticism to be that he is, in private at least, sharply critical of what he sees as excessive timidity in the writings of Campbell and Reid. In a letter to his friend, the blind poet Thomas Blacklock, about the origins of the *Essay on Truth* he distances himself from the respect which Reid's letter to Hume suggests was generally accorded the great sceptic by the members of the Aberdeen Philosophical Society: 'I could not approve', he writes, 'that extraordinary adulation which some of them paid to their arch-adversary. I could not conceive the propriety of paying compliments to a man's *heart*, at the very same time one is proving that his aim is to subvert the principles of truth, virtue, and religion; nor to his understanding, when we are charging him with the publishing the grossest and most contemptible nonsense' (Forbes (1806), vol. i, pp. 131–2). In an unpublished satire entitled, in the manner of Bunyan, 'The Castle of Scepticism', Beattie is severe in his mockery of Reid, who, though 'a person of great learning', is portrayed giving an absurdly contradictory speech about Hume, declaring, for instance, that 'His tenets obviously lead to the utter subversion of all truth, learning, and virtue: but he has always employed his greatest talents in promoting the cause of truth and the interests of mankind' (Beattie (1948), pp. 120–1).

[43] See Ulman (1990), pp. 134–5; and also pp. 38–9.

altogether the value of reasoning, but rather to limit its scope, and to show
that it is not our only means of arriving at truth. There is in addition
common sense, understood as

> that power of the mind which perceives truth, or commands belief, not by
> progressive argumentation, but by an instantaneous, instinctive, and irresistible
> impulse; derived neither from education nor from habit, but from nature; acting
> independently on our will, whenever its object is presented, according to an
> established law, and therefore properly called *Sense*; and acting in a similar manner
> upon all, or at least upon a great majority of mankind, and therefore properly called
> *Common Sense*. (*Essay on Truth*, p. 40)

Scepticism thrives where common sense, or, as Beattie sometimes calls it,
'instinct', is not given its due: where, in other words, belief is withheld
whenever a *reason* for belief is not apparent. 'The Cartesian philosophy', he
says later on, 'is to be considered as the ground-work of modern scepticism'
(*Essay on Truth*, p. 234), precisely in so far as Descartes 'reject[ed] the evidence of
sense, of intuition, and of mathematical demonstration' (*Essay on Truth*, p. 235).
The reference to mathematics is significant, since Beattie's vindication of the
distinction between reason and common sense takes the form of a proof 'by a
fair induction of particulars' that *every* form of reasoning, starting with the
most certain, rests on principles to which we assent intuitively and instinct-
ively. Mathematical axioms, Beattie points out, cannot be proved; nor do
they need to be, being 'already as evident as any thing whatsoever can be'
(*Essay on Truth*, pp. 55–6). After all, '[e]very proof must be clearer and more
evident than the thing to be proved' (*Essay on Truth*, p. 55). In areas of enquiry
where mathematical certainty is not to be hoped for, reliance on unproved
first principles is just as obvious. For example, Beattie argues that it is
impossible to give reasons why the evidence of memory should be trusted:
any argument for the reliability of memory must be an argument from past
experience, and any argument from past experience relies on the reliability of
memory. 'We trust to the evidence of memory', Beattie says, 'because we
cannot help trusting to it. The same Providence which endued us with
memory, without any care of ours, endued us also with an instinctive
propensity to believe in it, previously to all reasoning and experience' (*Essay
on Truth*, p. 93). In the same way, we cannot prove, but cannot doubt, that
every event has a cause, that the course of nature will continue in the future

to be as we have experienced it to be in the past, that 'similar causes in similar circumstances do probably produce, or will probably produce, similar effects' (*Essay on Truth*, p. 132), and that people are in general to be trusted even while we may have no prior experience of their honesty.

Particularly important as regards Beattie's approach to the question of liberty and necessity is what he says about 'the evidence of internal sense'. Natural philosophy rests upon the evidence of *external* sense, Beattie points out, and therefore upon the presupposition that our five senses can be relied upon to provide accurate information about the world around us; but scientific reasoning cannot prove the senses to be reliable, because scientific reasoning depends for its very possibility on the assumption that that is the case. The scientist who wanted to prove that he could rely on his senses before he began his experimental work would never get started. It is lucky for the scientist, then, and, of course, lucky for us all, that belief in the reliability of the senses is something that we cannot disown. Again: 'To believe our senses, is, . . . according to the law of our nature; and we are prompted to this belief, not by reason, but by instinct, or common sense' (*Essay on Truth*, p. 62). In the same way, belief in the veridicality of *internal* sense, or consciousness, is natural, and the moral philosopher should do as the natural philosopher does, which is to say, begin by feeling able to assume the reliability of his only source of information about his object of study. Hume's procedure was not to believe the evidence of internal sense: or, rather, he sought reasons why we should believe that evidence, and, finding that there are none, he (at least as Beattie reads him) recommended that we not believe, for example, in the continuing existence of an identical self. Because he refused to take the evidence of consciousness as veridical until proven otherwise, Hume also casts doubt on the deliverances of conscience. Hume asks why feelings should be taken as a guide to truth; but, Beattie complains, 'what standard of truth could he propose to me, more evident, and of higher authority, than my own feelings?' (*Essay on Truth*, p. 70). That I possess moral liberty, in the sense of being morally responsible for my actions, is what we cannot prove and cannot deny. Turning from Hume to Kames, Beattie notes that some advocates for necessity have endeavoured to prove the sense of moral liberty to be fallacious. He replies 'that if the real existence of this sense be acknowledged, it cannot be proved to be fallacious by any arguments, which may not also be applied to prove every power of nature fallacious, and, consequently, to show that man ought not believe anything at all' (*Essay on Truth*, p. 74). We shall return to the significance of this remark when discussing Reid's reply to Kames in Chapter 8. Beattie also at this point responds to an argument we will see Hartley and Priestley make in the next chapter, that we do not in fact have a sense of moral liberty at all. Beattie simply refuses to take this suggestion seriously. That we have this sense can no more be proven than can its reliability: it is obvious to all who are to any degree conscious of their feelings and beliefs.

After having considered the role of principles of common sense belief in reasoning of every kind, Beattie asks the question that we saw Oswald to have neglected, viz., 'by what criterion shall we know a sentiment of nature from a prejudice of education, a dictate of common sense from the fallacy of inveterate opinion?' (*Essay on Truth*, p. 162). '[A] full and satisfactory discussion' of this matter, he says, 'would do more real service to the philosophy of the human world, than all the systems of logic in nature; would at once exalt pneumatology to the dignity of a science, by settling it on a firm and unchangeable foundation; and would go a great way to banish sophistry from science, and rid the world of scepticism' (*Essay on Truth*, p. 163). It would not be true to say that a 'full and satisfactory' discussion is what Beattie proceeds to. Instead, he produces a long list of the ways in which Hume, as Beattie sees it, contradicts and seeks to subvert the natural and everyday beliefs upon which we proceed in both prudential and moral matters (see *Essay on Truth*, pp. 168–71). Again, Beattie contrasts Hume's mode of moral philosophy with the practices of the natural philosopher, who acknowledges that the external senses sometimes deceive, but who has means of identifying likely cases of deception from cases where natural confidence in their veridicality has no reason to be suspended. In the same way, Beattie argues, the moral philosopher should, if he is make progress in the study of the mind, trust in the ability of 'consciousness' to give us accurate information about how the mind functions. Consciousness, that is, should not be taken to be deceptive unless proven otherwise, and, in particular, should not be mistrusted just because of difficulties in finding an origin in 'impressions' for certain sentiments and beliefs. Where the feelings or sensations attended to are 'clear and definite, and such as I am, of my own accord, disposed to confide in without hesitation, as true, genuine, and natural', then they can be taken to be veridical, until there is 'positive reason to think them fallacious' (*Essay on Truth*, p. 212). If a feeling is always the same in similar circumstances; if, when acted on, the result is never hurt or inconvenience; and if it is not incompatible with feelings generated by other faculties; if experience suggests that all other men have similar feelings: if these conditions are satisfied, the feeling can be trusted. These are marks of truth, and suffice to provide reassurance of the existence of a distinction between natural belief, or common sense, on the one hand, and blind dogmatism on the other.

It is characteristic of Beattie's approach to the philosophy of mind to emphasize the importance of being able to act successfully and safely upon a putative natural feeling or sentiment. Hume himself had admitted in the Conclusion to Book I of the *Treatise* that his analysis of the mind left him paralysed, 'ready to reject all belief and reasoning', and 'utterly depriv'd of the use of every member and faculty'.[44] He had also described himself as forced into solitude, turned into 'some strange uncouth monster, who not being able to mingle and unite in society, has been expell'd all human commerce, and left utterly abandon'd and disconsolate'.[45] In order to rejoin society, and to take part in the everyday activities of common life, he had to forget all his philosophy, and to surrender to instinct at the expense of reason. Nothing makes it clearer, from Beattie's point of view, that Hume was wrong in his estimate of human nature: a true philosophy of the human mind is one that can be acted upon. If a belief is necessary to action, it can safely be regarded as true; if it cannot be acted upon, it may be taken to be deceptive. Thus, when turning to examples of candidates for the status of natural beliefs, Beattie contents himself with pointing out the practical absurdity of denying their veridicality. The two examples he focuses upon are belief that material substance exists, and belief in freedom of the will. In both cases, the absurdity manifests itself in three ways. First, to deny that matter exists or that we have freedom of choice is to set oneself against the beliefs of the vast majority of other people. Secondly, the arguments that those who deny these things put forward in support of their doubt fail to produce conviction, no matter how seriously one attends to them: even if the premises appear true, and the conclusion seems to follow from the premises, still belief in the conclusion is impossible to maintain. Thirdly, disastrous practical consequences would follow if one tried to act in the belief that matter does not exist or that the will is not free. When such are the results of denying a principle, Beattie believes, then it is reasonable to take the principle to be true, even if one cannot give arguments to support it. It will be obvious that, like Johnson and many other of his contemporaries, Beattie completely misunderstands Berkeley's immaterialism, interpreting it

---

[44] Hume (1739–40, 2000), p. 175.   [45] Ibid., p. 172.

as both a form of scepticism about the existence of an external world, and as inevitably solipsistic in tendency. Even if Berkeley did not represent himself as a sceptic, Beattie claims, 'is it not evident, from the use to which later authors have applied it, that his system leads directly to atheism and universal scepticism?' (*Essay on Truth*, p. 312).

Beattie's Reply to the Necessitarian

Like Butler and Berkeley before him, and doubtless inspired by Kames, Beattie equates the necessitarian's denial of human liberty with a denial of our responsibility for our actions. Necessitarianism is in Beattie's eyes the same thing as fatalism, and implies that there is no rationale for punishments and rewards. He claims that even those pagans who saw fate as the determinant of human affairs—Homer, Virgil, and the Stoics—tried to reconcile fate with moral responsibility, and that they therefore accept what modern necessitarians deny. This is why he feels able to say, with respect to the doctrine of necessity, that 'if any regard is to be had to the meaning of words, and if human actions may reasonably be taken for the signs of human sentiments, all mankind have, in all ages, been of a different opinion' (*Essay on Truth*, p. 347). People have also always *acted* as if they were free: for example, it is impossible, so Beattie says, to make sense of ambition, and especially the quest for power, without attributing to all men a belief in their own liberty. Again, 'all mankind distinguish between mere harm and injury', and 'this distinction is perfectly incomprehensible, except we suppose some beings to act necessarily, and others from free choice' (*Essay on Truth*, pp. 356–7).[46] We saw in Chapter 3 that Hume's case for necessity rests on the regularity and consequent predictability of human action. Hume exaggerates, Beattie claims: 'all men expect, with full assurance, that fire will burn to-morrow; but all men do not with full assurance expect, that a thief will steal tomorrow, or a miser refuse an alm to a beggar, or a debauchee commit

---

[46] Beattie returns to this theme later in the *Essay*, and devotes nearly thirty pages to a refutation of Hume's claim that there is a merely verbal distinction to be drawn between natural abilities and moral virtues (*Essay on Truth*, pp. 447–75). Beattie lists as another of the absurdities contained in the *Treatise of Human Nature* the implied claim 'That if thieves, cheats, and cutthroats, deserve to be hanged, cripples, idiots, and diseased persons, should not be permitted to live; because the imperfections of the latter, and the faults of the former, are on the very same footing, both being disapproved by those who contemplate them' (*Essay on Truth*, p. 484).

an act of intemperance, even though opportunities offer.... All general rules, that regard the influence of motives, admit of exceptions; but the general laws of matter admit of none' (*Essay on Truth*, pp. 358–9). It is true that, as Hume says, human nature has been essentially the same through the ages; but Hume's confidence that this is sufficient to establish the scheme of necessity is born of his having adopted the elevated perspective of a historian more interested in the large-scale changes in the nature of political society than in the details of everyday existence.[47] Beattie writes that 'if we come to particulars, we shall not perhaps find two human minds exactly alike. In two of the most congenial characters on earth, the same causes will not produce the same effects; nay, the same causes will not always produce the same effects even in the same character' (*Essay on Truth*, pp. 361–2). The experience of indecision and of hard choices, and of remorse after a wrong choice, should, Beattie argues, remind each of us of our tacit belief in liberty of will. It is in fact needless to insist on the universal acknowledgment of man's free agency: 'To me it is as evident, that all men believe themselves free, as that all men think. I cannot see the heart; I judge of the sentiments of others from their outward behaviour; from the highest to the lowest, as far as history and experience can carry me, I find the conduct of human beings similar in this respect to my own: and of my own free agency I have never been able to entertain the least doubt' (*Essay on Truth*, pp. 367–8).

Beattie's inability to doubt his own free agency is the focus of a second means of exposing the absurdity of necessitarianism. 'After giving the advocates for necessity a fair hearing', he reports, 'my belief is exactly the same as before. I am puzzled perhaps, but not convinced, no not in the least degree' (*Essay on Truth*, p. 369). Beattie thinks that others, even those who profess to be convinced, are in the same situation, since one would expect a genuine necessitarian to act according to his conviction; but, as has just been seen, everyone acts all the time as if they were free. Of course, as a necessitarian, you could 'admit that the instincts of your nature, the customs of the world, and the force of human laws, oblige you act like a free agent' (*Essay on Truth*, p. 371)—even though you are sure that you are really not free. But if you said that, you would be admitting that necessitarianism is 'contrary to nature and common sense', which is the very point that Beattie wants to prove. Some people are unable to reply to the arguments of the necessitarian,

---

[47] Beattie remarks in the Introduction to the *Essay*, *vis-à-vis* Hume, on the 'incongruity' of the fact '[t]hat he, who succeeds so well in describing the fates of nations, should yet have failed so egregiously in explaining the operations of the mind' (*Essay on Truth*, p. 11).

probably because deceived by dexterous conjuring with empty words; but even these people have the right to, and should, think of themselves as free regardless, since they are always also sure that the doctrine of necessity is false, 'though they cannot tell in what respect it is false' (*Essay on Truth*, p. 375). Turning to the 'dangerous consequences' of accepting the doctrine of necessity, Beattie claims that 'No genuine truth did ever of itself produce effects inconsistent with utility' (*Essay on Truth*, p. 377). What is dangerous in the doctrine of necessity is chiefly the fact that it renders impossible a vindication of the moral character of God, and therefore overturns 'the only durable foundation of human happiness' (*Essay on Truth*, p. 383). According to Beattie, this is what Hume himself infers from the doctrine of necessity at the end of the essay 'Of liberty and necessity'. The necessitarian renders incoherent the idea that God might punish some and reward others on the basis of their actions. One who believes in necessitarianism, therefore, has no reason to believe that his fate is in his own hands, and will give in to every passing whim and desire because he will believe that what he does is not up to him. He will give no heed to his conscience, being able to excuse himself for all that he does; nor will he be able to make promises, since he will say that 'my conduct tomorrow will certainly be determined by the motive that happens to predominate' (*Essay on Truth*, p. 391). Not only, then, will he ruin his chance of being accorded life after death, and consign himself to damnation; he will also cause chaos in the society in which he lives, and will in the end have to be imprisoned, or worse. The behaviour of 'the practical Fatalist' would be 'a series of adventures, more ludicrous, or at least more irrational than any of those for which the knight of La Mancha is celebrated' (*Essay on Truth*, p. 393). Thus, 'If God intended that men should be happy, and that the human race should continue for many generations, he certainly intended also that men should believe themselves free, moral, and accountable beings' (*Essay on Truth*, pp. 389–90).

Beattie does not detain himself in the *Essay on Truth* with what he terms 'a logical examination of the argument for necessity'. He urges the metaphysician 'to believe himself a free agent upon the bare authority of his feelings' (*Essay on Truth*, p. 342). 'If I have satisfied the reader, that the free agency of man is a self-evident fact', he says, 'I have also satisfied him, that all reasoning on the side of necessity, though accounted unanswerable, is, in its very nature, and previous to all confutation, absurd and irrational, and contrary to the practice and principles of all true philosophers' (*Essay on Truth*, pp. 394–5). It is in this connection that Reid and Beattie differ most strikingly in their approach to the question of liberty and necessity, for an integral part of Reid's case for liberty is a detailed, and sometimes brilliant, demolition of the usual arguments for the doctrine of necessity, and of arguments from the influence of motives in particular. It will be argued in Chapter 8 that Reid's argument against the idea that choices and actions are caused by motives has a role analogous to that played by the argument against the theory of ideas in his treatment of sensory perception. Reid's reply to scepticism is thus not restricted to a simple, fervent affirmation of 'the simple feeling of the understanding': the sceptic's arguments can be met head-on, and destroyed piece by piece. Beattie's version of the common sense philosophy is, however, identical to Reid's in so far as it refrains from attempting a direct proof of the veridicality of natural belief in liberty of will. Beattie sees as clearly as Reid does that it makes no sense to purport to provide a guarantee of the truth of principles which have been defined as basic or primary. There is, in particular, no sign that Beattie regards himself as able to appeal to the veracity of God in order to provide such a guarantee. Beattie's distinctive approach to the problem of scepticism is, as already noted, to emphasize the impossibility (apparently admitted by Hume) of sceptical *practice*. The sceptic dwells on the limitations of our cognitive faculties. Beattie replies that we are '[d]estined for action rather than know-ledge' (*Essay on Truth*, p. 430), and recommends that we be untroubled by the sceptic's worries just so long as we are able to secure happiness for ourselves. It is plainly the case that, by cultivating virtue and piety, we *are* able to win a lasting happiness, and while that is true, there is no need to be concerned about how little we know about the ultimate causes of things. The philo-sopher's best reply to scepticism is therefore to do all that can be done to strengthen the natural beliefs that are at the basis of virtue and piety, and thereby show, in a practical way, the baselessness of doubt concerning the faculties and powers of the mind.

Beattie discusses the question of liberty and necessity again in the *Elements of Moral Science* (1790–3), essentially a condensed transcript of Beattie's lecture course in moral philosophy. Two aspects of the later treatment are worth noting.[48] The first is Beattie's reiteration of the Clarkean claim that it is

---

[48] Beattie says that he will not here 'enter minutely into the question concerning liberty and necessity', principally because he has explained himself at length on the subject in the *Essay on Truth*. Most of the chapter 'Of Man's Active Powers' (152 out of 178 quarto pages) is given over to a detailed account of what are termed 'the principles of action', as divided into instincts, habits, appetites, passions or affections, and moral principles. Beattie more than once cites Reid's rather

absurd to regard *actions* as caused by motives, or as anything other than 'the work of an agent'. 'All action is the work of an agent, that is, of a being who acts; and every being who acts is the beginner of that motion which constitutes the action'; 'To ask therefore, and the question is almost as old as philosophy itself, whether man in any of his actions be a free agent, seems to be the same thing as to ask, whether man be capable of action.'[49] It is true that 'the will is determined by motives, purposes, intentions, or reasons'; but the determination is not necessary, since 'It is the will itself, or the self-determining power of the mind, that gives a motive that weight and influence whereby the will is determined: in other words, it depends on ourselves, whether we are to act from one motive, or from another.'[50] The second notable feature of the *Elements* chapter 'Of Free Agency' is Beattie's mockery of the necessitarianism of Joseph Priestley. Priestley claimed 'that nothing can be plainer than the doctrine of necessity, that it is as certain as that two and two are four: and yet he admits, that nine tenths of the generality of mankind will always disbelieve it': but if it is so plain, how is it that so many, including 'many of the acutest philosophers that have ever lived', do not believe it?[51] Priestley had admitted that, on his scheme, God is the cause of all evil and all good: but if this is so, Beattie writes, 'resentment and gratitude towards our fellow men are as unreasonable as towards the knife that wounds, or the salve that heals us; and . . . to repent of the evil I am conscious of having committed would be not only absurd but impious, because it would imply a dissatisfaction with the will of Him, who was the almighty cause of that evil, and was pleased to make me his instrument in doing it'.[52]

---

similar analysis in the third of the *Essays on the Active Powers*. Victor Cousin commented that throughout the *Elements*, Beattie 'suit Reid et le développe avec éloquence, mais sans y ajouter des vues nouvelles' (quoted in Morère (1980), p. 3).

[49] Beattie (1790–93), vol. i, pp. 196, 197.

[50] Ibid., p. 200.

[51] Ibid., p. 210.

[52] Ibid., pp. 211–12. In the *Essay* Beattie even seems prepared to countenance the idea that God cannot, in fact, foresee all human actions; after all, what is not certain cannot be foreseen as certain, and 'it implies not any reflection on the divine power, to say, that it cannot perform impossibilities' (*Essay on Truth*, p. 385). But he does not commit himself: 'That I am a free agent, I know and believe; that God foresees whatever can be foreseen, as he can do whatever can be done, I also know and believe: nor have the Fatalists ever proved, nor can they ever prove, that the one belief is inconsistent with the other' (*Essay on Truth*, pp. 386–7).

Beattie as Experimental Philosopher?

An emphasis on practical matters, and on the reinforcement of duties to self, to others, and to God, is ubiquitous in Beattie's writings. It seems to have been at the heart of his teaching as well. In the Introduction to the *Elements of Moral Science*, Beattie proclaims himself a follower of Bacon in his definition of philosophy as 'The knowledge of nature applied to practical and useful purposes'.[53] From the very beginning of his career at Marischal, he had given priority to the practical over the merely speculative, apparently condemning 'metaphysicians' such as Descartes, Malebranche, Locke, Berkeley, and Hume because their ideas could not be given practical application, and concluding his course with a reminder that 'the ultimate End of Man is Action; and that all Science which does not serve to make Men wiser and better, More profitable to themselves, Friends, and Country, is not only useless but also pernicious'.[54] Condemnations of 'metaphysics' are a prominent feature of the *Essay on Truth* as well. 'In the whole circle of human sciences, real or pretended', Beattie writes in a 'Postscript' added to the second edition of the *Essay*, 'there is not any thing to be found which I think more perfectly contemptible, than the speculative metaphysic of the moderns' (*Essay on Truth*, p. 534). Paul Wood has found reason in the combination of Beattie's hatred (this does not seem too strong a word) for 'metaphysics' with the practical orientation of both his lectures and his writings to claim that Beattie broke with the already entrenched Scottish tradition of uniting a concern for practical ethics with detailed inductive study of the anatomy of the mind. 'Beattie ... eschewed metaphysics in favour of polite letters and Addisonian moralising', Wood writes, 'and largely excluded from his purview a branch of philosophical inquiry which was central to the Scottish Enlightenment.'[55] Is this to say, then, that Beattie is

---

[53] Beattie (1790–3), vol. i, p. xi. For an account of the *Elements*, and of the circumstances surrounding its publication, see Robinson (1996b). It is a much more sober work than the *Essay on Truth*, and is rather less interesting as a result. In general, McCosh is not unfair when he writes in his article on Beattie in *The Scottish Philosophy* that 'In reading such a work as his "Moral Science," we feel as if we were walking along a road with pleasant grass and corn fields on either side, but without a turn in it, and without a rock or a stream, without a hill or a valley' (McCosh (1875), pp. 234–5).

[54] Quoted from notes taken by one of Beattie's students in 1762/3: Wood (1995), p. 121.

[55] Wood (1995), p. 129. For Wood's interpretation of Beattie, see Wood (1990); Wood (1995), pp. 119-29; Wood (1998b). As evidence for his reading, Wood quotes the following, deeply revealing passage from one of Beattie's letters: 'I wish rather to form the taste, improve the

not properly regarded as an 'experimental' reasoner, and that he has no place in a book such as this, concerned as it is with accounts of liberty and necessity that build on Locke's empirical investigation of human capacities in 'Of Power'? Is Beattie's treatment of the question of human freedom in the *Essay* just so much 'moralising', carried out with scant regard for the empirical evidence?

The first thing to say in answer to such questions is that, as should already be obvious from the account given above of Beattie's concern that moral philosophy be grounded in 'consciousness', Beattie himself would have rejected the charge that in his concern for practical matters he forsakes the project of constructing an empirically adequate account of the powers of the mind. He accepts the challenge issued by Hume in the Introduction to the *Treatise*, to replicate in moral philosophy the recent successes of natural. The appeal Beattie makes on behalf of the testimony of consciousness constitutes, in fact, a claim to the effect that Hume goes wrong in his model of what form a science of the mind should take. The task of the moral philosopher is not to look for the origins of our beliefs in sensory impressions; it is rather, and more simply, to attend to what introspection tells us is *natural* to believe, and to leave things at that. When the natural beliefs and sentiments of the mind are properly described, there will, for reasons already described, be shown to be no grounds for doubt about their veracity: for there will be seen to be no contradiction among them, they will be recognized to be beliefs that can be acted upon; they will appear steady and constant, and not erratic and fleeting; and so on. Beattie frequently criticizes Hume for failing to base his analyses upon experience. In his account of the distinction between virtue and natural ability, for example, Hume's reasoning 'is not philosophical, but metaphysical; being founded, not on fact, but on theory, and supported by ambiguous words and inaccurate experience' (*Essay on Truth*, p. 458). The author of *A Treatise of Human Nature*, Beattie says, 'seems indeed to have a singular aversion to that kind of curiosity which, not satisfied with knowing the names, is industrious to discover the natures of things' (*Essay on Truth*, p. 473). Like every Scottish

manners, and establish the principles, of young men, than to make them profound metaphy-sicians; I wish in a word, not to make Humes of them, or Leibnitzes, but rather, if that were possible, Addisons' (letter to William Creech, 28 March 1789; Wood (1995), p. 126). The reference to Addison alludes to the importance Beattie attached to the cultivation of *taste* in his students (and readers); for a brief sketch of the role of taste in Beattie's conception of virtue, see Harris (2004b).

philosopher of his day, Beattie criticizes 'the love of system', and praises Bacon for having proposed 'that the appearances of nature should be carefully observed, and that, instead of facts being wrested to make them fall in with theory, theory should be cautiously inferred from facts, and from them only' (*Essay on Truth*, p. 433). One source of error, for Beattie as for Locke, is the careless use of ill-defined terms; another is the assumption that the methods of natural philosophy can be carried over to the examination of the moral realm. 'When accidental discovery, long experience, or profound investigation, are the means of advancing a science', Beattie writes, 'it is reasonable to expect, that the improvements of that science will increase with length of time' (*Essay on Truth*, p. 492). Thus in 'natural philosophy, natural history, and some parts of mathematical learning' there has been significant progress since the ancients; '[b]ut the science of human nature, being attained rather by intuition than by deep reasoning or nice experiment, must depend for its cultivation upon other causes' (*Essay on Truth*, pp. 492–3).[56]

This contrast between 'deep reasoning' and 'nice experiment' on the one hand, and 'intuition' on the other, is significant. Hume himself had worried about the fact that moral philosophy 'in collecting its experiments, ... cannot make them purposely, with premeditation', since 'this reflection and premeditation wou'd disturb the operation of my natural principles, as must render it impossible to form any just conclusion from the phænomenon'.[57] Beattie (without acknowledging the parallel) also remarks on how 'the very act of studying, discomposes our minds a little, and prevents that free play of our faculties, from which alone we can judge with accuracy of their real nature' (*Essay on Truth*, p. 157). But here there is disagreement too: while Hume says in the Introduction to the *Treatise* that he 'wou'd esteem it a strong presumption against [the philosophy he is going to unfold], were it so very easy and obvious',[58] Beattie holds that 'the facts and experiments relating to the human mind, when expressed in proper words, ought to be obvious to all' (*Essay on Truth*, p. 18). This is, presumably, a tacit rejection of the Humean project of finding a source in impressions for all of our basic beliefs. The science of human nature relies, not on experimental ingenuity and

[56] As examples of what can be done with a combination of verbal ingenuity and inattention to experience, Beattie cites Spinoza's substance monism, Berkeley's immaterialism and his doctrine of passive resistance, Locke's denial of innate ideas, and Mandeville's extraction of public benefits from private vices: see *Essay on Truth*, pp. 444–7.

[57] Hume (1739–40, 2000), p. 6.

[58] Ibid., p. 4.

profound investigation, but simply on attention to consciousness, and on accurate characterization of the normal feelings of normal people. It would be misguided, these passages appear to suggest, to take Beattie's emphasis upon the practical problem of limiting the effects on manners and morals of a fashionable scepticism as a sign that he is uninterested in the question of how to answer Hume on his own terms, as a scientist of the mind, and not just as a moralizer. Beattie at least *thinks* of himself as engaged in the same project as Reid and Campbell. Nor would Beattie have recognized there to be tension between his interest in mental anatomy, on the one hand, and his practical concerns on the other: as he sees it, a reply to the sceptic is essential to the cause of virtue and piety, and the way the sceptic should be replied to is by replacing his travesty of the mental faculties with a picture of the mind as a unified, harmonious, and active whole. When the mind is seen as it really is, the sceptic's questioning of our capacities will no longer be able to sap our confidence in our natural beliefs and instincts. This said, however, it is to be admitted that Beattie *is* obviously far less concerned with the details of theoretical moral philosophy than are most of his peers, and Reid in particular. He does seem to have found precise philosophical analysis positively painful, and also a waste of time.[59]

The Success of the *Essay on Truth*

Beatie's *Essay on Truth* was an extraordinary success. Every critical review was favourable. A notice in the *Annual Register*, probably written by Edmund Burke, claims that Beattie 'has gone to the bottom of his subject, and vindicated the rights of the human understanding with such precision and sagacity, with such powers of reason and investigation, as will do him honour, when the systems he exposes will be remembered only in his refutation'.[60] Samuel Johnson declared to Boswell that Beattie had 'confuted'

---

[59] Beattie's feelings about philosophy come across very clearly in his most successful poem, *The Minstrel*, particularly where the protagonist dismisses 'ye, who snare and stupify the mind, / Sophists, of beauty, virtue, joy, the bane', and welcomes in their place 'ye might masters of the lay, / Nature's true sons, the friends of man and truth' (Book I, stanzas 41–2; Beattie (1866), p. 24). 'Would you know what ... genius is, and where it may be found?', Beattie asks in the *Essay on Truth*: 'Go to Shakespeare, to Bacon, to Montesquieu, to Rousseau; and when you have studied them, return if you can, to Hume, and Hobbes, and Malebranche, and Leibnitz, and Spinosa' (*Essay on Truth*, p. 481). See Phillipson (1978) on the emotional tenor of the *Essay on Truth*.

[60] Quoted in Robinson (1996a), pp. xxviii–xxix.

Hume.[61] The *Essay* brought praise for its author from every quarter, even from the King, and more tangible reward too, in the form of a royal pension of £200 a year, as well as an honorary doctorate from Oxford. Reynolds painted a portrait ('The Triumph of Truth') of Beattie vanquishing scepticism as represented by Hume and Voltaire.[62] The vagaries of literary fashion might explain Beattie's success in part, but surely not completely. Also needing to be taken into account, I suggest, is the widespread belief in this period that there is no need to answer on their own terms the arguments of those who would undermine natural and instinctive beliefs in, for example, liberty and moral responsibility. A faith in 'common sense' as the best possible reply to philosophical sophistry is not limited to a few Scottish opponents of Hume. Where the interests of morality and religion are felt to be in danger, there seems to have been a more general frustration with what Oswald calls 'reasoning', voiced in plain speech by such as Johnson, but also in more measured tones by writers like Dana, Butler, Berkeley, and Price. The eighteenth century's dislike of *a priori* argumentation and its confidence in experience as a guide to truth at times issue in a suspicion of philosophy as such. Beattie simply gave this distaste for 'reasoning' forceful, confident, and extended expression, thereby reassuring people that it was intellectually respectable, not mere unthinking dogmatism, to cleave to ordinary common sense, and to dismiss without taking seriously the arguments of the sceptic. What is to be trusted, before anything else, Beattie intimates, is how things feel. If it feels to you that you are free in choices and actions, then you *are* free in those things, whether or not you can answer the arguments of those who think they can show that appearances are deceptive. At a time when natural philosophy was showing that appearances very often are deceptive, this may well have been a comforting thing to be told.

---

[61] Boswell (1786, 1934–50), vol. v, p. 274.

[62] For a full account of Beattie's time in London, see his own 'London Diary' for 1773, in Beattie (1946). Oliver Goldsmith appears to have been the only dissenter: 'It very ill becomes a man of your eminence and character', he told Reynolds, 'to debase so high a genius as Voltaire before so mean a writer as Beattie. Beattie and his book will be forgotten in ten years, while Voltaire's fame will last for ever' (quoted in Morère (1980), p. 58).

7

Hartley, Tucker, Priestley

> If persons have the strength of mind not to be frightened by *names*, and be capable of attending to *things* only, the strongest objections to the doctrine of necessity will not affect them.
>
> Joseph Priestley, Preface to Collins's *Philosophical Inquiry concerning Human Liberty*

The second half of the century can appear to see the eclipse of English philosophical letters by the rise of the 'Scottish Enlightenment'. It could be taken as a sign of the ascendancy of the Scots that it was one of their number, James Beattie, and not an Englishman, who received acclaim in London for having 'confuted' the scepticism of David Hume. It is, however, not the case that philosophy in England hibernated while the Scots had their day. The version of Lockean empiricism developed by David Hartley in his *Observations on Man, His Frame, His Duty, and His Expectations* (1749) nourished a tradition of thought which challenged the fundamental assumptions of the science of the mind expounded by the Scottish philosophers of common sense. At the heart of this alternative version of the experimental approach to moral subjects was the association of ideas, and the claim that the role played by association in the workings of the mind is much more extensive than had hitherto been acknowledged. In this chapter we will be concerned first with Hartley's account of the consequences of his 'mechanistic' theory of mind for the question of liberty and necessity. We will then turn to two of the first English philosophers to be significantly influenced by Hartley: Abraham Tucker, and Joseph Priestley. Tucker's major work is his enormous and idiosyncratic *The Light of Nature Pursued* (1768–78). Tucker is an irenic and synthetic philosopher, either unaware of or untroubled by the very different theory of the mind espoused by Reid, Oswald, and Beattie. He lived a retired life, and made little impression on the contemporary philosophical scene.[1] Joseph Priestley, by contrast, was a polemicist and controversialist by nature, whose first contribution to the philosophy of mind was a vigorous attack on the common sense philosophy.[2] Unlike Tucker, Priestley was unafraid of embracing the more radical consequences of the Hartleyan philosophy. Where earlier necessitarians had sought to show that necessity is compatible with moral responsibility, Hartley and Priestley allow that it is not—and then deny that this matters.

Hartley on Association, Mechanism, and Providence

The *Observations on Man* is divided into two parts.[3] The first presents an analysis of the operations of the human mind; the second draws from that analysis conclusions concerning our duties in this life and what we can expect of the next. 'Part the First' has, in turn, two great themes: the doctrine of the association of ideas, and the doctrine of what Hartley calls 'vibrations'. In his development of the former, Hartley presents himself as building upon what 'Mr. *Locke*, and other ingenious Persons since his time' have demonstrated concerning 'the Power of Habit and Custom';[4] the doctrine of vibrations, on

[1] Tucker did not go completely without later adherents: William Paley and William Hazlitt both admired *The Light of Nature Pursued*; Hazlitt produced an abridgment in 1807. For details, see Harris (2003a), pp. xviii–xx.

[2] This was his *Examination* of 1774, which includes an attack on Beattie's treatment of liberty and necessity (pp. 166–87). In the third volume of his *Institutes of Natural and Revealed Religion*, also published in 1774, Priestley claims that the common sense philosophers have succeeded only in 'beclouding and puzzling a business, which, in the main, Mr Locke left very clear, and far advanced' (p. xxi). He expresses astonishment that they take no notice of Hartley, whose *Observations*, Priestley goes so far as to say, is 'without exception, the most valuable production of the mind of man'.

[3] In the present chapter all references to Hartley (1749) will be in the main body of the text. See Richard Allen (1999) for the best recent exposition of Hartley's thought in all its aspects; for a somewhat briefer summary, see Porter (1998), Nuovo (1999), or Harris (2002). An older but still useful account is given in Bower (1881). Hartley has tended to be of more interest to historians of psychology than to historians of philosophy: see, e.g., Boring (1929), pp. 195–202; Brett (1962), pp. 436–40; and Warren (1921), ch. III. See also Oberg (1976); Smith (1987); Sutton (1998); Part III; and Willey (1940), ch. VII.

[4] 'About Eighteen Years ago', Hartley writes in the Preface to the *Observations*, 'I was informed, that the Rev. Mr Gay, then living, asserted the Possibility of deducing all our intellectual Pleasures and Pains from Association. This put me upon considering the Power of Association' (*Observations*, Preface, p. v). Hartley is referring to Gay's 'Preliminary Dissertation. Concerning the Fundamental Principle of Virtue and Morality', first published with the 1731 English translation of King's *De Origine Mali*. It is possible that Hartley's belief that Locke places the association of

the other hand, 'is taken from the Hints concerning the Performance of Sensation and Motion, which *Sir Isaac Newton* has given at the end of his *Principia*, and in the *Questions* annexed to his *Optics*' (*Observations*, vol. i, p. 5).[5] Having proposed in an account of 'the general Laws, according to which the Sensations and Motions are performed, and our Ideas generated', Hartley proceeds to 'each of the Sensations and Motions in particular' (feeling, taste, smell, sight, hearing, sexual desire, and 'automatic' and voluntary bodily movement); then to 'the Phænomena of Ideas, or Understanding, Affection, Memory, and Imagination'; and, finally, to 'the Six Classes of intellectual Pleasures' (that is, the pleasures and pains of imagination, ambition, self-interest, sympathy, theopathy (i.e., 'the affections exerted towards God'), and the moral sense. At every stage Hartley supplements associationalist analysis with a sketch of the underlying physiological processes, and it is clear that he regards his two chief doctrines as mutually reinforcing. Nevertheless, when, at the end of the first part of the *Observations*, Hartley addresses the question of the freedom of the will, nothing seems to depend upon the doctrine of vibrations. Hartley goes out of his way to make it clear that his answer to the question holds good even 'if the Doctrine of Vibrations be rejected' (*Observations*, vol. i, p. 503). What he is principally concerned with are 'the Consequences flowing from the Doctrine of Association', and, in particular, that consequence which 'is thought by many to have a pernicious Tendency in respect of Morality and Religion': 'that of the Mechanism or Necessity of human Actions, in Opposition to what is generally termed Free-will' (*Observations*, vol. i, p. 500).[6]

Here, first, is Hartley's statement of 'my notion of the mechanism or necessity of human actions':

---

ideas at the heart of his theory of mind derives from Locke's *Some Thoughts Concerning Education*, and its discussion of the importance of the formation of the habits (see Locke (1693, 1989), e.g, pp. 121–2). For the influence of Locke's book on education on eighteenth-century thought, see Passmore (1965).

[5] Hartley alludes to Newton's hypothesis 'both that all sensation is performed, and also the limbs of animals moved in a voluntary manner, by the power and action of a certain very subtle spirit, i.e., by the vibration of this spirit, propagated by the solid capillaments of the nerves from the external organs of the senses to the brain, and from the brain into the muscles' (*Observations*, vol. i, p. 111; see Newton (1729, 1934), p. 547).

[6] In general, Hartley appears rather surer of the doctrine of association than of the doctrine of vibration: 'the Doctrine of Association', he says at one point, 'may be laid down as a certain Foundation, and a Clue to direct our further Inquiries, whatever becomes of that of Vibrations' (*Observations*, vol. i, p. 72).

By the mechanism of human actions I mean, that each action results from the previous circumstances of body and mind, in the same manner, and with the same certainty, as other effects do from their mechanical causes; so that a person cannot do indifferently either of the actions A, and its contrary a, while the previous circumstances are the same; but is under an absolute necessity of doing one of them, and that only. Agreeably to this I suppose, that by free-will is meant a power of doing either the action, A, or its contrary a; while the previous circumstances remain the same.

(Observations, vol. i, pp. 500–1)

This definition of 'free-will' amounts to the same thing as 'a power of beginning motion': such a power is also incompatible with the mechanism of the mind. But if by 'free-will' is meant merely 'the power of doing what a person desires or wills to do, of deliberating, suspending, choosing, &c. or of resisting the motives of sensuality, ambition, resentment &c.', then freedom ('under certain limitations') is compatible with mechanism, and even, so Hartley says, 'flows from it' (Observations, vol. i, p. 501). Mechanism, he goes on to say, is at odds only with a 'philosophical' understanding of liberty, and not with the 'popular and practical' sense of what it is to be free in one's actions.

Hartley thus situates himself squarely in the Hobbesian tradition, according to which the freedom that is incompatible with necessity is simply an invention of philosophers, and as such something that ordinary people with ordinary concerns have no thought of or interest in. He proceeds to three 'arguments which favour the opinion of mechanism'. The first is an argument from the fact that 'It is evident to, and allowed by all, that the actions of men proceed, in many cases, from motives' (Observations, vol. i, p. 501). Motives, moreover, 'seem to act like all other causes': that is, they influence action proportionately to their intrinsic strength, and interact with other according to their relative strength. Hartley approaches the influence of motive in inductivist manner, arguing that there is reason to think that 'where the motives are the same, the actions cannot be different; [and] where the motives are different, the actions cannot be the same'; and that the observable influence of motives is a guide to cases where motives are not detectable, either because of the 'minuteness' of the motives concerned, or 'through the inattention or ignorance of the observer' (Observations, vol. i, pp. 501–2). Hartley always characterizes motives in terms of the complex typology he has elaborated in the first part of the Observations, but his argument does not rest on that typology: no matter how you divide up motives, he says, it will still be clear to anyone who examines the matter, and who, in particular, examines himself, that motives influence action just as such 'mechanical' phenomena as 'heat, diet, or medicines' influence the state of the body. In light of the fact that what is supposed to be at issue here are the 'consequences' of the doctrine of association, it is striking that that doctrine does not seem to be doing any work in this argument from the influence of motives. The question of whether our actions are always caused by our motives in such a way as to rule out a freedom to do otherwise would seem quite independent of the question of whether the workings of the mind are governed by associative principles.

The doctrine of association is more obviously involved in the second argument Hartley gives for the mechanism of the mind. This is the argument, alluded to above, that invokes, but does not depend upon, the doctrine of vibrations as well. All human actions proceed from mechanical causes of some kind, just in so far as they proceed from muscular motion; and all muscular motions 'are either evidently of a mechanical nature, as in the automatic motions; or else have been shewn to be so in the account given of the voluntary motions' (*Observations*, vol. i, p. 503). By 'automatic' motions Hartley means, as he explains right at the start of the *Observations*, such motions as those of the heart and of the bowels, 'which arise from the mechanism of the body in an evident manner' (*Observations*, vol. i, p. iii). Voluntary motions, by contrast, are 'those which arise from ideas and affections, and which therefore are referred to the mind'. Examples given include walking, 'handling', and speaking. These are in our control, but, Hartley goes on to explain later in Part i, control is something that is learned by the human infant, and learned only by means of a complex associative process. The will, according to Hartley, is a product of early experiences of childhood, and, in particular, of accumulated experiences of pain and pleasure later to be associated with particular ideas, or states of mind: when the idea of a certain course of action comes into the mind, it will be associated with past experiences, and action will be pursued or refrained from accordingly. Later still, the movement from idea to action becomes almost immediate, as habits and dispositions are formed. This makes it seem as though control over action is natural in the sense of being something we are born with; but, so Hartley argues, there is always a mechanical process underlying and explaining what might seem not mechanical at all (see esp. *Observations*, vol. i, pp. 101–12, 256–63).

Hartley's third argument for necessity is a version of the charge that an act free in the libertarian sense of 'free' would be an act without a cause:

To suppose, that an action *A*, or its contrary *a*, can equally follow previous circumstances, that are exactly the same, appears to me the same thing, as affirming that one or both of them might start up into being without any cause; which, if admitted, appears to me to destroy the foundation of all general abstract reasoning; and particularly of that whereby the existence of the first cause is proved.

(*Observations*, vol. i, p. 503)

This is all that is said concerning the third argument. The governing assumption is clearly that a cause is to be understood as Hobbes (and Collins) understands it, as what necessitates its effect just in so far as it is sufficient for the production of that effect.[7] It will be obvious that this argument, like the argument from the influence of motives, does not depend in any way upon the truth of the doctrine of association.

In the Preface to the *Observations* Hartley tells the reader that when he began developing his theory of mind he 'was not at all aware' that the doctrine of necessity 'followed from that of Association' (p. vi). Nor, he says, did he admit the doctrine of necessity 'without the greatest Reluctance'. He does not say why he was reluctant to give up the freedom of the will. One standard libertarian objection to necessitarianism Hartley dismisses outright. We have seen that libertarians at this time set great store by a purported 'consciousness' or introspective awareness of power over decision and action. Necessitarians such as Hume and Kames admit that we do naturally feel that we are free, and then devise a means of explaining this feeling away: Hume describes the sense of freedom as a confusion born of the mind's tendency to confuse uncertainty with contingency; Kames presents it as a deception practised upon us for our own good by a benevolent God. Hartley, by contrast, simply denies that there is any such thing as an 'internal feeling' of freedom:

To prove that a man has free-will in the sense opposite to mechanism, he ought to feel, that he can do different things, while the motives remain precisely the same: and here I apprehend the internal feelings are entirely against free-will, where the motives are of a sufficient magnitude to be evident; where they are not, nothing can be proved.

(*Observations*, vol. i, p. 507)

---

[7] In light of the fact that Hartley shows himself familiar with Leibniz in the *Observations* (in connection with mind–body relations: see vol. i, pp. 110–11), and never refers to either Hobbes or Collins, it is possible that Leibniz's anti-libertarian application of the principle of sufficient reason (in, for example, the correspondence with Clarke) is Hartley's inspiration here.

Dugald Stewart claims that Hartley is the first necessitarian to refuse to accept the existence of consciousness of libertarian freedom of will.[8] Hartley as a result is able to argue that it is not true to say, as libertarians do, 'that men are perpetually imposed upon, unless they have free-will, since they think they have' (*Observations*, vol. i, p. 508).

With regard to punishment, and morality considered more generally, Hartley is rather more circumspect. His response to the charge that 'the denial of free-will destroys the distinction between virtue and vice' is that everything depends upon how virtue and vice are defined:

> If free-will be included in the definition of virtue, then there can be no virtue without free-will. But if virtue be defined obedience to the will of God, a course of action proceeding from the love of God, or from benevolence, &c. free-will is not at all necessary; since these actions may be brought about mechanically.
>
> (*Observations*, vol. i, p. 509)

In Part I of the *Observations* Hartley has presented an associationalist analysis of the genesis of the moral sense, rejecting the view that there is anything instinctual or innate about our moral sentiments, and arguing that we learn to approve and condemn actions to the extent that they further or harm the interests of others (see esp. pp. 493–9). In the first instance, we approve only what is in our own interests; but through sympathy is made possible a pure disinterested benevolence (see *Observations*, vol. i, pp. 471–85), as we come to regard the interests of others as our own. It is the thorough-going consequentialism of Hartley's understanding of the basis of the distinction between virtue and vice that entails that there is no need for an action to be freely performed to be approved of, or, indeed, disapproved of. The justice of punishment, one infers, is dependent on its conduciveness to the furtherance of the interests of the greatest possible number of people. There is, then, nothing to the moral sentiments that is incompatible with the doctrine of necessity.

But what, it might be asked, of the judgments made of human actions by God? It is in this connection that Hartley makes his boldest moves. For he appears prepared to accept that the doctrine of mechanism has the consequence that, literally speaking, God is the author of sin. Literally speaking, Hartley holds, God is the only agent in the universe: this is what it means to say that human beings do not have the power of beginning motion, and that

---

[8] See Stewart (1828), vol. ii, p. 510.

every event is wholly determined by a prior event. Therefore if God were to punish men for their sins, he would be being unjust, since he would be punishing others for what he himself is responsible for. Hartley's approach is simply to cut the hopelessly entangled knot that is the problem of evil by denying that God is an agent of punishment. God is, rather, purely benevolent, and wants, and acts to realize, the happiness of every one of his creatures.[9] No one, that is, is condemned to eternal punishment in hell.[10] 'If we suppose', Hartley writes, 'that all tends to happiness ultimately, this removes the difficulty so far as to produce acquiescence in the will of God, and thankfulness to him; and that just as much upon the system of mechanism as that of free-will' (*Observations*, vol. i, p. 509). There is a sense in which our ordinary moral judgments stand to be corrected by a more accurate view of things, in so far as we currently blame and praise as if human agents really are responsible for the good or ill that they do. Properly speaking, God does everything, and should be the only object of praise, and of blame, too, if there really is anything that he does that is blameworthy when considered in terms of the interests of the whole of creation. Even the convinced necessitarian, Hartley admits, finds it hard to stop reacting to others (and himself) in the usual way (see *Observations*, vol. i, p. 504). He finds it hard—but not impossible. In Part II of the *Observations* Hartley describes how the moral sense is gradually transformed by the opinion that God is the cause of all, as we approach the state that Hartley calls 'perfect Self-annihilation', the state of 'Resting in God as our Centre', or, more simply, of 'the pure Love of God' (see *Observations*, vol. ii, p. 281–2). The conclusion of the *Observations* taken as a whole is that the transformation of the mind that has been going on in each of us since birth, as experience and education slowly

---

[9] Correspondence between Hartley and his friend John Lister suggests that from very early on Hartley took the essence of the Christian message to be that God acts to ensure the happiness of all his creatures. 'The chief result of both Reason and Scripture as appears to me', he writes in 1735, 'is Universal Happiness in the most absolute sense ultimately'; 'I should be glad to know', he continues, what you think of Eternal Punishment' (Trigg (1938), p. 234). In 1734 the 'prayers and religious meditations' added to the fifth (1810) edition of the *Observations* cease dwelling on Hartley's sense of his own sinfulness, and focus instead on 'the all-beautiful and all wise system of the world, the system of benevolence' (Hartley (1810), vol. ii, p. 493). In the brief biography of his father added to later editions of the *Observations*, the younger David Hartley says that Hartley did not enter the Anglican ministry on account of being 'restrained by some scruples which made him reluctant to subscribe to the Thirty-nine Articles' (Hartley (1810), vol. i, p. ii). Article 17, 'Of Predestination and Election', may have been part of the problem.

[10] In fact, Hartley argues, from God's point of view 'all individuals are actually and always infinitely happy' (*Observations*, vol. II, p. 29).

mould our beliefs, sentiments, and behavioural dispositions, will carry on in the future, and that, in time, natural and moral evils will completely disappear from the face of the universe, such that 'all mankind will be made ultimately happy'.[11] Scripture, when read correctly, promises this, Hartley believes; but so does reason, that is, *experimental* reason, reason that uses an accurate account of the past and present of human nature in order to predict the future.

Not only, then, does the doctrine of association entail that of mechanism, according to Hartley, but it also shows the way to a solution of the most intractable problem of all for the necessitarian. That we have an idea that of evil, whether natural or moral, is something associationalist analysis can explain; and such analysis can also explain, or at least suggest, how the idea of evil will in time disappear, as our sentiments turn away from mortal concerns and towards what Hartley terms 'the reality and infinite value of the things of another world' (*Observations*, vol. i, p. 505). If there is, as Kames will suggest, deception inherent in the moral sense, that deception is not permanent, and can be transcended even now by those able to elevate themselves above everyday concerns. For the mind as Hartley conceives of it is essentially mutable. And if the mind is essentially mutable, then progress and improvement is possible. Hartley thus radicalizes the Lockean emphasis on the possibilities of education, expands the empire of habit to cover every aspect of the mental life, and is thereby freed from having to choose between regarding our natural sentiments as a guide to truth and depicting us as subject to deception by our maker. If it is the case *both* that necessity, or 'mechanism', is incompatible with praise and blame *and* that the moral sense has us thinking of ourselves and others as the proper subjects of praise and blame, there is an alternative to a hypothesis of divine deception, an alternative provided by the fact that the moral sense is to be regarded as a function of an intermediate stage of human development. It will be seen below that Priestley's approach to the question of liberty and necessity is shaped in its every aspect by Hartley's *Observations on Man*. But Hartley's influence on later philosophers extends beyond Priestley. Bentham and his followers dispensed with Hartley's theology, but they retained his notion of the mind as malleable and hence improvable.[12] Associationalism as developed by Hartley came to be the favoured weapon of those who could not accept

---

[11] A good account of Hartley's conception of progress is Leslie (1972).
[12] See Mandelbaum (1971), ch. 9.

the quasi-innatism of the philosophy of common sense. One could say that as the battle-lines were drawn between the 'Scottish' and the 'English' philosophies, the English side assembled under a Hartleyan banner.[13]

Tucker between Locke and Hartley

Tucker begins *The Light of Nature Pursued* with an account of the causes of human action, and argues that every action is performed in accordance with motives. He summarizes his view as being 'that each man's own satisfaction, interest, or happiness, is the primum mobile or the first spring of all his schemes and all his actions, as well rational as inconsiderate' (*Light of Nature*, vol. ii, p. 670).[14] Tucker takes his lead from Locke's notion that what prompts action is always a desire to escape from a feeling of 'uneasiness'. With Locke he stands opposed to 'your sticklers for indifferency of Will' (*Light of Nature*, vol. i, p. 61), such as King, who hold that a motive is not necessary to a particular exercise of the will. But he is careful to say that the satisfaction itself, or the relief from uneasiness, does not function as the motive for action: a motive is rather an *idea* of satisfaction to come. Therefore, even if satisfaction is, as Tucker puts it, 'always one and the same in kind', there is still room for great variety within the class of motives, since '[i]nnumerable are the ways men find at different times to satisfy themselves' (*Light of Nature*, vol. i, p. 146). Motives, then, need not be thought of as simply natural inclinations with which we are born. There are motives which 'may be termed natural, although not innate; because unavoidably fallen into by experience of those properties of affecting us, which nature has given to several sensations' (*Light of Nature*, vol. i, p. 149); but, as our ideas of satisfaction change, so also will our motives, which is to say that we are not constrained always to pursue the satisfactions of childhood. We can, as it were, educate and improve ourselves in our satisfactions. There are four general classes of motives, Tucker claims, connected with our ideas of pleasure, use, honour, and necessity. But these classes are not as distinct as they might seem. Our

---

[13] Such is the lesson of Elie Halévy's classic study of the rise of Benthamite 'philosophic radicalism': see Halévy (1928).

[14] Tucker (1840), vol. ii, p. 670. In this chapter all references to *The Light of Nature Pursued* will be in the main body of the text. Little work has been done on Tucker, but for synopses of the ideas developed in *The Light of Nature Pursued*, see Nuovo (1999b), or Harris (2003a); extracts, with an introduction, are to be found in Crimmins (1998).

notions of utility have their source in ideas of pleasure; our conceptions of honour, in notions of utility; and our understanding of necessities, including moral necessities or duties, can also be traced back through honour and utility to ideas of pleasures. Extremely sophisticated motivational dispositions, or 'passions', can thus develop, by means of 'translation', out of the permanent and ubiquitous desire for satisfaction. The account of the 'composition' of ideas, 'when they so mix, and as I may say melt together as to form one single complex idea' (*Light of Nature*, vol. i, p. 87), is clearly derived from Hartley, as is the description of the evolution of the higher pleasures out of the lower. Nevertheless, Tucker does not seem to want to advertise his debt to Hartley. He is critical of the speculations made by Hartley about the physical correlates of mental processes (see, e.g., *Light of Nature*, vol. i, pp. 28–9, 34ff, 144), believing that on Hartley's theory 'the mind remains totally inactive' (*Light of Nature*, vol. i, p. 28), and appearing to hold, as a result, that Hartley is a species of materialist.

Tucker does not commit himself to the view that motives *necessitate* our choices and actions. What prompts him to address question of the nature of human freedom is not the influence of motives as such, but rather the thought that liberty might be an obstacle in the way of believing in the existence of a 'universal Providence'.[15] Tucker says at one point in *The Light of Nature Pursued* that providence is 'a favourite topic with me' (*Light of Nature*, vol. ii, p. 311). He finds evidence of providence everywhere in both the natural and moral realms, and concludes that there is nothing whatsoever that happens by chance. It is undeniable, Tucker thinks, that everything that happens, happens because it is meant to happen. Indeed, this has always been acknowledged; but even so, Tucker notes, 'men could never be persuaded out of their liberty, nor prevailed upon to relinquish command of their own actions, a privilege they feel themselves possessed of by every day's and every moment's experience' (*Light of Nature*, vol. i, p. 539). Hence centuries of debate about freedom, foreknowledge, and fate. But there is no need to look upon the question of how there can be both providence and freedom as 'one of those mysteries which we are forced to admit though we cannot explain'

---

[15] Tucker (adopting the pseudonym Edward Search) published his chapter on 'Freewill' under the title *Freewill, Foreknowledge and Fate: A Fragment* in 1763. In this work, but not in *The Light of Nature Pursued*, there are annotations by 'Cuthbert Comment'. One of these informs the reader that the author's 'theology depends in great part upon the influence of motives: for he conceives 'tis by their intervention alone, that the government of Providence over the moral world may be explained' ([Tucker] (1763), pp. 72–3 fn).

(*Light of Nature*, vol. i, p. 540). Tucker believes that human freedom has been thought to be irreconcilable with providence because of a misunderstanding of what freedom really amounts to. Like several necessitarians before him, he intimates that the free will problem has 'more to do with words than with things' (*Light of Nature*, vol. i, p. 540). His point of departure in the definition of freedom is Locke's argument that the will, being a power, is not something that can properly be said to be free or unfree, since, as Tucker puts it, 'it would be absurd to affirm of a power that it has a power' (*Light of Nature*, vol. i, p. 541). Tucker's respect for Locke does not prevent him from finding there to be more in the idea of liberty than, simply, power to do what one desires to do: the idea also comprises 'a denial of restraint or force', Tucker claims; 'for when we say a man is free, we mean nothing else than that is there no hindrance against his doing or forbearing to what he has a mind' (*Light of Nature*, vol. i, p. 541). A careful consideration of various types of case suggests to Tucker that, *pace* Locke, there is a distinction to be drawn between liberty and power: for an agent can be free to do something but lack the power, and have the power to do something but lack the freedom. There is, however, no serious break made with what Tucker takes to be the essence of the Lockean position, the notion that 'Freedom relates to the event of our endeavours, not to the cause of them': 'For Liberty does not depend upon anything prior to the exercise of my power, but upon what would or would not stand in the way after having exerted it, and therefore is not inconsistent with any antecedent causes or dispositions of Providence influencing me to talk' (*Light of Nature*, vol. i, p. 545).

It is one of the virtues of Tucker's examination of the idea of freedom that it registers the difference between freedom of *action* and freedom of *will*. Tucker sees that 'the dispute turns, not upon our freedom to do as we will, but upon our freedom to choose out of several actions in our power' (*Light of Nature*, vol. i, p. 545). He considers two notions of freedom of will. The first, 'philosophical', conception of power over the will is a matter of the ability of an agent to determine now what will be his will at some point in the future; and in this connection Tucker can find no incongruity between liberty and 'prior causes', 'for if I do something because I had resolved upon it beforehand, and this we practise every day of our lives, the volition whereby I perform it must be acknowledged an effect of my former determination, nevertheless will be counted a free act in everybody's estimation, provided nothing hinders but that I might omit it' [i.e., if I decide to after the time of the initial resolution] (*Light of Nature*, vol. i, p. 546). The second, 'vulgar', conception of power over the will makes itself apparent in talk of conflict between various different *kinds* of will, for instance spiritual and carnal, and also in talk of an 'elective' power by means of which such conflicts are settled. Tucker refuses to take such talk seriously, on the grounds that whatever we do voluntarily we do because that is the thing we most want to do. Hard decisions are not made by a special elective faculty, but are settled when it is made clear which desire is strongest; and here, again, there is no need for choice to be isolated from prior causes. Tucker acknowledges that according to some there is a further matter to be addressed, concerning what he terms 'free Volency', or the power of an agent over any one particular volition, or of the will over itself; but he confesses himself unable to make much of such a power. Either choices are made in a state of complete indifference, or they are, in Tucker's words, 'dependent upon motives'; and if, as Tucker has argued, they are dependent upon motives, it is plain that there is no need of a power of the will over itself: 'for I never heard of anybody spinning the thread so fine as to suppose another election determining that which determines the Will' (*Light of Nature*, vol. i, p. 552). In no respect, Tucker concludes, is the idea of freedom impossible to reconcile with the doctrine of universal Providence—nor, as he also argues, with the doctrine of divine foreknowledge. Accurate philosophy is no enemy either to common sense or received philosophical wisdom. We now turn to a philosopher who positively delighted in contradicting the opinions of both the wise and the vulgar, and whose understanding of the consequences of the doctrine of necessity was unabashedly Hartleyan.

Priestley's 'Philosophical' Necessitarianism

Priestley's principal contribution to the question of liberty and necessity is *The Doctrine of Philosophical Necessity Illustrated*, added as a lengthy 'appendix' to the *Disquisitions on Matter and Spirit* of 1777, and revised for a second edition five years later.[16] Priestley defines his own position as follows:

All the *liberty*, or rather *power*, that I say a man has not, is that of *doing several things when all the previous circumstances* (including the *state of his mind*, and his *views of things*) are

---

[16] In the present chapter, references to this work will be given in the main body of the text. Little work has been done on Priestley's philosophy (as opposed to his scientific writings and theology). For a brief general account, see Stephens (1999). For a summary of Priestley's

precisely the same. What I contend for is, that, with the same state of mind (the same strength of any particular passion, for example) and the same views of things (as any particular object appearing equally desirable) he would always, voluntarily, make the same choice, and come to the same determination. For instance, if I make any particular choice to-day, I should have done the same yesterday, and shall do the same to-morrow, provided there be no change in the state of my mind respecting of the choice.

In other words, I maintain, that there is some *fixed law of nature respecting the will*, as well as the other powers of the mind, and everything else in the constitution of nature; and, consequently, that it is never determined without some real or apparent *cause*, foreign to itself, i.e. without some *motive of choice*, or that motives influence us in some definite and invariable manner: so that every volition or choice, is constantly regulated and determined by what precedes it. And this *constant* determination of the mind, according to the motives presented to it, is all that I mean by its *necessary determination*. This being admitted to be the fact, there will be a necessary connexion between all things past, present and to come, in the way of proper *cause and effect*, as much in the intellectual, as in the natural world; so that, how little soever the bulk of mankind may be apprehensive of it, or staggered by it, according to the established laws of nature, no event could have been otherwise than it *has been*, *is*, or *is to be*, and therefore all things past, present and to come, are precisely what the Author of nature really intended them to be, and has made provision for.

(*Philosophical Necessity*, pp. 7–9)

Priestley believes he can establish the truth of necessitarianism (his own term is 'necessarianism') simply by means of 'the consideration of cause and effect'.

In Section II of *The Doctrine of Philosophical Necessity*, he seeks to show that the libertarian commits himself to there being events without causes. A cause, Priestley says, 'can not be defined to be any thing, but *such previous circumstances as are constantly followed by a certain effect*; the *constancy* of the result making us conclude, that there must be a *sufficient reason* in the nature of things, why it should be produced in those circumstances' (*Philosophical Necessity*, p. 11). The cause of an event is what always immediately precedes that type of event in certain determinate circumstances. If, then, that type of event were to happen in those circumstances without its usual precedent, it would be an event without a cause. Obviously, this argument is a completely general one. It follows Hobbes in seeking to derive the doctrine of necessity simply from a

criticisms of Reid, see Sell (1979). For an account of his reply to Hume, see Popkin (1977). Harris (2001b), from which some of what follows is drawn, gives a fuller account of Priestley's argument for necessitarianism and also of his reply to Hume.

definition of 'cause'. But where Hobbes's definition of 'cause' makes no reference to the constant succession of 'previous circumstances' and 'effect', Priestley's definition is designed to identify him as a philosopher whose terms are taken from the practice of inductive science.[17] Another way of understanding Priestley's case for necessity is in terms of laws of nature. In so far as it is true that types of human action are constantly preceded by determinate types of 'previous circumstance', human actions fall under general laws. It follows that in order for it to be possible for an action to be performed without its usual precedent, with surrounding circumstances held constant, there must be a violation of a law of nature. And the libertarian, according to Priestley, is saying something more than that the laws of nature can change, or that there can at any time be instituted new regular pairings of types of event. The libertarian is saying that there are *no* laws of nature at all that apply to human actions: that in *any* situation, it is possible for something quite unprecedented to take place. Moreover, the libertarian is not going to restrict himself to asserting mere possibilities. He will say that human freedom is constantly manifesting itself in behaviour that does not fall under laws. For when it comes to the facts of the matter, either human behaviour is predictable, or it is not. If it is, Priestley has all he needs for his argument for necessity. Therefore it is going to matter to the libertarian, so Priestley is insinuating, to show that human behaviour is irregular, unpredictable, and under-determined by what motivates it.

As Priestley was well aware, this was an insinuation at which many eighteenth-century libertarians were liable to bridle. Those who write in criticism of Priestley's necessitarian argument are content to grant that human behaviour is regular, law-like, and therefore predictable. They do not follow William King and Isaac Watts in placing emphasis on the importance of the arbitrariness of at least some choices to a complete understanding of human freedom. What they contest is the claim that necessitation of choice by motive follows straightforwardly from regularity and certainty. Quite generally, they argue, even if consequence *B* has always been preceded

---

[17] According to Priestley, Hobbes was the first to distinguish 'the proper doctrine of philosophical necessity' from the fatalistic conception of predestination common to 'Mahometans', 'all the early reformers', and the Jansenists ((1782), vol. ii, pp. xxiii–xxiv). Hobbes thereby put the debate between Arminians and Calvinists on a philosophical footing. The confusion later caused by Locke's ambiguities was soon dispelled by Collins's reassuringly Hobbesian *Philosophical Inquiry concerning Human Liberty*: it was this work that converted Priestley himself to necessitarianism. Priestley produced an edition of Collins's *Inquiry* in 1790.

by circumstance *A*, there is no valid inference that *nothing but B* could ever follow *A*. Jacob Bryant speaks for all of Priestley's opponents when he says:

granting that people in the same circumstances would always act uniformly in the same manner: yet in respect to the mind and the freedom of choice, I do not see how they are at all affected. If I had full liberty to choose in one instance, I should have the same in another; and even if I were to repeat it an hundred times. You insist, that the repetition of the same act must be the effect of necessity. But if that, which I do, be the result of forecast and reason, it will at all times be an instance of my freedom in respect to election.[18]

The question is not whether my choices are influenced by motives in such a way that, given the same circumstances and motives, I always act in the same way. The question is what the nature of the influence of motives is. Do motives necessitate the will, or do they leave it at liberty?

Priestley's critics, in other words, counter his argument with the distinction between 'moral' and 'physical' necessity that, as we saw in Chapters 2 and 3, is central to the libertarianism of this period. Bryant complains to Priestley that 'you throughout make no distinction between inducement, and necessity; between inclination and force. Whenever we hesitate, deliberate, and choose, you think, we are impelled past all resistance: and from this freedom of election would infer a total want of liberty.'[19] When necessitarians represent the influence of motives 'as arising from a physical necessity, the very same with that which excites and governs the motions of the inanimate creation', Samuel Horsley writes in criticism of Priestley, 'here they confound Nature's distinctions':

A moral motive and a mechanical force are both indeed causes, and equally certain causes each of its proper effect; but they are causes in very different senses of the word, and derive their energy from the most opposite principles. Force is only another name for an *efficient* cause; it is that which impresses motion upon body, the passive recipient of a foreign impulse. A moral motive is what is more significantly called the *final* cause, and can have no influence but with a being that proposes to itself an end, chooses means, and thus *puts itself* into action.[20]

[18] Bryant (1780), p. 21.

[19] Ibid., pp. 21–2.

[20] Horsley (1811), vol. ii, p. 137. Horsley's criticism of Priestley's necessitarianism was originally published in 1778 with the title 'Providence and Free Agency'; it had been a Good Friday sermon. A reviewer for the *London Review* describes it as '[a]nother ingenious and fruitless attempt, among the many that have been made of late years, to reconcile divinity and philosophy, the wisdom of this world with that of the next' (*London Review* VII (1779), 122–3).

This is a theme developed in further responses to Priestley by both John Palmer and Richard Price. Moral necessity, Palmer insists, 'arises from the influence of motives, which, as they are not physical beings, or substances, cannot possibly act as one physical being does upon another'.[21] Price goes so far as to claim that while '[t]he views or ideas of beings may be the *account* or *occasions* of their acting; . . . it is a contradiction to make them the *mechanical efficients* of their actions'.[22]

Priestley's response is that Price is forgetting how it is that a 'philosopher'—that is, a natural philosopher—reasons:

Suppose a philosopher to be entirely ignorant of the constitution of the human mind, but to see, as Dr. Price, acknowledges, that men do, in fact, act . . . according to *motives*, would he not, as in a case of the doctrine of chances, immediately infer that there must be a *fixed cause* for this coincidence of motives and actions? Would he not say that, though he could not see into the man, the connexion was *natural* and *necessary*, because *constant*? And since the motives, in all cases, *precede* the actions, would he not naturally, i.e. according to the custom of philosophers in similar cases, say that the motive was the *cause* of the action?

(*Philosophical Necessity*, pp. 64–5)

Writing in reply to Joseph Berington's criticisms of Hartley's identical argument for necessity, Priestley says that the distinction between moral and physical causes is 'merely *verbal*' (*Philosophical Necessity*, p. 18). He elaborates in an answer to Price's claim that what 'informs and directs' the action is not the motive, but rather the mind that perceives the reasons the motive gives:

if the determination of the mind, which follows upon [the perception of reasons], be invariably *according to* that perception, I must conclude that the nature of the mind is such, as that it *could not* act otherwise, and therefore that it has no self-determination properly so called. A power manifested by no effects, must be considered as merely imaginary, it being from *effects* alone that we arrive at the knowledge of causes.[23]

The libertarian who admits that actions follow motives in a regular manner is *already* a necessitarian, according to Priestley. He tells several of his critics

---

[21] Palmer (1779), p. 45. As this quotation suggests, Palmer believes that Priestley's necessitarianism depends on his materialism. Priestley strenuously denies that this is so: see Priestley (1779), pp. 11–20.

[22] Price and Priestley (1778), p. 138.

[23] Ibid., p. 147.

that they are necessitarians without knowing it.[24] They themselves, he says, give no 'philosophical' reasons for us to think the will free. Their Clarkean insistence that motives, by their very nature, are unable to be causes, Priestley simply ignores. After all, the 'philosopher' forms his conclusions about the causes of phenomena solely on the basis of his observation of effects; and there is nothing to the observation of human behaviour to suggest that motives cannot be its cause.

In his writings on liberty and necessity, Priestley presents himself as one bringing the clarity of purely 'philosophical' reasoning to a question hitherto bedeviled by the imaginary distinctions of *a priori* metaphysics. The philosopher, he insists, reasons from observed effects to their causes, rather than in the other direction, from postulated causes to observed effects. His business is attention to experience, and he pays no attention to definitions and axioms forged in the dust and shadows of the schools. At the beginning of his *Disquisitions on Matter and Spirit*, Priestley claims that what distinguishes a *philosophical* treatment of a subject is a willingness to be guided in one's investigations by rules of reasoning 'such as are laid down by Sir Isaac Newton at the beginning of his third book of *Principia*'.[25] These rules are two in number.[26] The first is 'that we are to *admit no more causes of things than are sufficient to explain appearances*; and the second is, that *to the same effects we must, as far as possible, assign the same causes*'.[27] When it comes, then, to the question of the nature of the liberty bestowed upon a person in virtue of his possession of a faculty of will, enquiry is to be directed by these two rules. Whether or not human agents are subject to necessitation in their acts of volition is an empirical matter, to be resolved by the same style of reasoning as is used by the natural philosopher, the astronomer, and the anatomist.

Priestley's argument for necessity, however, draws attention to the fact that his interpretation of Newtonian reasoning is an idiosyncratic one. The idiosyncrasy is visible already in his translation of the first rule. Newton wrote: 'Causas rerum naturalium non plures admitti debere, quam quae *et verae sint* et earum phaenomenis explicandis sufficiant';[28] and Motte

---

[24] See, with respect to Berington and Horsley, *Philosophical Necessity*, pp. 208–9, 280–2; with respect to Price, Price and Priestley (1778), pp. 392–3; and with respect to Bryant, Priestley (1780), pp. 19–20.

[25] Priestley (1782), vol. i, p. 7.

[26] In the final version of the *Principia* there are four 'Rules of reasoning in philosophy'. But there were only two in the first edition.

[27] Priestley (1782), vol. i, p. 8.

[28] Newton (1726), p. 387; emphasis added.

translates as follows: 'We are to admit no more causes of natural things, than such as are both true and sufficient to explain their appearances.'[29] There is no reference to Newton's truth-condition in Priestley's translation. For Priestley, it seems, it goes without saying that what is sufficient to explain a phenomenon is that phenomenon's cause. There is no question as to whether what explains has the *power* or *ability* to cause the phenomenon in question. His critic John Palmer points out that Ockham's Razor might be thought to cut both ways with respect to the question of liberty and necessity. Given his emphasis on Newton's first rule, he writes, Priestley 'will then not think it improper in an advocate of liberty just to remind him, that the admission of that one principle of freedom in the human mind... will sufficiently account for all their actions, and that to seek after other causes, must, therefore, be wholly unnecessary'.[30] It does not follow from the fact that actions are not caused by motives that they have no causes at all, for a 'principle of freedom in the human mind' can account for actions just as well as motives can. 'Does it follow that because I am *myself* the cause, there is no cause?', asks Price.[31] Priestley says that to deny necessity is to admit events without causes. The libertarian says that the agent himself is the cause of action. In Berington's words: 'The truth... is, not that motives... impel or determine a man to act, but that a man from the view of the motives presented to his mind, *determines himself* to act, by the free exertion of his own innate powers.'[32]

The libertarian admits that neither the agent nor his self-determining power can explain why a particular action was chosen rather than another one. It is motives that do that kind of explanatory work. But motives are, precisely, not *agents*: they are not possessors of power, and so, the libertarian insists, they cannot be regarded as causes. Priestley's response is that the mind, considered independently of its motives, cannot be the cause of action because, considered as such, it is unable to *explain* why one determination was made rather than another.

If I ask the cause of what is called *wind*, it is a sufficient answer to say, in the first instance, that it is caused by the motion of the air, and this by its partial rarefaction, &c. &c. &c.; but if I ask why it blows *north* rather than *south*, will it be sufficient to say that *this* is caused by the motion of the air? The motion of the air being equally

---

[29] Newton (1729, 1934), p. 398.

[30] Palmer (1779), p. 36.

[31] Price and Priestley (1778), p. 136.

[32] Berington (1776), p. 166.

concerned in north and south winds, and can never be deemed an adequate cause of one of them in preference to the other.

In like manner, the self-determining power . . . can never be a sufficient cause one particular determination, in preference to another. Supposing, therefore, two determinations to be possible, and there be nothing but the mere self-determining power to decide between them, the disposition of mind and motives being all exactly equal, one of them must want a proper cause, just as much as the north or the south wind would be without a proper cause, if nothing could be assigned but the motion of the air in general, without something to determine why it should move this way rather than that.[33]

All that concerns the philosopher is what explains why *this* action was chosen rather than *that* one. There is no further question, Priestley believes, as to whether what explains an event is in fact the event's 'true' cause. In this way Priestley's economical translation of Newton's first rule allows him to move directly from the question of explanation to the identification of causes.[34]

Priestley on Consciousness and Responsibility

We have seen that Hartley broke with the necessitarian tradition by rejecting the notion of an internal feeling of liberty. Priestley does likewise. John

---

[33] Priestley (1779), p. 9–10.

[34] The libertarian reaction to Priestley's use of Newton reminds us that in eighteenth-century philosophy of science it is usual for there to be a distinction drawn between *physical* causes, on the one hand, and *efficient* causes, on the other. The scientist's business is to identify the physical causes of natural phenomena, and he does so by means of the canons of inductive reasoning. Yet physical causes are understood not to have powers of their own. While common sense may tell us that stones have the power to break windows and acids have the power to corrode metals, the truth is that all physical substances are entirely passive, and have their 'effects' on each other only by virtue of laws set up by God. The concern of the scientist is, then, the discovery of regularities in the succession of observable events, and the goal is an improved capacity on the part of human beings to predict what will succeed what in the future. What the scientist is *not* concerned with is, precisely, causal power, or efficiency. The question of why nature appears to us as it does, and whether the laws of nature might have been different from how they are, is a question for the metaphysician and the theologian. A particularly clear account of the distinction between physical and efficient causes is given by Dugald Stewart in the second volume of the *Elements of the Philosophy of the Human Mind*: see Stewart (1814), pp. 308–38. In Stewart (1805), a pamphlet written in defence of John Leslie's candidacy for the Edinburgh natural philosophy chair, Stewart argues that there was nothing novel or dangerous in Hume's claim that only constant conjunctions are *observable*. This had been said before Hume by Isaac Barrow, Clarke, Butler, Berkeley, and Peter Browne, and since Hume by Price, Reid, Adam Ferguson, and John Robison.

Palmer writes that 'if the *"phænomena of human nature"*, are to determine the question',

we must certainly include the whole of the *'phænomena'*; one of which is, that, let the actions be ever so *'definite in definite circumstances'*, [men] are still conscious of having had it in their power to determine otherwise than they actually did. This seems incontrovertible, from what they feel, in consequence of those volitions, which are of a moral nature.[35]

Here Palmer is drawing attention to the close connection between consciousness of an ability to have done otherwise and the self-directed moral attitude of remorse. Priestley is usually extremely dismissive of the former. His response is that it is incoherent to imagine that one could be 'conscious' of a *power*. One cannot be conscious of what one never did, nor of an ability to do what one never did. What one is conscious of are the motives one actually has, and Priestley denies that one ever has experience of acting against one's motives. He expects the libertarian to agree that one always acts in line with one's motives, and this concession, so Priestley believes, is equivalent to an admission of the truth of necessitarianism. Not only Palmer, but all of Priestley's critics counter his necessitarianism with a purported consciousness of liberty of will.[36] Writing in reply to Price, Priestley imagines a situation of being faced with the choice between two different kinds of fruit: all that a man can be *conscious of* in such a case, Priestley argues, is 'that nothing hinders his choosing or taking whichsoever of the fruits appears to him more desirable, or his not making any choice at all, according as the one or the other shall appear to him preferable upon the whole' (*Philosophical Necessity*, p. 58). There is therefore no deception in what consciousness tells an agent about the character of his freedom. We are conscious of all that we can be conscious of. Priestley admits that sometimes the agent will not know *which* motive prompted him to act in a certain way; but this is no evidence that the agent, rather than the motive, played the role of cause. Past experience, he thinks, justifies the belief that *some* motive was there to cause the action. For the question concerning consciousness is, again, what it is reasonable to *infer* from its deliverances. We are conscious of the contents of the mind, of our ideas, and not of the mind's powers; and we must form our conceptions of the mind's powers on the basis of experience. Criticizing those who appeal to

[35] Palmer (1780), p. 22.
[36] See Berington (1776), p. 163; Bryant (1780), p. 35; Horsley (1810), vol. iv, pp. 130–2; for Price, see, e.g., Price and Priestley (1778), p. 135.

consciousness as evidence against the hypothesis of the materiality of the mind, Priestley says we are particularly likely to be mistaken in what we infer from consciousness, because of 'the danger we are in of imagining that our knowledge of things relating to ourselves is *in the first instance*, when, in reality, it is in the *second*, or perhaps the *third* or *fourth*'.[37] At any rate, the facts of the matter regarding human liberty 'must be controverted by *argument*, and the question must not be decided by *consciousness*, or any pretended *feeling*'.[38]

Priestley's stand on the question of consciousness, however, creates a problem for him, in the form of the feeling of *remorse*. That people feel remorse for some, perhaps many, of their actions is not something Priestley can deny; and he is not willing to say that this feeling is erroneous, lest he be seen to countenance the fatalist's belief that nothing a man does is his own responsibility. 'Several persons, firmly persuaded of the truth of the doctrine of necessity, yet say, that it is not possible to *act upon it*', Priestley admits; 'and to put, what they think, a peculiarly difficult case, they ask, how it is possible for a Necessitarian to pray for the forgiveness of sin' (*Philosophical Necessity*, p. 142). 'Has not every man, who feels remorse for any evil he hath done', Palmer had asked him, 'an idea that he had it in his power not to have done it?'[39] To remove the basis for remorse is to come close to denying that one has the capacity for sin. Whatever evil is done becomes the subject of regret, rather than remorse: the evil one does is natural, rather than moral. Clearly, more than just remorse is at stake here. Moral attitudes directed at others might also be thought to lose their rationale if it is true, as Priestley has argued, that it is impossible for men to act otherwise than they do.

Priestley's first response to this worry is to deny that libertarian freedom provides any kind of foundation for morality. If remorse is felt to 'impl[y] a self-determining power', it is 'deceptive': 'The sense of *self-reproach* and *shame*, is excited by our finding that we have a disposition of mind, leading to vice, and on which motives to virtue, in particular cases, have had no influence' (*Philosophical Necessity*, p. 98). Moreover, the idea of a self-determining power 'is not at all adapted to excite any proper remorse'. He follows Hume and the later Kames in arguing that '[m]orals depend upon *inward dispositions of mind, and good or bad habits*; but this *self-determination* is a thing capable of counteracting all dispositions, and all habits, and not by means of *contrary dispositions* and

---

[37] Priestley (1782), vol. i, p. 133.

[38] Ibid., p. 137. For further discussion of consciousness from a Priestleyan point of view, see Dawson (1783), pp. 17–44.

[39] Palmer (1779), p. 10. See also Bryant (1780), p. 106.

contrary habits, but by a *power of quite another nature*' (*Philosophical Necessity*, p. 99). Quite generally, 'the doctrine of the *necessary influence of motives* upon the mind of man, makes him the proper subject of discipline, reward and punishment, praise and blame, both in the common and philosophical use of the words' (*Philosophical Necessity*, p. 97). The sense of remorse is, he says, only fully satisfied, and fully explained, where a man believes 'that his dispositions and habit of mind, *at that time* were so bad, that the vicious action was *unavoidable*' (*Philosophical Necessity*, p. 100). Consciousness of one's past badness will, in addition, cause one to try to act better in the future: it does not generate a fatalistic resignation in the face of a poor character, whereas the contingency associated by Priestley with libertarian freedom gives one no motive to try to mend one's ways in the future.

Thus far Priestley has followed the standard 'compatibilist' route, laid out by Hobbes and trodden after him by Collins, Hume, Kames, and Edwards. But things are not so simple for Priestley as they are for most of his necessitarian predecessors, because, like Hartley, he believes that, when the doctrine of necessity is properly understood, it will be seen that men are *not*, in fact, morally responsible for their actions. Priestley takes it to be a consequence of the doctrine that 'all things past, present and to come, are precisely what the Author of nature really intended them to be, and has made provision for' (*Philosophical Necessity*, p. 9). The 'real and unavoidable consequences' of the necessitarianism are, he says,

that nothing *could have been* otherwise than *it has been*, that every thing comes to pass in consequence of an established constitution of things, a constitution established by the author of nature, and, therefore, that God is to be considered as the proper and sole cause of all things, good and evil, natural and moral.

(*Philosophical Necessity*, p. 117)

Elaborating on this passage, Priestley says that while 'the bulk of mankind' 'look no farther for the causes of men's actions than to *men*', 'the philosopher considers them as necessary instruments in the hands of the first cause' (*Philosophical Necessity*, pp. 117–18). In the Dedication of *The Doctrine of Philosophical Necessity*, Priestley writes that if we accept that we are 'both *instruments* and *objects*' of God's designs, then 'we cannot but consider every *being*, and every *thing*, in a favourable light': 'Every person with whom we have any connexion is a *friend*, and every event in life is a *benefit*; while God is equally the father and friend of the whole creation' (*Philosophical Necessity*, pp. vii, x). If God is the cause of all things, then, despite appearances, all things must be good as well.

Priestley is thus not a necessitarian keen to affirm that his doctrine leaves everything as it appears to be in ordinary life. One's outlook on the world, and especially on the actions of one's fellow human beings, will change completely when one gives up on libertarian freedom. Morality as we presently know it stands to be radically transformed. As we meditate upon the central tenet of necessitarianism, the principle that God is the cause of all that happens in his creation, we will find that such passions as resentment and hatred, as well as pride and 'self-applause' will fade away and disappear, to be replaced by general love and benevolence. Priestley thus distances himself, just as Hartley does, from the Calvinist understanding of the character of necessitarianism. He writes approvingly of Edwards, but cannot quite believe that Edwards was earnest in his Calvinism. Edwards was the first Calvinist, Priestley remarks, to 'hit upon the true doctrine of *necessity*', and, surely, 'had this ingenious writer lived a little longer, and reflected upon the natural connection and tendency of his sentiments, as explained in his treatise, he could not but have seen things in a very different light'.[40] Necessitarianism, when properly understood, has none of Calvinism's gloomy consequences. It is a means of bridging, rather than widening, the divide between God and men.

[40] Priestley (1775), pp. xviii, xvi–xvii. For Priestley on the difference between 'philosophical' necessitarianism and Calvinism, see *Philosophical Necessity*, pp. 184–200. See also his preface to Collins's *Inquiry* (Priestley (1790)).

8

Science and Freedom in
Thomas Reid

This natural conviction of our acting freely, which is acknowledged by many who hold the doctrine of necessity, ought to throw the whole burden of proof upon that side: for, by this, the side of liberty has what lawyers call a *jus quæsitum*, or a right of ancient possession, which ought to stand good till it be overturned. If it cannot be proved that we always act from necessity, there is no need of arguments on the other side, to convince us that we are free agents.

Thomas Reid, *Essays on the Active Powers of the Human Mind*, Essay IV

It has often been noted that, concerning our most fundamental beliefs, Reid and Hume agree in one important respect: both hold that there is no reasoned justification of belief in, for example, the existence of an external world, the uniformity of nature, and the continuing existence of an identical self. We believe such things, according to both Reid and Hume, only because it is in our nature to do so.[1] There is, however, an important difference between how these two philosophers conceive of the naturalness of a belief. According to Hume, even a belief that is universally held must be found a source in experience, and if there is no obvious empirical origin for a belief, then Hume will look to the associative imagination, and to ways in which beliefs are sometimes produced indirectly, as a byproduct of custom

[1] Sir James Mackintosh reports having observed to Thomas Brown in 1812 that Reid and Hume 'differed more in words than in opinion'. Brown replied: 'Yes, Reid bawled out, We must believe in an outward world; but added in a whisper, We can give no reason for our belief. Hume cries out, We can give no reason for such a notion; and whispers, I own we cannot get rid of it' (Mackintosh (1836), p. 346 fn). Modern commentators who have drawn attention to what Reid and Hume have in common include Wolterstorff (1987), pp. 399–400; De Bary (2002), pp. 12–13; and Rysiew (2001), pp. 443–4.

or habit. From Reid's point of view, such explanatory stories involve precisely the kind of ungrounded speculation that the experimental philosopher has no business with. Fundamental beliefs are acquired so early that the philosopher is unable to observe the process of acquisition. The Humean appeal to processes of association is bound to be retrospective, and impossible to subject to experimental confirmation. Therefore Reid repudiates Hume's analytical ambitions, and holds that there is nothing of interest to be said about the origins of our fundamental beliefs. All we can say, according to Reid, is that if knowledge is to be possible, then there must be some principles whose truth can be taken for granted; for, as Reid puts it, 'every conclusion got by reasoning must rest with its whole weight upon first principles, as the building does upon its foundations'.[2] One of the main tasks of the philosopher of mind is to identify such principles, and to distinguish them from beliefs which are acquired from experience and education: to discover a set of beliefs that can be regarded as, in a phrase from the *Inquiry into the Human Mind on the Principles of Common Sense*, 'a part of the furniture which nature hath given to the human understanding'.[3] There are various means of identifying these beliefs. Attention to ordinary language can discover them; so can attention to facets of everyday behaviour. The most important means of access to the furniture of the mind, however, is provided by what Reid terms the 'way of reflection'. 'When the operations of the mind are exerted, we are conscious of them', Reid writes in the *Inquiry*; 'and it is in our power to attend to them, and to reflect upon them, until they become familiar objects of thought. This is the only way in which we can form just and accurate notions of these operations.'[4]

Like Kames, Beattie, and Oswald, Reid regards it as a satisfactory reply to the sceptic to show that a belief is natural in the sense of being part of the constitution of the mind. Yet Reid's way with the sceptic has another

---

[2] Reid (1785, 2002), p. 455.   [3] Reid (1764, 1997), p. 215.

[4] Ibid., p. 203. See the rest of Chapter 7 (pp. 203–18) for a distinction between the (legitimate) 'way of reflection' and the (illegitimate) 'way of analogy'. According to Reid, the mind is to be understood as something quite different from the rest of nature, and analogies drawn from natural philosophy are therefore to be avoided in the philosophy of mind. The architect of the 'way of reflection' was Descartes, whose method of doubt, however pernicious in other respects, 'naturally led him to attend more to the operations of the mind by accurate reflection, and to trust less to analogical reasoning upon this subject, than any philosopher had done before him' (p. 208). For Reid's understanding of scientific method, see Laudan (1970); Wood (1989), (1994), and (1995); Broadie (2003); and Tapper (2002). For further methodological pronouncements by Reid himself, see Essay I of Reid (1785, 2002); Reid (1989), *passim*; and Reid's criticisms of Hartley and Priestley in Reid (1995), esp. pp. 136–42.

dimension as well, one not found in these other philosophers of common sense. In addition to arguing for the naturalness of basic beliefs, Reid addresses on their own terms the arguments of those who would throw the trustworthiness of such beliefs into question. In the case of the funda- mental belief involved in sensory perception, the belief that the objects of perception are material things outside the mind, sceptical doubt is motivated by the theory of ideas, and so a large part of the *Inquiry* is devoted to showing, first, that there is no reason to think that such things as 'ideas' exist, and, secondly, that even if they did exist, they would not be able to explain smelling, tasting, hearing, touch, and seeing. With the theory of ideas discredited, Reid takes himself to have shifted the burden of proof onto the sceptic. Until the sceptic thinks of a new means of bringing the reliability of the senses into question, we have no reason to doubt that our senses provide us with information about objects external to the mind. It is important to see that this is the extent of Reid's reply to the sceptic. There is no attempt on his part to take up the sceptic's challenge of proving that the senses are reliable. Such an attempt would be incoherent, for it would involve Reid in simul- taneously claiming that certain principles are first principles and appealing to higher-order principles in order to prove those principles to be veridical. Plainly enough, if a principle is a first principle, it cannot be proved from some higher-order principle; and if it can be proved by some higher-order principle, it is not a first principle. Reid himself says that first principles do not require proof,[5] and he trenchantly criticizes what he takes to be the Cartesian fallacy of attempting to use the faculties of the mind in order to prove those same faculties to be trustworthy.[6]

My claim that Reid's reply to the sceptic consists in the first instance in a shifting back of the burden of proof is not a novel one.[7] What is not often noted, however, is the fact that Reid is as concerned with what might be

[5] See, e.g., Reid (1785, 2002), p. 41 (first principles 'require not proof, but to be placed in a proper point of view').

[6] See Reid (1785, 2002), pp. 480–1, 516–17.

[7] The case is powerfully made by De Bary (2002). Rysiew (2002) (without referring to De Bary's book) adds to this line of interpretation an argument to the effect that there is more to justify belief in first principles than a combination of their naturalness, or innateness, and the fact that there is no general reason to disbelieve them: it is rational to believe them, Rysiew's Reid believes, in light of 'the axiomatic, foundational or constitutive role they enjoy in all of our reasoning, thought and action' (p. 451). Developing a similar line of interpretation, Nicholas Wolterstorff construes Reid's way with the sceptic as a manifestation of his 'antirationalism' (see Wolterstorff (2001), pp. 185–214). 'When we have dug down to the deepest stratum of human understanding', according to Wolterstorff, '... [w]e find trust. Practical trust' (p. 213).

called practical scepticism as he is with theoretical scepticism. For Reid, as for Beattie, a reply to scepticism that focused only upon vindication of our cognitive capacities would be insufficient. Our natural, basic, fundamental beliefs stand and fall together, and among them, according to Reid is the belief 'That we have some degree of power over our actions, and the determinations of our will'.[8] To allow that belief in free will might be false, as Kames does in the first edition of the *Essays on the Principles of Morality and Natural Religion*, is to give the game away to the sceptic, for if one natural principle of belief might be untrustworthy, so might they all be. What reason could there then be, after all, to trust one fundamental principle, but not another? 'If any of our natural faculties be fallacious', Reid writes, in what is plainly an allusion to Kames's hypothesis, 'there can be no reason to trust any of them; for he that made one made all.'[9] It is vital, therefore, to the common sense reply to scepticism to show the harmoniousness of our basic beliefs, to show that they do not come into conflict with each other. It is essential, in particular, to show that Kames (and with him every other necessitarian of the period) was wrong to hold that belief in the freedom of the will is at odds with belief that every event has a cause. If it is true that a belief in power over the will is a basic and natural belief, all arguments against the truth of that belief have to be replied to before the common sense reply to the sceptic can be regarded as complete. Seen in this light, the *Essays on the Active Powers of the Human Mind* is just as important to the Reidian anti-sceptical strategy as the *Inquiry* and the *Essays on the Intellectual Powers*. Reid's discussion of the faculty of will has, in fact, exactly the same structure as his analysis of the cognitive powers of the mind. It has two principal components, which I shall describe in some detail: use of the way of reflection in order to characterize accurately the basic belief underlying human volition, and to show that that belief is not the product of education, custom, or prejudice; and a critical analysis of arguments that purport to show that belief in power over the will is false.[10]

---

[8] Reid (1785, 2002), p. 478.

[9] Reid (1788, 1969), p. 304 (iv.vi).References to this work will in this chapter be given in the main body of the text.

[10] Recently there has been a revival of interest in Reid's philosophy of action. Book-length treatments include Rowe (1991) and Yaffe (2004). See also Alvarez (2000); Duggan (1976); Harris (2001); Huoranszki (2002); Madden (1982); McDermid (1999); O'Connor (1994); Stalley (1989); Stecker (1992); Weinstock (1975). This new interest in Reidian 'agent causation' owes much to the writings of Richard Taylor and Roderick Chisholm: see, e.g., Taylor (1966) and Chisholm (1964) and (1966).

Freedom of the Will as a First Principle

Reid's first concern in the philosophy of mind is to resist simplification and reduction, and he therefore rejects the tendency of necessitarians to dissolve the distinction between, on the one hand, volitions, and, on the other, passions, appetites, and affections. According to Reid, motives and 'determinations to act or not to act' have nothing in common at all. Reid compares motives with advice: just as no one would say that advice and a decision to act on that advice are the same thing, so also no one should say that a motive and a decision to act in line with that motive are identical. There is a vital difference, then, between acts of will, and what Reid terms 'the principles of action'. Appetites, passions, and affections provide us with a variety of goals or purposes, but it is by means of the will that we choose between them. We do not, of course, choose randomly; or at least, we aim not to do so. What we aim to do is to choose rationally. The will's primary function is to bring the capacity for understanding, reflection, and judgment to bear upon our actions. This is not to say that the will simply *is* rationality used for practical purposes.[11] Reid is as careful to distinguish between volition and understanding as between volition and the various principles of action. Understanding and will are very closely tied together, in human minds in any case: acts of the understanding such as judgment and reasoning have an active element, and 'every act of the will must be accompanied by some operation of the understanding' (*Active Powers*, p. 76 (II.iii)). Nevertheless, the faculties of understanding and will 'are easily distinguished in thought'. The mental operations in which the will has the greatest and most obviously separate role are, Reid claims, '*attention, deliberation, and fixed attention, or resolution*'. When we attend to one thing rather than something else, when we make decisions about what to do, and when we resolve to do something in the future, we do something that is possible for us only because we possess a faculty of will: we exercise *control* over the mental domain, in the sense that we select from a variety of motives and attendant goals one motive as the one to act on, one goal as the one to pursue.[12] The understanding helps with this,

---

[11] I disagree, then, with Knud Haakonssen's suggestion that, according to Reid, 'power over one's will is ... the ability to judge rationally of what it is that one wills' (Haakonssen (1990), p. 45). It seems to me moreover to be simply false that Reid links willing with the power of judgment in order to 'sidestep' the issue of necessitarianism (see Haakonssen (1990), pp. 44–6; and also Weinstock (1975)).

[12] Here I follow Huoranszki (2002), pp. 531–4.

but it is not solely responsible. The understanding can provide no more than advice. It is always, as we say, up to us whether or not to take it, and this 'up to us'-ness is a function of possession of a faculty of will.

Underlying attention, deliberation, and the making of resolutions, then, is a conviction that our choices are in our power. For Reid, this is another way of saying that underlying these mental operations is the conviction that we are the causes of our choices. (Reid, for reasons that will become apparent below, holds that causes are all and only those things that act as a result of the interplay of understanding and will.) Reid seems to think that this conviction is generally held, rather than being, as one might suspect is more likely to be the case, something tacit in the sense of being *implied* by what people naturally do. Reid claims that a 'principle, which appears very early in the mind of man, is, that we are efficient causes in our deliberate and voluntary actions' (*Active Powers*, p. 269 (iv.ii)). Evidence for this claim, Reid continues, is provided by consciousness, and, in particular, by consciousness of making exertions, both mental and physical; by 'the language of all mankind'; and by ordinary human conduct.

In the previous chapter, we saw Priestley argue, in reply to libertarian talk of 'consciousness' of power over the will, that it makes no sense to talk of consciousness of a *power*. All one can be conscious of is what a power enables one to do. One cannot, that is, be conscious of an ability to have done things that, in the event, one did not do. Reid has an answer to this line of argument. In the very first chapter of the *Essays on the Active Powers*, Reid makes it clear that 'Power is not an object of any of our external senses, *nor even an object of consciousness*' (*Active Powers*, p. 5 (i.i); emphasis added). Consciousness is our means of knowing the operations of the mind, power is not an operation of the mind, and so power is not an object of consciousness. Nevertheless, according to Reid, it can be proved that we do have an idea of power over the will, for careful examination of the operations of the mind shows that we only engage in some of those operations because we *believe* ourselves to have such power. And here we have evidence, not only that Priestley is wrong to say that consciousness speaks only of actions performed in line with the strongest motives that we have, but also that it is wrong to say that all our ideas are derived from either sensation or reflection. We have a conception of power even though we never directly perceive power in either the world outside or the world within. Another consequence of the fact that we have no consciousness of power is that we may be deceived in believing that we possess it (see *Active Powers*, p. 6 (i.i)).

While consciousness, according to Reid, cannot deceive, a belief, unless it expresses a necessary truth (as is not the case with belief in power over the will), is always falsifiable in principle. For Reid, though, this is not a matter of great concern. The analysis of attention, deliberation, and resolution, and also of 'exertion', shows that belief in power over the will is so deeply embedded in the operations of the mind that it is to be regarded as, in Reid's words, 'the necessary result of our constitution' (*Active Powers*, p. 269 (IV.ii)). The belief is thus on a par with, for example, belief in the uniformity of nature, or in the existence of an external world of material bodies. It is not the kind of belief that can be, or needs to be, proven to be true.

Here, however, we meet with an interpretative problem. For having accorded belief in power over the will, or (what amounts to the same thing) belief that we are efficient causes with respect to our volitions, the status of a first principle, Reid proceeds in the essay 'Of the Liberty of Moral Agents' to give three arguments 'to prove that man is endowed with moral liberty' (*Active Powers*, p. 303 (IV.v)). 'Moral liberty' is Reid's name for the kind of freedom that control over the will gives an agent. There are other kinds of freedom, such as, for instance, the ability of an animal to do what it has an inclination to do, or the lack of impediment that allows a river to flow downhill. Moral liberty, however, 'supposes the agent to have understanding and will' (*Active Powers*, p. 259 (IV.i)), and is the kind of liberty normal adult human beings naturally believe they possess. Does Reid, then, think that in the case of this first principle, there is an argument available to show that what is naturally believed is truly believed?[13] In order to understand what Reid is doing in his arguments for moral liberty, it is helpful to look closely at Reid's discussion of first principles in the essay 'Of Judgment' in the *Essays on the Intellectual Powers*, and at the chapter 'Of first Principles in General' in particular. The governing concern of the chapter is the difficulty posed by the fact that through history philosophers have seriously disagreed about

---

[13] So argues McDermid (1999). McDermid charges Reid with violating his own strictures about the status of first principles (see p. 295); I sketch a reply on Reid's behalf in Harris (2003b), from which some of what follows is drawn. Yaffe (2004) suggests that, while first principles cannot be *proven*, they can nevertheless be *demonstrated*. 'A proof is an argument for a proposition that gives one greater epistemic reason to accept the proposition than one would have had in the absence of the argument; a demonstration is an argument for a proposition that offers premises from which the proposition is deduced' (p. 4). For Reid, according to Yaffe, the point of providing a demonstration is to convince an opponent that if he fails to grant the conclusion as much certainty as the premises, he does so on pain of irrationality. Thus, as Yaffe reads them, all three of the arguments are *ad hominem*.

what the first principles of reasoning actually are. The disagreement raises the question 'whether the differences among men about first principles can be brought to any issue?' Reid asks: 'Is there no mark or criterion, whereby first principles that are truly such, may be distinguished from those that assume the character without a just title?'[14] Priestley believed not. He held that to regard the central principles of philosophy as 'first principles' was to give up on reasoning altogether, and to appeal, simply, to the prejudices of the vulgar. Reid, we might say, wants to make it clearer than Beattie or Oswald had managed to do that such is *not* the character of an appeal to principles of common sense: that, in other words, the philosophy of common sense does not involve an abandonment of reason. Especially important in the context of the three 'arguments' for moral liberty is Reid's claim that 'although it is contrary to the nature of first principles to admit of direct or *apodictical* proof, yet there are certain ways of reasoning about them, by which those that are just and solid may be confirmed, and those that are false may be detected'.[15] The suggestion here is that there are *indirect* ways of reasoning about first principles, ways of reasoning that do not pretend to prove that first principles are true, but which show that philosophy can be brought to bear on the task of distinguishing genuine first principles from mere pretenders to that status.

These 'ways of reasoning' are five in number.[16] They are: (i) arguments *ad hominem*, which show that a certain principle stands on the same footing as principles admitted by one's opponent: thus the Cartesian sceptic is shown to be inconsistent when he exempts consciousness and reason from the scope of doubt; (ii) arguments *ad absurdum*, which show the ridiculous consequences that follow from denying the principle in question; (iii) adversion to 'the consent of ages and nations, the learned and the unlearned': this is not a simple appeal to authority, but rather an acceptance of the fact that it weakens one's belief in any theory if one finds oneself to be the only person who holds it; (iv) appeal to the early stage at which the opinion expressed by the principle enters the mind: a belief which we had before we could reason could not have been the product of instruction, and would seem as a result to be 'an immediate effect of our constitution'; and (v) illustration of the necessity of the opinion to the conduct of life: no principle which cannot sensibly be acted upon can be taken as a first principle. It is obvious that none of these ways of reasoning about a principle could hope to prove the

---

[14] Reid (1785, 2002), p. 454.   [15] Ibid., p. 463.   [16] Ibid., pp. 463–7.

principle to be true. They are merely means by which to show that it is not a 'vulgar error' or a 'prejudice'.[17] Reid's three arguments for moral liberty use combinations of these ways of reasoning to just this end.[18]

This is especially clear in the first argument, which is described by Reid himself as a consideration of 'the evidence of our having a natural conviction that we have some degree of active power', and is thus a recapitulation of and expansion upon arguments described above (*Active Powers*, p. 305 (iv.vi)). Reid says first that without such a conviction, we would have neither 'the notion of causes' nor 'the belief that every event must have a cause which had power to produce it'. This refers us back to earlier endorsements of the Humean claims that causation is not an object of sense experience and that, as a result, assent to the causal maxim cannot be derived from sensory experience either.[19] For present purposes, what is significant is that Reid is drawing the reader's attention to the fact that, because causation is not a datum of experience, 'This notion and this belief must have its origin from something in our constitution.' What he goes on to do is describe a number of 'rational operations' in which belief in our having active power is 'necessarily implied'. It is the fact that we engage in such operations that will explain our possession of 'the notion of causes' and our belief in the causal maxim. The crux of the matter, therefore, is whether the operations in question do in fact necessarily imply belief of our having active power; and to secure the claim that they do, Reid examines what, as a matter of fact, one believes when one makes voluntary exertions, deliberates about 'an action of moment', forms a resolution or purpose, plights one's faith in any promise or contract, and blames oneself for having done something. His conclusion is that one would not do any of these things unless one believed oneself to have power over the will. That belief, he infers,

must be coeval with our reason; it must be universal among men, and as necessary in the conduct of life, as those operations are.

We cannot recollect by memory when it began. It cannot be a prejudice of education, or of false philosophy. It must be a part of our constitution, or the necessary result of our constitution, and therefore the work of God.

(*Active Powers*, p. 308 (iv.vi))

---

[17] Cp. Rysiew (2002), p. 445: 'these are strategies for defending first principles as first principles, and are not intended as arguments for their truth'.

[18] For alternative interpretations of the three arguments for moral liberty, see, e.g., Lehrer (1989), ch. 14; Rowe (1991), pp. 94–121; Yaffe (2004), ch. 4.

[19] See *Active Powers*, pp. 22–32.

In this first argument for moral liberty, Reid is making most use of the fifth of the 'ways of reasoning about first principles': because belief that we have power over the will is necessary to the conduct of life, it is reasonable to take it to be a first principle that we have such power. He also employs the fourth way of reasoning: the belief appears so early in the mind that it cannot be 'the effect of reasoning, or of false reasoning',[20] and so, again, it is reasonable to take it to have the status of a first principle.

In the second argument, Reid addresses the conditions of moral responsibility, and lays it down as 'an axiom as self-evident as any in mathematics' 'That no man can be under a moral obligation to do what is impossible for him to do, or to forbear what it is impossible for him to forbear' (*Active Powers*, p. 316 (IV.vii)). The 'argument' is no more than a consideration of what some have claimed to be an exception to this principle. 'When a man, by his own fault, has disabled himself from doing his duty, his obligation, they say, remains, though he is now unable to discharge it.' Reid goes on to argue that in such cases, what the man is culpable for is only his original crime of disabling himself. The 'fundamental principles of morals', he claims, speak against the justice of punishing where the ability to do one's duty is absent. His conclusion is that there are no exceptions to what is today known as the principle of alternative possibilities. If an agent is to be accountable for a crime, it must have been possible for him not to have committed it; and in any given case this was a possibility, so Reid assumes, only if the agent possessed power over his will. 'Active power', Reid says, 'is necessarily implied in the very notion of a moral accountable being' (*Active Powers*, p. 319 (IV.vii)). Either, therefore, the necessitarian must renounce the very notion of accountability, or he must give the notion a content very different to the one the rest of us give it at present. The most that this argument could be said to show, of course, is that necessitarianism is at odds with generally accepted and deeply entrenched principles of morals. However, the strategy here seems to be that of an *argumentum ad absurdum*, dedicated to showing that one cannot deny belief in moral liberty without taking on an extremely heavy burden of consequences as a result. And a principle denial of which leads to such absurdity, Reid would appear to be suggesting, is one that has the right to be regarded as a first principle of the moral life.

The third argument, by contrast, seems to be an *argumentum ad hominem*. Necessitarians and libertarians alike will accept that man is 'capable of

---

[20] Reid (1785, 2002), p. 467.

carrying on, wisely and prudently, a system of conduct, which he has before conceived in his mind, and resolved to prosecute' (*Active Powers*, p. 321 (iv.viii)). But the necessitarian denies that such conduct shows that the agent possesses 'power over his own actions and volitions'. He holds that it demonstrates only that there is in the agent 'a certain degree of wisdom and understanding'. Reid's response is to argue 'That, if the actions and speeches of other men give us sufficient evidence that they are reasonable beings, they give us the same evidence, and the same degree of evidence, that they are free agents' (*Active Powers*, p. 324 (iv.viii)). For if the choices and decisions which go into the execution of a plan are not made by the agent himself, and are things over which he has no control, then there is no evidence left that the agent knew what he was doing. The agent could, for all that is shown by the appearances, be an automaton controlled by some other being. Reid sees that the committed necessitarian could accept the force of this argument, and assert that his fellow human beings 'may be mechanical engines for all that he knows'. The necessitarian could then say that human behaviour is evidence only of the intelligence of their divine creator. Reid counters this with a further *ad hominem* argument. What is evidence of God's intelligence is also evidence of his freedom of agency. And if design is evidence of God's power over his will, it is also evidence of human power over the will. Of course, the necessitarian could go one step further, and deny that order and purposiveness are evidence of any kind of designing intelligence. But the opponent Reid has in mind here is not one who goes that far. The third argument for moral liberty is intended to show only that the necessitarian has just as good a reason to infer power over the will from the appearance of purposive conduct as he has to infer a certain degree of wisdom and understanding. Therefore if the necessitarian accepts it to be a first principle that purposiveness is a sign of intelligence, he should by the same token take it to be a first principle that it is a sign also of moral liberty.[21]

Replies to the Necessitarian

There is reason to believe that Reid's three 'arguments' for moral liberty were conceived as responses to the case for necessitarianism made by Priestley

---

[21] The necessitarian could respond by simply denying the coherence of the notion of active power. Thus Reid's argument depends on his having vindicated the coherence of that notion.

in the *Doctrine of Philosophical Necessity Illustrated*.[22] Priestley allows there to be a natural conviction of moral liberty, but claims that it is the product of custom and the association of ideas; he denies that, properly speaking, we are morally responsible for our actions; and he allows (in fact, insists) that purposiveness is evidence of intelligent design. On the reading I have suggested, Reid at no point imagines himself to be able directly to prove Priestley wrong and himself right. The necessitarian is left able to claim that Reid has simply begged the important questions, and, in particular, the question of whether natural convictions, or principles of common sense, or first principles, are reliable as a guide to truth. Why trust natural, everyday convictions, Priestley might ask, when they are so misleading in other areas of philosophy? Reid's response to this question is, as I suggested above, best seen as comparable to his reply to scepticism about perception. Reid devotes much of the essay 'Of the Liberty of Moral Agents' to showing the untenability of the assumptions underlying various styles of necessitarian argumentation; just as, in response to the 'sceptical' arguments of Berkeley and Hume, he argues that there is no reason to think that there is a veil of ideas between the perceiver and the world of material objects. By means of a careful analysis of necessitarian argumentation, Reid wants to convince us that we have no reason to doubt the truth of the natural conviction of moral liberty, and that the burden of proof lies firmly with the necessitarian. The bulk of the essay 'Of the Liberty of Moral Agents' is given over to answers to a variety of arguments made against the doctrine of liberty. These arguments fall into five classes: (i) arguments from the incoherence, or 'inconceivability', of power over the will; (ii) arguments to the effect that moral liberty would be incompatible with the obvious influence of motives on choices and actions, and, relatedly, with the use of incentives and punishments to govern moral agents; (iii) *a priori* demonstrations of the 'impossibility' of libertarian freedom (from the principle of sufficient reason, the principle that every event has a cause, or the analogy between the deliberating mind and a pair of scales); (iv) claims that moral liberty would be dangerous to those that

---

[22] Among the Reid papers held at the University of Aberdeen is a transcription by Reid (dated 1 November 1780) of the rubric of a competition announced by 'Teyler's Theological Society' for the best answer to the question 'Wherein consists Mans reasonable Liberty; and how is it most clearly Demonstrable, that we are free Acting Beings' (see MS 2131/6/1/15). Other manuscripts strongly suggest that the essay 'Of the Liberty of Moral Agents' began as a proposed entry to this competition. However, there is no evidence that Reid did in the end submit the essay. I am very grateful to Martino Squillante for drawing my attention to these manuscripts.

possessed it; and (v) purported proofs that, as a matter of actual fact, men are not free agents (because of clashes between freedom and divine prescience, God's permission of evil, or the materiality of the mind). We have met with examples of most of these types of argument in earlier chapters. Some of them Reid takes more seriously than others. I shall begin with those he simply brushes off, and then turn to those he thinks warrant more detailed examination.

Reid says that it is generally believed by defenders of necessity that moral liberty is inconceivable and absurd. The supposed problem was first identified by Hobbes: freedom in the first instance is a matter of being able to act as we will; and so, if the will is free, it can only be in virtue of a prior act of will; and if that prior act of will is free, it can only be in virtue of another act of will; and so on in an infinite series of acts of will, which would be absurd.[23] We saw in Chapter 5 that this is Jonathan Edwards's chief argument against 'Arminian' liberty. It is an argument designed to prove that the only meaning that can be given to liberty is the ability to act voluntarily: to prove, in the terms that Hume borrows from the Schools, that 'liberty of spontaneity' is the only kind of freedom there is. Although he read Edwards fairly carefully (notes that he took from the *Inquiry* survive[24]), in the *Essays on the Active Powers* Reid makes no mention of Edwards in connection with the inconceivability argument, and, in fact, appears quite untroubled by it. He notes first that '[i]n every voluntary action, the determination of the will is the first part of the action, upon which alone the moral estimation of it depends' (*Active Powers*, p. 264 (i.i)). The question, then, is whether or not the determination of the will is a necessary consequence of the agent's constitution and circumstances. The inconceivability argument claims to be able to settle this question in the necessitarian's favour, on the grounds that no other kind of freedom than the necessitarian kind is conceivable. According to Reid, however, there is no difficulty in conceiving of an alternative to determination of choice by constitution and circumstances:

I consider the determination of the will as an effect. This effect must have a cause which had power to produce it; and the cause must either be the person himself, whose will it is, or some other being. The first is as easily conceived as the last. If the person was the cause of that determination of his own will, he was free in that

---

[23] See Hobbes (1654), p. 3 (Chappell (ed.), p. 16); cp. Locke (1690, 1975), p. 247 (II.xxi.25).
[24] The notes (MS 2131/3/II/06) are part of the Birkwood Collection of Reid manuscripts held at the University of Aberdeen.

action, and it is justly imputed to him, whether it was good or bad. But, if another being was the cause of this determination, either by producing it immediately, or by means and instruments under his direction, then the determination is the act and deed of that being, and is solely imputable to him.

(Active Powers, p. 265 (I.i))

What Reid says here does not depend upon his view that only a 'being' with a will and understanding can be a cause. The point is a very simple one. It is that there is an alternative to both the view that choices are determined by constitution and circumstances (for short: by motives) and the view that the choices can only be in our power if chosen. The alternative is that what determines, or causes, choice is the agent himself. It is disappointing that Reid does not see fit to discuss any of the problems associated with making sense of this approach to the causation of choice and action—problems that Edwards had already identified, and that still, to this day, beset the 'agent causal' theory of action.[25]

The problem with all attempted demonstrations that moral liberty is impossible, Reid argues, is that they beg the question at issue between the defender of liberty of determination and necessitarianism. Take, for example, Leibniz's deployment of the principle of sufficient reason. Reid can find no interpretation of this principle which is not either plainly false, or vacuous, or question-begging. If by 'sufficient reason' is meant 'a motive to the action sufficient to justify it to be wise and good, or at least, innocent, then it is quite plain that not every action has a sufficient reason (*Active Powers*, p. 329 (IV.ix)). If by 'sufficient reason' is meant, simply, a *cause*, then the libertarian will not contest the universal scope of the principle, but will deny that it implies the truth of necessitarianism, since he himself insists that every free action has the *agent* as its cause. If by 'sufficient reason' is meant 'something previous to the action which made it to be necessarily produced', then that every action has a sufficient reason is what the necessitarian has to prove.

Another argument that has been used to prove liberty of action to be impossible is, that it implies ' "an effect without a cause" ' (*Active Powers*, p. 332 (IV.ix)). Reid identifies this as the chief argument of 'a late zealous advocate for necessity': he means Priestley. A cause, Reid quotes Priestley saying (though without naming him), 'cannot be defined to be any thing but *such previous circumstances as are constantly followed by a certain effect*; the constancy of the

---

[25] For discussion of the problem, and a variety of 'Reidian' solutions, see, e.g., Rowe (1991), pp. 145–60; O'Connor (2000), pp. 46–9; Weinstock (1976); Yaffe (2004), pp. 150–8.

result making us conclude, that there must be a *sufficient reason*, in the nature of things, why it should be produced in those circumstances' (*Active Powers*, p. 333 (iv.ix)).[26] Reid agrees that if this is the only possible definition of cause, then to oppose the doctrine of necessity is to allow events that do not have causes. 'The matter therefore is brought to this issue, whether this be the only definition that can be given of cause?' Priestley's definition of cause is the same as Hume's, Reid observes, and therefore has all the problems that Hume's does: it makes night the cause of day, it allows that anything may be caused by anything, and it entails that we have no reason to conclude that every event must have a cause. More to the point, though, 'a definition of a cause may be given, which is not burdened with such untoward conse-quences': that is, a cause may be defined as 'a being that had power and will to produce the effect' (*Active Powers*, p. 335 (iv.ix)). As we have seen, Reid does not hold that a free action lacks a cause in this sense of 'cause'. Reid accepts that Priestley is entitled to argue that an appeal to such a distinction between types of cause is otiose, on the grounds that, as a matter of empirical fact, the same consequences invariably result from the same circumstances. But such invariability Priestley would have to *prove* to obtain. He cannot simply *assume* it, for, again, this is what is precisely what is at issue between him and the libertarian.

Eighteenth-century necessitarians like to see an analogy between the way in which choices are made and the way in which a balance behaves when weights are put in each pan. Just as a balance cannot move without weights, so also decisions cannot be made without motives; and just as a balance's movements are wholly determined by the difference between the weights, so also decisions are made by the relative strengths of motives. In Chapter 4, we saw Kames claim that 'it is involved in the very idea of the strongest motive, that it must have the strongest effect in determining the mind. This can no more be doubted of, than that, in a balance, the greatest weight must turn the scale'.[27] Kames attributes the 'real feeling of liberty' to something comparable to the oscillation that takes place before a balance comes to rest. In Chapter 5, we saw Edwards claim that 'Choice and preference can no more be in a state of indifference than motion can be in a state of rest, or than the preponderation of the scale of a balance can be in a state of equilibrium.'[28] Priestley, for his part, regards the analogy between the mind

---

[26] Compare Priestley (1782), vol. ii, p. 11   [27] Kames (1751), p. 167.
[28] Edwards (1754, 1957), p. 207.

and a weighing balance as 'obvious'.[29] The mind, he says, can no more be said to be the cause of one of its determinations than the beam of a balance can be said to be the cause of its own 'inclinations':

In the case of the beam it is immediately perceived that, bearing an equal relation to both the weights, it cannot possibly favour one of them more than the other; and it is simply on account of its bearing an equal relation to them both that it cannot do this. Now let the structure of the mind be ever so different from that of the balance, it necessarily agrees with it in this, that exclusive of motives...it bears as equal a relation to any determination, as the beam of the balance bears to any particular inclination; so that as, on account of this circumstance, the balance cannot of itself incline one way or the other, so neither, on account of the same circumstance, can the mind of itself incline, or determine, one way or the other.[30]

The beam of a balance cannot explain why it inclines as it does. Therefore it cannot be the cause of that inclination. Similarly, the mind, or, as Reid would have it, the 'person himself, whose will it is', cannot be the cause of a choice.[31] Reid's response is that this is another instance where the necessitarian begs the question (see *Active Powers*, p. 337 (IV.ix)). The analogy only works if it is assumed, first, that motives have intrinsic 'weights' or 'strengths', secondly, that they influence the mind in a purely mechanical fashion, and thirdly, that choices cannot be made without motives. The libertarian shares none of these assumptions.

'The modern advocates for the doctrine of necessity', Reid writes, 'lay the stress of their cause upon the influence of motives' (*Active Powers*, p. 283 (IV.iv)). This is born out by our examinations of the necessitarian arguments of Hume, Kames, Hartley, Tucker, and Priestley. Arguments from the influence of motives suit an age dedicated to the experimental analysis of the mind and its powers, for the bearing that our motives have upon our choices and actions is obvious to even the most superficial observer of human behaviour. If the scientific question is 'What are the causes of human choice and action?', the scientific answer, grounded in the constancy of connection between types of motives and types of actions, might plainly seem to be that motives are. I have alluded more than once in the present chapter to the fact that Reid has a distinctive account of the nature of causes, and it follows

---

[29] Priestley (1782), vol. ii, p. 65.

[30] Ibid., p. 25.

[31] Collins uses the balance analogy too: see Collins (1717), pp. 48–50. Stewart quotes Diderot saying that 'We can no more conceive a being acting without a motive, than we can one of the arms of a balance acting without a weight' (Stewart (1854–60), vol. i, p. 311).

directly from that account that a motive is, quite simply, not the kind of thing that can be a cause.[32] This doctrine bears upon his response to the claim that the influence of motives on choice and action shows that motives are the causes of choices and actions. To talk of causes, according to Reid, is to talk of *efficient* causes, of substances which have the power to make things happen, and the only conception we have of efficiency is drawn from ourselves, from the capacity we have to bring new states of affairs to pass using our powers of will and understanding. A motive, obviously enough, has neither understanding nor will, and so cannot be a cause. Motives, Reid says, 'suppose an efficient cause, and can do nothing without it' (*Active Powers*, p. 283 (IV.iv)). The same is true of putative physical, or non-mental, influences upon action. The point Reid is making is a general one: *nothing* that has neither will nor understanding can be a cause. No matter how constant the conjunction is between, say, a moving billiard ball's contact with another stationary billiard ball and movement of the stationary ball, it will always be improper to regard the moving ball as the cause of the stationary ball's movement. The scientist formulates laws to explain why billiard balls interact as they do, but to formulate laws is something very different from identifying causes.[33] Reid takes this to be the most important lesson to be found in Newton's natural philosophy, and it is a lesson he has recourse to in every aspect of his philosophy of mind. The distinction between laws and causes is a constant theme of correspondence with Kames and with James Gregory. Reid believes that it is only in a loose and improper sense that we talk of things lacking understanding and will as causes. Real causes are things that explain why the laws of nature are as they are, and the Newtonian scientist abjures all speculation about such things. Causes belong to the sphere of metaphysics, not physics—nor moral philosophy.[34]

[32] For Reid on the concept of cause, see the first of the *Essays on the Active Powers* ('Of Active Power in General'), and also the first two chapters of the essay 'Of Moral Liberty'. See also Reid (2001).

[33] Reid says something rather mysterious about the nature of motives: that a motive 'is not a thing that exists, but a thing that is conceived' (*Active Powers*, p. 283 (IV.iv)). For interpretation of this claim, see Yaffe (2004), ch. 5. It's worth noting that Reid says the same thing about laws of nature: he writes to Gregory that 'A *law of nature* can no more be an agent than can a motive. It is a thing conceived, and not a thing that exists; and therefore can neither act, nor be acted upon' (Reid (2002), p. 176).

[34] Reid writes to Kames that 'in Physicks we seek not the efficient Causes of Phenomena, but only the Rules of Laws by which they are regulated'; whether a body possesses in itself power to

Reid does not, of course, deny that motives influence our choices and actions. The question is *how* they do so. Do they influence our choices as billiard balls influence the movements of other billiard balls, or in a way that permits one to say that it is up to us what motives we act upon? This is a question that is best answered, according to Reid, by an empirical examination of human action. It cannot be settled *a priori*. At issue is whether there is, as the necessitarian claims, a law to the effect that 'every action, or change of action, in an intelligent being, is proportional to the force of motives impressed, and in the direction of that force' (*Active Powers*, p. 284 (iv.iv)).[35] If there is such a law of human nature, then there is no more reason to think that human beings have a capacity for self-determination (that is, are causes) than there is to think that material objects have. In that case, we would have to say, not that motives are causes, but that 'some other being', and not 'the person himself, whose will it is', is the cause of choice and actions. The chapter 'Of the Influence of Motives' in the essay 'Of the Liberty of Moral Agents' aims to show that human behaviour gives us no reason to think that the necessitarian's law obtains. It is important to keep in mind from the first that Reid does *not* think that what speaks most forcefully against the necessitarian and his law is the prevalence of random, unpredictable actions on the part of human agents. He believes that human beings are, in the main, reasonable beings, and that they are as a result generally predictable in what they do. But, he insists, they are only reasonable *in the main*, and are only *generally* predictable. The necessitarian's error is to read too much into the regularity of human behaviour. Reid is prepared to admit that '[w]hen it is proved that, though all nature, the same consequences invariably result from the same circumstances, the doctrine of liberty must be given up' (*Active Powers*, pp. 332–3 (iv.ix)). But this has not been proved so far. The necessitarian fails to restrict himself to what the empirical record actually shows, and, guided by a prior commitment to a theory, constructs a law which experience does not give him reason to believe in. Behind Reid's attack

---

continue moving once set in motion, or whether no such power of its own is needed, 'is a Question that belongs not to Physicks but to Metaphysicks' (Reid (2002), p. 127; see also, e.g., pp. 143, 158, 175–6).

[35] No necessitarian, so far as I know, explicitly affirms such a law. Reid should be taken to be discussing what he takes to be implicit in all versions of the doctrine of necessity. He may well have been influenced in this formulation by James Gregory's 'Essay on the Difference between the Relation of Motive and Action, and that of Cause and Effect', to be discussed in the next chapter.

on arguments from the influence of motives there is always and everywhere his commitment to strict inductivism and the avoidance of hypotheses.

Reid attacks first the necessitarian claim that every action performed by an intelligent being must have a motive. If this is not true, then the law that the necessitarian believes to govern human action is immediately undone. And Reid thinks that there are 'innumerable' actions performed by intelligent beings that have no motives. A man can deliberately, with foresight and will, coolly and calmly, do something for no reason at all. 'This must be appealed to every man's consciousness', Reid says:

I do many trifling actions every day, in which, upon the most careful reflection, I am conscious of no motive; and to say that I may be influenced by a motive of which I am not conscious, is, in the first place, an arbitrary supposition without any evidence, and then, it is to say, that I may be convinced by an argument which never entered into my thought.

(*Active Powers*, p. 285 (IV.iv))

For example, when I take from my pocket one coin rather than a number of identical others, I have no reason to take that particular coin. It is irrelevant that such actions are morally insignificant. They are important to the question of liberty nonetheless: 'For, if there ever was any action of this kind, motives are not the sole causes of human actions. And if we have the power of acting without a motive, that power, joined to a weaker, may counterbalance a stronger' (*Active Powers*, p. 286 (IV.iv)). Reid also rejects the claim that where there is a motive in favour of one side of a deliberative question, and no motive on the other, the motive must always determine the action. 'Is there no such thing as willfulness, caprice or obstinacy, among mankind? If there be not, it is wonderful that they should have names in all languages. If there may be such things, a single motive, or even many motives, may be resisted' (*Active Powers*, pp. 286–7 (IV.iv)). The privileged status Reid accords reflection upon consciousness is plainly vital here. Reid takes it as axiomatic that if one cannot introspectively detect a motive to act in a certain way, then no such motive exists. Not only is it impossible for consciousness to deceive, but also there cannot be more to the mind than one can be conscious of. Also doing some work in this connection is Reid's understanding of what a motive is. He tells James Gregory that he takes a motive, when applied to a human being and not to an animal, to be 'that for the sake of which [a human being] acts, and, therefore, . . . what he never was conscious of, can no more be a motive to determine his will, than it can be an argument to convince his judgment'.[36] It is to be admitted that it is hard to reconcile this strand of Reid's argument with his admission, earlier in the *Essays on the Active Powers*, of 'mechanical' and 'animal' principles of action.

Reid turns next to the necessitarian claim that when there are contrary motives, the strongest must prevail. '[T]his can neither be affirmed nor denied with understanding', he says, 'until we know distinctly what is meant by the strongest motive' (*Active Powers*, p. 287 (iv.iv)). If the necessitarian simply says, as Kames does, that 'it is involved in the very idea of the strongest motive, that it must have the strongest effect in determining the mind',[37] he says nothing to help with this problem, for what Reid is asking for is an account of motivational strength that tells us more than that the strongest motive is the motive that ends up determining choice. What is it, in other words, that makes one motive stronger than another? The necessitarian may feel that he can avoid having to answer this question by simply saying that, whatever it is, it is something that different motives have in different degrees, and the motive that has most of it is the one that will prevail. The problem with this, however, is that it assumes that, as Reid puts it, 'contrary motives are of the same kind, and differ only in quantity'. Such an assumption is, according to Reid, quite unwarranted, and begs an important question, for it is integral to libertarianism as Reid understands it that motives are of different kinds. In this connection, Reid is happy to recognize, indeed, insists upon, the distinction between 'rational' motives on the one hand, and 'animal' motives on the other. When all motives relevant to a deliberative situation are of the animal kind, it is acceptable to talk in terms of variations on a single scale of strength: the strength of an animal motive can be measured in terms of how hard it is to resist, and we can say that the motive that is hardest to resist is the one that is (or feels) strongest. Even here, however, it would be wrong, or at least begging a further question, to say that the strongest motive always will prevail, for, unlike animals, human beings appear to have powers of self-restraint. With respect to rational motives, strength has a different character, being a matter of what we judge to be the thing we have most *reason* to do, or of the thing we judge duty, or prudence, or some prior decision, requires us to do. Even if there is a single scale of strength along which rational motives can be compared, there will remain the question of how to compare the different strengths of an animal motive and a rational motive. 'The grand and the important

---

[36] Reid (2002), p. 232.   [37] See Kames (1751), p. 167.

competition of contrary motives is between the animal, on the one hand, and the rational on the other', Reid says; 'This is the conflict between the flesh and the spirit, upon the event of which the character of men depends' (*Active Powers*, p. 291 (IV.iv)). Experience suggests that sometimes the animal motive prevails, and that at other times the rational motive prevails. The necessitarian, therefore, has no reason to claim that the agent has no role in deciding which motive to act upon. Where there is conflict between animal and rational motives, strength, by itself, is unable to determine what will be chosen as the thing to be done.

Necessitarians, Hume prominent among them, claim that we reason from men's motives to their actions as we do from other causes to their effects. It is true that we use motives to predict what people will do in the future, Reid admits, and sometimes we do so with great probability.[38] But we never do so with absolute certainty. 'And to infer from this, that men are necessarily determined by motives, is very weak reasoning' (*Active Powers*, p. 291 (IV.iv)). It is weak reasoning because the appearances are no less compatible with the hypothesis of liberty of will than with the necessitation of choice by motives. Suppose that we were, in fact, free in Reid's sense of freedom, and that we possessed 'moral liberty'. What reason is there to believe that we would then act any differently from how we act in the present state of things? Some people would use their freedom to act prudently most of the time, some would use it to act short-sightedly. And this is how we see men act. 'Is it not very weak reasoning, therefore', asks Reid, 'to argue, that men have not liberty, because they act in that very way in which they would act if they had liberty?' (*Active Powers*, p. 292 (IV.iv)). For the same reasons, it is unreasonable for the necessitarian to conclude that if men had moral liberty, all their actions would be capricious and unpredictable. Liberty of will may be, and sometimes is, abused in this way, but that is no reason to believe that *anyone* possessed of such freedom will always act capriciously. On the assumption of liberty, some could be expected to act rationally, some could be expected not to. Again, there is no reason to believe that if agents were not necessarily determined by their motives, it would be pointless to use rewards and punishments in order to encourage virtue and discourage vice. The libertarian has to allow that sometimes, rewards and punishments will not influence us, and that it is a part of his understanding of freedom that a

---

[38] That there are general maxims pertaining to men's future actions, Reid says elsewhere, is 'the foundation of all political reasoning, and of common prudence in the conduct of life' (Reid (1785, 2002), p. 559).

person may commit a crime in the full knowledge of the penalty attached to such a course of action. But this is to allow no more than what sometimes happens in the present state of things. 'Upon the supposition of liberty, rewards and punishments will have a proper effect upon the wise and the good; but not so upon the foolish and the vicious, when opposed to by their animal passions or bad habits; and this is just what we see to be the fact' (*Active Powers*, p. 293 (iv.iv)).

The necessitarian theory has the added disadvantage that it entails that if men commit crimes, the fault must lie with the lawgiver and not with the criminals themselves. The job of the lawgiver is to fight the influence of motives that, on the necessitarian scheme, the agent is unable to fight himself. Upon the supposition of liberty, on the other hand, 'the transgression of the law implies no defect in the law, no fault in the lawgiver; the fault is solely in the transgressor' (*Active Powers*, p. 293 (iv.iv)). The implication, clearly enough, is that the necessitarian must accept that God himself is the cause of the evils to be found in the universe that he governs. Reid makes this charge explicit when, having argued that it is possible for a free action to be foreseen by God, he turns to the question of whether God can permit evil without at the same time being responsible for bringing it into existence. Reid accepts that it is difficult for the libertarian to make sense of why God permits evil. But, he argues, whatever problems are faced by the libertarian in this connection, the necessitarian's difficulties are much greater. The necessitarianism he has in mind here is, once again, that of Priestley, and of Hartley before him—rather than that of a Calvinist such as Edwards. Two aspects of this form of necessitarianism Reid finds particularly unpalatable and implausible: the notion that God's sole moral attribute is benevolence, along with the concomitant lack of a role for justice in God's dealings with men; and the suggestion 'that all the misery and vice that is in the world is a necessary ingredient in that system which produces the greatest sum of happiness upon the whole' (*Active Powers*, pp. 351–2 (iv.xi)). The first hypothesis limits God's moral character; the second limits his power. 'Priestly denies all Mysteries', Reid remarked to Kames.[39] If forced to choose between an implausible explanation and leaving something unexplained, Reid will always choose the latter course, and his treatment of the problem of evil presents no exception. The first of the first principles of morals, according to Reid, is that 'There are some things in human conduct, that merit

---

[39] Reid (2002), p. 91.

approbation and praise, others that merit blame and punishment; and different degrees either of approbation or of blame, are due to different actions' (*Active Powers*, p. 361 (v.i)). If the truth of this principle is hard to square with God's permission of evil, then that is something philosophers and theologians simply have to live with. A proper disdain for hypotheses obliges one to accept the reality and prevalence of evil without reaching for a means of explaining it away. Reid's affirmation of the natural freedom of the will is hard to square with the spirit of Calvinism, but his resistance to theorizing that plays down the significance of evil surely has its roots in the Calvinist tradition.

Reid and Kant: A Brief Comparison

In Chapter 6 we noted a fairly widespread tendency among eighteenth-century libertarians to combine the claim that the freedom of the will is a plain fact of experience with an admission that it is difficult to understand how such freedom might be possible. It might be supposed that this is evidence of the retreat of claims on behalf of human freedom in the face of the advances being made by the new science of nature. It might further be thought that it took Kant, with his distinction between a phenomenal world of scientific determinism and a noumenal realm of freedom, to explain how liberty of will might be reconcilable with a proper respect for the achievements of science. Such suppositions would be wrong on two counts. First, eighteenth-century worries about the possibility of human freedom had as much, if not more, to do with traditional cruxes in theology as with new scientific theories. Secondly, and, for present purposes, more importantly, Reid also strives to show how to reconcile science and human freedom. Reid's approach to this problem involves none of the deep metaphysical perplexities usually thought to attach to Kantian transcendental idealism. Instead, it asks us to be sure that we do not exaggerate the threat posed to human freedom by empirical science in general, and by an empirical science of human behaviour in particular. Priestley's aggressive claims to the effect that all that it takes to establish the doctrine of necessity is the application of Newton's *regulae philosophandi* to the connection between motives and actions is countered by proof that, properly applied, the rules of reasoning show no such thing. In order to obtain his result, Priestley has to do precisely what the Newtonian scientist never does, which is to say, extrapolate beyond available evidence. As things stand, according to Reid, there is no need to choose between science and freedom. Reflective analysis of consciousness, aided by attention to ordinary language, reveals a commitment to the reality of freedom to be deeply embedded in our lives as practically rational beings. There is every reason to think that this belief is innate to us, rather than being a philosopher's invention, or the product of education and custom. And every argument produced to show that that belief is false either begs the question or tries to draw more than is warranted from experience. In the next and final chapter of this study, we will look at debates about the freedom of the will in the decades immediately following the publication of Reid's *Essays on the Active Powers*.

9

Liberty and Necessity after Reid

The question, which has been attended with so long and obstinate debates, concerning the metaphysical doctrines of liberty and necessity, and the freedom of human actions, is not even yet finally and satisfactorily decided.

William Godwin, *Thoughts on Man*, Essay XII

Reid dedicated his *Essays on the Intellectual Powers of Man* to Dugald Stewart and James Gregory, both professors at Edinburgh; Stewart of moral philosophy, Gregory of 'the theory of physic'. Stewart had been a student of Reid's,[1] and acquired international renown as an exponent, albeit a critical one, of the philosophy of common sense. A letter of Reid's to Stewart survives, and tells us something of the elder philosopher's attitude to the manner in which his former pupil developed and modified his method in an analysis of the power of 'attention'.[2] We can only guess at what Reid would have made of Stewart's treatment of the question of liberty and necessity, published as an appendix to his *Philosophy of the Active and Moral Powers of Man* (1828). Stewart's approach to the question is very similar to Reid's, but he makes concessions to the necessitarians at which Reid would surely have bridled. On the other hand, Reid's correspondence tells us in some detail what he thought about our other principal concern in this chapter, Gregory's 'Essay on the Difference between the Relation of Motive and Action, and that of Cause and Effect in Physics: on Physical and Mathematical Principles' (1792).[3] Although

---

[1] Stewart took his MA at Edinburgh, but attended Reid's lectures at Glasgow 'during a considerable part of winter 1772' (Stewart (1811), p. 429).

[2] See Reid (2002), pp. 211–23. For commentary, see Daniel N. Robinson (1989) and Broadie (2003), pp. 71–4.

[3] Gregory's essay, with an Introduction and Appendix, was published as Volume One of *Philosophical and Literary Essays*; no subsequent volumes appeared. For Reid's comments on the essay, see Reid (2002), pp. 174–7, 178–9, 179–80, 181–6, 205–8, and 241–59.

he nowhere declares allegiance to the philosophy of common sense, and is critical of appeals to 'consciousness' such as are characteristic of Reid's philosophical method, Gregory can also be understood as working within a Reidian framework. His 'physical and mathematical' approach to the nature of the influence of motives is, despite appearances, not an attempt to prove the truth of a Reidian first principle. It is, rather, an attempted *reductio ad absurdum* of the opposing position, of the kind that in the previous chapter we saw Reid endorse as a means of identifying which beliefs are to be counted as principles of common sense. Reid appears to have been unsure that Gregory achieves what he attempts to; and still less sure that the attempt was necessary. Others, on both sides of the debate, were more forthright: the author of the article 'Metaphysics' in the third edition of the *Encyclopædia Britannica* declares that 'the philosophical world is much indebted to Dr. Gregory for an argument which, in our opinion, can neither be overturned nor evaded';[4] while the necessitarian Alexander Crombie 'cannot help observing, that [Gregory's] Essay discovers throughout, extreme vanity, arrogance, and ostentation, qualities highly offensive, and generally characteristic of a weak and little mind'.[5] Gregory's essay will occupy us for the first part of this chapter. We will then turn to necessitarian criticisms of both Gregory and Reid, and to latter-day expositions of Priestleyan 'philosophical' necessitarianism. The chapter will conclude with a consideration of Stewart's recapitulation and revision of the Reidian doctrine of liberty.

James Gregory's 'Essay'

More than once in this study we have seen libertarians insist upon the importance of distinguishing between the influence of motives upon choices and actions, on the one hand, and the influence of physical causes on their effects, on the other. For Samuel Clarke and those who followed his lead, it is essential to the libertarian position that motives be allowed to have an influence upon free choices and actions: as we saw in Chapter 2, Clarke rejects the extreme libertarian view, associated with William King, according to which freedom manifests itself most clearly in cases of completely arbitrary choice. But the influence of motives is, Clarke holds, merely 'moral': a motive does not literally necessitate a certain choice or course of action, and

---

[4] [Gleig] (1797), p. 597.   [5] Crombie (1793), p. 326.

always leaves an agent at liberty to do something else, or to do nothing at all. The interpretation of Hume's reconciling project in Chapter 3 hinged on the thesis that Hume argues that all the idea of necessity we ever have, whether in the natural world or the moral, is of a merely 'moral' necessity. When the necessitarian position is properly understood, if Hume is right, it will be seen that it amounts to no more than the Clarkean libertarian already grants. Priestley's necessitarianism has none of Hume's subtlety, and excites among its libertarian critics the charge of having blurred (to quote Jacob Bryant) the 'distinction between inducement, and necessity; between inclination and force'.[6] For Gregory, too, the central issue between libertarians and necessitarians is, as he puts it himself, 'What is the relation between [motives] and our actions? and, Is it the same with that of physical cause and effect?'[7] The question, that is, is whether the connection between appetites, passions, and the like is constant and regular enough to be comparable with, or perhaps even identical to, the connection between events in the law-bound physical world.[8]

One thing that Reid finds to criticize in Gregory's essay is the younger philosopher's adherence to the view that physical things can be regarded as genuine causes.[9] As we saw in the previous chapter, Reid holds that a cause must have both understanding and will, and therefore regards neither material substances nor motives as causes, properly speaking. But Reid accepts that the central question between the libertarian and the necessitarian is whether there are constant and regular relations between motives and causes: 'It is a question of fact, whether the influence of motives be fixed by laws of nature, so that they shall always have the same effect in the same circumstances', he writes to Gregory; 'Upon this, indeed, the question about liberty and necessity hangs.'[10] Reid is a libertarian because he sees no reason to believe that there are 'laws of nature' connecting motives and actions. Gregory is a libertarian because he thinks he can prove that if motives determined actions in the same way as physical causes determine their effects, human beings would act very differently from how everyday

---

[6] Bryant (1780), p. 21.

[7] Gregory (1792), pp. 133–4.

[8] The only modern work on Gregory is an unpublished Edinburgh Ph.D. thesis by Michael Barfoot, 'James Gregory (1753–1821) and Scottish Scientific Metaphysics, 1750–1800' (1983). See also McCosh (1875), pp. 264–5.

[9] See Reid (2002), pp. 174–6, 181–5, 205–8, 242–4.

[10] Ibid., p. 176.

experience shows them to act. For Gregory, then, there is no danger that further information might come in to show that the influence of motives *is* fixed by laws of nature. This suggests that there is in fact only a rather attenuated sense in which Gregory is an 'experimental' philosopher. Other aspects of the 'Essay' provide further confirmation of Gregory's lack of interest in several of the characteristic concerns of eighteenth-century libertarianism. It does not matter to Gregory, for example, what it is inside the agent, as it were, that connects motives and actions. Nothing rests on the distinction between motives, on the one hand, and volitions, on the other; nor is it important to clarify the role of the understanding in deliberation and decision-making. Accurate description of the powers or faculties of the mind is no part of Gregory's defence of the doctrine of liberty. Gregory seems in fact not to value talk of faculties very highly. His focus is upon the influence of motives upon the agent considered as a whole, and he writes disparagingly of 'the *fancied acts* of many *imaginary agents*, such as will, judgement, understanding, power, &c.'.[11] For Gregory it is visible bodily actions, and not invisible acts of will, that establish the absurdity of necessitarianism.

Gregory disdains to attach importance to an autonomous will principally because he is loath to rely in any way whatsoever upon 'appeals to consciousness'. He accepts that it is possible to acquire accurate knowledge of the laws of the mind by means of 'direct and very strict attention' to our thoughts; but most of those who have attempted this 'have begun and continued such attempts with some preconceived opinion, or system, or hypothesis, . . . , concerning that part of the philosophy of the human mind which they wished to investigate';[12] and the person under the influence of a prior attachment to a system 'is no longer perfectly *candid* in his observations and reflections; nor can he be altogether trusted in the account which he gives of them'.[13] Necessitarians (such as Hartley and Priestley) claim that the constant conjunction of certain motives and certain actions is a datum of consciousness. Gregory says that he has reflected carefully upon his own case, and came to an opposing conclusion. Who is to be regarded as correct, and how would that decision be made?

As in all these cases the question of fact was to be decided by a direct appeal to consciousness; and as those with whom I had occasion to argue gave an account of consciousness, and their sentiments, diametrically opposite to what I found to be true with respect to mine; and as I was sensible that I had no superiority over them,

---

[11] Gregory (1792), p. 604.   [12] Ibid., p. xci.   [13] Ibid., pp. xci–xcii.

which could intitle my thoughts to greater regard, or my assertions to greater credit; I thought it expedient to drop entirely the consideration of such cases, and to turn my attention towards those other cases which related merely to the actual conduct, or overt actions, of mankind.[14]

Gregory's interest in the actual conduct of mankind, however, should not be taken to amount to the historian's or social scientist's concern with tracing the nature of the laws that appear to govern human behaviour. The absurdity and falsity of the doctrine of necessity can be demonstrated without there being a need for further enquiry.[15]

Gregory eschews appeals to common sense, 'which appeals many philosophers might regard as nugatory and contemptible'.[16] Nevertheless, he advertises the fact that '[t]he very peculiar mode that I have employed in treating this subject' was suggested to him by an example Reid gives in the first of the *Essays on the Intellectual Powers* of manner in which analogies drawn from natural philosophy can be a 'fruitful source of error' in the philosophy of mind.[17] This is the analogy between the deliberating mind and a balance, or pair of weighing scales, an analogy that Kames, Edwards, and Priestley all employ. Reid points out that the analogy is only a good one if it is assumed that there is no difference between a living creature and a dead one, and this observation captures one essential component of necessitarianism as Gregory understands it: the thesis that the human agent is entirely passive and inert, in the sense that we cannot change from a state of rest to motion, or from motion to rest, without being acted upon by something external to us. The necessitarian thus supposes that we are just as plainly without a power of self-movement, or, as Gregory usually calls it, self-government, as are material bodies such as stones and planets. The other essential component of necessitarianism, according to Gregory, is the claim that the relation between types of motives and types of actions is identical to the relation between types of physical causes and effects, and is describable in terms of regular or constant conjunction. Gregory regards Hume as having introduced the notion of constant conjunction into the free will debate: Priestley's necessitarianism

---

[14] Ibid., pp. civ–cv.

[15] Another element of the common 'experimental' case of libertarianism that Gregory dispenses with is the experience of acting where there are no motives to act in that way: see Gregory (1792), pp. 692, and the references given there by Gregory to the relevant parts of the 'Essay'.

[16] Gregory (1792), p. ccxxxii.

[17] Ibid., p. ccxxxiii; see Reid (1785, 2002), pp. 54–5.

is, he thinks, identical to Hume's. Earlier necessitarians had regarded motives and actions as 'separable', and had rested their case solely upon the inertia of the mind.[18] Gregory's principal target is a 'modern' and self-consciously 'philosophical', or scientific, necessitarianism that insists (as both Hume and Priestley do) on the similarities between the regular and law-bound world of bodies and the sphere of human action. He aims at this target with a modern and scientific weapon, the doctrine of forces described and explained in Newton's *Principia*. Especially relevant to the question of the influence of motives is the first corollary drawn by Newton from the three laws of motion: 'A body, acted on by two forces simultaneously, will describe the diagonal of a parallelogram in the same time as it would describe the sides by those forces separately.'[19] 'It is well known to all who know anything of science', Gregory writes, 'that this corollary is the basis of a vast fabric of the most important physical knowledge, which all who understand it admit to be as firmly established as the abstract truths of pure geometry'; for it 'enabled [Newton] to make such wonderful progress in the theory of astronomy, and in other branches of mechanical philosophy'.[20]

To assert that motives and actions are constantly conjoined, Gregory is assuming, is to assert that the laws that describe those constant conjunctions are identical to the laws of contact mechanics. Human beings, if the doctrine of necessity is true, should therefore behave under the influence of motives in the same way as do bodies under the influence of forces. But human beings do not behave that way under the influence of motives; and so the doctrine of constant conjunction, and *a fortiori* the doctrine of necessity, is false. Such, in bare outline, is Gregory's *reductio* of necessitarianism. Physical causes can interact in three ways: they can concur with each other, they can directly oppose each other, and they can combine with each other. The crux of the matter as regards the analogy between motives and physical causes is the case of combination. Gregory imagines a porter standing at a point A offered a guinea per mile for carrying a letter in the direction AB, and also offered half a guinea per mile for carrying another letter in another direction AC.

---

[18] See Gregory (1792), pp. 337–54 for an argument to the effect that old or 'common' necessitarianism fares no better in the face of Gregory's *reductio* than the new or 'philosophical' variety. The old-style necessitarian, according to Gregory, is *also* committed to there being events without causes.

[19] Newton (1729, 1934), p. 14.

[20] Gregory (1792), pp. 166, 198.

The porter is assured that he cannot earn both the guineas and the half-guineas. Between directions AB and AC is direction AD: if AB were to the east, and AC were to the south, then AD might be to the south-east. Gregory asks: 'Will [the porter] go in the direction AB, or in the direction AC, or in the direction AD, or will he remain at rest at the point A?'[21] He will not remain at rest at the point A, Gregory argues, because then the motives would have no influence at all on action, which would be contrary to the principle of constant conjunction. For the same reason, he will not go in either the direction AB or the direction AC, since then one or other of the two motives influencing him would be, as Gregory puts it, 'completely separated from its proper action'.[22]

The porter, then, according to the principle [of constant conjunction], has nothing for it but to go peacefully, and without murmuring in the diagonal AD: for in this case both motives are conjoined with their actions, as far as is consistent with their mutual interference and modification: the result partakes of both, and is different from what either action would have been singly, as from the application of one of the motives by itself. And the difference between the result of the combination of the two motives, and that which would have taken place if only one of them had been applied, will be exactly equal to the full (supposed) effect of the other motives. . . .[23]

The porter, this is to say, will proceed in the direction AD even though he cannot earn, and knows that he cannot earn, anything by doing so. But this is plainly contrary to experience. Therefore the doctrine of necessity is false. We know that, all things being equal, the porter would set off in the direction AB, and this proves that the influence of motives is not the same as the influence of physical causes upon their effects. Gregory's 'Essay', when taken together with its Introduction and Appendix, is close to 700 pages long, but here we already have its essence.[24]

---

[21] Ibid., p. 226.

[22] Ibid., p. 230.

[23] Ibid., pp. 231–2.

[24] Another important aspect of the 'Essay' is Gregory's claim that all necessitarians propound their doctrine in bad faith, since their actions show that they do not really believe what they claim to believe. As noted above, in letters to Gregory Reid commented on the 'Essay' in some detail. He asks: 'May it not be objected to your reasoning, that you apply the three laws of motion to motives; but motives may be subject to other laws of nature, no less invariable than the laws of motion, though not the same' (Reid (2002), p. 177).

Replies to Gregory: Allen and Crombie

Gregory's 'Essay' never reached a second edition. It did, however, excite a certain amount of critical debate immediately after publication.[25] In 1795 John Allen, a former student of Gregory's, published (anonymously) *Illustrations of Mr. Hume's Essay concerning Liberty and Necessity, in Answer to Dr. Gregory of Edinburgh*. Allen charges Gregory with misrepresenting the necessitarian position, and, in particular, with neglecting the importance of a condition to the effect that, in order for similar motives always to produce similar actions, the surrounding circumstances must be held constant. Where the circumstances change, Allen argues, there is no knowing *a priori* what action will be produced by a particular motive: then only observation and experiment can determine what the agent will do.[26] Allen also has an *ad hominem* reply to Gregory's porter argument. Gregory himself admits that we are not free with respect to the determinations of the understanding. But, by Gregory's own principles, this should mean that if I hear a report that a man was walking in the direction AB, and another report that he was walking in the direction AC, I will believe that he was in fact walking in the direction AD. And that, presumably, is not a result that Gregory would welcome. As already noted, Gregory's argument is rather more favourably reviewed in the 'Metaphysics' article of the third (1797) edition of the *Encylopædia Britannica*. However, the author of the article—George Gleig, a Scots episcopalian divine—is less sceptical than Gregory of the contribution that can be made by consciousness to the question of liberty and necessity. 'What is the particular nature of that relation which subsists between the voluntary actions of men, and the motives from which they proceed, can be known to every individual only by an attentive and unbiassed reflection on the operations of his own mind', he writes; 'Without this reflection, no man can be made to understand it by the reasonings of philosophers, and with it no man can need the aid of those reasonings.'[27]

---

[25] For a survey of contemporary reviews, see Fieser (2001), pp. x–xiii.

[26] See [John Allen] (1795), p. 31. Allen is a sensitive reader of Hume, and declares himself unable to see what might be subversive of morals and religion in a theory 'founded in our own experience of the uniformity of human conduct, as evinced by the records of past time, and implied in the daily intercourse of society' (p. 22).

[27] [Gleig] (1797), p. 598. Gleig goes on to recommend 'the last edition of King's Origin of Evil, by Dr Law late bishop of Carlisle'. It is also worth noting that, where Gregory takes Hume to provide the best representation of the necessitarian position, Gleig draws most heavily on Kames's *Sketches of the History of Man*.

The fullest contemporary discussion of Gregory's 'Essay' is in the third chapter of Alexander Crombie's *Essay on Philosophical Necessity* (1793).[28] Crombie was taught by Beattie at Marischal College, Aberdeen, and was himself a libertarian until he read and was convinced by Priestley's *Doctrine of Philosophical Necessity Illustrated*.[29] Unsurprisingly, like Allen, he charges Gregory with misrepresenting the necessitarian position; and, again like Allen, he emphasizes the importance of factoring surrounding circumstances into estimations of how motives will influence actions.[30] He accepts the importance of the thesis of constant conjunction to 'philosophical' necessitarianism; '[b]ut that the same external motive, considered simply, or *per se*, should produce the same quantity of all action in all cases, independently of any change of concomitant circumstances, ... is a supposition as absurd, as that the same physical cause, in every possible situation, and in every change of circumstances, should be accompanied with precisely the same effect'.[31] The fact that man acts necessarily, Crombie insists, does not mean that he acts blindly, without reflection: Gregory goes wrong in focusing only upon motives and actions, and ignoring the contribution made by the faculty of choice to determining the effect of motives upon action. 'External' motives, the things 'for the sake of which' we act, are always mediated in their influence by 'internal' motives, such as the agent's state of mind, or his own particular conception of good and evil. 'I may chuse a certain proposed good to-day; but it does not follow, that, if my state of mind is changed, I should make the same choice to-morrow; and yet both elections may be necessary.'[32] With respect to Gregory's porter analogy, Crombie argues that it has a veneer of plausibility solely because of the supposition that the two motives oppose each other only indirectly, so as to interact, like indirectly opposing forces, by combination. And this supposition is false. In fact, the motives in such a case are *directly* opposed to each other. The porter, knowing

[28] For a brief account of Crombie's life and works, see Harris (2002b) or McCosh (1875), pp. 265–6; for discussion of the *Essay* see Vesey (1989) and Fieser (2001). Crombie sent a draft of his *Essay* to Gregory, who in turn passed it on to Reid. Reid comments on it in a surviving letter to Gregory: see Reid (2002), pp. 232–5. It is in this letter that Reid makes the criticisms of the notion of unconscious motives described in Chapter 8: see pp. 197–8 above.

[29] See Crombie (1793), pp. i–iii.

[30] Crombie makes no reference to Allen, which is of course not surprising, given that Allen's pamphlet was published two years after Crombie's *Essay*. Crombie does, however, discuss Gleig's endorsement of Gregory in the *Encylopædia Britannica* 'Metaphysics' article, which was not published until 1797: see Crombie (1793), pp. 499–508.

[31] Crombie (1793), pp. 385–6.

[32] Ibid., pp. 389–90.

that he cannot walk at the same time in both the directions AB and AC, where B is to the east and C is to the south, is in precisely the same situation as if B were to the east and C to the west. There is therefore no reason to imagine him being forced to walk to the south-east, in the direction AD.[33] What Gregory fails to appreciate is the fact that the porter, unlike a brute material substance, is 'a being endowed with a capacity, of thinking, judging, and willing, and who feels, at the same time, a desire to obtain the proffered good'.[34] The desire for money will combine with the capacity of thought, judgment, and choice to ensure that the porter proceeds in either direction AB or AC. Crombie points out that the cornerstone of the necessitarian system is that for every action there is a motive, and that the porter has no motive whatsoever to move off in the direction AD.[35]

The first and fourth chapters of Crombie's *Essay* present a cogent restatement of Priestley's case for the doctrine of necessity. Like most necessitarians of the period, Crombie believes that attention to the everyday meanings of words and a clear presentation of 'the state of the question' of liberty and necessity will reveal there to be underlying agreement between the two parties. Once the libertarian admits the influence of motives upon choices and actions, he in effect adopts the necessitarian position. To deny that motives are the causes of free actions is to endorse the notion of events without causes, and to undermine the possibility of a distinction between virtue and vice, of what Crombie calls 'moral culture', and of divine foreknowledge of human actions. Libertarianism is also at odds with Scripture: like Priestley, Crombie is a necessitarian not just because experience shows the falsity of libertarianism, but also because of the way in which necessitarianism harmonizes with the central teachings of the Christian religion. The effect of embracing the truth of necessitarianism, he says, is 'to render the Deity the chief object of our attention and regard, and to impress the mind with an habitual sense of his supreme government and continual agency'.[36] 'Regarding every event with the same eye as he who

---

[33] Crombie (1793), p. 354.

[34] Ibid., p. 355.

[35] See ibid., p. 356. There is more to Crombie's reply to Gregory than we have space for here. Perhaps worth noting in brief is his utilization of the scales analogy against Gregory. Just as the smallest difference between the weights in the two pans is sufficient to depress one pan beneath the other, so also the smallest difference in the relative strengths of two motives is sufficient to produce a decision in favour of one of them: see Crombie (1793), pp. 374–8. The rather badtempered dispute between Gregory and Crombie is continued at length in Gregory and Crombie (1819).   [36] Crombie (1793), p. 453.

ordains it,' Crombie writes of the necessitarian at the end of the *Essay*, 'evil vanishes before him, and he beholds nothing but good'.[37] The necessitarian, unlike the libertarian, is able to regard his enemy as 'purely an instrument in the hand of God, for effectuating his wise and benevolent designs'.[38] There is no consolation in events being merely *foreseen* by God: better is to be able to regard every event, and so every human action, as performed by God himself for the best possible reasons. Moral evil, when seen from this perspective, is comparable to the noxious qualities of an animal or plant, and can be assumed to have a place in the larger providential scheme. Crombie admits that this makes a problem out of remorse, which usually involves a belief that one might have acted otherwise than one in fact did. The consistent necessitarian cannot, strictly speaking, feel remorse; but he can feel 'anguish' at his actions, and '[a]s pain accompanies a diseased body, so anguish is the concomitant of a distempered soul;—and this anguish will operate like remorse, as a stimulus to correct that disposition or temper of mind, which is the immediate cause of it'.[39] Here we have also a rationale for punishment, conceived of as a means of curing distempered souls by en-couraging better behaviour in the future. According to Crombie, a judge does not enquire whence the depraved dispositions of a criminal have originated. The judge, in other words, is not interested, as the libertarian thinks he should be, in whether or not those dispositions can be said to be the criminal's responsibility. 'It is sufficient to authorise punishment, that the crime was voluntary, that it proceeded from evil propensities in the offender—that this crime has injured his neighbour, and that the temper, whence it proceeded, will still prove pernicious to happiness and good social order'.[40]

Crombie's criticisms of the libertarian position, and of Reid in particular, are sometimes fairly telling. Take, for example, Reid's claim that libertarian-ism, in denying that motives cause actions, does not postulate events without causes, because it regards the *agent* as the cause of his actions. '[T]he fact is', Crombie replies, 'when Libertarians contend, that man is the only efficient cause of his actions, that he acts, and is not acted upon, they erroneously consider him as a creature distinct from himself, as abstracted from the affections, passions, appetites, and sentiments of his mind, which are the principle and immediate cause of his actions; not attending to this obvious truth, that these passions and appetites are part of himself, nay, I may say the

---

[37] Ibid., p. 496.   [38] Ibid., p. 466.   [39] Ibid., p. 480.   [40] Ibid., p. 437.

man himself; for without these, he is nothing.'[41] The Reidian agent is as hard
to characterize as the property-less 'substratum' discussed by Locke in the
Essay concerning Human Understanding's chapter 'Of the complex Ideas of Substance'. One of the reasons why Reid rejects the notion that motives cause
actions is that the necessitarian is unable to give a non-circular account of
why this motive rather than that one is a particular action's cause. The
necessitarian says that the motive that causes an action is, by definition, the
strongest motive; but, according to Reid, has no means of explaining what it
is for a motive to be stronger than another. The necessitarian, Reid concedes,
can say that 'by the strength of a motive is not meant its prevalence, but the
cause of its prevalence';[42] and this is what Crombie does say, claiming, in
addition, that 'We have no standard by which to estimate the strength of any
cause, but the effect which it produces. I ascribe the preponderance of one
scale, as an effect, to the superiority of weight in that scale, as the cause of its
preponderance. In like manner I attribute the predominance of a motive, or
a system of motives over others, to a superiority of force in the predominant
motives, as the cause of that prevalence.'[43] Reid rejects the balance analogy,
of course, but, Crombie claims, in doing so he merely begs the question at
issue.[44]

The influence of motives upon the will, Reid suggests, can be compared
with the influence of counsel upon a judge. Motives provide grounds for a
decision, but leave the will free to decide what is to be done. But *why*,
Crombie asks, does a judge decide as he does? Is there not always a motive
for the decision? Something must explain why one decision was made rather
than another; and that is the same thing as to say that something necessitated the decision. The only alternative is to portray the decision as arbitrary,
made on a whim.[45] The distinction between moral and physical necessity is of
no help to the libertarian, for so long as the conjunction between motives
and decisions is constant (in given circumstances), there is the same reason to
regard motives as the causes of decisions as there is to regard any physical
thing as the cause of the effect with which it is constantly conjoined.[46] The

---

[41] Crombie (1793), p. 111.

[42] Reid (1785, 1969), p. 288 (IV.iv).

[43] Crombie (1793), p. 109.

[44] Crombie is careful not to say that, because a motive prevails, it must be, as he puts it, *per se*
the strongest motive. We can be wrong about what we have most reason to do. But we always
act on what *seems to us* the strongest motive: see Crombie (1793), pp. 161–2.

[45] See Crombie (1793), p. 113.   [46] See ibid., pp. 114–23.

libertarian might point to decisions made when the motives are equal—and perhaps also to actions performed for no motives at all. Such cases, the libertarian might say, and Reid does say, undo the analogy between mind and balance. If there is reason to think that *sometimes* the mind can act free of the influence of motives, then, the libertarian claims, there is no reason to say that it loses its liberty when it acts in line with their influence. And the evidence for an ability to choose even where motives are equal, and to act where motives are lacking, is provided by consciousness. In reply to this line of argument, Crombie introduces the notion that there might be motives of which the agent is not conscious. He notes that 'many instinctive impulses or motives . . . escape our notice, or at least operate uniformly by the constitution of our frame, while we are unconscious of it'.[47] Habit, he argues, or elements of our constitution (such as being left rather than right-handed) can prompt us to act in ways while leaving us unaware of why we so act. This is one reason why consciousness is not a reliable guide when it comes to determining the causes of our choices and actions. Crombie gives three other reasons as well: '[t]he argument of consciousness' has often been urged in favour of obvious absurdities, as when a man declares himself 'conscious' of something of which others have no conception at all (such as an immaterial soul); there is too often substantive disagreement about the content of consciousness; and the evidence of consciousness can be opposed by the evidence of memory, 'a faculty, in such cases, much less fallacious'.[48] This last reason for scepticism as to the ability of consciousness to establish the freedom of the will pits the first-person present-moment perspective against the capacity of retrospective reflection to discover motives where it seemed at the time of action there were none. Crombie thus shares Gregory's scepticism about the usefulness of consciousness as a means of answering the question of liberty and necessity.

Philosophical Necessity after Priestley

The only one of Reid's three arguments for moral liberty that Crombie regards as worth taking seriously is the second, the argument from moral responsibility. Nevertheless, he thinks that a distinction between vulgar and philosophical ways of talking about agency and morality is sufficient to rob it

---

[47] Ibid., p. 104.   [48] Ibid., p. 135.

of force.[49] Properly speaking, every human action is the work of God; but this does not undermine the point of ascribing to men responsibility for their actions, since praise and blame are useful as a means of cultivating virtue and discouraging vice. The notion that the doctrine of necessity is consonant with the interests of morality and religion grows increasingly widespread towards the end of the eighteenth century. Crombie is not alone in having been impressed by the way in which Priestley rid necessitarianism of its association with the supposed scepticism and libertinism of Hobbes, Spinoza, Collins, and Hume. The anti-Subscription campaigner John Jebb, to whom Priestley dedicated the *Doctrine of Philosophical Necessity Illustrated*, cites Hartley in support of the view that '[t]he natural liberty of man' consists only 'in having the will to act, and an exemption from all restraints, arising from defects in the instruments of action, such as in hands, feet, from palsies, &c. as well as from the restraints arising from natural external circumstances'.[50] In his *Tracts Ethical, Theological and Political* (1789), Thomas Cooper, another friend of Priestley's, feels able to take for granted the truth of 'the doctrine of *philosophical necessity*', and uses it as a basis for arguing (against King and Clarke) that God is just as much a 'necessary agent' as human beings are. In creating the universe, according to Cooper, God acted 'from some *motive* or *inducement*, which occasioned him to become the cause of it'; the motive or inducement 'operated *necessarily*, in the strict sense of the word, exclusive of the possibility of liberty, or free agency'; and the motive was 'the *greater sum of happiness* which would arise upon the whole from the existence of the effect, than from its none existence' [sic].[51] The Unitarian William Belsham opens two volumes of *Essays Philosophical and Moral, Historical and Literary* (1789) with an essay 'On Liberty and Necessity', in which is presented a clear and compact statement of Priestley's case for necessity. 'As to the immoral and pernicious consequences which our adversaries pretend to deduce from Necessarian principles', Belsham writes towards the end of the essay, 'it is easy to show that they are founded in a gross misapprehension of their nature and tendency.'[52] Belsham's brother Thomas, also a Unitarian, considers the question at greater length in his *Elements of the Philosophy of the Mind* (1801), but comes to the same conclusions. Belsham allows that philosophical liberty is *possible*, and that it might need to be attributed to God so as to allow him to act when presented with motives of equal strength, or when no motive presents itself; but he

---

[49] For Crombie's criticisms of Reid's three arguments, see Crombie (1793), pp. 251–82.

[50] Jebb (1787), vol. ii, p. 146.   [51] Cooper (1789), pp. 124–5.

[52] William Belsham (1789), vol. i, p. 14.

argues that such liberty cannot be attributed to men because it would obstruct divine prescience, that experience proves men to lack it, and that the doctrine of necessity has many beneficial practical consequences.[53] Belsham does not refer to Crombie, but there is no great difference between their arguments. He takes Gregory as representative of the libertarian position. Stewart, in turn, will take Belsham's 'Discussion of the Doctrines of Liberty and Necessity' as the epitome of modern necessitarianism.

All of these writers advocate Priestleyan or Hartleyan 'philosophical' necessity as an element of rational, often Dissenting, religion. William Godwin, in *An Enquiry concerning Political Justice* (1793) is unusual among late eighteenth-century necessitarians in showing no interest at all in the theological ramifications of the doctrine of necessity.[54] His concern is with morality and the possibility of improving it, and he rejects free will because of its deleterious consequences for virtue and education. '[S]o far as we act with liberty, so far we are independent of motives', Godwin argues, 'our conduct is as independent of morality as it is of reason, nor is it possible that we should deserve either praise or blame for a proceeding thus capricious and indisciplinable.'[55] Like Hartley and Priestley, however, Godwin acknowledges that our ideas of the nature virtue and vice change once necessitarianism is adopted: 'our disapprobation of vice will be of the same nature as our disapprobation of an infections distemper', he writes;[56] and punishment will be seen solely as a means of reforming error. 'Whenever punishment is employed under this system, it will be employed, not for any intrinsic recommendation it possesses, but just so far as it shall appear conducive to general utility.'[57] There are no pretensions to novelty in Godwin's presentation of the arguments for necessity and against liberty. He acknowledges the influence of Hume, and adds to it arguments from Edwards. Where Godwin does innovate, it is with respect to the connotations of regarding the mind as mechanistic in its operations. He thinks that Hartley's version of this claim tends to make the mind as such look irrelevant to the generation of at least some bodily motions: external substances act upon the nerves, create vibrations in the brain, which in turn cause the body to

---

[53] See Belsham's 'recapitulation' of his argument: Thomas Belsham (1801), pp. 297–318.

[54] However, for an interpretation of Godwin on liberty and necessity that emphasizes what Godwin has in common with Priestley and Hartley, see Philp (1986), pp. 89–95.

[55] Godwin (1793), vol. i, p. 304.

[56] Ibid., p. 313.

[57] Ibid., p. 314.

react. What Godwin wants to establish is that 'thought is the medium through which the motions of the animal system are generally carried on', and he thinks that one thing that will make this more compatible with the mechanism of the mind is the notion of thoughts that are 'unattended with consciousness'.[58] In this connection Godwin develops the notion of 'unperceived thoughts' further than does Crombie. He argues that several mental phenomena suggest that thought need not be attended with reflexive awareness. We are constantly subject to many more perceptions than we can attend to. The mind cannot be aware of more than one thought at a time, but—in order to understand the entirety of a speech, say, or even of a sentence—we must in fact be able to retain many perceptions at once. Even when the mind is at its most obviously mechanical—in the performance of habitual actions, say—thought may yet be responsible for each movement of the body.[59]

Stewart on the Active and Moral Powers of Man

In 1793 Dugald Stewart published *Outlines of Moral Philosophy*, designed 'to exhibit such a view of the Arrangement of my Lectures, as may facilitate the studies of those to whom they are addressed'.[60] This elegant synopsis of Stewart's thought sketches his conception of our intellectual and 'active and moral' powers, and also (in the first edition, at least) his approach to man

---

[58] Godwin (1793), vol. i, pp. 324–33.

[59] In his late work *Thoughts on Man* (1831), Godwin appears much more worried than in the *Enquiry* about the tension between philosophical and vulgar perspectives on human action. '[E]very man', he writes, 'the necessarian as well as his opponent, acts on the assumption of human liberty, and can never for a moment, when he enters into the scenes of real life, divest himself of his persuasion' (Godwin (1831, 1993), p. 164). He endorses the solution proposed by Kames in the first edition of the *Essays on the Principles of Morality and Natural Religion*. For discussion of this change of view, see Don Locke (1980), pp. 323–7. For another early proponent of secular necessitarianism, see Hazlitt (1834, 1931). Hazlitt, however, was more impressed by Edwards (despite Edwards's Calvinism) than by Priestley: 'Dr. Priestley's whole aim seems to be evade the difficulties of the subject, Edwards's to answer them' (p. 261).

[60] Stewart (1801), p. v. The only modern biography of Stewart is Macintyre (2003). There is no comprehensive modern study of Stewart's philosophy considered as a whole, but for a comparative study of Reid and Stewart, see Griffin-Collart (1980). Madden (1986) also discusses the ways in which Stewart 'enriches' the Reidian philosophy of common sense. The most reliable brief account is Haakonssen (1999). In an examination of the history of the Edinburgh moral philosophy chair in the eighteenth century, Richard Sher stresses Stewart's 'debt to Ferguson as a didactic moralist': see Sher (1990), pp. 123–5.

considered as a member of political society.[61] It also contains a compact statement of Stewart's philosophical method: 'As all our knowledge of the material world rests ultimately on facts ascertained by observation', Stewart writes, 'so all our knowledge of the human mind rests ultimately on facts for which we have the evidence of consciousness. An attentive examination of such facts will lead in time to the general principles of the human constitution, and will gradually form a science of the mind not inferior in certainty to the science of body.'[62] Of this species of investigation', he adds, 'the works of Dr Reid furnish many valuable examples.'[63] Insistence on the importance of attention to consciousness is a recurrent theme in the methodological chapters of Stewart's writings. Like natural philosophy, the science of the mind can only hope to make progress in so far as it follows the inductive method of reasoning laid out in Bacon's *Novum Organum*; but it is nevertheless vital that investigation into the powers of the mind be kept distinct and separate from the study of nature. The philosophy of mind, Stewart writes in the first volume of his *Elements of the Philosophy of the Human Mind*, 'borrows its principles from no other science whatever'.[64] Like Reid, Stewart is always alert to the manner in which analogies drawn from the science of matter distort and falsify our views of the operations of mind. From infancy onwards we tend to be more concerned with outward things than inward ones, and this makes it all too easy to import alien presuppositions into moral philosophy. To take an example particularly relevant to our concerns in this study, Stewart complains about the fact that 'We are apt to forget what *the Will* is, and to consider it as something inanimate, which can have its state changed only by the operation of some foreign cause.'[65] It is significant, and potentially misleading, 'that the names of almost all our mental powers and operations are borrowed from sensible images', Stewart says: thus we talk of, for example, 'weighing the *motives* our actions', and of 'yielding to that *motive* which is the strongest', and sometimes do not notice that this is already to talk as the necessitarian talks.[66] For 'motives' are by definition things which move the mind to act in a certain way, while the question between the

---

[61] Stewart dropped the articles on political economy from the second edition, 'substituting in their stead, a few others, calculated to illustrate the peculiar and intimate connexion between this department of Politics and the more appropriate objects of Ethics' (Stewart (1801), p. ix).

[62] Ibid., pp. 7–8.

[63] Ibid., p. 8.

[64] Stewart (1792), p. 19.

[65] Stewart (1815–21, 1854), p. 593; cp. Stewart (1828), vol. ii, p. 474.

[66] Stewart (1814), p. 425.

libertarian and necessitarian concerns, precisely, whether or not the mind is moved to act by anything other than itself. It is by cleaving to consciousness as the only wholly reliable source of information about the mind's operations that the distinctive character of those operations will be revealed. Gregory, as we have seen, was suspicious of appeals to consciousness as a means of settling the question of liberty and necessity; Stewart, by contrast, is prepared to say that consciousness is 'the only tribunal competent to pass any judgment whatever on the question at issue'.[67]

In the *Philosophy of the Active and Moral Powers of Man*, Stewart sets himself two tasks: to classify and analyse the principles of action that influence the human will, and to delineate our duties to God, to others, and to ourselves. The focus of the book is thus somewhat different from that of Reid's *Essays on the Active Powers*. Where Reid devotes three out of five essays to the proper definition of power, volition, and moral liberty, Stewart relegates to an appendix consideration of the 'metaphysical subtleties' attaching to the question of whether or not the will is free. Nor is this the end of the differences between the two books. Where Reid had divided up the principles of human action into three classes—the mechanical, the animal, and the rational—Stewart's principal concern, so he tells the reader in the Introduction, is to mark 'the essential distinction between those active principles which originate in man's rational nature, and those which urge him, by a blind and instinctive impulse, to their respective objects'.[68] For the same reasons as Godwin, Stewart does not think that any principle of action is properly called mechanical.[69] The class of instinctive principles comprises the appetites (hunger, thirst, sexual appetite), the desires (of knowledge, society, esteem, power, and superiority), and the affections (benevolent and malevolent); the class of 'rational and governing' principles comprises self-love and the moral faculty. Self-love for Stewart is not the same as selfishness: rather, we act out of self-love when we use the desire for happiness as the structuring principle of life; and it is entirely possible to find happiness in serving the interests of others. We act out of a consideration for morality, by contrast,

---

[67] Stewart (1810), p. 136.

[68] Stewart (1828), vol. i, p. 7. Stewart also says that 'it is chiefly by attending to what passes in our own minds that we can reasonably hope to ascertain the general laws of our constitution as active and moral beings' (p. 11): it is very hard to be certain as to the principles upon which another human being acts.

[69] See Stewart's chapter on attention (Stewart (1792), pp. 103–31). Both Hartley and Reid are wrong, he claims, to regard habitual actions as mechanical: they remain voluntary, but the acts of will are unconscious, in the sense that they are not attended to, and cannot be recollected.

when we use obedience to the call of duty as the structuring principle of life. Stewart takes it as obvious that freedom of the will is required in order to act out of both self-love and duty. In both cases, one employs reason in order consciously to formulate a plan of action and then to execute it over time, and in order to do this one must be in control over one's choices and decisions.[70] When we act on rational principles, according to Stewart, we act freely. And it is so obvious that we do act on rational principles that there is no need to spend time proving that the will is not subject to necessity. Stewart writes at the end of his analysis of the principles of action that 'All the foregoing inquiries concerning the moral constitution of man proceed upon the supposition that he has a freedom of choice between good and evil; and that, when he deliberately performs an action which he knows to be wrong, he renders himself justly obnoxious to punishment.'[71] 'That this supposition is agreeable to the common apprehensions of mankind', he continues, 'will not be disputed.'[72] It is only a few 'speculative men' who have questioned whether the will is really free, and that is why the matter merits only an appendix.

Stewart begins 'Of Man's Free Agency' with an attempt to clarify what we mean when we talk of the *will*, on the one hand, and of *motives*, on the other. The power of will should be distinguished from the volitions that are its acts; and volitions should be kept distinct from such things as desires, inclinations, and pleasures. Once the will is confused with volitions, and volitions with desires, it is easy to lose sight of the fact that the will, properly considered, is by definition something active, or rather, something by means of which its possessor acts. The will, like every other power of the mind, cannot be given a proper definition: the meanings of the terms *will* and *volition*, Stewart writes, are 'to be learned only from careful reflection on what passes in our own minds, and to multiply words upon the subject would only involve it in obscurity'.[73] The will, being a power, is not properly said to be something that can act, or upon which anything else can act: the question of the

[70] In the *Outlines* Stewart writes that animals 'are incapable of looking forward to consequences, or of comparing together the different gratifications of which they are susceptible; and accordingly, as far as we are able to perceive, they yield to every impulse. But man is able to take a comprehensive survey of his various principles of action; and to form a plan for the attainment of his favourite objects. Every such plan implies a power of refusing occasionally to particular active principles, the gratification which they demand' (Stewart (1801), pp. 109–10).

[71] Stewart (1828), vol. i, p. 325.

[72] Ibid.

[73] Stewart (1828), vol. ii, p. 471.

relation between motives and will is, properly speaking, the relation between motives and the *agent*.[74] Inanimate things can only be altered by some foreign or external cause; but, whatever the relation between motives and volitions, volitions are (again, by definition) things that can only have agents as their causes. As we have already noted, Stewart thinks that to use the term 'motive' for the principles of action is already to import necessitation into our picture of agency. 'To say that the *will* is determined by *motive* powers', he claims, 'is to employ a language which virtually implies a recognition of the very point in dispute.'[75] It is only metaphorically that one can describe as 'motives' the intentions or purposes which, as Stewart puts it, 'accompany our voluntary actions'. Like Gregory, Stewart thinks that to talk of 'motives' is really to talk of the *ends* for the sake of which we act. Despite these misgivings, however, Stewart conforms to contemporary practice, and employs motive terminology throughout his discussion. He first concedes that every action is 'performed from some motive': there is no point in denying this. He concedes also that the merit of every action depends on its motive. But, for Stewart as for almost every eighteenth-century libertarian, these concessions settle nothing: the libertarian is not worried by motives as such. 'The great question is, *How* do these motives determine the will?'[76]

As Stewart understands it, the necessitarian claim is that 'all human actions are as necessarily produced by motives as the going of a clock is necessarily produced by the weights, and that no human action could have been otherwise than it really was'.[77] Stewart thinks this claim generates obvious absurdity, but not for the reasons given by Gregory. Stewart in fact shares the reservations of Allen and Crombie about Gregory's way with the necessitarian, pointing out that the importance of identical circumstances to the constant conjunction thesis, and arguing also that, even if the relation between motive and action were the same as cause and effect, 'it might happen that no constant conjunction between them should be observable, in consequence either of some alteration in the state of the intellectual powers, or of the active principle'.[78] The problem he takes the necessitarian to face is, rather, that the argument from the influence of motives is a completely general one, such as applies to the divine mind just as surely as to the human, yielding the conclusion that *no* event in the universe

[74] Stewart (1828), vol. ii, p. 474.   [75] Ibid., p. 474.   [76] Ibid., p. 481.
[77] Ibid., pp. 481–2.   [78] Ibid., p. 478 fn.

could have happened otherwise than it did. The upshot of necessitarianism, in other words, is Spinozism. Stewart's response lays no claim to originality: he takes it that Clarke proved satisfactorily that God must be a free agent; that, therefore, free agency is *not* impossible; and that there is no reason to attach absurdity to the idea that God made man a free agent. There is nothing new to the argument of the necessitarian, Stewart thinks, and so no new reply is needed. In other parts of the appendix he is content to rely on moves already made by Reid: Hobbes's claim that we can conceive of no greater liberty than the power to act as we will is falsified by the obvious conceivability of a liberty opposed to necessity; and Leibniz's argument from the principle of sufficient reason is convicted of begging the question in exactly the manner described by Reid in the essay 'Of Moral Liberty'. But it is Clarke to whom Stewart returns most frequently. '[A]lmost every page of the subsequent history of this controversy', he says at one point, 'may be regarded as an additional illustration of the soundness of Clarke's reasonings, and of the sagacity with which he anticipated the fatal errors likely to ensue from the system which he opposed.'[79] Clarke's 'sagacity' reveals itself in the fact that some necessitarians have accepted his principal contention, that necessity is incompatible with moral agency and the distinction between virtue and vice. Stewart has in mind Hartley, Priestley, and their disciples, particularly Thomas Belsham. Clarke's demonstration of the *possibility* of moral liberty is, however, just as adequate a reply to the modern necessitarian as it was to Hobbes, Spinoza, and Collins. Moreover, the desire to attribute everything to God may originate in piety, but it must in the end generate a (Spinozistic) conception of God that no pious man could accept.

Freedom of will being possible, the only question that remains is whether, in fact, we possess it; and this question Stewart believes each person can settle for himself by reflecting upon what he is conscious of when he acts. The question of liberty necessity, this is to say, is the same as the question, 'Is the evidence of consciousness in favour of the scheme of free-will, or of that of necessity?' 'It may ... be regarded as one great step gained in this controversy', Stewart writes, 'if it may henceforth be assumed as a principle agreed on by both parties, that this is the *only* question which can be philosophically stated on the subject.'[80] He is aware that 'some late writers' have claimed that it is only on a partial view of the subject that actions appear, from the agent's

---

[79] Ibid., p. 501.   [80] Ibid., p. 508 fn.

perspective, not be necessitated by their motives. Again, Stewart quotes Hartley, Priestley, and Thomas Belsham, and draws attention to their equivocations over remorse, which they are bound in the end to regard as born of a mistaken conception of who is responsible for what appear to be moral evils. But it is not the retrospective view of human action that best makes the case for liberty. Stewart asks:

> why have recourse with Belsham and Priestley, in this argument, to the indistinct and imperfect recollection of the criminal, at a *subsequent* period, with respect to the state of his feelings while he was perpetrating the crime? Why not make a direct appeal to his consciousness at the very moment when he was doing the deed? Will any person of candour deny, that, in the very act of transgressing an acknowledged duty, he is impressed with a conviction, as complete as that of his own existence, that his will is free; and that he is abusing, contrary to the suggestions of reason and conscience, his moral liberty?[81]

In this way Stewart wants to focus the reader's thoughts upon what it feels like when one is actually choosing and performing an act one knows to be wrong. Then one is conscious that one is not being forced to do the thing in question. There are reasons, or motives, to do the virtuous thing as well; and reasons, perhaps, to do nothing at all. The reasons one has, whatever they are, to act viciously are not felt to force one to act that way. Reid's analysis of the assumptions built into deliberation, choice, and promise-keeping has no echo in Stewart's treatment of the question of liberty and necessity. Indeed, at times Stewart's expression of his confidence in the testimony of consciousness is rather reminiscent of Beattie's impatience with the arguments of the necessitarian. With respect to connections sometimes forged between divine prescience and the notion of an irresistible fate or destiny, for example, Stewart contrasts, in the manner of the author of the *Essay on Truth*, 'the impotence of... scholastic refinements' with 'the feelings of nature'.[82] It

---

[81] Stewart (1828), vol. ii, p. 513.

[82] Ibid., p. 525. Like Beattie (but unlike Reid), Stewart is prepared to countenance the idea that it is impossible for God to have foreknowledge of free human actions: see Stewart (1828), vol. ii, pp. 523–6. In a manuscript letter in the Fettercairn Collection held at the National Library of Scotland, Stewart declares himself very pleased by the *Essay on Truth*: 'In a work professedly polemical', he writes, 'it was impossible for the author to aim at unity or elegance of design; but what was really practicable, he appears to me to have executed with an uncommon degree of skill and judgment.' Stewart also signals his anxiety 'to do everything in my power to promote the usefulness of the "Essay on Truth"'. See MS Acc 4796, Box 93.

must be admitted that there is something of a contrast between the adventurousness of some of Stewart's earlier work and these bluff assertions of trust in consciousness of power over the will.

Stewart on Kant

Unlike Reid, Stewart was aware of the metaphysical writings of Kant – even if, because he had no German, he was forced to read the *Critique of Pure Reason* in a Latin translation.[83] Stewart shows himself unimpressed by the sage of Königsberg, however, finding in his analysis of the *a priori* elements of experience nothing that is not at least implicit in Reid,[84] and more obvious still in Cudworth and Price.[85] Nor does Stewart believe that Kant does much to establish the possibility of the freedom of the human will. Kant appears, rather, to be a proponent of the doctrine of necessity; and the doctrine of transcendental idealism, so far as Stewart can see, does not serve to make room for freedom: 'For if the reasonings of the Necessitarians be admitted to be satisfactory, and if nothing can be opposed to them but the incomprehensible proposition, that man neither exists in space nor in time, the natural inference is, that this proposition was brought forward rather to save appearances, than as a serious objection to the universality of the conclusion.'[86] When combined with his necessitarianism, Stewart claims, Kant's claim that freedom is implied in the notion of *practical reason* is indistinguishable from Kames's hypothesis of a deceitful sense of liberty. 'In both cases, the reader is left in a state of most uncomfortable scepticism, not confined to this particular question, but extending to every other subject which can give employment to the human faculties.'[87] For Stewart, as for Reid, there is no need of either Kamesian or Kantian ingenuity in order to preserve the freedom of the will in the face of the achievements of an inductive science of mind.

We see, then, that at the close of the long eighteenth century of British philosophy there remains substantive disagreement about the consequences of experimental reasoning for the question of liberty and necessity. I hope to have shown that it would not be true to say that the libertarianism of this

---

[83] See Stewart (1810), p. 98 fn; and Stewart (1854), p. 389 fn.
[84] See Stewart (1810), p. 99.   [85] See Stewart (1854), pp. 397–408.
[86] Ibid., p. 410.   [87] Ibid., p. 411.

period goes along with a reluctance to regard the human mind as a proper object of scientific investigation. Libertarians believe, rather, that what persuades some to adopt the doctrine of necessity is a misunderstanding and misapplication of the experimental method. In the brief Postscript that follows, I suggest that this continues to be true throughout the nineteenth century. The British nineteenth-century free will debate is in fact rather similar, in outline at least, to the debate described in this book. It is not until the early twentieth century that there are significant changes in the manner in which British philosophers discuss the freedom of the will.

Postscript
The Nineteenth Century and Afterwards

On the Determinist side there is a cumulative argument of great force. The belief that events are determinately related to the state of things immediately preceding them is now held by all competent thinkers in respect of all kinds of occurrences except human volitions. It has steadily grown both intensively and extensively, both in clearness and certainty of conviction and in universality of application, as the human mind has developed and human experience has been systematised and enlarged. Step by step in successive departments conflicting modes of thought have receded and faded, until at length they have vanished everywhere, except from this mysterious citadel of Will.

Henry Sidgwick, *The Methods of Ethics*, Chapter v

One reason to see Dugald Stewart as marking the endpoint of eighteenth-century British philosophy is that it is only in the years after his death that German thought finally begins to make a significant impression on philosophers in Britain.[1] The influence of Kantian and post-Kantian ideas is particularly obvious in Sir William Hamilton, whose first philosophical work appeared in the *Edinburgh Review* in 1829.[2] Stewart had died the previous year. In its terminology and in its abstruseness, Hamilton's philosophy is very different from anything written in English in the period covered in this study: the 1829 article ('The Philosophy of the Unconditioned') was judged by Francis Jeffrey to be 'the most unreadable thing that ever appeared in the

[1] For the reception of Kant in Britain, see Wellek (1931).
[2] For Kant's influence on Hamilton, see Madden (1985); Kuehn (1990); Tropea (2001).

Review'.[3] Nevertheless, Hamilton regards himself as continuing with the project of an 'experimental' philosophy of mind; and, like Reid and Stewart before him, he takes introspection to be the most important source of information about our mental powers. 'Consciousness is to the philosopher', Hamilton writes in an essay on 'Philosophy of Perception', 'what the Bible is to the theologian'.[4] And when, in the course of a discussion of 'the law of Causality' in his *Lectures on Metaphysics*, Hamilton addresses the freedom of the will, what he takes to testify against 'Fatalism' and 'Atheism' is 'the positive consciousness,—the affirmative deliverance, that we truly are the authors,— the responsible originators, of our actions, and not merely links in the adamantine series of effects and causes'.[5] Hamilton is prepared to endorse this 'affirmative deliverance' even though he believes that *how* the will can be free is something we do not and cannot know. He argues that we cannot so much as *conceive* of an 'absolute commencement' or a 'free volition'—and in his edition of Reid brings this to bear on Reid's assertions to the contrary in a series of hostile footnotes to Reid's essay 'Of the Liberty of Moral Agents'.[6] In these notes, Hamilton endorses Leibniz's deployment of the principle of sufficient reason against Clarke's libertarianism, and argues that in order that we be able to make sense of choice, there must always be 'some cause' by which an agent is 'determined' to exert his volition. However, this does not push Hamilton towards the Kamesian hypothesis that the sense of freedom of will is an illusion, since Hamilton is not prepared to say that what we can and cannot conceive is a reliable guide to things as they are in themselves. It is sufficient to establish the freedom of the will that we have 'positive consciousness' of it: there is no need to be able to show how it is possible.

It is perhaps not surprising that in his *Examination of Sir William Hamilton's Philosophy*, John Stuart Mill finds this supposed solution of the problem of liberty and necessity unsatisfactory. Hamilton's own case for the inconceivability of free volition, Mill says, 'saved his opponents the trouble of answering his friends', in so far as it provides 'a strong indication that some form of necessity is the opinion naturally suggested by our collective experience of life'.[7] Experience 'makes known' that 'in the case of all things within the

---

[3] Quoted in Tropea (2001), p. xiv.
[4] Hamilton (1830, 1853), p. 86.
[5] Hamilton (1859), vol. ii, p. 412.
[6] See Hamilton (ed.) (1863), pp. 608–11 fn.
[7] John Stuart Mill (1865, 1979), p. 445. A fairly large number of Hamilton's 'friends' went into print to defend him against Mill. In the chapter on free will in the third edition of the *Examination*, Mill replies to two of them: [Phillips] (1866) and Alexander (1866).

range of our knowledge' there is 'an invariable connection between every event and some special combination of antecedent conditions, in such sort that wherever and whenever that union of antecedents exists, the other event does not fail to occur'.[8] Experience makes known, in other words, the general truth of the doctrine of necessity. All the necessitarian demands is that parity of reasoning extend to the case of volition, for there is the same invariability in the connection of 'moral antecedents' and exercises of the will as there is in every other domain of experience. This, Mill argues, is evidenced by each person's observation of his own actions; by observation of the actions of those with whom we come into contact; and by the application of statistical modes of analysis to human beings acting in large numbers. At any rate, there is no more reason to deny invariability of conjunction with respect to human actions than there is to deny it with respect to *physical* causes and effects. Here Mill echoes Hume. In his reply to Hamilton's argument from consciousness, Mill echoes Priestley and Crombie. 'Consciousness tells me what I do or feel. But what I am *able* to do, is not a subject of consciousness. Consciousness is not prophetic; we are conscious of what is, not of what will or can be.'[9] In retrospect, we are conscious only of having been able to act differently had there been a motive for such an action: had, in other words, the circumstances been different. Consciousness of effort is merely consciousness of the existence of mental conflict. There is, moreover, no force to the Reidian argument from the circularity of appealing to the superior strength of a motive to explain why it was the one that determined choice, for the strongest motive is simply that 'which is strongest in relation to pain and pleasure'.[10] But unlike Priestley, and like Hume, Mill is extremely careful to make it clear that constant conjunctions, or invariable connections, are all there are to necessity as he understands it. In particular, Mill insists that there is no implication of a tie or link between causes and their effects, and no implication of the cause forcing or compelling the effect to take place. Mill's best explanation of his understanding of the doctrine of necessity is given in Book VI of *A System of Logic*. 'It would be more correct to

---

[8] John Stuart Mill (1865, 1979), pp. 445, 446.

[9] Ibid., p. 449.

[10] Ibid., p. 468. In this connection, Mill's target is Hamilton's follower Henry Mansel rather than Reid himself. For Mansel's version of the circularity objection, see Mansel (1851), p. 302. Mill also cites and attacks Mansel's argument from introspection. (Mansel claims that 'in every act of volition, I am fully conscious that I can at this moment act in either of two ways, and that, all the antecedent phænomena being precisely the same, I may determine one way to-day and another way to-morrow' (p. 152).)

say that matter is not bound by necessity', Mill says there, 'than that the mind is so.'[11]

Necessitarianism has been widely misconstrued, according to Mill, by its enemies and adherents alike. Its proper meaning was established by 'Hume's and Brown's analysis of Cause and Effect'. Mill read Thomas Brown at an early age, and the influence of Brown's version of the Humean approach to the causal relation is plain in both the *Examination* and the *System of Logic*. Brown himself made no contribution to the question of liberty and necessity, but he can nevertheless be regarded as having had a significant influence on nineteenth-century discussions of the free will problem.[12] In addition to providing a theory of causation perfectly in tune with the period's increasingly positivistic understanding of scientific method, he challenged the taxonomic approach to the philosophy of mind championed by Reid and Stewart, and paved the way for the resuscitation of the analytic associationism of Hartley, Tucker, and Priestley.[13] For Brown, the science of the mind may be compared to chemistry: its goal is the reduction of complex wholes to their simpler components.[14] And the key to such reduction are various processes of 'suggestion', which, Brown argues, obviate the need to postulate distinct 'faculties' of the mind.[15] Another means of dating the commencement of distinctively nineteenth-century British philosophy is provided by the Brown-inspired return to Hartley; and, by a nice coincidence, the first fruit of the reinvigorated tree appeared in 1829, the same year as Hamilton's 'The Philosophy of the Unconditioned'. This was James Mill's *Analysis of the Phenomena of the Human Mind*.[16] Associationism of the kind developed by Mill is

---

[11] John Stuart Mill (1843, 1973), p. 838.

[12] Brown's *Lectures on the Philosophy of the Human Mind* was taken by some to be plainly necessitarian in tendency: see Hamilton (1830, 1853), p. 98; Ballantyne (1828), pp. 27–8; Morell (1846), vol. ii, p 27. (I am endebted to Dixon (2003), pp. 116, 124, for the latter two references.) Cairns (1844) provides an example of an attempt to reconcile Brownian philosophy of mind with a libertarian theory of the will.

[13] The case for Brown's influence on later philosophers such as James Mill, Bain, and Spencer is made in Dixon (2003), ch. 5. It should be noted, however, that Brown himself was enough of a product of the 'Scottish school' to reject the 'mechanistic' tendencies and 'fanciful' analogies of Hartley's system: see Brown (1828), pp. 279–81.

[14] See Brown (1828), pp. 64–5.

[15] See ibid., pp. 253–81 (where Brown proposes a 'reduction of certain supposed mental faculties to simple suggestion': the faculties in question being conception, memory, imagination, and habit).

[16] In his Preface to the 1869 edition of the *Analysis*, John Stuart Mill cites Brown's comparison of the philosophy of mind with chemistry as defining and characterizing the task his father set

by its nature incompatible with the libertarian conception of the will. The will is conceived of, not as a power or faculty, but merely as, in Mill's words, 'that peculiar state of mind or consciousness..., by which action is preceded'.[17] The difficulty is to explain what exactly this state of mind consists in, and how it is formed. It is assumed from the outset that volition, whatever it is, is part of a causal chain linking mental states and bodily movements—though Mill begins his chapter on the will by citing Brown's account of the causal relation, in order to make it clear that there should be nothing disturbing in the idea of the volitions being caused by preceding states of mind. Herbert Spencer and Alexander Bain also portray volition as having a history which it cannot transcend. Bain explicitly rejects the notion of freedom of will—and rejects talk of necessity too. The only thing worth discussing in this connection is the truth or falsity of 'the doctrine, of invariable sequence in human actions', and this is a purely empirical question.[18] According to Spencer, 'Psychical changes either conform to law, or they do not. If they do not conform to law, this work [*The Principles of Psychology*], in common with all works on the subject, is sheer nonsense: no science of Psychology is possible. If they do conform to law, there cannot be any such thing as free-will.'[19] Again, this is a purely empirical matter.

Spencer and Bain share a belief in the importance to physiology, and especially the physiology of the nervous system, to the science of the mind. The mind is not for them (as it is for Reid and Stewart, and also for the Mills) a self-contained sphere, separated off, at least for the purposes of investigation into its powers, from the rest of nature.[20] T. H Huxley took 'psycho-physiology' to its logical extreme when he identified scientific progress with

himself. He also describes his father as the 'reviver and second founder of the Association psychology'. The first founder was Hartley—'But his book made scarcely any impression upon the thought of his age' (Mill (1869), pp. xi–xii).

[17] James Mill (1829), vol. 2, p. 255.

[18] Bain (1859), pp. 543–9.

[19] Spencer (1855), p. 620. Spencer also argues that 'that every one is at liberty to desire or not to desire, which is the real proposition involved in the dogma of free-will, is negatived as much by the internal perception of every one as by the contents of the preceeding chapters' (p. 617).

[20] In a study of 'mid-nineteenth-century British psycho-physiology', Kurt Danziger writes that 'What was involved was a new recognition of the relevance of biological or physiological perspectives for psychology. Rather than constituting a world apart, the mind was now to be viewed in terms of its place in nature' (Danziger (1982), p. 120). Bain's innovations in the study of emotion and volition are clearly explained in Mischel (1966). Mischel ends this article by remarking that 'there is no place for an agent who is "able to do" in these explanations of how our organs and viscera get "moved"' (p. 144).

'the extension of the province of what we call matter and causation, and the concomitant banishment from all regions of human thought of what we call spirit and spontaneity'.[21] To many of Huxley's contemporaries, this looked like an elimination of the mind from the domain of science, and was therefore something to be vigorously contested. Writers such as W. B. Carpenter, James Ward, and James Sully insist that the first duty of the psychologist is to characterize accurately the subjective phenomena of consciousness, irrespective of whether there promises to be a means of giving those phenomena a basis in physiology. 'No sound psychology is possible', Sully argues, 'which does not keep in view the fundamental disparity of the physical and the psychical, and the consequent limits of the physiological explanation of mental facts.'[22] The subjective experience of volition, in particular, was used as evidence of the impossibility of regarding the mind as a mere collateral product or epiphenomenon of physical change. Somehow— and it is left unclear how it is to be done—the psychologist has, according to Carpenter, to do justice to *both* 'the dependence of the Automatic activity of the Mind upon conditions which bring it within the *nexus* of physical causation' *and* 'the existence of an independent Power, controlling and directing that activity, which we call Will': 'I cannot regard myself, either Intellectually or Morally, as a mere puppet, pulled by suggesting-strings; any more than I can *dis*regard that vast body of Physiological evidence, which proves the direct and immediate relation between Mental and Corporeal agency.'[23]

Ward's article on psychology in the ninth edition of the *Encyclopædia Britannica* contains an especially clear description of the phenomena that the scientist of mind must save:

the rigidly determinist position can only be psychologically justified by ignoring the activity of the experiencing subject altogether. At bottom it treats the analysis of conduct as if it were a dynamical problem pure and simple. But motives are never merely so many quantitative forces playing upon something inert, or interacting entirely by themselves. At the level of self-consciousness especially motives are reasons, and reason is itself a motive. In the blind struggle of so-called 'self-regarding' impulses might is the only right; but in the light of principles or practical maxims right is the only might.[24]

Ward, like Hamilton, studied in Germany, and there is a marked Kantian element to his writings—though he criticizes Kant's architectonic for 'pre-

---

[21] Huxley (1868, 1893), p. 159.   [22] Sully (1884), p. 4.
[23] Carpenter (1874), pp. ix–x.   [24] Ward (1910–11), pp. 600–1.

vent[ing] [Kant] from working out his philosophy from the standpoint of experience as life'.[25] Andrew Seth also manifests the influence of Kantian thought when he complains of the manner in which 'the "new" psychology' reduces the conscious subject to the status of 'an inactive spectator of... psychological happenings, which are themselves the inert accompaniments of certain transformations of matter and energy'. Will, he argues, is an 'inexpugnable and irreducible aspect of experience'; he approvingly cites Fichte's claim that the motivational force of ideas lies not in the ideas themselves, but in the will of the person who adopts them as his.[26] These writers are not, it is important to recognize, opposed to the idea of a science of the mind. They do not believe that the freedom of the will places the mind outside the scientific realm. Rather, they take it to be one of the things that a science of the mind must be able to accommodate. Edward Buchner expresses this point of view succinctly when he writes that 'To eliminate volition as a scientific datum, would be a virtual subversion of the science of psychology so long as it is developed with the intent of representing the nature of mental activity and the course of its development in terms of a real and acceptable knowledge of the facts.'[27]

What this brief sketch of nineteenth-century discussion of the will suggests is, I believe, that the death of Dugald Stewart was not immediately followed by a radically different approach to the question of liberty and necessity. In other words, there is a degree of arbitrariness to my decision to bring this book's narrative to close with Stewart's *Philosophy of the Active and Moral Powers of Man*. Treatments of the will and its relation to the determinants of choice and action appear to remain first and foremost 'experimental' for the duration of the nineteenth century. If there is a growing sense in some quarters that associationistic analysis and physiology are the keys to a deeper understanding of the mind, the associationists and psycho-physiologists

---

[25] Ward (1922), p. 179. Ward believes that it is the active mind that should be the focus of moral science. He therefore rejects what he takes to be Kant's decision in the first *Critique* to give priority to analysis of the understanding over analysis of practical reason: 'It is not on the analogy of what we *find* that we interpret what we are. On the contrary, it is the modes of the conscious self *as knowing, feeling, and willing*, which are the source of the categories; and it is we who then apply these analogically to the Not-self which is there confronting us, and with which we interact' (p. 176; emphases added).

[26] Seth (1898), pp. 566, 569, 570.

[27] Buchner (1900), p. 507. Buchner makes it fairly plain that he opposes the mechanistic tendencies of 'recent discussions in psychology'. In this paragraph I have been reliant upon Daston (1978) and (1982), and Dixon (2003), ch. 6.

want to convince their readers that their accounts of volition are in accord with experience—as does a necessitarian such as John Stuart Mill, who makes no reference to either associational factors or physiology in his case against libertarianism. If there is in other quarters an increasing interest in Kantian and post-Kantian philosophical strategies, this does not go along with a rejection of the value of 'consciousness' to accurate moral philosophy.[28] Even towards the end of the nineteenth century, the notion of the agent as in control of determinations of his will, and of the will as an autonomous faculty of the mind, was regarded by some as compatible with a genuinely scientific approach to the mental realm. By the early twentieth century, however, the situation had changed dramatically. After 1900 the will more or less disappeared from experimental study of the mind.[29] It would seem likely that this was a product of, or at least went along with, the turn-of-the-century entrenchment of 'psychology' as an autonomous discipline.[30] At this time 'experimental' mental science began to be contrasted with armchair appeals to introspection: experiments were henceforth things conducted in laboratories, and needed to be repeatable and objectively confirmable. Purely internal and subjective phenomena such as volitions did not have a place in the conception of mind that went along with the new experimentalism. Faculties of all kinds were banished from psychology.

Discomfort with the will grew also in philosophy, now, at last, firmly separated from empirical enquiry into the functioning of the mind.[31] Gilbert Ryle very influentially dismissed the 'ghostly thrusts' of the will from his 'logical geography' of the concept of mind. Volition, he argued, like phlogiston and animal spirits, is an out-dated technical concept now completely lacking in utility.[32] In the twentieth century, the free will debate centred, in the first instance, upon the question of whether or not the *concept* of moral

[28] It is to be admitted, though, that some nineteenth-century British philosophers regarded Kant as having demonstrated that philosophy is not, after all, an empirical science: James Ferrier is among the first to argue that the subject-matter of philosophy is not experience but the *conditions* of experience, and he is followed in this by T. H. Green.

[29] Daston draws attention to the rapidity with which articles relating to volition disappeared from the listings of *Psychological Abstracts* in the first half of the twentieth century. By 1969 there were no longer subject headings for Will and Volition. See Daston (1978), p. 207.

[30] 'The first experimental psychological laboratories were opened in British universities in 1897 at Cambridge and University College London; the British Psychological Association was founded in 1901; and the *British Journal of Psychology* was launched in 1904' (Rylance (2000), p. 5).

[31] On the separation of psychology from philosophy, see Reed (1994).

[32] See Ryle (1949), ch. III. It is only fairly recently that the case has begun to be made again for the will as a component of the philosophy of mind and action: see especially O'Shaughnessy

responsibility is compatible with the *concept* of determinism. The debate was conducted in the conditional mood: *if* determinism is true, some argued, then we cannot ever do otherwise than what we do (and so we cannot be responsible for what we do); *if* determinism is true, others replied, then there is in fact a sense in which can we do otherwise (and so we can be responsible for what we do). Even if we cannot do otherwise than what we do, still others argued, we can nevertheless be responsible for what we do. Such remains the way in which philosophers argue about the will and its freedom.[33] What the eighteenth-century philosopher can offer the twenty-first, perhaps, is a reminder that the question of the will and its freedom is also a question that arises in everyday experience, when reflective agents seek to reconcile their introspective experience of making choices with the regularities plain in the behaviour of humankind at large.

(1980). It is probably true to say, however, that the majority view among Anglophone philosophers remains similar to Ryle's.

[33] See, e.g., the introduction to Watson (ed.) (2003).

REFERENCES

Primary Sources

Where two dates are given, the first indicates when the work was first published. A date in square brackets indicates when the first edition of the work was published. An author's name in square brackets indicates that the work was published anonymously or under a pseudonym. Where not stated, the place of publication is London.

Alexander, Patrick Proctor (1866). *Mill and Carlyle: An Examination of Mr. John Stuart Mill's Doctrine of Causation in Relation to Moral Freedom with an Occasional Discourse on Sauerteig, by Smelfungus*, Edinburgh.

[Allen, John], (1795). *Illustrations of Mr. Hume's Essay concerning Liberty and Necessity, in Answer to Dr. Gregory of Edinburgh*.

Ames, William (1639). *Conscience with the Power and Cases Thereof*.

Anderson, George (1753). *An Estimate of the Profit and Loss of Religion, personally and publicly stated*, Edinburgh.

[Anon.] (1751). Review of *Essays on the Principles of Morality and Natural Religion*, *The Monthly Review* 5: 129–55.

[Anon.] (1753). *Some late Opinions concerning the Foundation of Morality, Examined in a Letter to a Friend*.

[Anon.] (1755). *Observations upon a Pamphlet, Entitled, An Analysis of the Moral and Religious Sentiments of Sopho and David Hume, Esq.*, Edinburgh.

[Anon.] (1756). *Objections against the Essays on Morality and Natural Religion Examined*, Edinburgh.

[Anon.] (1760). *Essay towards the Demonstrating the Immateriality and Free Agency of the Soul*.

Bain, Alexander (1859). *The Emotions and the Will*.

Balfour, James (1768). *Philosophical Essays*, Edinburgh.

Ballantyne, John (1828). *An Examination of the Human Mind*, Edinburgh and London.

Bayle, Pierre (1727). *Oeuvres diverses*, 4 vols., La Haye.

Beattie, James (1771 [1770]). *An Essay on the Nature and Immutability of Truth*, second edition, Edinburgh.

—— (1786). *Evidences of the Christian Religion*, 2 vols., Edinburgh.

—— (1790–3). *Elements of Moral Science*, 2 vols., Edinburgh.

—— (1866). *The Poetical Works*, The Aldine Edition of the British Poets.

—— (1946). *James Beattie's London Diary 1773*, ed. Ralph S. Walker, Aberdeen.

—— (1948). 'The Castle of Scepticism', ed. Ernest Campbell Mossner, *The University of Texas Studies in English* 27: 108–45.

—— (2004). *Correspondence*, ed. Roger J. Robinson, 4 vols., Bristol: Thoemmes Continuum.

Belsham, Thomas (1801). *Elements of the Philosophy of the Mind.*

Belsham, William (1789–91). *Essays Philosophical and Moral, Historical and Literary*, 2 vols.

Berington, Joseph (1776). *Letters on Materialism and Hartley's Theory of the Human Mind.*

Berkeley, George (1732, 1950). *Alciphron: or the Minute Philosopher*, in *The Works of George Berkeley*, ed. A. A. Luce and T. E. Jessop, 9 vols.

Blair, Hugh (1783). *Lectures on Rhetoric and Belles Lettres*, 2 vols.

[Bonar, John] (1755). *An Analysis of the Moral and Religious Sentiments contained in the Writings of Sopho and David Hume, Esq.*, Edinburgh.

Boswell, James (1791, 1934). *Life of Johnson*, ed. C. B. Tinker, 4 vols., Oxford.

Bramhall, John (1655). *A Defence of True Liberty from Antecedent and Extrinsecall Necessity, Being an answer to a late Book of Mr. Thomas Hobbs of Malmsbury, intituled, A Treatise of Liberty and Necessity.*

—— (1658). *Castigations of Mr. Hobbes his last Animadversions.*

Brown, Thomas (1828 [1820]). *Lectures on the Philosophy of the Human Mind*, Edinburgh.

Bryant, Jacob (1780). *An Address to Dr. Priestly [sic], upon his Doctrine of Philosophical Necessity Illustrated.*

Buchner, Edward Franklin (1900). 'Volition as a Scientific Datum', *Psychological Review* 7: 494–507.

Burke, Edmund (1757, 1998). *A Philosophical Enquiry into the Sublime and the Beautiful*, ed. David Womersley, Harmondsworth.

Butler, Joseph (1726, 1897). *Sermons*, in W. E. Gladstone (ed.), *The Works of Joseph Butler*, 2 vols., Oxford.

—— (1736, 1897). *The Analogy of Religion, Natural and Revealed, to the Constitution and Course of Nature*, in W. E. Gladstone (ed.), *The Works of Joseph Butler*, 2 vols., Oxford.

Butterworth, Lawrence (1792). *Thoughts on Moral Government and Agency, and the Origin of Evil; in opposition to the doctrine of Absolute, Moral, Christian, and Philosophical Necessity*, Evesham.

A. C. (1729). *A Dissertation on Liberty and Necessity. With some Remarks upon the Reverend Dr. Clarke's Reasoning on this Point.*

Cairns, William (1844). *A Treatise on Moral Freedom.*

Campbell, George (1762). *A Dissertation on Miracles; Containing an Examination of the Principles Advanced by David Hume Esq.; in an Essay on Miracles*, Edinburgh.

Carpenter, William. B. (1874). *Principles of Mental Physiology, with their applications to the Training and Discipline of the Mind, and the Study of its Morbid Conditions*.

Chambers, Ephraim (1728). *Cyclopædia: or, An Universal Dictionary of Arts and Sciences*, 2 vols.

Chappell, Vere (ed.) (1999). *Hobbes and Bramhall on Liberty and Necessity*, Cambridge.

Cheyne, George (1715). *Philosophical Principles of Religion: Natural and Reveal'd*.

Clarke, John (1720). *An Enquiry into the Cause and Origin of Evil. In which the Principal Phenomena of Nature are Explained according to the True Principles of Philosophy*.

Clarke, Samuel (1738). *The Works of Samuel Clarke, D.D.*, 4 vols. Referred to here:

[1705]. *A Demonstration of the Being and Attributes of God: More Particularly in Answer to Mr. Hobbs, Spinoza, And their Followers. Wherein the Notion of Liberty is Stated, and the Possibility and Certainty of it Proved, in Opposition to Necessity and Fate* (vol. II, pp. 521–77).

[1717]. *Letters to Dr. Clarke concerning Liberty and Necessity; from a Gentleman of the University of Cambridge; with the Doctor's answers to them* (vol. IV, pp. 711–18).

[1717]. *Remarks upon a Book, Entitled, A Philosophical Enquiry concerning Human Liberty* (vol. IV, pp. 719–35).

Clayton, Robert (1753). *Some Thoughts on Self-Love [etc.] . . . occasioned by reading Mr. Hume's Works*.

Clerc, Jean le (1707). Review of the fifth edition of Locke's *Essay concerning Human Understanding: Bibliotheque Choisie, pour servir de suite à la bibliotheque universelle* 12: 80–123.

Collins, Anthony (1707). *An Essay concerning the Use of Reason in Propositions, The Evidence whereof depends upon Human Testimony*.

—— (1710). *A Vindication of the Divine Attributes. In some Remarks on his Grace the Archbishop of Dublin's Sermon, intituled, Divine Predestination and Foreknowledg consistent with the Freedom of Man's Will*.

—— (1717). *A Philosophical Inquiry concerning Human Liberty*.

Cooper, Thomas (1789). *Tracts Ethical, Theological and Political*, Warrington.

[Corry, William] (1761). *Reflections upon Liberty and Necessity*.

Crombie, Alexander (1793). *An Essay on Philosophical Necessity*.

Cudworth, Ralph (1838, 1996). *A Treatise of Freewill*, included with *A Treatise Concerning Eternal and Immutable Morality*, ed. Sarah Hutton, Cambridge.

[Dana, James] (1770). *An Examination of the late President Edwards's Enquiry on Freedom of the Will*, Boston.

Dawson, Benjamin (1783). *The Necessitarian: or the question concerning Liberty and Necessity stated and discussed, in XIX Letters*.

Descartes, René (1984–5). *The Philosophical Writings of Descartes*, translated by John Cottingham, Robert Stoothoff, and Dugald Murdoch, 2 vols., Cambridge.

Dudgeon, William (1739, 1765). *A View of the Necessitarian or Best Scheme: freed from the Objections of Mr. Crousaz, in his examination of Mr. Pope's Essay on Man*, in *The Philosophical Works of Mr. William Dudgeon, Carefully Corrected*, no place.

Edwards, Jonathan (1731, 1999). 'God Glorified in the Work of Redemption, By the Greatness of Man's Dependence upon Him, in the Whole of it', in *Sermons and Discourses 1730–1733*, ed. Mark Valeri, New Haven and London (vol. 17 of the Yale edition of *The Works of Jonathan Edwards*).

—— (1741, 1999). 'Sinners in the Hands of an Angry God', in *The Sermons of Jonathan Edwards: A Reader*, ed. Wilson H. Kimnach, Kenneth P. Minkema, and Douglas R. Sweeney, New Haven and London.

—— (1754, 1957). *A careful and strict Enquiry into The modern prevailing Notions of that Freedom of Will, Which is supposed to be essential to Moral Agency, Virtue and Vice, Reward and Punishment, Praise and Blame*, ed. Paul Ramsey, New Haven and London (vol. i of the Yale edn of *The Works of Jonathan Edwards*).

—— (1758a, 1957). *Remarks on the Essays on the Principles of Morality and Religion, in a Letter to a Minister of the Church of Scotland*, appended to Edwards (1754, 1957).

—— (1758b, 1970). *The Great Christian Doctrine of Original Sin Defended; Evidences of it's Truth produced, and Arguments to the Contrary answered*, ed. Clyde A. Holbrook, New Haven and London (vol. iii of the Yale edn of *The Works of Jonathan Edwards*).

—— (1765, 1989). *Two Dissertations, I. Concerning the End for which God created the World. II. The Nature of True Virtue*, in *Ethical Writings*, ed. Paul Ramsey, New Haven and London (vol. viii of the Yale edn of *The Works of Jonathan Edwards*).

—— (1806). *A Treatise on Religious Affections*, abridged by John Wesley.

—— (1980). *Scientific and Philosophical Writings*, ed. Wallace E. Anderson, New Haven and London (vol. vi of the Yale edn of *The Works of Jonathan Edwards*).

—— (1994). *The Miscellanies (entry nos. a-z, aa-zz, 1–500)*, ed. Thomas A. Schafer, New Haven and London (vol. xiii of the Yale edn of *The Works of Jonathan Edwards*).

—— (2000). *The Miscellanies (entry nos. 501–832)*, ed. Ava Chamberlain, New Haven and London (vol. xviii of the Yale edn of *The Works of Jonathan Edwards*).

Enfield, William (1791). *The History of Philosophy, from the Earliest Times to the Beginning of the Present Century; drawn up from Brucker's Historia Critica Philosophiæ*, 2 vols.

Episcopius, Simon (1678 [1665]). *Opera Theologia*, 2nd edn, 2 vols.

Fancourt, Samuel (1729). *An Essay concerning Liberty, Grace, and Prescience*.

[Franklin, Benjamin] (1725). *A Dissertation on Liberty and Necessity, Pleasure and Pain*.

[Gleig, George] (1797). 'Metaphysics', *Encyclopædia Britannica*, 3rd edn, eds. Colin Macfarquhar and George Gleig, 18 vols., Edinburgh.

Godwin, William (1793). *An Enquiry concerning Political Justice*, 2 vols.

—— (1831, 1993). *Thoughts on Man, his Nature, Productions, and Discoveries*, in *Essays*, ed. Mark Philp, vol. v of *Political and Philosophical Writings of William Godwin*, London.

Gregory, James (1792). *Philosophical and Literary Essays*. Edinburgh.

—— (1819). *Letters from Dr. James Gregory of Edinburgh, in defence of his essay on the difference of the relation between motive and action and that of cause and effect in physics: with replies by the Rev. Alexander Crombie, LL. D.*

Gretton, Phillips (1730). *Remarks on two Pamphlets written by the late A. C. Esq; concerning Human Liberty and Necessity.*

Hamilton, Sir William (1830, 1853). 'Philosophy of Perception', in *Discussions on Philosophy and Literature, Education and University Reform*, 2nd edn, London and Edinburgh.

—— (1863 [1846]). *Preface, Notes and Supplementary Dissertations to The Works of Thomas Reid, D.D. Now Fully Collected, With Selections from his Unpublished Letters.*

—— (1859–60). *Lectures on Metaphysics and Logic*, 4 vols., ed. H. L. Mansel and John Veitch, Edinburgh and London.

Hartley, David (1749). *Observations on Man, His Frame, His Duty, and His Expectations*, 2 vols.

—— (1810). *Observations on Man, His Frame, His Duty, and His Expectations*, 5th edn, 2 vols.

Hazlitt, William (1834, 1931). 'On Liberty and Necessity', in *The Complete Works of William Hazlitt*, ed. P. P. Howe, 21 vols., London and Toronto, 1930–34, vol. II, pp. 245–70.

Highmore, Joseph (1766). *Essays, Moral, Religious and Miscellaneous*, 2 vols.

Hobbes, Thomas (1654). *Of Libertie and Necessity. A Treatise, Wherein all Controversie concerning Predestination, Election, Free-will, Grace, Merits, Reprobation &c. is fully decided and cleared, in answer to a Treatise written by the Bishop of London-Derry, on the same subject.*

—— (1656a). *The Questions Concerning Liberty, Necessity, and Chance. Clearly Stated and Debated Between Dr. Bramhall Bishop of Derry and Thomas Hobbes of Malmesbury.*

—— (1656b, 1839). *Elements of Philosophy. The first section, Concerning Body, written in Latin . . . and translated into English*: vol. I of Sir William Molesworth (ed.), *The English Works of Thomas Hobbes of Malmesbury.*

Horsley, Samuel (1811). *Sermons*, 3 vols., Dundee.

Hume, David (1739–40, 2000). *A Treatise of Human Nature*, ed. David Fate Norton and Mary J. Norton, Oxford.

—— (1740, 2000). *An Abstract of a Book lately published, entitled, A Treatise of Human Nature, &c. Wherein the Chief Argument of that Book is Farther Illustrated and Explained*, in Hume (1739–40, 2000), pp. 403–17.

—— (1745). *A Letter from a Gentleman to his Friend in Edinburgh*, Edinburgh.

—— (1748, 2000). *An Enquiry concerning Human Understanding: A Critical Edition*, ed. Tom L. Beauchamp, Oxford.

—— (1754–62, 1983). *The History of England, from the Invasion of Julius Caesar to the Revolution of 1688*, ed. William B. Todd, Indianapolis.

—— (1932). *The Letters of David Hume*, ed. J. Y. T. Greig, 2 vols., Oxford.

—— (1987). *Essays Moral, Political, and Literary*, ed. Eugene F. Miller, revised edition, Indianapolis.

Hutcheson, Francis (1730, 1993). 'Inaugural Lecture on the Social Nature of Man', trans. Thomas Mautner, in *On Human Nature*, ed. Thomas Mautner, Cambridge.

Huxley, Thomas H. (1868, 1893). 'On the Physical Basis of Life', in *Collected Essays*, 9 vols., London, vol. I, pp. 130–65.

Jackson, John (1730). *A Vindication of Humane Liberty, in Answer to a Dissertation on Liberty and Necessity, by A. C.*

Jebb, John (1787). *The Works Theological, Medical, Political, and Miscellaneous*, 3 vols.

Kames, Lord (Henry Home) (1751). *Essays on the Principles of Morality and Natural Religion.*

—— (1754). 'Of the Laws of Motion', in [Various authors], *Essays and Observations, Physical and Literary, Read before a Society in Edinburgh, and published by them, Volume I*, Edinburgh.

—— (1758). *Essays on the Principles of Morality and Natural Religion*, 2nd edn.

—— (1779). *Essays on the Principles of Morality and Natural Religion*, 3rd edn, Edinburgh.

—— (1785 [1762]). *Elements of Criticism*, 6th edn, 3 vols., Edinburgh.

—— (1778 [1774]). *Sketches of the History of Man*, 2nd edn, 3 vols., Edinburgh.

King, William (1709, 1727). *Divine Predestination and Fore-knowledge, consistent with the Freedom of Man's Will. A Sermon Preached at Christ-Church, Dublin. May 15. 1709*, 3rd edn, Dublin.

—— (1731). *An Essay on the Origin of Evil*, translated and edited by Edmund Law, Cambridge.

Leibniz, Gottfried Wilhelm (1710, 1985). *Theodicy: Essays on the Goodness of God, the Freedom of Man and the Origin of Evil*, translated by E. M. Huggard, Chicago and La Salle.

Leibniz, Gottfried Wilhelm and Clarke, Samuel (1717, 1956). *The Leibniz–Clarke Correspondence*, ed. H. G. Alexander, Manchester.

Leland, John (1754–6). *A View of the Principal Deistical Writers of the Last and Present Century*, 2nd edn, 2 vols.

Limborch, Philip (1713). *A Compleat System or Body of Divinity, Both Speculative and Practical, Founded on Scripture and Reason*, trans. William Jones, 2nd edn, 2 vols.

Locke, John (1690, 1975). *An Essay concerning Human Understanding*, ed. Peter Nidditch, Oxford.

—— (1693, 1989). *Some Thoughts Concerning Education*, eds. John W. and Jean S. Yolton, Oxford.

—— (1954). *Essays on the Law of Nature and Associated Writings*, ed. W. von Leyden, Oxford.

Locke, John (1976–1989). *The Correspondence of John Locke*, ed. E. S. De Beer, 8 vols., Oxford.

Mackintosh, Sir James (1821). Review of Stewart (1854 [1815–21]): *The Edinburgh Review, or Critical Journal* 36: 220–67.

—— (1836). *Dissertation on the Progress of Ethical Philosophy, Chiefly During the Seventeenth and Eighteenth Centuries*, Edinburgh.

Maclaurin, Colin (1748). *An Account of Sir Isaac Newton's Philosophical Discoveries.*

Mansel, Henry Longueville (1851). *Prolegomena Logica. An Inquiry into the Psychological Character of Logical Processes*, Oxford.

Mill, James (1829). *Analysis of the Phenomena of the Human Mind*, 2 vols.

—— (1869 [1829]). *Analysis of the Phenomena of the Human Mind*, a new edition by John Stuart Mill, with notes by Alexander Bain, Andrew Findlater, and George Grote, 2 vols.

Mill, John Stuart (1843, 1973). *A System of Logic Ratiocinative and Inductive, Being a Connected View of Evidence and the Methods of Scientific Investigation*, ed. J. M. Robson (vols. VII and VIII of the *Collected Works of John Stuart Mill*).

—— (1865, 1979). *An Examination of Sir William Hamilton's Philosophy and of The Principal Questions Discussed in his Writings*, ed. J. M. Robson (vol. IX of the *Collected Works of John Stuart Mill*).

—— (1869). Introduction to James Mill, *Analysis of the Phenomena of the Human Mind*, 2 vols.

Morell, J. D. (1846). *An Historical and Critical View of the Speculative Philosophy of Europe in the Nineteenth Century*, 2 vols.

Newton, Isaac (1726 [1687]). *Philosophiae naturalis principia mathematica*, 3rd edn.

—— (1729, 1934). *The Mathematical Principles of Natural Philosophy*, trans. Andrew Motte, trans. revised by Florian Cajori, Berkeley.

Oswald, James (1766). *An Appeal to Common Sense in Behalf of Religion*, vol. I, Edinburgh.

—— (1772). *An Appeal to Common Sense in Behalf of Religion*, vol. II, Edinburgh.

Palmer, John (1779). *Observations in defence of the Liberty of Man as a Moral Agent*.

—— (1780). *An Appendix to the Observations in defence of the Liberty of Man as a Moral Agent*.

[Phileleutherus] (1751). *A Letter to a Friend, upon Occasion of a late Book, intitled, Essays upon Morality and Natural Religion*, Edinburgh.

[Phillips, Lucy] (1866). *The Battle of the Two Philosophies*, London.

Price, Richard (1758). *A Review of the Principal Questions and Difficulties in Morals*.

Price, Richard and Priestley, Joseph (1778). *A Free Discussion of the Doctrines of Materialism, and Philosophical Necessity*.

Priestley, Joseph (1772–4). *Institutes of Natural and Revealed Religion*, 3 vols.

—— (1774). *An Examination of Dr. Reid's Inquiry into the Human Mind, Dr. Beattie's Essay on the Nature and Immutability of Truth, and Dr. Oswald's Appeal to Common Sense*.

—— (1775). *Hartley's Theory of the Human Mind on the Principle of Association of Ideas*.

—— (1779). *A Letter to the Rev. Mr. John Palmer, in defence of the Illustrations of Philosophical Necessity*, Bath.

—— (1780a). *A Letter to Jacob Bryant, Esq. in Defence of Philosophical Necessity*.

—— (1780b). *A Second Letter to the Rev. Mr. John Palmer, in defence of the Doctrine of Philosophical Necessity*.

—— (1782 [1777]). *Disquisitions relating to Matter and Spirit* and *The Doctrine of Philosophical Necessity Illustrated; being an Appendix to the Disquisitions relating to Matter and Spirit. To which is added, An Answer to several Persons who have controverted the Principles of it*, 2nd edn, 2 vols., Birmingham.

—— (1787 [1780]). *Letters to a Philosophical Unbeliever*, 2nd edn, 2 vols.

—— (1790). 'Preface' to Anthony Collins, *A Philosophical Inquiry concerning Human Liberty*, Birmingham.

Ramsey, John (1888). *Scotland and Scotsmen in the Eighteenth Century*, ed. Alexander Allardyce, 2 vols., Edinburgh.

Reid, Thomas (1764, 1997). *An Inquiry into the Human Mind on the Principles of Common Sense*, ed. Derek R. Brookes, Edinburgh.

—— (1785, 2002). *Essays on the Intellectual Powers of Man*, ed. Derek R. Brookes, Edinburgh.

—— (1788, 1969). *Essays on the Active Powers of the Human Mind*, Cambridge, MA.

—— (1858). *The Works of Thomas Reid, D. D.*, ed. Sir William Hamilton, fifth edition, Edinburgh.

—— (1989). *The Philosophical Orations of Thomas Reid*, ed. D. D. Tod, translated by S. D. Sullivan, Carbondale.

—— (1990). *Practical Ethics*, ed. Knud Haakonssen, Princeton.

—— (1995). *Thomas Reid on the Animate Creation: Papers Relating to the Life Sciences*, ed. Paul Wood, Edinburgh.

—— (2001). 'Of Power', *The Philosophical Quarterly* 51: 1–12.

—— (2002). *The Correspondence of Thomas Reid*, ed. Paul Wood, Edinburgh.

Ryle, Gilbert (1949). *The Concept of Mind*, London.

Seth, Andrew (1898). 'The "New" Psychology and Automatism', *The Contemporary Review* 63: 555–74.

Shaftesbury, Anthony Ashley Cooper Third Earl of (1711, 1999). *Characteristics of Men, Manners, Opinions, Times*, ed. Lawrence Klein, Cambridge.

Sidgwick, Henry (1907 [1874]). *The Methods of Ethics*, 7th edn.

Smith, Adam (1759, 1984). *The Theory of Moral Sentiments*, ed. D. D. Raphael and A. L. Macfie, Indianapolis.

Spencer, Herbert (1855). *The Principles of Psychology*.

Spinoza, Baruch (1982). *The Ethics and Selected Letters*, ed. Seymour Feldman, translated by Samuel Shirley, Indianapolis.

Stewart, Dugald (1792). *Elements of the Philosophy of the Human Mind*.

—— (1801). *Outlines of Moral Philosophy*, Edinburgh.

—— (1810). *Philosophical Essays*, Edinburgh.

—— (1811). *Biographical Memoirs, of Adam Smith, LL. D. of William Robertson, D. D. and of Thomas Reid, D. D. Read Before the Royal Society of Edinburgh*, Edinburgh.

—— (1814). *Elements of the Philosophy of the Human Mind, Volume Second*, Edinburgh.

Stewart, Dugald (1828). *The Philosophy of the Active and Moral Powers of Man*, 2 vols., Edinburgh.

—— (1854 [1815–21]). *Dissertation: Exhibiting the Progress of Metaphysical, Ethical, and Political Philosophy, Since the Revival of Letters in Europe*, 2nd edn, in vol. ɪ of Stewart's *Collected Works*, ed. Sir William Hamilton, 11 vols, Edinburgh.

Strutt, Samuel (1730). *A Defence of the late Learned Dr. Clarke's Notion of Natural Liberty: in answer to Three Letters wrote to him by a Gentleman of the University of Cambridge, on the Side of Necessity.*

Sully, James (1884). *Outlines of Psychology with special reference to the Theory of Education*, London: Longmans, Green and Co.

Taylor, Jeremy (1740). *The Scripture Doctrine of Original Sin proposed to Free and Candid Examination.*

Trigg, W. B. (1938). 'The Correspondence of Dr. David Hartley and Rev. John Lister', *Transactions of the Halifax Antiquarian Society*, pp. 230–78.

Tucker, Abraham [pseud. Edward Search] (1763). *Freewill, Foreknowledge and Fate: A Fragment.*

—— (1840 [1768–1778]). *The Light of Nature Pursued*, 5th edn, 2 vols.

Voltaire, François-Marie Arouet de (1733). *Letters concerning the English Nation*, trans. anon..

Ward, James (1910–11 [1886]). 'Psychology', *Encylopædia Britannica*, eleventh edition, Cambridge: Cambridge University Press.

—— (1922). *A Study of Kant*, Cambridge: Cambridge University Press.

Watts, Isaac (1732). *On the Freedom of the Will in God and Creatures.*

—— (1733). *Philosophical Essays on Various Subjects . . . With some Remarks on Mr. Locke's Essay on the Human Understanding.*

Wesley, John (1774). *Thoughts upon Necessity.*

Witherspoon, John (1763 [1753]). *Ecclesiastical Characteristics: or, the Arcana of Church Policy*, 5th edn, Edinburgh.

Secondary Sources

Aarsleff, Hans (1994). 'Locke's influence', in Chappell (ed.) (1994).

Allen, Alexander V. G. (1889). *Life and Writings of Jonathan Edwards*, Edinburgh: T. and T. Clark.

Allen, Richard C. (1999). *David Hartley on Human Nature*, Albany, NY: State University of New York Press.

Alvarez, Maria (2000). 'Reid, Agent Causation and Volitionism', *Reid Studies* 3: 69–87.

Anderson, Wallace E. (1980). 'Editor's Introduction' to Edwards (1980).

Ardley, Gavin (1980). *The Common Sense Philosophy of James Oswald*, Aberdeen: Aberdeen University Press.

Barfoot, Michael (1990). 'Hume and Culture of Science in the Early Eighteenth Century', in Stewart (ed.) (1990).

Bennett, Jonathan (2001). *Learning from Six Philosophers*, 2 vols., Oxford: Clarendon Press.

Berman, David (1976). 'Introduction' to *Archbishop King's Sermon on Predestination*, Dublin: The Cadenus Press.

—— (1982). 'Enlightenment and Counter-Enlightenment in Irish Philosophy', *Archiv für Geschichte der Philosophie* 64: 148–65.

—— (1988). *A History of Atheism in Britain from Hobbes to Russell*, London: Routledge.

Blackburn, Simon (1990). 'Hume and Thick Connexions', *Philosophy and Phenomenological Research* 50, Supplement, 237–50.

Boring, E. G. (1929). *A History of Experimental Psychology*, New York: D. Appleton-Century Co.

Botterill, George (2002). 'Hume on Liberty and Necessity' in Millican (ed.) (2000).

Bower, George (1881). *Hartley and James Mill*, London.

Brandt, Frithiof (1928). *Thomas Hobbes' Mechanical Conception of Nature*, Copenhagen and London: Levin and Munksgaard.

Brett, G. S. (1962). *History of Psychology*, ed. and abridged by R. S. Peters, revised edn, London: George Allen and Unwin Ltd.

Broadie, Alexander (2002). 'The Association of Ideas: Thomas Reid's Context', *Reid Studies* 5: 30–53.

—— (ed.) (2003). *The Cambridge Companion to the Scottish Enlightenment*, Cambridge: Cambridge University Press.

—— (2003). 'The Human Mind and its Powers', in Broadie (ed.) (2003).

Brookes, Derek R. (1997). 'Introduction' to Reid (1764, 1997).

Brown, Stuart (ed.) (1991). *Nicolas Malabranche: His Philosophical Critics and Successors*, Assen: Van Gorcum.

Buchdahl, Gerd (1961). *The Image of Newton and Locke in the Age of Reason*, London and New York: Sheed and Ward.

Buckle, Stephen (1999). 'British Sceptical Realism: A Fresh Look at the British Tradition', *European Journal of Philosophy* 7: 1–29.

—— (2001). *Hume's Enlightenment Tract: The Unity and Purpose of An Enquiry concerning Human Understanding*, Oxford: Clarendon Press.

Cassirer, Ernst (1932, 1951). *The Philosophy of the Enlightenment*, trans. Fritz C. A. Koelln and James P. Pettegrove, Princeton: Princeton University Press.

Chai, Leon (1998). *Jonathan Edwards and the Limits of Enlightenment Philosophy*, New York and Oxford: Oxford University Press.

Chamberlain, Mary Ava (1990). *Jonathan Edwards against the Antinomians and Arminians*, Columbia University PhD dissertation.

Chappell, Vere (1994). 'Locke on the Freedom of the Will', in G. A. J. Rogers (ed.), *Locke's Philosophy: Content and Context*, Oxford: Clarendon Press.

—— (ed.) (1994). *The Cambridge Companion to Locke*, Cambridge: Cambridge University Press.

—— (2000). 'Locke on the Suspension of Desire', in Gary Fuller, Robert Stecker, and John P. Wright (eds.), *John Locke:* An Essay concerning Human Understanding *in focus*, London: Routledge.

Cherry, Conrad (1966). *The Theology of Jonathan Edwards: A Reappraisal*, Bloomington and Indianapolis: Indiana University Press.

Chisholm, Roderick M. (1964, 1982). 'Human Freedom and the Self', in Gary Watson (ed.), *Free Will*, Oxford: Oxford University Press.

—— (1966). 'Freedom and Action', in Keith Lehrer (ed.), *Freedom and Determinism*, New York: Random House.

Colie, Rosalie (1957). *Light and Enlightenment: A Study of the Cambridge Platonists and the Dutch Arminians*. Cambridge: Cambridge University Press.

Colman, John (1983). *John Locke's Moral Philosophy*, Edinburgh: Edinburgh University Press.

Craig, Edward (1987). *The Mind of God and the Works of Man*, Oxford: Clarendon Press.

—— (ed.) (1998). *The Routledge Encyclopedia of Philosophy*, 10 vols., London: Routledge.

Crimmins, James E. (ed.) (1998). *Utilitarians and Religion*, Bristol: Thoemmes Press.

M. Dalgarno and E. Matthews (eds.) (1989), *The Philosophy of Thomas Reid*, Dordrecht: Kluwer.

Danziger, Kurt (1982). 'Mid-Nineteenth-Century British Psycho-Physiology: A Neglected Chapter in the History of Psychology', in Woodward and Ash (eds.) (1982).

Darwall, Stephen (1995). *The British Moralists and the Internal 'Ought': 1640–1740*, Cambridge: Cambridge University Press.

Daston, Lorraine (1978). 'British Responses to Psycho-Physiology, 1860–1900', *Isis* 69: 192–208.

—— (1982). 'The Theory of the Will versus the Science of the Mind', in Woodward and Ash (eds.) (1982).

De Bary, Philip (2002). *Thomas Reid and Scepticism: His Reliabilist Response*, London: Routledge.

Dixon, Thomas (2003). *From Passions to Emotions: The Invention of a Secular Psychological Category*, Cambridge: Cambridge University Press.

Duggan, Timothy (1976). 'Active Power and Liberty of Moral Agents', in Stephen F. Barker and Thomas Beauchamp (eds.), *Thomas Reid: Critical Interpretations*, Philadelphia: Philosophical Monographs (1976).

Elwood, Douglas J. (1960). *The Philosophical Theology of Jonathan Edwards*, New York: Columbia University Press.

Erdt, Terrence (1980). *Jonathan Edwards: Art and the Sense of the Heart*, Amherst: University of Massachusetts Press.

Feingold, Mordechai (1988). 'Partnership in Glory: Newton and Locke through the Enlightenment and Beyond', in P. B. Scheurer and G. Debrock (eds.), *Newton's Scientific and Philosophical Legacy*, Dordrecht: Kluwer.

Ferguson, J. P. (1974). *The Philosophy of Samuel Clarke and its Critics*, New York: Vantage Press.

—— (1976). *An Eighteenth Century Heretic: Dr Samuel Clarke*, Kineton: The Roundwood Press.

Fiering, Norman (1981). *Jonathan Edwards's Moral Thought and Its British Context*, Chapel Hill: University of North Carolina Press.

Fieser, James (2001). 'Introduction' to a facsimile reprint of Gregory (1792), Crombie (1793), and Gregory and Crombie (1819), *Philosophical and Literary Essays, and Letters*, Bristol: Thoemmes.

Flew, Antony (1961). *Hume's Philosophy of Belief: A Study of his First* Inquiry, London: Routledge and Kegan Paul.

Foisneau, Luc (1999). 'Introduction' to Thomas Hobbes, *Les Questions concernant la Liberté, la Nécessité et le Hasard*, trans. Foisneau and Florence Perronin, Paris: Libraire Philosophique J. Vrin.

Forbes, Duncan (1975). *Hume's Philosophical Politics*. Cambridge: Cambridge University Press.

Forbes, Margaret (1904). *Beattie and his Friends*, London: Archibald Constable and Co.

Forbes, William (1806). *Life and Writings of Beattie*, 2 vols., Edinburgh.

Force, James (1990). 'Hume's Interest in Newton and Science', in Force and Popkin (eds.), *Essays on the Context, Nature, and Influence of Isaac Newton's Theology*, Dordrecht: Kluwer, 181–206.

Garrett, Don (1997). *Cognition and Commitment in Hume's Philosophy*. Oxford: Oxford University Press.

Gay, John H. (1963). 'Matter and Freedom in the Thought of Samuel Clarke', *Journal of the History of Ideas* 24: 85–105.

Gert, Bernhard (1996). 'Hobbes's psychology', in Sorell (ed.) (1996).

Griffin-Collart, Evelyne (1980). *La philosophie écossaise du sens commun: Thomas Reid and Dugald Stewart*, Brussels: Palais des Académies.

Guelzo, Allen C. (1989). *Edwards on the Will: A Century of American Theological Debate*, Middletown: Wesleyan University Press.

Haakonssen, Knud (1990). 'Introduction' to Reid (1990).

—— (1999). 'Stewart, Dugald' in Yolton, Price, and Stephens (eds.) (1999).

Halévy, Elie (1928). *The Growth of Philosophic Radicalism*, trans. Mary Morris, London: Faber and Gwyer.

Harris, James A. (2001a). 'Reid's Challenge to Reductionism about Human Agency', *Reid Studies* 4: 33–42.

—— (2001b). 'Joseph Priestley and "the proper doctrine of philosophical necessity" ', *Enlightenment and Dissent* 20: pp. 23–44.

—— (2002a). 'Hartley, David', in P. Dematteis and P. Fosl (eds.), *Dictionary of Literary Biography, vol. 252: British Philosophers 1500–1799*, Bruccoli Clark Layman.

—— (2002b). 'Crombie, Alexander', in Mander and Sell (eds.) (2002).

—— (2003a). 'Introduction' to a facsimile reprint of Tucker (1840), Bristol: Thoemmes Press.

—— (2003b). 'On Reid's "Inconsistent Triad": a Reply to McDermid', *British Journal for the History of Philosophy* 11: 121–7.

—— (2003c). 'Hume's Reconciling Project and "the common distinction betwixt *moral* and *physical* necessity" ', *British Journal for the History of Philosophy* 11: 451–71.

—— (2004b). 'Introduction' to James Beattie, *Selected Philosophical Writings*, ed. James A. Harris, Exeter: Imprint Academic.

—— (2005). 'Hume's use of the rhetoric of Calvinism', in Marina Frasca Spada and Peter Kail (eds.), *Impressions of Hume*, Oxford: Oxford University Press.

Harrison, A. W. (1937). *Arminianism*, London: Duckworth.

Hatfield, Gary (1995). 'Remaking the Science of the Mind: Psychology as Natural Science', in Christopher Fox, Roy Porter, and Robert Wokler (eds.), *Inventing Human Science: Eighteenth-Century Domains*, Berkeley and Los Angeles: University of California Press.

Helm, Paul (1969). 'John Locke and Jonathan Edwards: A Reconsideration', *Journal of the History of Philosophy* 7: 51–61.

Helo, Ari (2001). 'The Historicity of Morality: Necessity and Necessary Agents in the Ethics of Lord Kames', *History of European Ideas* 27: 239–55.

Houaranszki, Ferenc (2002). 'Common Sense and the Theory of Human Behaviour', *The Philosophical Quarterly* 52: 526–43.

James, Susan (1997). *Passion and Action: The Emotions in Seventeenth-Century Philosophy*, Oxford: Clarendon Press.

Jesseph, Douglas (1996). 'Hobbes and the Method of Natural Science', in Sorell (ed.) (1996).

Jolley, Nicholas (1999). *Locke: His Philosophical Thought*, Oxford: Oxford University Press.

Jones, Peter (1982). *Hume's Sentiments: Their Ciceronian and French Context*. Edinburgh: Edinburgh University Press.

Kail, Peter (2001). 'Projection and Necessity in Hume', *European Journal of Philosophy* 9: 25–55.

Kuehn, Manfred (1987). *Scottish Common Sense in Germany, 1768–1800: A Contribution to the History of Critical Philosophy*, Kingston: McGill-Queen's University Press.

Kuklick, Bruce (2001). *A History of Philosophy in America 1720–2000*, Oxford: Clarendon Press.

Kuypers, Mary Shaw (1930). *Studies in the Eighteenth-Century Background of Hume's Empiricism*, New York: Russell and Russell.

Laudan, Larry (1970). 'Thomas Reid and the Newtonian Turn of British Methodological Thought', in Robert E. Butts and John W. Davis (eds.), *The Methodological Heritage of Newton*, Oxford: Basil Blackwell.

Laurie, Henry (1902). *Scottish Philosophy in its National Development*, Edinburgh.

Lee, Sang Hyun (2000). *The Philosophical Theology of Jonathan Edwards*, expanded edn, Princeton: Princeton University Press.

Lehmann, William C. (1971). *Henry Home, Lord Kames, and the Scottish Enlightenment*, The Hague: Martinus Nijhoff.

Lehrer, Keith (1989). *Thomas Reid*. London: Routledge.

Leijenhorst, Cees (1996). 'Hobbes's Theory of Causality and its Aristotelian Background', *The Monist* 79: 426–47.

Leslie, Margaret (1972). 'Mysticism Misunderstood: David Hartley and the Idea of Progress', *Journal of the History of Ideas* 33: 625–32.

Lessay, Franck (1993). 'Introduction' to Thomas Hobbes, *De la Liberté et de la Nécessité*, trans. Lessay, Paris: Libraire Philosophique J. Vrin.

Locke, Don (1980). *A Fantasy of Reason: The Life and Thought of William Godwin*, London: Routledge and Kegan Paul.

Lowe, E. J. (1995). *Locke on Human Understanding*, London: Routledge.

Lyon, Georges (1888). *L'idéalisme en angleterre au XVIIIe siècle*, Paris: Ancienne Librairie Germer Baillière.

Macintyre, Gordon (2003). *Dugald Stewart: The Pride and Ornament of Scotland*, Brighton: Sussex Academic Press.

Maclean, Kenneth (1936). *John Locke and English Literature of the Eighteenth Century*, New Haven: Yale University Press.

Madden, Edward H. (1982). 'Commonsense and Agency Theory', *Review of Metaphysics* 36: 319–41.

—— (1985). 'Sir William Hamilton, Critical Philosophy, and the Common Sense Tradition', *Review of Metaphysics* 38: 839–66.

—— (1986). 'Stewart's Enrichment of the Commonsense Tradition', *History of Philosophy Quarterly* 3: 45–63.

Magri, Tito (2000). 'Locke, Suspension of Desire, and the Remote Good', *British Journal for the History of Philosophy* 8: 55–70.

Mandelbaum, Maurice (1971). *History, Man, and Reason*, Baltimore: Johns Hopkins Press.

Mander, W. F. and Sell, Alan P. F. (eds.) (2002). *The Thoemmes Dictionary of Nineteenth-Century British Philosophers*, 2 vols., Bristol: Thoemmes.

Marsden, George (2003). *Jonathan Edwards: A Life*, New Haven: Yale University Press.

McClymond, Michael J. (1998). *Encounters with God: An Approach to the Theology of Jonathan Edwards*, New York and Oxford: Oxford University Press.

McCosh, James (1875). *The Scottish Philosophy, Biographical, Expository, Critical, From Hutcheson to Hamilton.*

McCracken, Charles (1983). *Malebranche and British Philosophy*, Oxford: Clarendon Press.

McDermid, Douglas (1999). 'Thomas Reid on Moral Liberty and Common Sense', *British Journal for the History of Philosophy* 7: 275–303.

McGuinness, Arthur (1970). *Henry Home, Lord Kames*, New York: Twayne.

McIntyre, Jane L. (1994). 'Hume: Second Newton of the Moral Sciences', *Hume Studies* 20: 3–18.

Miller, Perry (1973 [1949]). *Jonathan Edwards*, reprinted at Newport, CT: Greenwood Press.

Millican, Peter (ed.) (2002). *Reading Hume on Human Understanding: Essays on the First Enquiry*. Oxford: Clarendon Press.

—— (2002a). 'The Context, Aims, and Structure of Hume's First *Enquiry*', in Millican (ed.) (2002).

—— (2002b). 'Hume's Sceptical Doubts concerning Induction', in Millican (ed.) (2002).

Mintz, Samuel (1962). *The Hunting of Leviathan*. Cambridge University Press.

Mischel, Theodore (1966). ' "Emotion" and "Motivation" in the Development of English Psychology: D. Hartley, James Mill, A. Bain', *Journal of the History of the Behavioral Sciences* 2: 123–44.

Morère, Pierre (1980). *L'Oeuvre de James Beattie: tradition et perspectives nouvelles*, Paris: H. Champion.

—— (1999). 'Beattie, James', in Yolton, Price, and Stephens (eds.) (1999).

Murphy, Arthur E. (1959). 'Jonathan Edwards on Free Will and Moral Agency', *Philosophical Review* 68: 181–202.

Neiman, Susan (1994). *The Unity of Reason: Rereading Kant*, New York and Oxford: Oxford University Press.

Norton, David Fate (1979). 'Hume and his Scottish Critics', in David Fate Norton, Nicholas Capaldi, and Wade Robison (eds.), *McGill Hume Studies*, San Diego: Austin Hill Press.

—— (1982). *David Hume: Common-Sense Moralist, Sceptical Metaphysician*, Princeton: Princeton University Press.

Noxon, James (1973). *Hume's Philosophical Development: A Study of Hume's Methods*. Oxford: Clarendon Press.

Nuovo, Victor (1999a). 'Hartley, David', in Yolton, Price, and Stephens (eds.) (1999).

—— (1999b) 'Tucker, Abraham', in Yolton, Price, and Stephens (eds.) (1999).

O'Connor, D. J. (1967). *John Locke*, New York: Dover.

O'Connor, Timothy (1994). 'Thomas Reid on Free Agency', *Journal of the History of Philosophy* 32 (1994): 605–22.

—— (ed.) (1995). *Agents, Causes, and Events: Essays on Indeterminism and Free Will*, New York: Oxford University Press.

—— (2000). *Persons and Causes: The Metaphysics of Free Will*, New York: Oxford University Press.

O'Higgins, James (1970). *Anthony Collins: The Man and his Works*, The Hague: Martinus Nijhoff.

—— (1976). 'Introduction' to *Determinism and Freewill: Anthony Collins'* A Philosophical Inquiry Concerning Human Liberty, The Hague: Martinus Nijhoff.

O'Shaughnessy, Brian (1980). *The Will: A Dual-Aspect Theory*, 2 vols., Cambridge: Cambridge University Press.

Oberg, Barbara Bowen (1976). 'David Hartley and the Association of Ideas', *Journal of the History of Ideas* 37: 441–54.

Owen, David (2000). *Hume's Reason*, New York: Oxford University Press.

Passmore, John (1951). *Ralph Cudworth: An Introduction to his Thought*, Cambridge: Cambridge University Press.

—— (1965). 'The Malleability of Man in Eighteenth-Century Thought', in Earl R. Wasserman (ed.), *Aspects of the Eighteenth Century*, Baltimore: The Johns Hopkins Press.

Pécharman, Martine (1990). 'Philosophie première et théorie de l'action selon Hobbes', in Yves Charles Zarka and Jean Bernhardt (eds.), *Thomas Hobbes: Philosophie première, théorie de la science et politique*, Paris: Presses Universitaires de France.

Penelhum, Terence (2000). 'Hume and the Freedom of the Will', in *Themes from Hume: The Self, The Will, Religion*, Oxford: Clarendon Press.

Phillipson, N. T. (1978). 'James Beattie and the Defence of Common Sense', in Bernhard Fabian (ed.), *Festschrift für Reiner Gruenter*, Heidelberg.

Philp, Mark (1986). *Godwin's Political Justice*, London: Duckworth.

Popkin, Richard (1977). 'Joseph Priestley's Criticisms of David Hume's Philosophy', *Journal of the History of Philosophy* 15: 437–47.

Poppi, Antonino (1988). 'Fate, fortune, providence and human freedom', in Charles B. Schmidt and Quentin Skinner (eds.), *The Cambridge History of Renaissance Philosophy*, Cambridge: Cambridge University Press.

Porter, Roy (1998). 'Hartley, David', in Craig (ed.) (1998).

—— (2000). *Enlightenment: Britain and the Creation of the Modern World*, London: Penguin.

Ramsey, Paul (1957). 'Editor's Introduction' to Edwards (1754, 1957).

Read, Rupert, and Kenneth Richman (eds.) (2000). *The New Hume Debate*, London: Routledge.

Reed, Edward S. (1994). 'The Separation of Psychology from Philosophy: Studies in the Science of Mind 1815–1879', in C. L. Ten (ed.), *The Nineteenth Century*, London and New York: Routledge (vol. vii of the *Routledge History of Philosophy*).

Rickless, Samuel C. (2000). 'Locke on the Freedom to Will', *The Locke Newsletter* 31: 43–67.

—— (2001). Review of Yaffe (2000), *Locke Studies* 1: 235–55.

Rivers, Isabel (1991–2000), *Reason, Grace and Sentiment: A Study of the Language of Religion and Ethics in England, 1660–1780*, 2 vols., Cambridge: Cambridge University Press.

Robinson, Daniel N. (1989). 'Thomas Reid's Critique of Dugald Stewart', *Journal of the History of Philosophy* 3 (1989): 405–22.

Robinson, Roger J. (1996a). 'Introduction' to James Beattie, *An Essay on Truth*, London: Routledge and Thoemmes.

—— (1996b). 'Introduction' to James Beattie, *Elements of Moral Science*, London: Routledge and Thoemmes.

Rogers, G. A. J. (1978). 'Locke's *Essay* and Newton's *Principia*', *Journal of the History of Ideas* 39: 217–32.

Ross, Ian Simpson (1972). *Lord Kames and the Scotland of his Day*, Oxford: Clarendon Press.

—— (2000). 'The Natural Theology of Lord Kames', in Wood (ed.) (2000).

Rowe, William (1991). *Thomas Reid on Morality and Freedom*. Ithaca, NY: Cornell University Press.

Russell, Paul (1995a). *Freedom and Moral Sentiment*. Oxford: Oxford University Press.

—— (1995b). 'Hume's *Treatise* and the Clarke–Collins Controversy', *Hume Studies* 21: 95–115.

—— (1999). 'Dudgeon, William', in Yolton, Stephens, and Price (eds.) (1999).

Rylance, Rick (2000). *Victorian Psychology and British Culture 1850–1880*, Oxford and New York: Oxford University Press.

Rysiew, Patrick (2002). 'Reid and Epistemic Naturalism', *The Philosophical Quarterly* 52: 437–56.

Schneewind, Jerome (1998). *The Invention of Autonomy: A History of Modern Moral Philosophy*, Cambridge: Cambridge University Press.

Schouls, Peter A. (1992). *Reasoned Freedom: John Locke and Enlightenment*, Ithaca, NY: Cornell University Press.

Sell, Alan P. F. (1979). 'Priestley's Polemic Against Reid', *The Price–Priestley Newsletter* 3: 41–52.

Sher, Richard (1985). *Church and University in the Scottish Enlightenment: The Moderate Literati of Edinburgh*, Edinburgh.

—— (1990). 'Professors of Virtue: The Social History of the Edinburgh Moral Philosophy Chair in the Eighteenth Century', in Stewart (ed.) (1990).

Sleigh, Robert, Chapell, Vere, and Della Rocca, Michael (1998). 'Determinism and Human Freedom', in Daniel Garber and Michael Ayers (eds.), *The Cambridge History of Seventeenth-Century Philosophy*, Cambridge: Cambridge University Press.

Smith, C. U. M. (1987). 'David Hartley's Newtonian Neuropsychology', *Journal of the History of the Behavioural Sciences* 23: 123–36.

Sorell, Tom (1986). *Hobbes*, London: Routledge and Kegan Paul.

—— (ed.) (1996). *The Cambridge Companion to Hobbes*, Cambridge: Cambridge University Press.

Stalley, R. F. (1986). 'The Will in Hume's *Treatise*', *Journal of the History of Philosophy* 24: 41–53.

—— (1989). 'Causality and Agency in the Philosophy of Thomas Reid', in M. Dalgarno and E. Matthews (eds.), *The Philosophy of Thomas Reid*, Dordrecht: Kluwer.

Stecker, Robert (1992). 'Thomas Reid's Philosophy of Action', *Philosophical Studies* 66: 197–208.

Stephen, Leslie (1902, 1962). *History of English Thought in the Eighteenth Century*, 3rd edn, 2 vols., New York: Harbinger.

Stephens, John (1999). 'Priestley, Joseph', in Yolton, Price, and Stephens (eds.) (1999).

Stewart, M. A. (ed.) (1990). *Studies in the Philosophy of the Scottish Enlightenment*, Oxford: Clarendon Press.

—— (1990). 'An early fragment on evil', in Stewart and Wright (eds.) (1995).

—— (2002). 'Two Species of Philosophy: The Historical Significance of the First *Enquiry*', in Millican (ed.) (2002).

Stewart, M. A. and Wright, John P. (eds.) (1995). *Hume and Hume's Connexions*, University Park: Pennsylvania University Press.

Strawson, Galen (1989). *The Secret Connexion: Causation, Realism, and David Hume*, Oxford: Clarendon Press.

—— (2000). 'David Hume: Objects and Power', in Read and Richman (eds.) (2000).

Stroud, Barry (1977). *Hume*, London: Routledge and Kegan Paul.

Sutton, John (1998). *Philosophy and Memory Traces*, Cambridge: Cambridge University Press.

Tapper, Alan (2002). 'Reid and Priestley on Method and the Mind', *The Philosophical Quarterly* 52: 511–25.

Taylor, Richard (1966). *Action and Purpose*, Englewood Cliffs, NJ: Prentice Hall.

Tropea, Savina (2001). 'Introduction' to *Works of William Hamilton*, 7 vols., Bristol: Thoemmes Press.

Tyacke, Nicholas (1987). *Anti-Calvinists: The Rise of English Arminianism c. 1590–1640*. Oxford: Clarendon Press.

Tytler, Alexander Fraser (1807–9). *Memoirs of the Life and Writings of the Honourable Henry Home of Kames*, 2 vols., Edinburgh.

Ulman, H. L. (ed.) (1990). *The Minutes of the Aberdeen Philosophical Society 1758–1773*, Aberdeen: Aberdeen University Press.

Vailati, Ezio (1990). 'Leibniz on Locke on Weakness of Will', *Journal of the History of Philosophy* 28: 213–28.

—— (1997). *Leibniz and Clarke: A Study of their Correspondence*. New York: Oxford University Press.

Vesey, Godfrey (1989). 'Introduction' to a fasimile reprint of Crombie (1793), Bristol: Thoemmes Press.

Vienne, Jean Michel (1991). 'Malebranche and Locke: The Theory of Moral Choice, a Neglected Theme', in Brown (ed.) (1991).

Warren, Howard C. (1921). *A History of Association Psychology*, London: Constable and Co.

Watson, Gary (ed.) (2003). *Free Will*, 2nd edn, Oxford: Oxford University Press.

Weber, Donald (1981). 'Introduction' to a new imprint of Miller (1949), Amherst: University of Massachusetts Press.

Weinstock, Jerome (1975). 'Reid's Definition of Freedom', *Journal of the History of Philosophy* 13: 335–45.

Wellek, René (1931). *Immanuel Kant in England, 1793–1838*, Princeton: Princeton University Press.

Willey, Basil (1940). *The Eighteenth-Century Background: Studies on the Idea of Nature in the Thought of the Period*, London: Chatto and Windus.

Winkler, Kenneth (1991). 'The New Hume', *The Philosophical Review* 100: 541–79; reprinted in Read and Richman (eds.) (2000).

Wolterstorff, Nicholas (1987). 'Hume and Reid'. *The Monist* 70: 398–417.

—— (2001). *Thomas Reid and the Story of Epistemology*, Cambridge: Cambridge University Press.

Wood, Paul (1989). 'Reid on Hypotheses and the Ether: A Reassessment', in Dalgarno and Matthews (eds.) (1989).

—— (1990). 'Science and the Pursuit of Virtue in the Aberdeen Enlightenment', in Stewart (ed.) (1990).

—— (1994). 'Hume, Reid and the Science of the Mind', in M. A. Stewart and John P. Wright (eds.), *Hume and Hume's Connexions*, Edinburgh: Edinburgh University Press.

—— (1995). 'Introduction' to Reid (1985).

—— (1998 (a)). 'The Aberdeen Philosophical Society', in Craig (ed.) (1998).

—— (1998 (b)). 'Beattie, James', in Craig (ed.) (1998).

—— (ed.) (2000). *The Scottish Enlightenment: Essays in Reinterpretation*, Rochester, NY: University of Rochester Press.

Woodward, William, and Ash, Mitchell G. (eds.) (1982). *The Problematic Science: Psychology in Nineteenth-Century Thought*, New York: Praeger.

Woolf, Robert P. (1960). 'Kant's Debt to Hume via Beattie', *Journal of the History of Ideas* 21: 117–23.

Wright, John P. (1983). *The Sceptical Realism of David Hume*, Manchester: Manchester University Press.

—— (1991). 'Hume's Criticism of Malebranche's Theory of Causation', in Brown (ed.) (1991).

—— (2000). 'Hume's Causal Realism: Recovering a Tradition Interpretation', in Read and Richman (eds.) (2000).

Yaffe, Gideon (2000). *Liberty Worth the Name: Locke on Free Agency*, Princeton: Princeton University Press.

—— (2001). 'Locke on Refraining, Suspending, and the Freedom to Will', *History of Philosophy Quarterly* 18: 373–91.

—— (2004). *Manifest Activity: Thomas Reid's Theory of Action*, Oxford: Clarendon Press.

Yolton, John (1983). *Thinking Matter: Materialism in Eighteenth-Century Britain*, Oxford: Basil Blackwell.

Yolton, John, and Yolton, Jean (1985). *John Locke: A Descriptive Bibliography*, Bristol: Thoemmes.

Yolton, John, John Price, and John Stephens (eds.) (1999). *The Dictionary of Eighteenth-Century British Philosophers*, 2 vols., Bristol: Thoemmes.

Zarka, Yves Charles (2001). 'Liberty, Necessity and Chance: Hobbes's General Theory of Events', *British Journal for the History of Philosophy* 9: 425–37.

Zebrowski, Martha K. (1997). '"Commanded of God, because 'tis Holy and Good": The Christian Platonism and Natural Law of Samuel Clarke', *Enlightenment and Dissent* 16: 3–28.

INDEX